Catholicism and the Great

MW00805457

This transnational comparative history of Catholic everyday religion in Germany and Austria-Hungary during the Great War transforms our understanding of the war's cultural legacy. Challenging master narratives of secularization and modernism, Houlihan reveals that Catholics from the losing powers had personal and collective religious experiences that revise the decline-and-fall stories of Church and state during wartime. Focusing on private theologies and lived religion, Houlihan explores how believers adjusted to industrial warfare. Giving voice to previously marginalized historical actors, including soldiers and women and children on the homefront, he creates a family history of Catholic religion, supplementing studies of the clergy and bishops. His findings shed new light on the diversity of faith in this period and how specifically Catholic forms of belief and practice enabled people from the losing powers to cope with the war much more successfully than previous cultural histories have led us to believe.

PATRICK J. HOULIHAN received his PhD in History from the University of Chicago in 2011. He is Assistant Director of Student Preparation in the Career Advancement Office at the University of Chicago, where he has also taught in the History Department.

Studies in the Social and Cultural History of Modern Warfare

General Editor

Jay Winter, *Yale University*

Advisory Editors

David Blight, *Yale University*
Richard Bosworth, *University of Western Australia*
Peter Fritzsche, *University of Illinois, Urbana-Champaign*
Carol Gluck, *Columbia University*
Benedict Kiernan, *Yale University*
Antoine Prost, *Université de Paris-Sorbonne*
Robert Wohl, *University of California, Los Angeles*

In recent years the field of modern history has been enriched by the exploration of two parallel histories. These are the social and cultural history of armed conflict, and the impact of military events on social and cultural history.

Studies in the Social and Cultural History of Modern Warfare presents the fruits of this growing area of research, reflecting both the colonization of military history by cultural historians and the reciprocal interest of military historians in social and cultural history, to the benefit of both. The series offers the latest scholarship in European and non-European events from the 1850s to the present day.

This is book 42 in the series, and a full list of titles in the series can be found at: www.cambridge.org/modernwarfare

Catholicism and the Great War

Religion and Everyday Life in Germany and Austria-Hungary, 1914–1922

Patrick J. Houlihan

University of Chicago

CAMBRIDGE
UNIVERSITY PRESS

University Printing House, Cambridge CB2 8BS, United Kingdom

One Liberty Plaza, 20th Floor, New York, NY 10006, USA

477 Williamstown Road, Port Melbourne, VIC 3207, Australia

4843/24, 2nd Floor, Ansari Road, Daryaganj, Delhi - 110002, India

79 Anson Road, #06-04/06, Singapore 079906

Cambridge University Press is part of the University of Cambridge.

It furthers the University's mission by disseminating knowledge in the pursuit of education, learning and research at the highest international levels of excellence.

www.cambridge.org
Information on this title: www.cambridge.org/9781108446020

© Patrick J. Houlihan 2015

This publication is in copyright. Subject to statutory exception and to the provisions of relevant collective licensing agreements, no reproduction of any part may take place without the written permission of Cambridge University Press.

First published 2015
First paperback edition 2017

A catalogue record for this publication is available from the British Library

Library of Congress Cataloging in Publication data
Houlihan, Patrick J., 1980–
Catholicism and the Great War : religion and everyday life in Germany and Austria-Hungary, 1914–1922 / Patrick J. Houlihan, University of Chicago.
    pages   cm. – (Studies in the social and cultural history of modern warfare ; 41)
Includes bibliographical references and index.
ISBN 978-1-107-03514-0 (alk. paper)
1. Catholic Church – Germany – History – 20th century.   2. Catholic Church – Austria – History – 20th century.   3. Catholic Church – Hungary – History – 20th century.   I. Title.
BX1536.H68   2015
282′.4309041 – dc23   2015003499

ISBN 978-1-107-03514-0 Hardback
ISBN 978-1-108-44602-0 Paperback

Cambridge University Press has no responsibility for the persistence or accuracy of URLs for external or third-party internet websites referred to in this publication, and does not guarantee that any content on such websites is, or will remain, accurate or appropriate.

To Bettina, Elisabeth, and Alexander

"If war is an act of force, the emotions cannot fail to be involved."
– Karl von Clausewitz, *On War*, translated and edited
by Michael Howard and Peter Paret (Princeton, NJ:
Princeton University Press, 1976 [1832]), 76

"The war is being conducted not only with guns and cannons
but also with weapons of piety and prayer."
– Sven Hedin, *Ein Volk in Waffen* (Leipzig: F. A.
Brockhaus, 1915), 461

Contents

Figures

SOURCES

Bibliothek für Zeitgeschichte (Stuttgart), Ktn. 214.

Lipusch, Viktor, ed. *Österreich-Ungarns katholische Militärseelsorge im Weltkriege.* Vienna: Verlag für Militär- und Fachliteratur Amon Franz Göth, 1938.

Rudl, Siegmund. *Kriegsvaterunser: Andenken an den Weltkrieg für alle Mitkämpfer und ihre Angehörigen.* Prague: Bonifatia Verlag, 1917.

Acknowledgments

This book benefited from the support of many people and institutions, and it is a pleasure to thank them in print. I only regret that I will not be able to name all the people involved and inevitably will have to stop writing at some point, for which I apologize.

This project began as a dissertation at the University of Chicago, and I had a stellar committee. John W. Boyer, my dissertation chair, offered an inspiring model of a scholar/teacher/administrator, always making time for me amid his myriad other responsibilities. Michael Geyer and Leora Auslander were incredible dissertation committee members and attentive readers. As a whole and as individuals, this committee constantly gave advice that challenged and improved my scholarship on all levels. Words cannot fully express how grateful I am for such a wonderful dissertation committee.

Jay Winter, whose work has deeply influenced my own and many others in Great War studies, took an early interest in my project and has offered supportive feedback throughout the process. Michael Watson, Executive Publisher at Cambridge University Press, and the Press support staff worked with a combination of patience and efficiency that reflects the high standards of academic publishing. In particular, copy editor Tim West saved me from multiple stylistic and grammatical infelicities. Two anonymous referees for the Press offered incredibly helpful criticisms that vastly improved the draft. Among the numerous colleagues to whom I sent parts of the manuscript, Roger Chickering and Benjamin Ziemann offered particularly superlative feedback. I alone bear responsibility for any errors of fact or interpretation that remain.

The research for this project has been supported by grants and fellowships from the University of Chicago, the Fulbright Program, and the American Philosophical Society. Without the financial support of organizations like these, this book would not exist, and I am truly grateful. I also thank the Office of Career Advancement, and its Executive Director, Meredith Daw, for allowing me opportunities to complete the research and writing of the book.

Numerous individuals and institutions offered perspectives that vastly improved the work. At the University of Chicago, the Modern Europe Workshop provided an incredible scholarly forum. Centered in this community, but going beyond it, I have benefitted from the friendship and scholarship of Jennifer Amos, Morgan Aycox, Michael Baltasi, Doris Bergen, Jim Bjork, John Deak, Jean Bethke Elshtain, Thomas Grischany, Jonathan Gumz, Joachim Häberlen, Paul Hanebrink, Derek Hastings, Maureen Healy, Cynthia Hillman, Ke-chin Hsia, Lonnie Johnson, Ari Joskowicz, Dan Koehler, Thomas Kselman, Lesley Lundeen, Corinne Lyon, Lynn Page, Sara Panzer, Mearah Quinn-Brauner, Richard Rosengarten, Jake Smith, Michael Snape, Ronen Steinberg, Allie Tichenor, and Kati Vörös. Francis Cardinal George and Justin Cardinal Rigali provided letters of support that opened some archival doors for me. Many archivists and libraries in Europe and America patiently dealt with numerous requests and offered generous assistance. Martin Geyer and Lothar Höbelt were gracious sponsors during my Fulbright time in Central Europe. In Europe and America, my family was fortunate to find supportive communities, including Collegium Sapientiae in Freiburg and St. Thomas the Apostle Parish in Hyde Park, Chicago. We also benefitted from the University of Chicago undergraduate community, both in my classes and particularly in Coulter House ("Which House?"), our residence. Friends who have stayed with me for the long haul include Matt Fesak, Lindsay Fraschilla, and, last but not least, my friend since we were seven years old, Chris Maston.

Conference participants at many venues offered disparate perspectives that improved my work. These forums included the American Historical Association, the National Endowment for the Humanities, the National World War I Museum (Kansas City, MO), the UK Armed Forces Chaplaincy Center, the German Studies Association, Internationales Forschungszentrum Kulturwissenschaften (Vienna), the Polish Academy of Sciences, New York University Kandersteg Seminar (Switzerland), and the University of Notre Dame (London Centre).

The journals *Central European History* and *First World War Studies* graciously allowed me to reprint earlier published materials. The flood of publications will only increase as the Great War centenary anniversaries continue. Looking backward 100 years since the assassination in Sarajevo, I have tried to incorporate material published through July 2014, when this manuscript went to press.

As any scholar of the Great War knows, homefront and battlefront are inextricably linked. For my bookish battle, my family has provided love and support beyond measure, without which this project would not be possible; from the beginning, we were together "in the trenches," as it were. My parents, Pat and Mary Houlihan, and my sister, Jessica, provided a loving family environment and happy childhood. My extended family, most particularly my maternal grandparents, Alexander and Dorothy Poplawsky, inspired my love of Europe, history, and culture: a project that has established transnational connections with my in-laws in Europe, particularly Joachim and Traute Domnick.

Ultimately, from the perspective of everyday life, this project directly benefitted most from the love and support of my wife, Bettina, and our children, Elisabeth and Alexander. They keep me focused on what is truly important. Consequently, it is to them that the present work is dedicated.

PJH
Chicago USA
July 28, 2014

Note on the text

Geographic naming is a perennial issue in European history, and there is no singular satisfactory solution that will account for all contingencies of identity politics. My imperfect method has been to remain close to the archival sources, replicating the names most prevalent in the documents that I have read. I hope that this will help future researchers effectively follow up on the paths I have trodden. I make exceptions, however, for place names that are widely known in English, such as Vienna (not Wien) and Prague (not Praha/Prag).

Except as noted, scriptural references derive primarily from Donald Senior and John J. Collins, eds., *The Catholic Study Bible*, 2nd edn. (New York: Oxford University Press, 2006).

Abbreviations

AAS	Acta Apostolicae Sedis
AASI	Archivum Provinciae Austriae Societatis Iesu
ABF	Archiv der Bayerischen Franziskaner
AFV	Apostolisches Feldvikariat
AOK	Armeeoberkommando
ASV	Archivio Segreto Vaticano
BA-MA	Bundesarchiv-Militärarchiv
BHStA	Bayerisches Hauptstaatsarchiv
BfZ	Bibliothek für Zeitgeschichte (Stuttgart)
DAG	Diözesanarchiv Graz
DLA	Dokumentationsarchiv Lebensgeschichtlicher Aufzeichnungen (Vienna)
DTA	Deutsches Tagebucharchiv (Emmendingen)
EAF	Erzbischöflichesarchiv Freiburg
EAK	Erzbischöflichesarchiv Köln
EAM	Erzbischöflichesarchiv München-Freising
EAW	Erzbischöflichesarchiv Wien
KAS	Konsistorialarchiv Salzburg
KBKM	Königlich-Bayerisches Kriegsministerium
KM	Kriegsministerium
k.u.k.	kaiserlich und königlich
MKSM	Militärkanzlei Seiner Majestät
NL	Nachlass
NFA	Neue Feldakten
ÖStAKA	Österreichisches Staatsarchiv-Kriegsarchiv
PH	Preussisches Heer
TLA	Tiroler Landesarchiv
TLVA	Tiroler Landesverteidigungsakten

Introduction

On August 20, 1914, the invading German Army entered Brussels, marching through Belgium and into northern France. Also on that day, Pope Saint Pius X, the declared anti-modernist "peasant pope," died suddenly after a short illness. Soon after, in the midst of unfolding war, cardinals from across Europe gathered in Rome to elect the new supreme pontiff, and the mood was anxious. At the conclave in the corridors of the Vatican, Cardinal Felix von Hartmann of Germany greeted his colleague Cardinal Désiré Mercier of Belgium, saying, "I hope that we shall not speak of war." Mercier responded, "And I hope that we shall not speak of peace."[1] The national rancor between bishops would escalate as the war dragged on, and episcopal enmity and clerical nationalism have become cultural shorthand for the religious experience of the Great War. However, the sound and fury of the bishops has helped to conceal the experiences of ordinary religious believers.

This book argues that, seen through the religious experiences of everyday Catholics from the losing powers, the Catholic story of the Great War challenges standard interpretations of the war's disillusioning legacy. In particular, the study of lived religion for people from the losing powers provides counter-narratives to stories of secularization and artistic modernism. Specifically Catholic forms of belief and practice allowed Catholics in the losing powers to cope with the war's devastation remarkably better than standard cultural histories of secularization and literary modernism would have readers believe. This Catholic spirituality included intercession, sacramentality, dolorous cyclical history in the long term, and worship of female spirituality. These modes of faith provided relief and comfort in extreme situations of distress. Catholic spirituality, both liturgically and theologically, provided traditional means of

---

[1] The exchange between the cardinals is recounted in Michael Burleigh, *Earthly Powers: The Clash of Religion and Politics in Europe from the French Revolution to the Great War* (New York: HarperCollins, 2005), 457. For the official documents on the conclave, see Anon., *Acta Apostolicae Sedis: Commentarium Officiale* (Rome: Typis Polyglottis Vaticanis, 1909–), 6:473–500.

understanding tremendous upheaval, allowing the Great War's devastating new horrors to be relativized as one episode in the story of human existence. Catholicism portrayed war as necessary suffering, diminished belief in divine-right nationalism, and created a nostalgic vision of idyllic domesticity. While the homefront vision may have been delusive, it was nonetheless a powerful motivator and source of hope, especially in the war-torn world struggling to rebuild itself during the interwar period.

This book goes beyond instrumental and functional analyses that reduce religion to an epiphenomenon. Instead, it argues that Catholics from the losing powers had a wide and deep variety of autonomous, meaningful, and irreducible religious experiences. Using a personalized source base of reports, letters, diaries, and memoirs, the book explores how religious believers adjusted to the new industrial warfare in various contexts: ecclesiastical, imperial, national, local, and personal. Revising Church-oriented histories of the bishops and clergy that focus on clerical nationalism and "just war" theology, it incorporates the perspectives of not only soldiers at the battlefront but also women and children on the homefront, viewed comparatively and transnationally in the context of two different empires, with Catholics a favored majority in Austria-Hungary and a suspect minority in Germany.

Throughout history, religion's relation to violence and war can be seen as both classical and contemporary.[2] With reference to the Great War, the study of religion taps into historiographical debates about the nature of consent and coercion; enthusiasm and remobilization after the failure of an early decisive victory; and the nature of ideology as both incitement of hatred and source of social pacification. As Hew Strachan and Jay Winter, among others, have argued, the historiography of the Great War has reached a new transnational threshold, but national histories remain deeply entrenched.[3] For Austria-Hungary, condemned to declining irrelevance before the conflict began, the war provides a convenient narrative end point for the shattering of a seemingly incoherent jumble of ethnicities. For Germany, the Great War is a prelude to the destructive vengeance of the Nazi movement.[4]

---

[2] For an excellent overview, see Mark Juergensmeyer, Margo Kitts, and Michael Jerryson, eds., *The Oxford Handbook of Religion and Violence* (New York: Oxford University Press, 2013).

[3] Hew Strachan, "Epilogue," in *The Legacy of the Great War: Ninety Years On*, ed. Jay Winter (Columbia: University of Missouri Press, 2009), 185–98; Jay Winter, "Approaching the History of the Great War: A User's Guide," in Winter, *The Legacy of the Great War*, 1–17, esp. 6–7.

[4] For a superlative historiographical overview, see Jay Winter and Antoine Prost, *The Great War in History: Debates and Controversies, 1914 to the Present* (Cambridge: Cambridge University Press, 2005).

The First World War had a Catholic dimension that has not received attention as a pan-European phenomenon, especially for the losing powers of Central and Eastern Europe. Aside from high-level diplomacy and research on the radical right-wing fringe, very few studies of the Great War view Germany and Austria-Hungary together as related but distinct entities.[5] Although religiosity is difficult to quantify, even the sheer empirical data on nominal religious affiliation suggest the need to examine a Catholic experience of the war: according to one set of figures from 1920, those nominally identified as Catholics made up 194.83 million of a total European population of 353.57 million people, or 55.10%. The regional data are even more pronounced, especially viewed in terms of Protestant–Catholic differences. In Central Europe, Catholics made up 59.99 million out of a total of 114.90 million people, or 52.21%, while Protestants made up 44.90 million, or 39.08%. Regional disparities in Eastern and Southern Europe, long-neglected areas of First World War studies, are more lopsided. In Eastern Europe, Catholics represented 12.93 million out of 43.08 million total inhabitants, or 30.01%, whereas Protestants made up 3.61 million, or 8.38%. In Southern Europe, Catholics formed 66.28 million out of a total of 75.41 million, or an overwhelming 87.89%, whereas Protestants numbered around 168 000, or a mere 0.22%.[6]

Why, then, does one find this neglect of a major component of belief during a transformative global event? As Michael Snape has argued, the Christian history of the First World War remains understudied because of a narrow national or denominational focus;[7] the present book aims to correct this for the losing powers. There is also the issue of the war's cultural legacy, in large part dominated by representations of avant garde modernism. Many cultural histories of the war argue that the dominant master-narrative of its cultural legacy is, in the pointed words of Modris Eksteins, the emergence of "orgiastic-nihilistic irony," with

---

[5] The neglect of comparative studies of the losing powers is striking, especially in comparison to works about Britain and France. For a pioneering countervailing work, see Holger H. Herwig, *The First World War: Germany and Austria-Hungary, 1914–1918* (London: Arnold, 1997). An important recent transnational study of counter-revolutionary movements in Central Europe is Robert Gerwarth, "The Central European Counter-Revolution: Paramilitary Violence in Germany, Austria and Hungary after the Great War," *Past and Present* 200, no. 1 (2008): 175–209.

[6] These statistics are taken from Gabriel Adriányi, ed., *History of the Church*, vol. 10: *The Church in the Modern Age* (New York: Crossroad, 1981), 5–6. Figures originally taken from H. A. Krose, ed. *Kirchliches Handbuch für das katholische Deutschland*, vol. 7, 1930–1 (Cologne, 1931), 263.

[7] Michael Snape, "The Great War," in *World Christianities, c.1914–c.2000*, ed. Hugh McLeod (Cambridge: Cambridge University Press, 2006), 131–50. For brief preliminary studies that indicate a historiographic shift is imminent, see Martin Greschat, *Der Erste Weltkrieg und die Christenheit. Ein globaler Überblick* (Stuttgart: Kohlhammer, 2014).

Germany "the modernist nation par excellence" of the twentieth century.[8] Tempering this view, Jay Winter's path-breaking work of comparative and transnational cultural history demonstrates the persistence of traditional motifs and means of understanding, particularly the modes of classical, romantic, and religious culture. On a pan-European level, Winter argues that traditional ways of representation provided comfort, helping bereaved survivors mourn the dead and thus cope with human loss on an unprecedented scale.[9] Despite the more recent pull of studies of popular culture, given the impact of modernism, there is still a strong tendency to view culture in terms of high culture.[10]

Nevertheless, the religious history of the war has now become an established component of its cultural history. Annette Becker's pioneering book on Catholic France, *War and Faith: The Religious Imagination in France, 1914–1930*, represented a new approach to the cultural history of religion during the war, deliberately focusing on the religious experiences of lay believers and thus counterbalancing the previous dominance of the papacy and priests.[11] After the historiographical cultural turn in First World War studies, powerful recent histories of religion have stressed the power of religion as an enduring source of identity for everyday believers; however, these studies are largely limited to the framework of a single nation-state.[12] Recent histories of religion in the capital cities of Paris, London, and Berlin have shown that even paramount centers of modernism should not inherently be categorized as engines of secularization during the war.[13] Further complicating cultural stereotypes about the experience of the First World War grounded in the archetypal hellish

[8] Modris Eksteins, *Rites of Spring: The Great War and the Birth of the Modern Age* (Boston, MA: Houghton Mifflin, 1989), xiv–xvi. For a seminal work about the Great War as a foundational moment in the emergence of literary modernism, see Paul Fussell, *The Great War and Modern Memory* (Oxford: Oxford University Press, 1975).

[9] Jay Winter, *Sites of Memory, Sites of Mourning: The Great War in European Cultural History* (Cambridge: Cambridge University Press, 1995).

[10] See, for example, the essays in Aviel Roshwald and Richard Stites, eds., *European Culture in the Great War: The Arts, Entertainment, and Propaganda, 1914–1918* (Cambridge: Cambridge University Press, 1999).

[11] Annette Becker, *War and Faith: The Religious Imagination in France, 1914–1930*, trans. Helen McPhail (Oxford: Berg, 1998).

[12] In addition to Annette Becker's *War and Faith*, see Jonathan H. Ebel, *Faith in the Fight: Religion and the American Soldier in the Great War* (Princeton, NJ: Princeton University Press, 2010), and Michael Snape, *God and the British Soldier: Religion and the British Army in the First and Second World Wars* (London: Routledge, 2005). For a work that blends analysis of the USA and the UK, see Richard Schweitzer, *The Cross and the Trenches: Religious Faith and Doubt among British and American Great War Soldiers* (Westport, CT: Praeger, 2003).

[13] Adrian Gregory and Annette Becker, "Religious Sites and Practices," in *Capital Cities at War: Paris, London, Berlin*, vol. 2: *A Cultural History*, ed. Jay Winter and Jean-Louis Robert (Cambridge: Cambridge University Press, 2007), 383–427.

landscape of the Western Front trenches, Alexander Watson's effective recent study of combat motivation and morale in the British and German armies firmly argues that endurance, not psychological collapse, was the normative condition of most soldiers fighting at the front. Watson highlights religion as a key factor in explaining this endurance. He argues that, "For most [soldiers], religion or superstition lent sense and meaning to the chaotic environment and offered an opportunity of imposing order on it. The human capacity for hope, optimism and, not least, self-deception made the war subjectively less threatening and lent men peculiar powers of resilience."[14] The archetypal hopeless, hellish anomie in the trenches of the Western Front simply does not adequately represent the variety of ways people experienced the war.

In Europe and around the world, societies drew upon religion to make sense of the Great War. Focusing on the global reordering of the twentieth century, Philip Jenkins has recently written, "Religion is essential to understanding the war, to understanding why people went to war, what they hoped to achieve through war, and why they stayed at war."[15] The study of religion during wartime must study both similarities and differences within a global framework. Overall, as Adrian Gregory has recently written, wartime religion should be "highly sensitive to the nuances and complexities of actual religions in their practices and beliefs." While the concept of religion should be analytically limited (and not all-encompassing and circular), nevertheless, "religious practices, languages, and imagery were intimately engaged in making sense of 'war experience.'"[16]

Yet, for religion in Central Europe, the historiographical teleology of modernization and Nazism remains strong: Weberian disenchantment followed by the substitute messianism of Adolf Hitler. For religious history in Central Europe, the story moves quickly from 1914 to 1933. George S. Williamson has argued that, despite qualifications, the religious history of Central Europe is dominated by a Protestant *Sonderweg*.[17] As Mark Lilla's recent appraisal of religiosity *The Stillborn God* admits,

---

[14] Alexander Watson, *Enduring the Great War: Combat, Morale and Collapse in the German and British Armies, 1914–1918* (Cambridge: Cambridge University Press, 2008), 234; see esp. pp. 92–100.

[15] Philip Jenkins, *The Great and Holy War: How World War I Became a Religious Crusade* (New York: HarperOne, 2014).

[16] Adrian Gregory, "Beliefs and Religion," in *The Cambridge History of the First World War*, ed. Jay Winter (Cambridge: Cambridge University Press, 2014), 3:418–44; quote from 443.

[17] George S. Williamson, "A Religious Sonderweg? Reflections on the Sacred and the Secular in the Historiography of Modern Germany," *Church History* 75, no. 1 (2006): 139–56.

the story of secularization is often a tale of legacies of Protestantism and Judaism, with Catholicism left out.[18] Applied to First World War studies, the "war cultures" approach relies on a notion of ideological crusade between combatants, which accentuates religious cultural difference and uses Protestant Prussia as the reductive symbol for Germany. While the crusading element was certainly one important part of religious belief, the focus on combatant animosity tends to highlight escalating brutality, especially of occupied regions, as a formative period for genocide.[19]

In the historiography of Central European Catholicism on the eve of the Great War, the milieu remains an analytical starting point. Despite many advances, the work on the milieu often highlights the ghettoization of Catholic historiography within Central Europe. Contrasted with the permeation of Roman Catholicism, both officially and unofficially, in Austria-Hungary, as a minority religion in Protestant-dominated Germany the Catholic milieu was a defensive subculture that provided a life-world for believers, eventually, at the national level, translating into the political power of the Center Party.[20] The top-down reassertion of papal primacy known as "ultramontanism," in its extreme form, gave rise to the model in which the priest was "manager" of the milieu.[21] The Franco-Prussian War did not last long enough to create a true sense of shared suffering capable of integrating Protestants and Catholics.[22] By contrast, the enormous bloodletting of the Great War would help to

[18] Mark Lilla, *The Stillborn God: Religion, Politics, and the Modern West* (New York: Knopf, 2007).

[19] For a recent statement of the "war cultures" approach to religion, see Annette Becker, "Faith, Ideologies, and the 'Cultures of War,'" in *A Companion to World War I*, ed. John Horne (Malden, MA: Wiley-Blackwell, 2010), 234–47. For the "war cultures" approach more generally, see Stéphane Audoin-Rouzeau and Annette Becker, *14–18: Understanding the Great War*, trans. Catherine Temerson (New York: Hill and Wang, 2002).

[20] For a recent review article that expertly outlines debates about the twentieth-century transformation of the Catholic milieu in Central Europe, ultimately arguing for the milieu's analytical viability in terms of "lived religion," see Michael E. O'Sullivan, "From Catholic Milieu to Lived Religion: The Social and Cultural History of Modern German Catholicism," *History Compass* 7, no. 3 (2009): 837–61. Earlier foundational statements include Münster Arbeitskreis für kirchliche Zeitgeschichte, "Katholiken zwischen Tradition und Moderne: Das katholische Milieu als Forschungsaufgabe," *Westfälische Forschungen* 43 (1993): 588–654, and Oded Heilbronner, "From Ghetto to Ghetto: The Place of German Catholic Society in Recent Historiography," *Journal of Modern History* 72, no. 2 (2000): 453–95.

[21] Olaf Blaschke, "Die Kolonialisierung der Laienwelt: Priester als Milieumanager und die Kanäle klerikaler Kuratel," in *Religion im Kaiserreich: Milieus, Mentalitäten, Krisen*, ed. Olaf Blaschke and Frank-Michael Kuhlemann (Göttingen: Vandenhoeck & Ruprecht, 1996), 93–135.

[22] Christian Rak, *Krieg, Nation und Konfession: die Erfahrung des deutsch-französischen Krieges von 1870/71* (Paderborn: F. Schöningh, 2004).

fuse confessional differences along a model of Christian sacrifice for the nation, which also accentuated the exclusion of Jews from the national community.

Standard accounts of Catholicism in Central Europe during the Great War focus on the bishops, and particularly their aggressive "war theology" in defense of interests of state. These tend to represent war experience solely through published war sermons circulated in pastoral letters and published in religious periodicals.[23] Even religious histories of the churches during the war tended to focus on the actions of the bishops in a very top-down fashion.[24] Because of its accessible source base and readily identifiable actors, military chaplaincy has provided a way for talking about religion in a largely military context at the battlefront.[25] Thus, despite historiographical shifts that argue for essential connections between homefront and battlefront, religion in Central Europe during the war is often represented through the perspectives of the military administrative state and the leading churchmen psychologically invested in it, thus instrumentalizing religion and privileging the nation-state. The focus on church men also highlights the extent to which the religious history of Central Europe has been largely gendered by exclusively

[23] Wilhelm Achleitner, *Gott im Krieg: Die Theologie der österreichischen Bischöfe in den Hirtenbriefen zum Ersten Weltkrieg* (Vienna: Böhlau Verlag, 1997); Karl Hammer, *Deutsche Kriegstheologie, 1870–1918* (Munich: Deutscher Taschenbuch Verlag, 1974); Heinrich Missalla, *"Gott mit uns": Die deutsche katholische Kriegspredigt, 1914–1918* (Munich: Kösel Verlag, 1968); Wilhelm Pressel, *Die Kriegspredigt 1914–1918 in der evangelischen Kirche Deutschlands* (Göttingen: Vandenhoeck und Ruprecht, 1967).

[24] Heinz Hürten, "Die katholische Kirche im Ersten Weltkrieg," in *Der erste Weltkrieg: Wirkung, Wahrnehmung, Analyse,* ed. Wolfgang Michalka (Munich: Piper Verlag, 1994), 725–35; Richard van Dülmen, "Der deutsche Katholizismus und der Erste Weltkrieg," *Francia* 2 (1974): 347–76. More recently, see Martin Lätzel, *Die katholische Kirche im Ersten Weltkrieg. Zwischen Nationalismus und Friedenswillen* (Regensburg: Friedrich Pustet, 2014).

[25] For an overview of military chaplaincy in both the Habsburg and the Hohenzollern monarchies, see Patrick J. Houlihan, "Clergy in the Trenches: Catholic Military Chaplains of Germany and Austria-Hungary during the First World War" (Ph.D. dissertation, University of Chicago, 2011). See also Claudia Ham, "Von den Anfängen der Militärseelsorge bis zur Liquidierung des Apostolischen Feldvikariates im Jahr 1918," in *Zwischen Himmel und Erde: Militärseelsorge in Österreich,* ed. Roman-Hans Gröger (Graz: Styria Verlag, 2001), 13–98; Arnold Vogt, *Religion im Militär: Seelsorge zwischen Kriegsverherrlichung und Humanität: Eine militär-geschichtliche Studie* (Frankfurt a.M.: Peter Lang, 1984); and Benjamin Ziemann, "Katholische Religiosität und die Bewältigung des Krieges: Soldaten und Militärseelsorger in der deutschen Armee, 1914–1918," in *Volksreligiosität und Kriegserleben,* ed. Friedhelm Boll (Münster: Lit, 1997), 116–36. The published diaries of chaplains, with valuable scholarly commentary, are also an excellent source. See Frank Betker and Almut Kriele, eds., *Pro fide et patria! Die Kriegstagebücher von Ludwig Berg 1914/18: Katholischer Feldgeistlicher im Grossen Hauptquartier Kaiser Wilhelms II* (Cologne: Böhlau, 1998), and Hans-Josef Wollasch, ed., *Militärseelsorge im Ersten Weltkrieg: Das Kriegstagebuch des katholischen Feldgeistlichen Benedict Kreutz* (Mainz: Matthias Grünewelt Verlag, 1987).

male stories. Catholic women and children remain a marginalized group of historical actors. The present work represents this group in order to more accurately depict the religious experiences of believers.

The landscape of Central European war history is starting to change. Benjamin Ziemann's *Front und Heimat*, a fundamental work on Bavaria (a heavily Catholic region of the German Empire), brilliantly dismantles Nazi myths of combat solidarity at the front, arguing that ties between homefront and battlefront were much more consequential. Ziemann finds that for soldiers from Bavaria, a heavily agricultural area, regional loyalties of farm, family, and faith were extremely important markers of identity.[26] Bavaria, as a key Catholic region of the German Empire and a vital point of transnational affiliation between Germany and Austria-Hungary, also figures largely in the present study. This book builds on this work by incorporating other regions and firmly keeping in mind the comparative dynamics of the different empires.

On a pan-European level, religion during the First World War remains vastly understudied, particularly in comparison to the Second World War and its aftermath.[27] Catholics were immersed in processes of globalization that took formative shape in the nineteenth century and continue into the twenty-first.[28] Many works of Catholic history rightly point out that the Church's story of adaptation to the modern world took huge strides forward with the Second Vatican Council of 1962–65. Thus, the present book highlights how the Catholic story of the twentieth century, as seen through the losing powers, does not fit with standard narratives of the Great War as an epic moment of disillusioning modernism.

Prescient analyses of wartime Catholicism have called attention to the need to place the experiences of the laity at their center.[29] Especially in historical long-term analyses, structural factors tend to compress the era of the world wars into a rubric of clerical nationalism, in which the power structure of religion-nation-power has remained the definitive experience of religiosity since the French Revolution.[30] The focus on clerical

---

[26] Benjamin Ziemann, *Front und Heimat: Ländliche Kriegserfahrungen im südlichen Bayern, 1914–1923* (Essen: Klartext, 1997). Recently translated as Benjamin Ziemann, *War Experiences in Rural Germany, 1914–1923*, trans. Alex Skinner (Oxford: Berg, 2007).

[27] Nicholas Atkin and Frank Tallett, *Priests, Prelates, and People: A History of European Catholicism since 1750* (New York: Oxford University Press, 2003).

[28] Vincent Viaene, "International History, Religious History, Catholic History: Perspectives for Cross-Fertilization (1830–1914)," *European History Quarterly* 38, no. 4 (2008): 578–607.

[29] Andreas Holzem and Christoph Holzapfel, "Kriegserfahrung als Forschungsproblem: Der Erste Weltkrieg in der religiösen Erfahrung von Katholiken," *Theologische Quartalsschrift* 182, no. 4 (2002): 279–97.

[30] Andreas Holzem, ed., *Krieg und Christentum: Religiöse Gewalttheorien in der Kriegserfahrung des Westens* (Paderborn: Schöningh, 2009).

nationalism, however, tends to instrumentalize religion in service of state aims: that is, to emphasize that religious enthusiasm was "successful" to the extent that it sustained social cohesion, advancing mobilization for a victorious political outcome in the war.

Instead, this study focuses on the losing powers in a transnational context, showing that even though political entities in Central Europe lost a disastrous war, religious believers there had a wide variety of religious experiences. These religious experiences certainly included the nation, but they were not exclusively, or even primarily, defined by it. Religious believers made sense of the war at many levels: individual, familial, local, national, imperial, and transnational. The nation was only one of many valences of loyalty. Studies of popular religion have rightly insisted that the boundary between institutional religion and superstition is blurred.[31] In the realm of popular religion, forms of Catholic spirituality drew on pagan and folk cultures, adapted by individuals to fit the new circumstances of war.

The Great War was an epic moment in the religious history of modern Europe, and yet the voices of ordinary believers remain marginalized by the sound and fury of the war's immense cultural legacy. This book analyzes themes on a broad scale across national boundaries, relating huge swaths of Central and Eastern Europe to more pan-European developments. It exemplifies the classical theoretical tension between the "horizon of expectation" (*Erwartungshorizont*) and "realm of experience" (*Erfahrungsraum*) articulated by Reinhart Koselleck.[32] Avoiding simplistic starting and stopping points such as 1914 or 1918, the book's narrative instead shows how the Great War as experienced by religious believers does not fit standard twentieth-century chronological signposts.

Thus, this book is a study of how a very traditional religion, stereotyped as archaic, confronted and adjusted to the new horrors of industrial warfare. At the level of the nation, collective symbolic loss was an important part of the conflict, but this was only one level at which religious believers conceived of the war. The book examines the bishops' infamous war theology and its transmission to the masses of believers, but it also represents the lesser-known positions of the papacy and of lay believers. It examines fundamental contrasts between national/imperial visions of collective sacrifice and what these meant for individual believers in terms

---

[31] Christine Beil, Thomas Fliege, Monique Scheer et al., "Populare Religiosität und Kriegserfahrungen," *Theologische Quartalsschrift* 182, no. 4 (2002): 298–320; Gottfried Korff, ed., *Alliierte im Himmel: Populare Religiosität und Kriegserfahrung* (Tübingen: Tübinger Vereinigung für Volkskunde, 2006).

[32] Reinhart Koselleck, *Vergangene Zukunft. Zur Semantik geschichtlicher Zeiten* (Frankfurt a.M.: Suhrkamp, 1979).

of personal piety, especially after it became apparent that the war was lost. Institutional prescriptions of the Catholic faith formed important orientation points for believers. Whenever possible, however, this work stresses the lived reality of individual experiences of transcendence. It places emphasis on pastoral forms of theology and religious practice, showing the popular reception of ideas, the transmission to action of the faithful, and the autonomous modes of spirituality that developed against Church guidelines. Thus, this work highlights both Church and state authorities' instrumentalization of faith and individual lay believers' assertion of their faith as a form of personal identity and experience.

Methodology

Impossible to articulate fully for one person, and even more so for millions of believers in two empires, a focus on religion and everyday life will inevitably fall short of an adequate representation of personal religiosity. Nevertheless, one should clarify some of the guiding methods. In studying religious phenomena, where does one draw the line for classifying something as a religious experience? Scholars of religious studies will continue to debate whether the existence of a concept of "religion" makes sense.[33] In order not to get bogged down in endless wrangling over this issue, this book has been generous in classifying according to an ideal-type characteristic of Catholicism defined by both scholars and believers. Nevertheless, in order to better represent cultural flow and personal agency, it also incorporates a model of concentric, overlapping circles of commitment.[34] At the center of the circle lie the doctrine and dogma of the Catholic Church seated in Rome under the authority of the Pope, but the direction of commitment to that center has two-way movement: both centripetal and centrifugal.

This study focuses on Catholicism specifically, although other religions and confessions will be discussed throughout. Occasionally, in order to compare and contrast forms of Christianity, the book discusses Protestant spirituality in particular. There are obvious areas of overlap: for instance, in loyalty to Kaiser Wilhelm II as the highest state authority in Imperial Germany. In some cases, the book has used Protestant archival material, and one may wonder at the scholarly legitimacy of including

---

[33] For excellent discussion of these issues, see Robert A. Orsi, ed., *The Cambridge Companion to Religious Studies* (New York: Cambridge University Press, 2011).

[34] John Taylor, "The Future of Christianity," in *The Oxford History of Christianity*, ed. John McManners (Oxford: Oxford University Press, 1993), 644–83. See also David B. Barrett, George Thomas Kurian, and Todd M. Johnson, eds., *World Christian Encyclopedia: A Comparative Survey of Churches and Religions in the Modern World*, 2nd edn., 2 vols. (New York: Oxford University Press, 2001).

this. For example, in Chapter 5, it discusses Red Cross sisters and the historigraphically neglected experiences of women and children. In these cases, Christian material was selected as the most clear empirical example of a larger point that exclusively Catholic sources do not adequately address. For instance, Red Cross nurse Hilda Galles, a Christian of uncertain denomination, provided a vivid and immediate contrast of differing representations of war experience: a laconic, dutiful letter to her parents and her personal diary entries written at the same time, the latter of which record a hospital world of hellish chaos and depression. These two documents highlight important points of difference between personal subjectivity and semi-public images of war: factors crucial to the varieties of religious experience and gendered representations of duty.

Perhaps most offensive to scholars and some religious believers will be this book's claims that Catholicism provided an extra measure of comfort beyond Protestantism during the Great War. On one level, these criticisms are correct: there are no quantifiable benchmarks to demonstrate something like this with a social scientific degree of numerical accuracy. On another level appropriate to religious studies, however, argumentation must be qualitatively suggestive rather than quantitatively conclusive, and this book does not pronounce infallible judgments *ex cathedra*; rather, it posts theses for disputation.

There is a qualitative difference that this book insists upon: firmly rooted in historical theology between Christian denominations, wartime Catholicism's emphasis on belief *and* practice, or faith *and* works, simply provided more ways in which Catholic believers could understand and potentially shape their own beliefs. This was especially relevant for increasingly atomized national or imperial communities as the collective sacrifice that began in 1914 became increasingly hopeless by 1918. Particularly for the losing powers of Central Europe, the Protestant justification by individual faith alone, especially when the war seemed lost, did not allow religious believers additional ways in which to understand the chaos of war that made communal sense outside of national defeat and frustration. As religion became tangled with nationhood in German history, the consequences of defeat in 1918 were especially traumatizing for the Protestant collective imaginary that had, the year before, celebrated the 400th anniversary of the Reformation begun by Martin Luther in 1517. By contrast, Catholic spirituality emphasized such matters as intercessory saint culture, the tangibility of devotional objects, and a universal Church community beyond the nation – and these were modes of faith that proved comforting during collective imperial defeat for the Central Powers.

Instead of stressing religion's ecumenical similarity, which prejudices analysis toward the nation-state, this book stresses religious differences.

Rooted in war experience, Protestant theology in Central Europe, represented by towering figures such as Karl Barth and Paul Tillich, took a decisive turn during the Great War. By contrast, Central European Catholic theology and its exponents, such as Max Scheler, Romano Guardini, and Karl Adam, viewed the years of 1914–18 much more traditionally and continuously, not as a decisive rupture. The Catholic Church, represented ultimately by the papacy and institutional networks such as a caritas network for social welfare, dealt with the Great War in terms of adapted tradition, not fundamental disruption and reorientation.

Catholic specificities remain at the heart of this transnational and comparative work. In his classic work on Catholicism, Father Richard McBrien argued for a more inclusive reading of Catholicism that represented the Church's self-conceptualized universalistic mission. Nevertheless, McBrien identified three themes that have helped to differentiate Catholic belief and practice from alternative variants of Christianity: sacramentality, mediation, and communion.[35] Sacramentality emphasizes tangible practices and concerted actions; mediation stresses the intercessory culture in the hierarchical Church, where clergy members and saints intervene on behalf of all believers, communicating with the group of spirits ultimately led by God; and communion underscores the united community of believers, transcending all boundaries of distinction. These themes will recur often in the present work.

Given the interreligious ecumenism in modern studies of religion, the focus on one religion might seem strange, especially considering the intertwined relations and deep history of Protestants, Catholics, and Jews in Central Europe.[36] Focusing on Catholicism was also a strategic choice, however, made for two primary reasons. First, because of the multi-ethnic nature of the Habsburg monarchy, a study of Germany and Austria-Hungary that dealt with the major official state religions would have to talk about not only Protestantism, Catholicism, and Judaism, but also Eastern Orthodoxy and Islam. In the course of a single monograph, comparing so many religions would result in a superficial level of empirical representation, detracting from the desire to represent the everyday thoughts and beliefs of ordinary believers. Second, the empirical archival data available at the state and local level simply exist in much richer detail for Catholicism than for other religions, especially Protestantism in a military context in Germany. Significantly, the destruction of the

---

[35] Richard P. McBrien, *Catholicism*, rev. edn. (San Francisco: HarperSanFrancisco, 1994), 8–17.

[36] For one of the best approaches, see Helmut Walser Smith, ed., *Protestants, Catholics, and Jews in Germany, 1800–1914* (New York: Berg, 2001).

German military archives in Potsdam during an air raid in 1945 caused much archival material on the German Army during the First World War to be lost forever, complicating the study of Protestantism in particular. However, at German federal and ecclesiastical archives, particularly the ecclesiastical archives in Munich and Cologne and the military archives in Freiburg im Breisgau, enough material on Catholic religiosity during the war has survived to permit a substantial comparison to Catholicism in Austria-Hungary. Although much of the empirical material of this book is focused on ethnically German speakers, the book's Catholic transnationalism integrates other nationalities into discussions of the war's impact for Central and Eastern European Catholicism. Thus, this book opens up avenues for further research, integrating previously marginal individual Catholics from these regions into discussions of the war's cultural history, which were previously focused on bishops and artists. Areas of overlap between Christian denominations can be extended to allow analysis of other religions during the war.

Thus, Catholicism in Germany and Austria-Hungary represents a transnational and comparative history of everyday religion during wartime. It is transnational in that it examines Catholicism, an ancient religious community of believers affiliating with the Pope in Rome as the successor of Saint Peter, the supposed leader of the initial Church organized by Jesus Christ – and thus oriented across the political boundaries of two empires. But the comparative aspect is also important, for Catholics in Germany and Austria-Hungary were also political members of two different empires. In Germany, Catholics were a suspect minority, around thirty-six percent of the population in a Protestant- and Prussian-dominated empire, while Catholics in Austria-Hungary were around eighty percent of the population (over ninety percent in the "Austrian" half of the monarchy), a favored majority in a monarchy affiliated with a throne-and-altar alliance of privilege. Recent works of Habsburg history have done much to complicate the standard story of an unstable monarchy doomed to dissolution by the unruly forces of nationalism; indeed, the category of "national indifference" has helped to reintroduce contingency and identity on a local level: key parts of a complicated picture of state-building.[37] The nation and emerging

---

[37] Gary B. Cohen, "Nationalist Politics and the Dynamics of State and Civil Society in the Habsburg Monarchy, 1867–1914," *Central European History* 40 (2007): 241–78; Jonathan Kwan, "Nationalism and All That: Reassessing the Habsburg Monarchy and Its Legacy," *European History Quarterly* 41, no. 1 (2011): 88–108. For a pioneering work of "national indifference," see Tara Zahra, *Kidnapped Souls: National Indifference and the Battle for Children in the Bohemian Lands, 1900–1948* (Ithaca, NY: Cornell University Press, 2008).

national consciousness mattered, but this was not the only source of loyalty.[38]

This book keeps the power relations of national sacrifice firmly in mind, while also representing multiple layers of religious affiliation above and below the nation: a universalistic Church, regional affiliations, family relations, and personal identities – all of which were unified by a centripetal–centrifugal relation to the Church of Rome. Politically speaking, the most represented contingent in this study remains a pan-Germanic version of Catholicism, in which German-speaking ethnicity played a large part. However, the book contextualizes pan-German Catholicism within other layers of Central European identities.

The comparison of Germany and Austria-Hungary also focuses on the losing powers for reasons of historiographic strategy. One could, for instance, make intriguing comparative studies between Catholic "winners" and "losers" during the war: France and Austria-Hungary or Italy and Austria-Hungary. However, the focus on Germany and Austria-Hungary allows a transnational focus on Catholicism that is both similar and different. It problematizes a pan-Germanic Central European Catholicism, while also relating to the emerging nationality question for Central and Eastern Europe. Most importantly, it allows a pointed historiographic engagement with narratives of disenchantment and loss, which is especially paramount in studies of the First World War's cultural legacy. The dominant narratives of the war's cultural history represent well the story of secularization and literary modernism. This, however, has created a negative teleology. Focusing on the experiences of the losing powers allows engagement with the metanarratives of secularization and modernism, pointing the way toward a Church history of Central Europe that goes beyond the words of bishops toward the beliefs and actions of individual Catholics. It shows that religious believers, even from the losing powers, had formative life experiences that have not been sufficiently represented in the Great War's cultural history.

How does one represent a religious experience, either one's own or, especially, someone else's? There is, at the outset, a fundamental problem of subjectivity: the inability to "peer into hearts," as the Protestant theologian Friedrich Wilhelm Graf has put it.[39] There is also the problem of evidence. As Annette Becker, one of the foremost historians of religion in

---

[38] Gerd Krumeich and Hartmut Lehmann, eds., *"Gott mit uns": Nation, Religion, und Gewalt im 19. und frühen 20. Jahrhundert* (Göttingen: Vandenhoeck & Ruprecht, 2000).

[39] Friedrich Wilhelm Graf, "'Dechristianisierung.' Zur Problemgeschichte eines kulturpolitischen Topos," in *Säkularisierung, Dechristianisierung, Rechristianisierung im neuzeitlichen Europa*, ed. Hartmut Lehmann (Göttingen: Vandenhoeck & Ruprecht, 1997), 66.

France during the Great War, has written, "Traditional religious services and spiritualism, prayers and amulets, the suffering of Christ and the intercession of the saints, ordinary piety and extraordinary revelations all contributed to the religion of wartime. Yet it is hard to reconstitute prayers, fears, and suffering when they leave few archival traces."[40] Perhaps more than other historical questions, religiosity is a problem that tends toward an unreachable limit. Yet the attempt must be made, given the sources at hand.

This is a religious history that gives an impressionistic portrait. For those who seek a quantitatively grounded social scientific history of religion, this book will be especially unsatisfactory: for the most part, it does not chase after representation of religion by measuring statistics such as official communion reception and burial records (even when such records exist), with a few pointed exceptions. Existing statistical data on religious personnel, even for an institution with such deep bureaucratic ties as Catholic military chaplaincy in Germany, are often non-comprehensive and plagued with uncertainty.[41] As a statistical portrait, the "evidence" will be problematic, in some cases relying on one person's retrospective account of what he or she thought, sometimes written down years afterward. Nevertheless, supporting evidence for the book's argument draws on multiple archival sources across Europe, representing other voices marginalized in the historiography of the Great War. This book has surveyed existing archives in an unprecedented breadth and depth for its subject matter, including ecclesiastical, federal, state, and local archives across Central Europe, including Vatican City. Building on previous histories of military religion in Central Europe, this work particularly incorporates sources from Catholic areas of Germany, including Bavaria and the Rhineland, as well as the records of the Austro-Hungarian monarchy centralized in Vienna. This archival detail helps to demonstrate that previously marginalized "epiphenomena" of religious belief were, in fact, pan-European phenomena of utmost importance to how masses of people understood and experienced the war.

Whenever possible, this study seeks the perspectives of the history of everyday life of ordinary believers. Although the pope, bishops, and prominent clerics are an important part of the story, this book strives to give voice to the lay believers, especially women and children. It

---

[40] Becker, "Faith, Ideologies," 241.

[41] The pioneering work of a research team in the Catholic Military Bishop's office has brought a much more comprehensive approach. Nevertheless, this team freely admits being hampered by lack of knowledge of their office's holdings before 1918. See Hans Jürgen Brandt and Peter Häger, eds., *Biographisches Lexikon der Katholischen Militärseelsorge Deutschlands 1848 bis 1945* (Paderborn: Bonifatius, 2002), xii–xiii.

incorporates a topically unparalled source base of personalized ego-documents, such as letters, diaries, and memoirs. Other, more conventional sources also provide context: periodicals and bureaucratic sources such as chaplains' reports to their religious and military superiors. However, in contrast to previous religious histories of the conflict, this work contextualizes the "war theology" rhetoric of the bishops and prominent members of the clergy, especially as represented in official publications. The book lets believers speak in their own voices as much as possible, with relevant context, because the extant personal written sources are the best way of accessing their "life-worlds." As Brad Gregory has recently argued, a history of religion must not seek some instrumentalized social scientific explanation of religion that reduces it to something else; rather, a genuine inquiry about religious belief should seek to clarify "what did it mean to them?"[42] Consequently, whenever possible, one needs to hear believers in their own voice. This does not imply that readers should necessarily believe them, but it does require that we take seriously historical actors' viewpoints as one possibility of what their experience meant. When believers' viewpoints are shared by others, the beliefs in question achieve more social significance. Consequently, we should keep in mind the words of Richard McBrien, who has written that the Catholic Church is, in the minds of believers, "not simply a religious community, institution, or movement (although it is all of these and more)" but also a "mystery, or sacrament... the corporate communal presence of the triune God in the world."[43] In any event, the plurality of Catholic experiences complicates standard notions of the cultural history of the Great War and its religious legacy for twentieth-century Europe.

In line with studies of "total war," this book blurs the boundaries between homefront and battlefront. The book seeks to introduce a "family" history of Catholicism into larger debates about the changing nature of war. It argues that women, children, and family relations connected homefront and battlefront as both a problematic nostalgic ideal and an unsettling new political reality. By incorporating homefront religiosity, this book recasts a religious history of the war that, for Central Europe, has been almost exclusively male and very much focused on the clergy, especially the bishops and the papacy.

Recent works on the history of everyday life in Central Europe have done much to introduce women and children as socio-political actors into

---

[42] Brad S. Gregory, "The Other Confessional History: On Secular Bias in the Study of Religion," *History and Theory* 45, no. 4 (2006): 132–49.

[43] Richard P. McBrien, *The Church: The Evolution of Catholicism* (New York: HarperOne, 2008), 354.

the history of the war, but their religious worldviews have not received adequate attention. The notion of religion as a "lived condition" firmly anchors religious inquiry in a history of everyday life, and this historiographical field has seen marked advances applied to the study of Central Europe during the Great War. Recent works have focused on the breakdown of social relations in capital cities, emphasizing the importance of material conditions, especially food supplies. Maureen Healy's pathbreaking work on the collapse of Imperial Vienna, *Vienna and the Fall of the Habsburg Empire*, shows that women and children became political actors with grievances against the state, and that the imperial patriarchy lost its authority when people realized that the government could not provide food for its citizens.[44] Similarly, with a staggering amount of empirical detail, Roger Chickering's urban history of Freiburg, *The Great War and Urban Life in Germany*, is a pioneering attempt to give a "total history" of "total war" using massive documentation to portray the experiences of a single city. As Chickering freely admits, such histories of everyday life are very good at capturing the "structural and material changes that the war occasioned" but struggle "to accommodate the many different ways in which urban residents made their own war – how they understood, interpreted, or otherwise 'constructed' the war's meaning as they dealt with its mounting burdens."[45] Urban histories showing the socio-political breakdown of the state are a vital component of the war, although one cannot assume that wartime cities were inherent engines of secularization. In contrast, this work is an attempt to recover the religious actions and spiritual worldviews of masses of ordinary Catholic believers across Central Europe. Thus, this book historically problematizes the religious emotions of everyday life,[46] articulating transnational Catholic beliefs in imperial frameworks of the losing powers.

Regarding the structure of the book, Chapter 1 gives a sketch of Catholicism in Germany and Austria-Hungary. While providing a portrayal of religious life in the pre-1914 world, it outlines the structural factors of Catholicism as a minority religion in Germany and a majority religion in Austria-Hungary. Chapter 2 takes up the question of theological worldviews, beginning with the infamous war theology of bishops and

---

[44] Maureen Healy, *Vienna and the Fall of the Habsburg Empire: Total War and Everyday Life in World War I* (Cambridge: Cambridge University Press, 2004).

[45] Roger Chickering, *The Great War and Urban Life in Germany: Freiburg, 1914–1918* (Cambridge: Cambridge University Press, 2007), 7.

[46] For approaches to the burgeoning subfield of the history of religious emotions in Central Europe, see Pascal Eitler, Bettina Hitzer, and Monique Scheer, "Feeling and Faith: Religious Emotions in German History," *German History* 32, no. 3 (2014): 343–52. More generally, see Nicole Eustace et al., "AHR Conversation: The Historical Study of Emotions," *The American Historical Review* 117, no. 5 (2012): 1487–531.

clerics but quickly moving on to discover alternative strands of theology that were to be much more influential for the course of twentieth-century Catholicism. The chapter includes both famous theologians (and their implications for Vatican II) and "little theologies" of everyday experience, including strains of virulent anti-Semitism that would help to lay the groundwork for genocidal complicity during the Second World War. Overall, the chapter stresses how Catholic theology ran on a different time scale of deep continuities, thus minimizing the horror and destruction of the Great War. Moving into the experience of battle directly, Chapter 3 represents the most pointed association of religion with state administration: Catholic military chaplains as state-sponsored clergy members ministering to troops in battle. This chapter shows that even chaplains, the stereotypical fire-breathers of "Praise God and pass the ammunition," were often sensitive and nuanced observers of the upheaval and catastrophe of war. This chapter also highlights the insufficiency of official representations and clerical agency, arguing that religious experiences during the war went well beyond possibilities of clerical control. Nevertheless, chaplains represented an essential source of commentary, simply because of their liminal position and the records they left behind. Chapter 4 goes into the realm of personal spirituality, arguing for recognition of the blurred spectrum of officially sanctioned forms of piety and of "superstitious" elements, showing a mix of folk belief, magic, and official devotion. Catholicism's culture of tangible devotions and intercessory saint culture provided its believers with a wide spectrum of comfort measures and ways of interpreting the chaos of war.

While the first four chapters stress homefront connections as integral to an understanding of total war, Chapter 5 puts more of a focus on the homefront itself. It especially highlights the role of women and children, stressing that the dream of peaceful order was often a form of delusive nostalgia, but was nonetheless a powerful motivating factor in healing societies shattered by war. More concretely, the chapter stresses the essential roles of religious women as members of a caritas network that helped to ameliorate suffering and rebuild the war-torn world; this was especially important as religious resources had to supplement areas that the state was unable to cover. Catholicism's emphasis on the role of the Virgin Mary played a key role in creating a picture of female devotion to Christian sacrifice. Chapter 6 looks at the role of the papacy, arguing that more attention should be paid to the transformative role that Benedict XV had in shaping the Church as a humanitarian political actor both during and after the war. Institutionally speaking, the Church and its new Code of Canon Law from 1917 emerged from the war strengthened, more believable as a non-partisan actor, and poised for a period of interwar renewal and growth through such movements as the youth movement, the liturgical movement, and Catholic Action. Finally, Chapter 7 examines processes of memory and mourning, highlighting how traditional Catholic representations of grief and destruction such as the Mass in Time of War and the motif of the Pietà helped believers understand the chaos of war and mourn the loss of their loved ones. Catholic modes of grief were centered on feminine and familial means of representation, which helped especially to comfort the losing powers. Catholic universalism was a transnational ideal that helped to generate reconciliation but also allowed new nation-states to flourish as new or reborn identities that championed both political particularity and common religious identity.

This book portrays the wide and deep varieties of religious experience. Seen through the everyday lives of Catholic believers from the Great War's losing powers, the Catholic story of the twentieth century does not fit with standard narratives of the First World War as an epic moment of disillusionment. Ultimately, this book shows how the futility of trench warfare on the Western Front is an inadequate master narrative for talking about religion and the European cultural history of the twentieth century.

1   Catholicism on the eve of the Great War in Germany and Austria-Hungary

Through a sketch of pre-1914 developments of Catholicism in Germany and Austria-Hungary, one can properly assess the continuities and changes that the war represented. Religious mentalities were absolutely essential to people's worldviews on the eve of the Great War. Religious belief and practice helped form an essential part of everyday life, particularly in peasant and rural regions.[1] These religious traditions would adapt to the upheavals of war, demonstrating resilence and comfort in the face of potentially atomizing chaos.

This chapter proceeds in a hierarchical fashion that respects the power of different institutional politics at the elite level but also recognizes cultures of everyday life for the majority of rural inhabitants in the empires. Although much of the religious history of Central European Catholics is a story of shared overlap in peasant regions, important imperial differences remain. The methodology of the chapter highlights certain structural features based on their historiographical significance to the respective empire. For example, the "nationalities" question is treated in the section about Austria-Hungary and ultramontanism remains in the context of the *Kulturkampf* in Germany. One could also speak about the "Polish" or "Alsatian" members of the Hohenzollern monarchy and the rise of ultramontanism after the post-1855 Concordat in the Habsburg monarchy. Thus, examining these issues as placed is not a claim of imperial exclusivity but rather a matter of historiographical prominence. Nevertheless, the historiography gives an idea of the disparate political contours of the empires. As the chapter proceeds to discuss matters of everyday life for Catholics, irrespective of political frameworks, it becomes much more of an "entangled history" of a common Catholic way of life in Central Europe.[2]

---

[1] Jenkins, *The Great and Holy War*, 14–16.
[2] Heinz-Gerhard Haupt and Jürgen Kocka, eds., *Comparative and Transnational History: Central European Approaches and New Perspectives* (New York: Berghahn Books, 2009). See also Jürgen Kocka, "Comparison and Beyond," *History & Theory* 42, no. 1 (2003): 39–44.

The chapter begins by examining the socio-political scene in comparative frameworks. Catholics in Austria-Hungary were a favored majority religion and part of the throne-and-altar alliance. In Germany, by contrast, Catholics were a suspect minority religion newly integrated into a Protestant-dominated German Empire largely controlled by Prussia. After laying out how Catholicism fit into the official frameworks in the Habsburg and Hohenzollern Empires, the chapter proceeds to examine religious life at a more personal level of lived experience for the adherents of the Catholic religion. This can be no more than a cursory sketch that falls short of the unreachable ideal inherent in individual religious subjectivity. Nevertheless, the chapter offers an impressionistic sketch in order to address the question of personal worldviews, outlooks, and ways of life, which is often obscured by larger narratives about secularization and the course of the Great War. Finally, in order to emphasize the comparative aspects of conflict across time, the chapter concludes with a brief examination of religion during the last major wars that Central Europe fought before 1914: the Austro-Prussian War of 1866 and the Franco-Prussian War of 1870–71.

Austria-Hungary

At the turn of the twentieth century, the Catholic throne-and-altar alliance was alive and well in Austria-Hungary; indeed, the Habsburg Empire was the most Catholic of the Great Powers.[3] On the eve of the Great War, Austro-Hungarian Catholics were a favored religious majority, part of a medieval dynasty that dated back to the year 1273 and the founding of the Habsburg monarchy. More recently in an era of rising nationalism, Catholicism was a cultural element with unifying, transnational tendencies. Religious affiliation, even for nominal believers, was a form of communal participation in a non-national imagined community. Measured in purely quantitative confessional statistics, Catholics made up over seventy-nine percent of the monarchy's inhabitants. In the Cisleithanian or "Austrian" half of the Dual Monarchy established in 1867, Roman Catholics made up over ninety-three percent of citizens.[4]

---

[3] Deep into the war, Austro-Hungarian diplomats would interpret the interest of their country as the indispensible "Catholic superpower" of Europe in their conversations with Eugenio Pacelli, the new Apostolic Nuncio in Bavaria and future Pope Pius XII. See HHSA, PA IV, Ktn. 59: "Bayern: Berichte, Weisungen, Varia, 1917–18" Berichte 1917 (folder), pp. 146–51, "Erster Empfang bei neuen Nuntius Mgr. Pacelli."

[4] Maximilian Liebmann, "Von der Dominanz der katholischen Kirche zu freien Kirchen im freien Staat – vom Wiener Kongreß 1815 bis zur Gegenwart," in *Geschichte des Christentums in Österreich*, ed. Rudolf Leeb, Maximilian Liebmann, and Georg Scheibelreiter, *Österreichische Geschichte* (Vienna: Ueberreuter, 2003), 379. In the Transleithanian or

In some areas of the Habsburg Empire, Catholic identity was largely based on a lack of alternatives. The 1905 statistics for the diocese of Laibach (Ljubljana), for instance, had the highest proportion of Catholics in the Habsburg lands: 99.76% of all inhabitants were registered as Catholic.[5] Describing the All Saints' festival, filled with holy water, incense, prayer, and candles placed on graves, the rural farm laborer Richard Puchner, from Nikolsdorf in east Tyrol, revealed almost parenthetically that many in these communities viewed public demonstrative piety as the observable belief of the overwhelming majority. Puchner noted that during such events, "The believers – for this purpose numbered actually everyone . . . "[6] Of course, communal religious belief and practice, never mind individual religious subjectivity, varied greatly across disparate localities that can only be unpacked through thickly descriptive anthropologies.[7] Nevertheless, the majority of Central and Eastern Europeans inclined toward more long-established traditions and customs, including a religious worldview. As a pre-1914 trend, the notion of avant garde modernism remains hollow without a majority of *garde* as the movement's backdrop.

Viewed dynastically, Catholicism stood as a redoubt against pressures from both inside and outside the monarchy's borders. As the oldest Great Power monarchy in Europe, with deep continuities that began several hundred years before the Romanovs, the Habsburg monarchy held fast to the deep-seated historical symbolic value of the throne-and-altar alliance. In its own conceptualization, the monarchy felt itself to be the premier Catholic dynasty of Europe – an impression that, with regard to other governments on the European scene, was not mistaken. The Habsburgs steeped themselves in a demonstratively and highly symbolic Catholic public piety of the early modern era, especially that of the Baroque era, with its Counter-Reformation aesthetics and sensibilities.[8]

Nevertheless, Habsburg Catholicism had to account for the secularizing rationalist tendencies of the reformist Emperor Joseph II, who, among other measures, seized Church property and closed monasteries that appeared "unproductive" to state aims; Joseph had introduced

"Hungarian" half of the monarchy, Roman Catholics nominally made up 58% of the population.

[5] Rupert Klieber, *Jüdische, Christliche, Muslimische Lebenswelten der Donaumonarchie 1848–1918* (Vienna: Böhlau, 2010), 101.

[6] Norbert Ortmayr, ed., *Knechte. Autobiographische Dokumente und sozialhistorische Skizzen, Damit es nicht verlorengeht* (Vienna: Böhlau, 1992), 91.

[7] For a ground-breaking scholarly work of local religious anthropology, see William A. Christian, *Person and God in a Spanish Valley*, rev. edn. (Princeton, NJ: Princeton University Press, 1988).

[8] Anna Coreth, *Pietas Austriaca*, trans. William D. Bowman and Anna Maria Leitgeb (West Lafayette, IN: Purdue University Press, 2004).

a rationalizing conception of state that would remain as a prominent motive in discussions of Central European governance.[9] At the mid-century point, the Revolution of 1848 had shaken the foundations of the empire, but military intervention had preserved the monarchy and reinforced the conservatives. In the aftermath, Emperor Franz Joseph tended toward a policy of Neo-Absolutism that would reassert historical traditionalism in the face of centrifugal nationalist, socialist, and modernist tendencies.

At the turn of the twentieth century, the monarchy based its political legitimacy on the symbolic traditionalism of the monarch and the dynasty's association with the Catholic Church. It was a policy that underscored adaptive traditionalism, both entrenched and flexible to the needs of the moment. Perhaps most explicitly demonstrated to the public was the emperor's annual pre-Easter participation in the Holy Thursday ceremony of the foot-washing of twelve men, in direct imitation of the behavior of Christ and the apostles – with the emperor playing the role of Christ, the foot-washer. Another highpoint of Habsburg symbolism was the annual procession in Vienna for the festival of Corpus Christi, held three weeks after Trinity Sunday based on the liturgical calendar. With equal parts humility and majesty, the procession explicitly linked the Emperor, Franz Joseph, with both the medieval heritage of his ancestors, especially the founder of the dynasty, Rudolf von Habsburg, and the cult of the Eucharist, thus forming a direct link to Christ as a defender of the faith. The 1898 procession, following close on the heels of the Badeni crisis, which introduced acrimony about German–Czech language disputes into official bureaucratic policy, highlighted the dynasty's attempt to reinforce its image as the main supranational, centripetal force uniting the peoples of the Habsburg realm.[10]

On the eve of the Great War, the main supranational pillars were the dynasty, the military, and the bureaucracy. Before 1914, centrifugal forces were stirring but were not yet strong enough to bring down the imperial edifice. Nevertheless, there was a growing sense of more exclusive localism and the formation of separate imagined communities. Even in such stereotypically "traditional" Catholic areas of "Poland," Imperial spectacles with explicit religious symbolism, such as processions in Galicia, showed that local actors appropriated the imperial dynasty to suit local needs of symbolic representation and the legitimation of authority.

---

[9] Derek Beales, *Joseph II. Against the World, 1780–1790* (Cambridge: Cambridge University Press, 2009).

[10] For the account of the Corpus Christi procession, see *Neue Freie Presse* June 10, 1898, p. 1. For analysis of the symbolism, see James Shedel, "Emperor, Church, and People: Religion and Dynastic Loyalty During the Golden Jubilee of Franz Joseph," *Catholic Historical Review* 76, no. 1 (1990): 71–92.

Yet the local actors, in this case Galician nobles and gentry, remained loyal to the dynasty.[11]

In order to give a narrative framework to the confusing jumble of sovereignties and peoples that has existed since the medieval era, for a long time even scholarly grand narratives of the Habsburg monarchy tele-ologically characterized the polity as unviable in an age of rising nationalism. A generation of scholarship has done much to revise the notion that Austria-Hungary on the eve of the Great War was one of the "sick men" of Europe, hobbled by centrifugal nationalism. Viewed in terms of church–state policies, religion added another layer of complexity to the nationalist movements. In the Cisleithanian ("Austrian") half of the monarchy, national sentiment for disparate ethnicities focused on achieving leadership gains for that particular ethnicity as a leading people of the empire. Foremost in this category were Germans, Hungarians, Poles, and Italians. On the other hand, for the other ethnicities of the monarchy, primarily Czechs, Slovaks, Croats, Serbs, Slovenes, and Ruthenes, there was a more revolutionary and emancipating aspect to religious national movements. This involved achieving more autonomy vis-à-vis the dominant ethnic groups. In the Transleithanian ("Hungarian") half of the monarchy, for instance, the government policies of cultural magyarization generated resistance in non-magyar minorities.[12] Although the religious aspects of nationalist policy remain underexplored on an imperial level, before 1914, and even late into the Great War, nationalist movements in the Habsburg monarchy were not separatist. With the exception of a few nationalist leaders such as Thomas Masaryk who eventually did seek polities separate from the Habsburgs, most nationalists wanted a greater share of autonomy within the imperial framework, usually at the expense of other nationalities. The nationalists wanted greater freedom within the political imaginary that had structured social relations for centuries. No one foresaw the destruction, political reordering, and ethno-national separatism that were consequences of the Great War.[13]

The politics of nationality and language highlighted the complexities of religious identity in the Habsburg monarchy. The emergence of a singular chosen form of language was rightly one of the important moments in the emergence of nationalism. Yet at a very personal level for

---

[11] Daniel L. Unowsky, *The Pomp and Politics of Patriotism: Imperial Celebrations in Habsburg Austria, 1848–1916*, Central European Studies (West Lafayette, IN: Purdue University Press, 2005).

[12] Andreas Gottsmann, *Rom und die nationalen Katholizismen in der Donaumonarchie. Römischer Universalismus, habsburgische Reichspolitik und nationale Identitäten 1878–1914* (Vienna: Verlag der Österreichischen Akademie der Wissenschaften, 2010), 299–331.

[13] Cohen, "Nationalist Politics," 241–78; Kwan, "Nationalism and All That," 88–101.

religious believers, language mattered for the performance of sacramental rituals from birth to death. Perhaps most pointedly and frequently, there was the issue of what language the priest should use to deliver the sermon at Mass. For instance, as decreed by the Council of Trent, Church Slavonic was an officially accepted language of liturgy. However, especially in the South Slav regions of the Habsburg Empire, a more pan-ethnic concept of Church Slavonic developed as both clergy and laity confused Church Slavonic with the concepts of disparate ethno-national languages. Even a direct decree issued in 1907 by the reactionary Pope Saint Pius X proved unenforceable in its aim of reining in the privileges of Church Slavonic as a liturgical language.[14] As in many matters of Church doctrine, local implementation did not coincide with central direction.

In a similar vein, seminaries were not simply points of Vatican authority and could often serve as hotbeds of nationalist fervor, depending on the shifting whims of the bishops responsible for staffing teachers. For the papal nuncio Emidio Taliani, for instance, the seminary in Zara was the nexus of a South Slav nationalist movement centered in Dalmatia, led by the priest, journalist, and politician Ivan Prodan and the newspaper *Katolička Dalmacija*. Despite his misgivings, however, Taliani could do little to change the Zara seminary, as it enjoyed the support of strong bishops: Frane Uccellini and Josip Marčelić. Both Uccellini and Marčelić had been former professors in the Zara seminary and supported it as a cultural beacon for nationalist awakening.[15] As educated spokesmen and community leaders, these clerics gradually became caught up in national movements, particularly in the South Slavic regions of the monarchy.[16]

In their political imaginations, priests, as leaders of national awakening, were not part of a centrifugal nationalist movement away from the Habsburg monarchy. Drawing inspiration from Herder's notion of difference rather than Fichte's superiority principle, the priests' individual visions of nationalism were within the universalism of Church. Bishops from the South Slavic regions, like Johann Josef Strossmayr, cultivated national awakening as a facet of particularistic cultures rooted in language. However, the deeply ingrained notion of hierarchical authority focused on loyalty to the sovereign authority of the emperor, based on scripture such as Romans 13:1–2: "Let every person be subordinate to the higher authorities, for there is no authority except from God, and those that exist have been established by God. / Therefore, whoever resists

---

[14] Gottsmann, *Rom und die nationalen Katholizismen*, 308–11.   [15] Ibid., 320.
[16] Peter Leisching, "Die römisch-katholische Kirche in Cisleithanien," in *Die Habsburg-ermonarchie, 1848–1918*, ed. Adam Wandruszka and Peter Urbanitsch (Vienna: Verlag für die Österreichische Akademie der Wissenschaften, 1980), 232–7.

authority opposes what God has appointed, and those who oppose it will bring judgment upon themselves."

At the local level, a foremost point of Catholic authority was the priest. In both Austria-Hungary and Germany, lower-ranking Catholic clergy members were closer in social origin to the peasant peoples to whom they ministered. This was especially striking when seen in contrast to other religious groups in the Austro-Hungarian monarchy: Jewish, Eastern Orthodox, Muslim, and Protestant religious leaders were mostly from bourgeois backgrounds.[17] Catholic clergy members were leaders of laity, without competition for leadership of the religious community. In their self-perception as an imitation of Christ, they were shepherds of the flock. Viewed more sociologically, the clerics were on-the-ground point men for the interpretation and translation of old and new values, as well as distributors of sacramental rites deemed essential to believers. In contrast to other religious groups, Catholic priests were a celibate caste that had to be newly recruited each generation. There was a pronounced democratization and indeed active recruitment of peasant and underprivileged groups, especially through small priestly seminary training schools in the nineteenth century. This reinforced the "ideal of the selfless Priest and pastor" committed to the Church, and democratized the Church leadership, particularly compared to religious leaders of other faiths. In no other religious social group could the sons of peasants rise within one generation to become bishops, cardinals, or even pope.[18] At the same time, these priests also had a large measure of gratitude toward the institutional Church for their improved social station.

In 1914, Austria-Hungary remained an overwhelmingly agrarian country populated by peasants. During the nineteenth century, some industrialization had taken place, diffusing from west to east and from north to south. In particular, there were pockets of industry in the Bohemian lands and the areas around Vienna and other large cities. Yet on the whole, Austria-Hungary remained socio-economically similar to many rural and agrarian regions in the southern and eastern parts of the German Empire.[19]

There were, however, movements of modernization associated with increasing urbanization and the rise of political liberalism and its

[17] Rupert Klieber, "Soziale Integration durch Religion? Die konfessionelle Milieus der Habsburgermonarchie und ihr Einfluss auf die Lebenspraxis der Bevölkerung," in *Die Habsburgermonarchie 1848–1918*, vol. 9: *Soziale Strukturen*, ed. Helmut Rumpler and Peter Urbanitsch (Vienna: Verlag der Österreichischen Akademie der Wissenschaften, 2010), 746–9.

[18] Ibid., 759–60.

[19] Roman Sandgruber, ed., *Ökonomie und Politik: österreichische Wirtschaftsgeschichte vom Mittelalter bis zur Gegenwart* (Vienna: Ueberreuter, 1995).

opponents in the post-1848 era. The rise of the Christian Social Party in Austria highlighted ways in which a modern political party could claim a religious mantle, especially in contrast to its opponents, and yet operate its own agenda largely independent of the Church, beyond symbolic gestures. Although sometimes classified as a Fascist mass-party prototype, the Christian Social Party was in fact a movement of particular urban politics applied to local conditions peculiar to the curia voting system of Vienna. Through successive appeals to different voting blocs, the movement harnessed disillusionment with Liberal governance and channeled especially lower middle-class artisan discontentment into a coherent program of urban renewal fostered by the dynamic and particularly Viennese mayor, Karl Lueger.[20] The Christian Social Party modernized the urban infrastructure of Vienna, while using the renovated city as a springboard into imperial political aspirations.[21] It was also infamous for its electoral appropriation of anti-Semitism.

As in much of Central and Eastern Europe, popular anti-Semitism had a long tradition in Germany. However, in Germany, anti-Semitic discourse acquired a much more explicitly racial tinge, associated with the singularity of the incipient German nation. In the nineteenth century, the civic "bonds of community" between Jews and Christians were not yet snapped but were being decisively weakened, precisely as the concept of German nationalism became more exclusivist, with strong Christian overtones.[22]

The old artificial distinctions between religious anti-Semitism (that is, doctrinally based, drawing on ancient roots) and racist anti-Semitism (blood-based, beginning in the nineteenth century) had considerable overlap in Central Europe, which increased at the turn of the twentieth century.[23] The dual anti-Semitisms as a form of cultural code represented one aspect of the triumph of ultramontanism and its hostility toward outsiders, and this helped pave the way for the eventual triumph of eliminationist racism.[24] As Urs Altermatt has shown at the liturgical level, devotional practices helped to reinforce the ideological presuppositions. At Good Friday services among Swiss Catholics, priests knelt in prayer to

[20] John W. Boyer, *Political Radicalism in Late Imperial Vienna: Origins of the Christian Social Movement, 1848–1897* (Chicago: University of Chicago Press, 1981), ix–xiv.

[21] John W. Boyer, *Culture and Political Crisis in Vienna: Christian Socialism in Power, 1897–1918* (Chicago: University of Chicago Press, 1995).

[22] Helmut Walser Smith, *The Continuities of German History: Nation, Religion, and Race across the Long Nineteenth Century* (Cambridge: Cambridge University Press, 2008), 39–73.

[23] John Connelly, "Catholic Racism and Its Opponents," *Journal of Modern History* 79, no. 4 (2007): 813–47.

[24] Olaf Blaschke, *Katholizismus und Antisemitismus im Deutschen Kaiserreich* (Göttingen: Vandenhoeck & Ruprecht, 1997).

atone for every group except the Jews; furthermore, the tumult of rattles during the Good Friday Way of the Cross was said to represent the clamor of Jewish voices mocking Christ. There was even overlap between liturgy and more deep-seated forms of popular religion: Easter bonfires were known as "Jew burnings" in many regional dialects.[25]

The rise of modern political anti-Semitism in Central Europe developed against a background of coming to terms with wide-ranging modernization. Industrial capitalism was rapidly changing the agrarian social structures that had been in place for centuries. Rising life expectancies combined with better methods of public health, and the new masses of workers created new social classes that threatened established social orders, especially the lower middle class. Movements for political emancipation and full equality of voting rights caused the rise of demagogic politicians who harnessed anti-modern critiques of convenient scapegoats, particularly the Jews. For the anti-Semites, critique of the Jews was a rage against the progressive developments of political liberalism.[26] The beginnings of anti-Semitic political movements represented a "politics in a new key" as the ossified political structures of the Habsburg Empire generated increasing discontent vented culturally. The most visible and prominent anti-Semite, Georg Ritter von Schönerer, was the leader of the pan-German movement in the Habsburg monarchy. Since the movement was explicitly anti-Habsburg and anti-Catholic, it faced an uphill battle against deeply ingrained social structures, never capturing more than four percent of the popular vote. Schönerer's increasing troubles with the law eventually caused his public disgrace and caused him to be more of an ideological figurehead than a practical leader.[27]

Long-simmering ideological hatreds could fester in areas where Catholics were either a minority or a majority. On the level of popular anti-Semitism, especially among rural populations, lower clergy members drew on ancient stereotypes of hatred against Jews, which helped to fan the ideological flames against perceived non-belongers in the organic and hierarchical Christian community. Although official pogroms did not exist, unlike, for example, in Russia, popular resentments could nonetheless combine with official persecution, perhaps most spectacularly in the

---

[25] Urs Altermatt, *Katholizismus und Antisemitismus: Mentalitäten, Kontinuitäten, Ambivalenzen: zur Kulturgeschichte der Schweiz 1918–1945* (Frauenfeld: Huber, 1999).

[26] Peter Pulzer, *The Rise of Political Anti-Semitism in Germany and Austria*, rev. edn. (Cambridge, MA: Harvard University Press, 1988), 3–26.

[27] For the classic examination of this phenomenon, see Carl E. Schorske, *Fin de siècle Vienna: Politics and Culture* (New York: Alfred A. Knopf, 1980), 116–80.

form of "blood libel" trials against Jews who were accused of purport-edly killing Christian children and using their blood for religious rituals. Blood libels erupted into public persecutions in places like Tiszaeszlár, Polná, and Zabolotiv.

Along with the influential Catholic noble convert Baron Karl von Vogelsang, publisher of *Vaterland*, clerical anti-Semites such as Sebastian Brunner and Albert Wiesinger, publishers of the *Wiener Kirchenzeitung*, disseminated vulgar anti-Jewish stereotypes to a wide audience. They later began to combine these outbursts with a more refined anti-modern social critique against the liberal-capitalist order.[28]

Nevertheless, on the eve of war in 1914, the position of Jews in Ger-many and Austria-Hungary seemed remarkably favorable to contempo-raries; indeed, it seemed a "golden era" in the history of Central and Eastern European Jewry. Built on the traditions of Emperor Joseph II, in Austria-Hungary the Emperor Franz Joseph, who ruled from 1849 to 1916, had fostered a policy of religious tolerance. It was an age in which Jews had made remarkable progress toward civic equality in their integration into majority Christian societies.[29]

Germany

On the eve of the Great War, the political situation of Catholics in Ger-many could not have been more different from that of their counter-parts in Austria-Hungary. In the homeland of the Protestant Reforma-tion begun by Martin Luther in 1517, the split between Protestants and Catholics formed a long-standing and essential part of the cultural his-tory. While other cultural nations such as England and France became politically unified in the early modern period, Germany remained polit-ically fragmented into the nineteenth century. The late formation of the German political nation after the Franco-Prussian War of 1870–71 rein-forced the tendency for German Catholics to be viewed as second-class citizens of the Wilhelmine Empire. Perhaps overly anxious concerning its parvenu status among the European great powers, this German Empire remained profoundly suspicious of its citizens with transnational loyal-ties, especially Catholics and Socialists.

Making up around thirty-six percent of the empire's citizens, Catholics were a sizeable and problematic minority viewed from the vantage point of centralizing, homogenizing Protestant Prussia. As a group, Catholics

[28] Bruce F. Pauley, *From Prejudice to Persecution: A History of Austrian Anti-Semitism* (Chapel Hill: University of North Carolina Press, 1992), 17–40.
[29] Ibid., 45–60.

were large enough to form an ideological problem for Protestant nationalists, yet small enough that the powers of state could oppress them with
comparative impunity. In the German Empire founded in 1871, persecution of Catholics became official state policy as part of the culture
war (*Kulturkampf*) waged by Chancellor Otto von Bismarck from 1871
to 1878. Bismarck's plans foresaw an emphatically Protestant Prussia
as the leading force in the unification of German states. In a progressive modern era of nineteenth-century liberal advancement, Catholicism
seemed to many liberals to be the antithesis of the modern, and indeed,
anti-Catholicism was a key part of the German liberal self-identity.[30]

Among other means, Bismarck's official measures of repression
included prohibiting Catholic electoral candidates, closing Catholic
schools, imprisoning bishops, and fining clergy members who spoke
against the government. Enacted in the Reichstag, the "pulpit paragraph"
of 1871 was a national law that forbade the use of Catholic pulpits for
political purposes, with considerable interpretive leeway given to state
authorities about what was considered "political." The following year, the
entire Jesuit order was banned from Germany.[31] More direct attempts
followed in the state of Prussia with the famous "May Laws" of 1873,
which attempted to gain unquestioned state control over religious education and clerical appointments. However, most of these initial repressive
measures did not achieve their full aims, leading to a second, harsher wave
of measures in 1874–75, primarily in Prussian lands. These new measures focused on removing state funds from priests who refused to swear
allegiance to government policy. This led to clerical imprisonments, as
well as to priests hiding within Germany and going into exile abroad.
Dioceses went without bishops (at one point, there were only three bishops officially on their seats in the whole of the German Empire), and
1400 parishes (nearly one-third of all German parishes) were left without
priests. State authorities confiscated Church property and administered
it as their own. At the end of the conflict, over 1800 priests had been
jailed or exiled and German authorities had seized over 16 million marks'
worth of Church property.[32]

In the end, however, Catholic resistance overcame the *Kulturkampf*.
The repression, which some Catholics melodramatically likened to the

---

[30] Michael B. Gross, *The War against Catholicism: Liberalism and the Anti-Catholic Imagination in Nineteenth-Century Germany* (Ann Arbor: University of Michigan Press, 2004).

[31] Róisín Healy, *The Jesuit Specter in Imperial Germany* (Boston, MA: Brill, 2003). Though
the law prohibiting the Jesuits was substantially reduced by the turn of the twentieth
century, it remained officially on the books until 1917.

[32] For an overview of the *Kulturkampf*, see Atkin and Tallett, *Priests, Prelates, and People*,
130–47 and Burleigh, *Earthly Powers*, 320–36.

ancient Roman persecutions by Nero and Diocletian, caused Catholic solidarity to coalesce around resistance to the persecutors. This happened not only locally but especially on an imperial level, as a strong Catholic group identity developed. Foremost among the leaders was the dynamic new force in German politics, the Catholic Center Party, and its adroit leader, Ludwig Windthorst. By 1879, the *Kulturkampf* had died down, and Bismarck set his sights on other targets, namely the Socialists.[33]

Bismarck's anti-Catholicism was based on a vision of Catholicism as an undesired competing loyalty for the modern unitary German state. This was not an unfounded suspicion. German theologians in particular, led by Ignaz von Döllinger in Munich, had publicly opposed the infallibility decree, but infallibility gained widespread acceptance among most clergy members and lay Catholics. Although a few bourgeois Central European Catholics had formed a movement known as "Old Catholicism" that did not recognize the decree of infallibility, this never gained a mass following. Instead of causing another radical splintering of the Church, the infallibility decree was a "victory for ultramontanism" that represented a Rome-oriented move toward centralization and greater authoritarian and hierarchical clerical control.[34] After the *Kulturkampf* wound down, most of the official anti-Catholic measures were quietly repealed. But the unofficial confessional cleft remained strong, and mutual suspicion continued. The German Kaiser remained the official head of the Protestant Church in Germany, and anti-Catholicism remained a strong undercurrent in German politics.

German Catholicism had two strong elements that sometimes worked at cross-purposes: ultramontanism and regionalism. Viewed from Germany, ultramontanism, or "beyond the mountains" (i.e., the Alps), meant a Catholic orientation toward Rome.[35] In key ways, Catholic defensiveness against *Kulturkampf* persecutions had solidified German Catholic orientation toward a more homogenous social milieu. In actual practice, the boundaries of the social world of the milieu were porous, but as a social orientation point, it was an ideological ghetto.[36] These various milieus formed both a worldview and a way of daily life. They

---

[33] Gross, *War against Catholicism*, 288–91.

[34] Thomas Nipperdey, *Religion im Umbruch: Deutschland, 1870–1918* (Munich: C. H. Beck, 1988), 9–13.

[35] As the example of the Archdiocese of Freiburg shows, even within the relatively progressive enclave of the state of Baden, the formation of priests and monks in the seminaries was becoming more ultramontane in the late nineteenth and early twentieth centuries. Irmtraud Götz von Olenhusen, *Klerus und abweichendes Verhalten: zur Sozialgeschichte katholischer Priester im 19. Jahrhundert: die Erzdiözese Freiburg* (Göttingen: Vandenhoeck & Ruprecht, 1994).

[36] Heilbronner, "From Ghetto to Ghetto," 453–95.

provided a cradle-to-grave point of identity according to which people could define their allegiances. The primary bulwarks of the milieu
were the press media and the networks of associations (*Vereine*) that
gave German Catholics a specifically religious content as their locus of
identity.[37]

Regionalism in German Catholicism meant the regional dynamics of
four core regions: Bavaria, Silesia, Baden, and Rhineland-Westphalia.[38]
Across the whole of Germany, many German Catholics were more
inclined than their Austro-Hungarian counterparts to identify with the
singular modern German nation. Nationalization was taking place con-
currently with ultramontanization in the years leading up to 1914.[39] Yet
Germany, and especially German Catholics, remained regionally fragmented, and even the incipient national consciousness often saw the
nation as a local metaphor.[40] The deep-seated notion of *Heimat* was
rooted in localisms, not progressively superseded by nationalism. Particularly in outlying areas of the Wilhelmine Empire, such as Silesia and
Alsace-Lorraine, pluralities of identity and religious affiliation existed.
Often contrary to the wishes of exclusive nationalists, Silesian Catholics
were "neither German nor Pole"; they instead identified themselves based
on locality and varying degrees of religious commitment.[41]

Within these regions, there was a wide range of social-class orientation between areas in Rhineland-Westphalia and their Bavarian counterparts. Overall, the social structures of many German Catholics from
rural regions, most particularly Bavaria, were similar to those of Catholics
in the Austro-Hungarian monarchy. This was a world that was focused

---

[37] This defensive subculture originated in studies of German electoral behavior and took
on broader social implications. On multiple regional levels, culminating at the imperial
level, scholars portrayed the Catholic milieu in Germany in opposition to various other
milieus, primarily Protestant, Socialist, Liberal, and National (Arbeitskreis für kirchliche Zeitgeschichte, "Katholiken zwischen Tradition und Moderne," 588–654). For
a pointed argument about clerics as "milieu managers," see Blaschke, "Die Kolonialisierung der Laienwelt."

[38] Thomas Mergel, "Milieu und Religion. Überlegungen zur Ver-Ortung kollektiver Identitäten," in *Sachsen in Deutschland. Politik, Kultur und Gesellschaft 1830–1918*, ed. James
N. Retallack (Bielefeld: Gütersloh, 2000), 265–79.

[39] Rudolf Morsey, "Die Deutsche Katholiken und der Nationalstaat zwischen Kulturkampf und Erstem Weltkrieg," *Historisches Jahrbuch* 90, no. 3 (1970): 31–64. More
recently, see Barbara Stambolis, "Nationalisierung trotz Ultramontanisierung oder:
'Alles für Deutschland. Deutschland aber für Christus': mentalitätsleitende Wertorientierung deutscher Katholiken im 19. und 20. Jahrhundert," *Historische Zeitschrift* 269
(1999): 57–97.

[40] Alon Confino, *The Nation as a Local Metaphor: Württemberg, Imperial Germany, and
National Memory, 1871–1918* (Chapel Hill: University of North Carolina Press, 1997).

[41] James E. Bjork, *Neither German nor Pole: Catholicism and National Indifference in a Central
European Borderland* (Ann Arbor: University of Michigan Press, 2008).

on petite-bourgeois and agrarian concerns. It was a world that was pre-capitalist, pre-industrial, and in many ways, pre-modern. Most Catholics lived in communities of under 10 000 inhabitants. According to the figures of the 1907 census, Catholics formed 36.5% of all the citizens of the German Empire. Yet, Catholics were statistically overrepresented in the primary sector of the economy, where they made up 44.2% of all workers, and underrepresented in the tertiary sector, where they made up 29.9% of workers.[42]

Catholics in Germany came from a wider spectrum of socio-economic development than did their counterparts in Austria-Hungary. Rapidly developing industrialization, especially in western areas of Prussia such as the Ruhr and Rhineland-Westphalia, caused major socio-economic shifts in heavily Catholic areas. In Münster, for instance, the number of Catholics per parish district went from a little over 3000 in 1845 to a highpoint of 6500 in 1899. Studies of advancing urbanization in cities like Münster and Bochum indicated that even the rapid industrialization had much less of a secularizing effect on the Catholic milieu than it did on Protestant adherents.[43] Especially in the mining regions and in places of heavy industry in Silesia and Rhineland-Westphalia (and in further regional strongholds like Upper Silesia and the Saar region, respectively), the Christian workers' movement organized 350 000 workers by 1912, and these numbers would increase during and after the war. Despite more coercive labor measures deployed by the military administrative state, membership in Christian trade unions rose dramatically during the war, from 178 907 in 1916 to 538 559 in 1918 and 1 000 070 in 1919.[44] Faced with the specter of socialism, Christian trade unions provided an attractive alternative for union members. Nevertheless, one should not equate industrialization with progressively secular modernity. Daily existential rhythms of hard labor with little hope of social advancement, as well as the omnipresent threat of serious injury or death, caused Catholic religion to be a source of comfort and consolation to miners, iron smelters, and machine operators. This was especially so in contrast to a more ideal-type "bourgeois religion" of relatively abstract pure personal faith, distinct from traditional elements of popular religion.[45] The

---

[42] Nipperdey, *Religion im Umbruch*, 38–9.

[43] Antonius Liedhegener, *Christentum und Urbanisierung: Katholiken und Protestanten in Münster und Bochum 1830–1933* (Paderborn: F. Schöningh, 1997), 174.

[44] Hans-Georg Aschoff, "Von der Revolution 1848/49 bis zum Ende des Ersten Weltkrieges," in *Laien in der Kirche*, ed. Erwin Gatz, *Geschichte des kirchlichen Lebens* (Freiburg: Herder, 2008), 171–4, 190–1.

[45] Josef Mooser, "Katholische Volksreligion, Klerus, und Bürgertum in der zweiten Hälfte des 19. Jahrhunderts: Thesen," in *Religion und Gesellschaft im 19. Jahrhundert*, ed. Wolfgang Schieder (Stuttgart: Klett-Cotta, 1993), 150–4.

war would provide yet another source of chaos and death, and religion would again provide comfort and interpretive orientation.

As both a defensive reaction and a declaration of independent identity during the *Kulturkampf*, the Catholic press media began to expand rapidly in the 1870s during the consolidation of the majority Protestant Wilhelmine Empire. The main daily newspapers that achieved an imperial circulation were the *Kölnische Volkszeitung* and *Germania*. These were supplemented by magazines and journals such as the *Historisch-Politische Blätter*. In many cases, the most prominent periodicals had further subcultural themes within Catholicism, such as *Stimmen aus Maria Laach* (later *Stimmen der Zeit*), which served Jesuit audiences, and the yearbooks of the *Görres Gesellschaft*, for the academic and scientific communities.

The network of associations formed an important part of German Catholicism, giving adherents a strong sense of identity vis-à-vis non-Catholics, but also permitting a degree of regional variability and personal independence within the subculture. Meetings of quasi-national groups at yearly "Catholic Days" (*Katholikentage*) had taken place since 1848. The foundation of the *Volksverein für das katholische Deutschland* in 1890 represented a decisive step forward, especially defined in opposition to Social-Democratic mass organizations. In 1891, the *Volksverein* registered 105 000 members; by 1914, this number had risen to around 800 000.[46] The thick network of *Vereine* had important regional variations. The *Vereine* were strongest in areas of increasing industrialization and helped ease the move toward a more differentiated class structure. Thus, Rhineland-Westphalia remained the center of the strongest *Verein* movements, while in Bavaria, the parish church remained the heart of village religious life.[47]

Germany, as a rapidly advancing industrial nation, put women at the forefront of debates about modernization – and Catholicism's perceived anti-modernity. Across Europe, the nineteenth century witnessed a remarkable feminization of the Catholic Church. Larger processes of industrialization and the rise of new social classes – the bourgeoisie and the proletariat – led to a restructuring of social relations as women and children became increasingly visible on the socio-political scene. Both official doctrine and public piety operated dialectically. Women began to enter religious congregations and orders in larger numbers and made up a larger proportion of those parishioners who attended church regularly.

---

[46] Nipperdey, *Religion im Umbruch*, 24–5.
[47] Josef Mooser, "Das katholische Milieu in der bürgerlichen Gesellschaft. Zum Vereinswesen des Katholizismus im späten Deutschen Kaiserreich," in *Religion im Kaiserreich. Milieus, Mentalitäten, Krisen.*, ed. Olaf Blaschke and Frank-Michael Kuhlemann (Gütersloh: Chr. Kaiser, 1996), 59–92.

Across Europe, sharper distinctions began to emerge between practicing and non-practicing Catholics, with more men gradually seeing religion as a "women's sphere." Even if religious men chose to associate with the established Church or its associational networks, husbands left ever more religious matters to the control of their wives, daughters, and other female relatives.[48] Particularly within the Catholic Church, women and children became visible and prominent historical actors, with unprecedented degrees of authority compared to their Protestant and Jewish counterparts in the public sphere. This was especially demonstrated through the ecstatic visionaries of Marian apparitions, such as the children of Marpingen and of Lourdes.[49]

Yet in the Catholic Church, women were in a particularly ambiguous position symbolically and practically. Although women were central to the nineteenth-century revival, hierarchically, in terms of Church governance structures, they held no formal power, being excluded from the celibate, all-male clergy. As David Blackbourn has noted, the Virgin Mary, so central to ideas of nineteenth-century Catholic resurgence, presented a "model at once chaste, domesticated, and submissive."[50] Despite the persistence of patriarchy, however, the Catholic revival and feminization of the Church offered a new and unprecedented relative freedom for religious women: patriarchy without the paterfamilias in charge. Catholic lay women could go to their priest as a "countervailing locus of power" to escape from the domination of a father, brother, or husband.[51] Women in religious orders had an even greater degree of freedom, as they were removed from the burdens of reproduction and childcare.[52] Hence, the cult of the Virgin Mary was much more complicated than a mere opiate for the female masses. Blackbourn has observed that, "In the Marian century, the Virgin remained a richly ambiguous symbol, fusing the potent myths of virginity and motherhood, combining the 'womanly' virtues with power."[53]

As another distinct movement within the Catholic subculture, Catholic women also had a prominent corporate voice in the public sphere. The women's association, the *Katholische Deutsche Frauenbund*, founded in

---

[48] Hugh McLeod, *Religion and the People of Western Europe, 1789–1989*, 2nd edn. (Oxford: Oxford University Press, 1997), 28–35.

[49] David Blackbourn, *Marpingen: Apparitions of the Virgin Mary in Nineteenth-Century Germany* (New York: Knopf, 1994); Ruth Harris, *Lourdes: Body and Spirit in the Secular Age* (New York: Viking, 1999).

[50] Blackbourn, *Marpingen*, 31.

[51] Ralph Gibson, *A Social History of French Catholicism, 1789–1914* (London: Routledge, 1989), 187.

[52] Ibid., 117–19.

[53] Blackbourn, *Marpingen*, 31.

1903, achieved national status as a mass organization. Largely free from clerical control, the *Frauenbund* was led by Elisabeth Gnauck-Kühne, Emmy Gordon, Agnes Neuhaus, and Hedwig Dransfeld. This organization gave German Catholic women a national voice in the public sphere, while remaining devoted to holistic and traditional Catholic conceptions of the family, especially focused on the role of the mother. In contrast to Socialist organizations, the *Frauenbund* did not advocate for women's equality; it argued instead for women's distinctness and for a unique role that was essential to a holistic, well-ordered domestic family, complementary to the role of the husband. While women would not gain the vote until the time of the Weimar Republic, the Catholic women's movement contributed to future developments. Indeed, many of the Catholic Center Party's first female parliamentarians during the Weimar Republic were leaders from the former *Frauenbund*, now operating in a radically different social-political landscape altered by the experience of the Great War.[54]

Closely linked to the associational movement, and the women's movement in particular, were the stirrings of a Catholic social-caritative network. By 1914, however, this network was comparatively small, underdeveloped, and uncoordinated at an imperial level. The pre-war caritas network in Austria-Hungary was less developed and was fragmented regionally, coming under the auspices of the *Reichsverband der katholischen Wohltätigkeitsorganisationen in Österreich* only at the end of the war.[55] There were already some strides in the pre-war era, however. Franziska Lechner, a poor wagoner's daughter from Bavaria, founded the caritas order of the "Congregation of the Daughters of Divine Love." Financed solely through money raised by Lechner and her followers (over 500 women at the time of Lechner's death in 1894), the Congregation of the Daughters of Divine Love created a small empire of girls' schools, orphanages, and practical training institutes for female domestic servants, stretching from Krakow to Sarajevo, that was unprecedented in the religious history of the Habsburg monarchy. It was a decisive shift from a patronized, patriarchal care of women to a more self-assertive care for women by women – but one which nonetheless often ran into conflict with churchmen concerning overall hierarchical control.[56]

---

[54] Gisela Breuer, *Frauenbewegung im Katholizismus: der Katholische Frauenbund 1903–1918* (Frankfurt: Campus Verlag, 1998).

[55] Michaela Kronthaler, "Caritasorganisation in Österreich bis zum Ende des Zweiten Weltkrieges," in *Caritas und soziale Dienste*, ed. Erwin Gatz, *Geschichte des kirchlichen Lebens in den deutschsprachigen Ländern seit dem Ende des 18. Jahrhunderts* (Freiburg im Breisgau: Herder, 1997), 213–26.

[56] Klieber, "Soziale Integration durch Religion?", 757.

Catholic women featured prominently in the Catholic press, both as authors and as themes, unlike in its Protestant and Jewish equivalents. Though containing deep-seated traditional practices, the Catholic world was adjusting to the "social question" on the eve of the Great War.

Everyday life

The daily worldviews of Catholics in the Austro-Hungarian and German Empires formed a complex arrangement of behaviors that can only be cursorily sketched here. Nonetheless, some minimum Catholic ideal-type classification is necessary to establish common ground for a transnational analysis of what Catholicism actually meant. Furthermore, the Great War's fundamental continuities and changes, assessed in later chapters, can also be better seen from a common starting point. Future chapters will explore such questions as how parish priests, in pre-war days responsible for several hundred souls, handled the pastoral care of several thousand men in a division; how a "feminized" religion such as Catholicism dealt with the gender upheavals that the war caused; and how a Catholic theology of the body dealt with body-obliterating shell hits and poison gas.

Ideology and questions of religious belief are contingent on everyday practice, subject to constant adaption, negotiation, and reformulation based on local circumstances.[57] Religiosity was less an either/or proposition of "belief" or "unbelief" than a series of concentric levels of commitment and practice in which the analytical boundaries are permeable.[58]

The Catholic Church's pre-1914 self-conceptualized worldview was a cradle-to-grave, all-encompassing network of commitment that believed itself to be a universal magisterium, an organic and hierarchical means of ordering the world in which all human beings were assigned a place in creation. Catholic belief stressed humanity's deep-seated and omnipresent sinfulness as a legacy of Adam and Eve's original sin, and thus inherent to the human condition. Although the state of humanity was indeed fallen, the Church was the City of God on Earth and provided Catholic believers a means of eventual salvation in the afterlife, through the intercession of the institutional Church and its sacramental priesthood as the symbolically apostolic representatives of Christ on Earth.[59]

---

[57] In his recent work, Charles Taylor has emphasized the need to "understand belief and unbelief better as lived conditions, not just as theories or sets of beliefs subscribed to." See Charles Taylor, *A Secular Age* (Cambridge, MA: Belknap Press of Harvard University Press, 2007), 8.

[58] Taylor, "The Future of Christianity," 650–1. See also Barrett, Kurian, and Johnson, eds., *World Christian Encyclopedia*.

[59] McBrien, *The Church*.

It is important to distinguish levels of concentric commitment to the official dogmas of the Church. At the center, embodied by the ultramontanism during the papacy of Pius IX (1846–1878) – a period which included the infamous "Syllabus of Errors" and the decree of papal infallibility – there was indeed an ultrareactionary anti-modernism that was hostile to outsiders and intent on preserving tradition at all costs against real or perceived enemies of the Church. Inward-seeking, and often idealizing the rural village, this was a worldview founded on a traditional order of centuries-old socio-economic patterns.[60] Especially following the papacy of Leo XIII (1878–1903), however, there was also an increasingly accommodating perspective, often rooted in a respect for a pluralistic political process since the French Revolution, and in particular a willingness to engage with social questions raised by industrial modernity. The notion of electoral competition brought home to many members of the clergy that their worldview was one among others.[61] Outside of direct clerical control, practices of popular religion filtered varying degrees of centralized dogma through local traditions and customs.[62]

The tension between center and periphery reflected notions of adapted tradition, but there was no simple categorization of authenticity. The reactionary Pope Saint Pius X (1903–1914) chose his papal name to identify with Pius IX and stressed his humble rural origins, devoting his attention to poor rural peoples. Nevertheless, the "peasant pope" introduced such innovations as a movement for lay parishioners to receive communion frequently: that is, during each Mass, not just at Easter, Christmas, and select other occasions. Although Saint Pius X's communion innovations would become standard practice in the Church, during his pontificate, widespread acceptance remained limited: against his orders, Catholics went about their traditional ways of life, which did not include frequent communion reception. Yet they believed themselves authentically Catholic.[63]

Particularly beyond the dogmas and decrees of individual popes, the basic question remains: Who was a Catholic, and how did one live a

---

[60] The Church believed itself both historical (i.e., rooted in a succession of authority dating to the Apostles of Jesus Christ) and ahistorical (as a timeless universal magisterium representing God's plan for the salvation of humanity).

[61] For the role of Catholic priests as practitioners of democratic politics, see Margaret Lavinia Anderson, *Practicing Democracy: Elections and Political Culture in Imperial Germany* (Princeton, NJ: Princeton University Press, 2000).

[62] Urs Altermatt, *Katholizismus und Moderne: zur Sozial- und Mentalitätsgeschichte der Schweizer Katholiken im 19. und 20. Jahrhundert* (Zürich: Benziger, 1989), 72–95.

[63] Richard P. McBrien, *Lives of the Popes: The Pontiffs from St. Peter to John Paul II* (San Francisco: HarperSanFrancisco, 1997), 351–5.

Catholic way of life? Modern scholarly studies have focused on three basic related ideal-type categories: sacramentality, mediation, and communion. Sacramental practices involved rites endowed with special significance by the Church as signs of revealed grace. In contrast to the "priesthood of all believers" advocated by many Protestants, mediation was the fundamental idea that Catholics required other people to intercede and implore God on their behalf: a "communion of saints." In the visible realm, this took the form of the hierarchical clerical structures of the Church, and in the invisible realm, the communion of deceased saints, as well as the Trinitarian aspects of God in the form of Jesus Christ and the Holy Spirit. Finally, communion meant that Catholic believers, in order to be considered "in communion with the Church" obeyed the precepts of the Catholic Church embodied in the ultimate authority of the Bishop of Rome (i.e., the Pope), as the successor of the power given by Christ to Saint Peter.[64]

At a minimum, the rites of practice included a Catholic baptism at infancy and a Catholic burial at death, as well as reception of the sacraments of first communion, penance, marriage or holy orders, and extreme unction (also known as last rites). According to the ideal, in the course of one's religious life, one lived according to the Catechism of the Catholic Church, which defined the official belief structures and interpreted them in a practical sense through the priestly hierarchy. As the symbolic center of the Christian reenactment of the Last Supper, the Mass was a focal point of contact between clergy and laity. The minimum Mass attendance was succinctly stated by the Viennese Jesuit Heinrich Abel, who advocated a reinvigorated "practical Christianity" in which to "live Catholic" meant, above all, a "good Sunday," a "Good Friday," and a "good Easter"; that is, weekly attendance at Sunday Mass, as well as participation in the Easter celebrations.[65] Beginning in the 1890s, Abel led a movement to evangelize and reinvigorate male interest in the Church. Yet Abel's minimum was explicitly directed to encourage masculine participation at a bare minimum. The stereotypical "feminization" of Catholicism during the nineteenth century nonetheless raised questions about differing male and female commitment to the Church in a publicly observable sense among the laity.

As part of Church regulations, decrees included strictures about fasting and abstinence that attempted to regulate basic norms of food consumption. These measures included eating no meat on Fridays, during Lent,

---

[64] McBrien, *Catholicism*, 8–17.

[65] Josef Leb, *P. Heinrich Abel, S.J., Der Männerapostel Wiens: ein Lebensbild* (Innsbruck: Marianischer Verlag, 1926), 46–7.

and on special fast days. However, the rules often included many exceptions: for factory workers, miners, and tram conductors, as well as children, the elderly, and the infirm. Though some Catholics no doubt violated such provisions, others followed them in detail, for instance using
linseed oil on fast days, instead of pig fat, which was the normal fat
used in many cooking preparations.[66] When food and the politics of food
became hotly contested issues during the Great War, the Church's stance
acquired increased attention.

Other areas in which the Catholic Church attempted regulation
included sexuality. Marriage laws in Catholic Central Europe were inflexible and existed for purposes of procreation between a husband and a
wife. Once a marriage was contracted and consummated, death, not
divorce, was the only way out.[67] Even the famous composer Johann
Strauss II, born and raised Catholic in Vienna, could not escape the marriage laws on a formal level: the Church did not grant Strauss a divorce
from his second marriage (an earlier wife had died), so in order to marry
his third wife, Adele, he gave up his Habsburg citizenship and Catholic
religion. Legally, Strauss became a Protestant citizen of Saxe-Coburg-
Gotha in July 1887. Strauss and his bride then returned to Vienna,
where he lived the rest of his life, dying in 1899. Thus, in the official eyes
of Church and state, the "Waltz King of Vienna" spent the reminder of
his life in the Habsburg capital as a technical apostate and a foreigner.[68]
Already in the heady days of August 1914, as the soldiers marched off
to war, thousands of quick marriage requests overwhelmed Church and
state authorities, challenging previously accepted forms of tradition. As
the war lengthened seemingly without end, conservative conceptions of
the family would be shaken by such issues as state-sanctioned bordellos
and women as increasingly independent heads of households.

The agency of priests was a critical focal point of debates about the
nature of Catholicism and its social reception. Priests at a local level held
an enormous degree of power, interpreting the maxims of the Church
and dispensing sacramental precepts. The overwhelming majority of the
peasantry was illiterate, and consequently obtained news of the outside
world from the village priest. The local clergy retained correspondingly

---

[66] *Wiener Diözesanblatt* 2 (1913), 15ff.

[67] See Canons 1012–1143 in Edward N. Peters, ed., *The 1917 or Pio-Benedictine Code of
Canon Law: In English Translation with Extensive Scholarly Apparatus* (San Francisco:
Ignatius Press, 2001), 351–92.

[68] Grove Music Dictionary (online, subscription required), http://www.oxfordmusic
online.com/subscriber/article/grove/music/52380pg2?q=johann+strauss+ii&search=
quick&pos=1&_start=1#firsthit (last accessed October 31, 2014).

great power, not only to interpret dogma and religious practice but also to influence political views.[69] Robert Schellnburger, the youngest of twelve children in a family of miners from Carinthia, remembered his priest as a "shadow mayor" whose assent to unpopular political decisions by the official mayor was necessary in order for the measures to take effect.[70]

The daily life of priests corresponded to classic Tridentine formulations about serving the laity and the Church according to well-ordered schedules and rhythms. Priests rose early, at 4:00 a.m. (or 5:00 a.m. during the winter), and attended daily Mass. After breakfast, they distributed the sacraments, composed and delivered sermons, worked on catechesis, and then occupied the rest of their time with care of the poor and sick. Increasingly in the nineteenth century, priests also became more involved in serving as educators, which formed one of the main flashpoints for conflicts with the secularizing liberal state.[71] But one must not imagine an idealized, harmonized Catholic community under the leadership of priests as self-conceptualized shepherds: there were tensions within the flock, sometimes directed at the shepherds. Richard Pucher, from Nikolsdorf in East Tyrol, for instance, remembered vividly confrontations between the town tailor and the town priest escalating to the point where the tailor publicly denounced the priest as "not caring for souls but rather caring for money."[72]

The Catholic Church's liturgical calendar structured believers' lives in a yearly cycle that lent strength to the Church's claim to be an ordering presence in a chaotic world. It was a world especially attuned to cyclical agrarian practices, where the sounds of parish church bells regulated notions of time.[73] The year began with the Advent season and the consequent preparation for Christmas. After the New Year and Epiphany

---

[69] Margaret Lavinia Anderson, "Voter, Junker, Landrat, Priest: The Old Authorities and the New Franchise in Imperial Germany," *American Historical Review* 98, no. 5 (1995): 1448–74. Cf. Klieber, "Soziale Integration durch Religion?", 759–60.

[70] Rupert Maria Scheule, ed., *Beichten: Autobiographische Zeugnisse zur katholischen Bußpraxis im 20. Jahrhundert, Damit es nicht verlorengeht* (Vienna: Böhlau, 2001), 125–6.

[71] For an excellent overview of priests' daily lives, see Erwin Gatz, "Zur Kultur des priestlichen Alltages," in *Die Diözesanklerus*, ed. Erwin Gatz, *Geschichte des kirchlichen Lebens in den deutschsprachigen Ländern seit dem Ende des 18. Jahrhunderts* (Freiburg: Herder, 1995), 304–5. The conflicts in education can be approached through Christopher Clark and Wolfram Kaiser, eds., *Culture Wars: Secular-Catholic Conflict in Nineteenth-Century Europe* (Cambridge: Cambridge University Press, 2003).

[72] Ortmayr, *Knechte*, 103–5. "Lieber Herr Pfarrer, du bist kein Seelsorger, sondern ein Geldsorger."

[73] Altermatt, *Katholizismus und Moderne*, 268–80.

in early January, the liturgical calendar became lunar-based in the late winter/early spring. Following Ash Wednesday, the season of Lent culminated in Holy Week and the beginning of the Easter season. As the symbolic highpoint of the Christian calendar, the events leading up to Easter Sunday symbolized the suffering, crucifixion, and resurrection of Jesus Christ as the central elements of Christian religious belief. Cooked with the symbolic "holy fire" of Holy Saturday bonfires, special foods such as consecrated Easter bread (for many, the only time white bread was eaten during the entire year) went along with the comparative opulence of finest clothing and elaborate ceremonies, emphasizing spiritual regeneration and celebration, the triumph of everlasting life over death. Following the celebration of Easter, a series of holidays during the spring and summer months reinforced the intercessory nature of the institutional Catholic Church. The month of May was popularly known as the "month of Mary" and included many kinds of Marian devotion, focused especially on motherhood, but also on sainthood. These included processions and the consecration of altars and statues of the Virgin Mary. Fifty days after Easter Sunday came the Feast of Pentecost, symbolizing the Church as Christ's deputation of his apostolic mission to his disciples through the intercession of the Holy Spirit. Pentecost was immediately followed by Trinity Sunday one week later, emphasizing the crucial notion of the three aspects of the divine presence – God the Father, God the Sun, and God the Holy Spirit – as a foundational theological conception of the Church. Soon after Trinity Sunday came the Feast of Corpus Christi, which stressed the body of Christ, symbolized in the form of the consecrated Eucharist. The summer months were less filled with high feasts, but as throughout the year, were dotted with festivals for individual saints, such as Ignatius of Loyola (July 31), Augustine of Hippo (August 28), and Thérèse of Lisieux (October 1). Individual saints such as Wenceslas (September 28) in the Czech areas and Elisabeth of Hungary (November 17) were regional figures of intense devotion. Before the next repetition of Advent, the Church's liturgical year wound to a close with the major Feasts of All Saints (November 1) and All Souls (November 2), with their linkages to inevitable mortality, further underscoring the intercessory saint culture that formed a prominent part of Catholic belief.

The religion of Austro-Hungarian and German Catholics in agrarian regions in Central Europe was rooted in traditional, pre-modern practices and ideas. Child mortality was high: in 1881–90, around half of the children born in these regions would not live to see their fifth year. Those that did survive entered into a world of big families focused on fruitful harvests and the care of the land and animals that made such produce possible. Bad weather, animal sickness, and the constant specter of early death were all existential threats to this style of life. In this agrarian world, traditional agricultural practices valued time-tested methods as the best guarantee of a sustaining harvest. This reinforced a conservative worldview against new experiments and refinements.[74]

In this highly patriarchal world of village religious life, women had limited roles. Due to the closures of many female cloisters since the eighteenth century, most religious women faced a stark choice: either marriage or domestic service in another household. In the province of Bukovina, for instance, around sixteen percent of women remained unmarried. Following biblical prescriptions of ritual impurity, women were barred from church for 40 days after the birth of every child. A wife's supposed "uselessness," which in practice often meant an inability to bear children, was often grounds for divorce for Eastern Rite believers, some of whom fell under the authority of the Roman Catholic Church. Unlike their Roman Catholic counterparts, however, Eastern Rite Catholic women could be married to priests, and thus achieve a measure of social power, especially in areas of Galicia and Bukovina, among Ruthenian communities in the monarchy's eastern lands.[75]

This was a religious world in which official dogma provided only a bare minimum of religious content. The vast majority of daily religious life was a blend of superstitious and folk practices.[76] In the rural regions of Bohemia, for instance, believers lit candles that had been blessed at a Mass of Light held on every February 2, both to ward off thunderstorms (in which case the candles were called "thunder candles" [hromnicky]) and to accompany the dying. Similarly, in order to guide the dying during their final hours, the German inhabitants of Bohemia began to ring handbells by the bedside. After death occurred, the handbells were rung in a procession to lead the spirit out of the house, so that future inhabitants would not be haunted.[77]

More isolated regions such as the Alpine valleys south of the Brenner Pass were heavily steeped in long-established local cultures, in some cases with Roman and Ladin roots. These areas could be favorable to fantasts, visionaries, seers, and prophets. In such cases, religious continuities stretched back beyond early modern times, often into ancient practices. Believers with stigmata, such as Maria von Mörl from Kaltern,

---

[74] Klieber, *Jüdische, Christliche, Muslimische*, 104–5.   [75] Ibid., 80–1.
[76] Altermatt, *Katholizismus und Moderne*, 261–341.
[77] Klieber, *Jüdische, Christliche, Muslimische*, 105–6.

Domenica Lazzari in the Lazzari region, and Krezentia Niglutsch from Lana, became sources of popular devotion, as did the mystic "sick, blind woman" from Eppan, the farmer's daughter Ursula Mohr. In highly patriarchal societies, these prominent roles allowed women to gain a measure of leadership through their religious authority.[78]

In the eastern regions of the Habsburg and Hohenzollern Empires, religious believers lived in a more isolated and less socio-economically-developed world than the increasingly industrialized countries of Western Europe. Eastern Rite Catholics, particularly Greek Catholics and Armenian Catholics, practiced their religious rites similarly to their Orthodox brethren but maintained loyalty to the Bishop of Rome. Especially in the eastern regions of the empire, in Galicia and surrounding areas, the Eastern Rite Catholic peasants, mostly ethnic Ruthenes (Ukranians), lived in a world that was out of step with the industrial modernization that had overtaken much of the western regions of Europe. Much of religious life, such as the mass pilgrimages to see the relics of Saint John of Suczawa, took place according to the Julian calendar, which by the twentieth century was nearly two weeks different from the Gregorian one. Living in dimly-lit, one-room straw-thatched cottages with dirt floors, the main pieces of decorative art were icons and objects of worship, which resided on the eastern wall of every cottage, lying next to bundles of blessed herbs. Whether a scene of the crucifixion or a portrait of a saint such as the Virgin Mary or Saint Nicholas, these religious pictures were objects of deep veneration. Farm worker, servant, and day laborer were the primary occupations of people living in these regions. These ideal types were often based on ethnographic categories, particularly those of the documented property owners. Although it is difficult to peer into the hearts of the peasant religious, major festivals were prominent expressions of communal solidarity celebrated virtually without exception in the countryside. The two biggest festivals were the blessing of food at Easter time and the blessing of water for the River Jordan celebration in January.[79]

Though the official structure of the Catholic Church's liturgy and dogma provided the unifying theory, in practice all religion was local. Nevertheless, Catholic priests often formed important contact points for local communities' interactions with the wider world, even if they were not "milieu managers." Priests shaped but did not control their communities.

---

[78] Ibid., 106–7. Cf. Bruno Grabinski, *Weltkrieg und Sittlichkeit* (Hildesheim: Franz Borgmeyer, 1917).

[79] Klieber, *Jüdische, Christliche, Muslimische*, 68, 79–80.

Central European wars before 1914

The two major Central European wars between 1815 and 1914 did not last long enough to shift religious social structures and mentalities. The Austro-Prussian War of 1866 lasted a mere seven weeks, but it decisively shaped the course of Central European history on a diplomatic level. Allied with Italy, Prussia quickly advanced its army into Habsburg lands, and the main clashes took place in Bohemia, culminating in the battle of Königgrätz on July 3. Austria lost the war because it was outgunned and outgeneraled. Superior Prussian arms, particularly the breech-loading needle-gun, were deployed according to the strategic plans of General Helmuth von Moltke the Elder. Moltke's armies shattered the Austrian units, which were poorly led by General Ludwig von Benedek. Casualties for the entire war were limited to around 70 000 for the Austrians and 37 000 for the Prussians. This quick war did not have time to shake the belligerents' social structures. The diplomatic consequences, however, were enormous. In a war that most outside observers at the outset expected Austria to win, the decisive Prussian victory settled important issues that had lingered since the Congress of Vienna. The territorial unification of an empire of German-speaking peoples would be conducted by Protestant Hohenzollern Prussia, to the exclusion of Catholic Habsburg Austria, and especially to the exclusion of non-German-speaking Habsburg lands.[80]

In the historically conceived Habsburg throne-and-altar alliance, little changed as a result of Austria's decisive quick defeat. "Let others make war; you, happy Austria, marry," was the famous slogan that encapsulated the dynastic mission to consolidate the empire through marriage alliances, rather than battlefield victories. Catholic Habsburg publications remained fixated on the past glories of the dynasty, particularly the seventeenth and eighteenth centuries and the era of the Counter-Reformation, with its Baroque and Rococo aesthetics. The official history of Habsburg military chaplaincy, published in 1901, ended its chronology in 1757 with the story of the victory of Habsburg forces at the battle of Krichnau in Bohemia against none other than the Prussians.[81]

The defeat at Königgrätz caused alarm among Austrian liberals in the government, who clamored for more efficient modernization to reform the army and other state structures; however, an overall conservatism prevailed. Most notably, the Compromise (*Ausgleich*) of 1867 created

[80] Geoffrey Wawro, *The Austro-Prussian War: Austria's War with Prussia and Italy in 1866* (Cambridge: Cambridge University Press, 1996).
[81] Emerich Bielik (sic), *Geschichte der k.u.k. Militärseelsorge und des Apostolischen Feld-Vicariates* (Vienna: Selbstverlag des Apostolischen Feld-Vicariates, 1901), 11–16.

the polity of Austria-Hungary. On many internal matters, the two halves of the monarchy functioned as independent states, and the existence of a "Hungarian" half gave many nationalist groups a target on which to focus demands for greater participation in affairs of state. However, viewed externally, Austria-Hungary shared a set of common institutions and acted as one power on the level of foreign policy. Viewed in retrospect, this confusing entity seemed to have accelerated the centrifugal nationalist movements. To contemporary observers, however, the political imaginary was fixated on the Habsburg dynasty as the unifier of disparate lands and peoples. Even within nationalist movements, most nationalists clamored for a greater share of influence within the Habsburg polity, not outside of it in an independent state. The Habsburg Army, and above all its officer corps, remained resistant to reform, and viewed in the long term, held together strikingly well as protector of the realm and enforcer of social cohesion.[82] Overall, the military, the bureaucracy, and the Catholic Church remained three interlocked centralizing sources of support for the Habsburg dynasty on the eve of the Great War.

For Germany, the Franco-Prussian War of 1870–71 similarly did not radically alter established internal Central European social structures, although the effects for France were much more profound. It was also a relatively short and limited war, basically the result of one campaign fought entirely on French soil. The casualty figures were heavier: 134 000 for the Germans and 756 000 for the French. Again, the superiority of German arms and generalship – particularly the continued strategic maneuvering of Helmuth von Moltke – won decisive results. The diplomatic results were important. As German states rallied to the Prussian cause, the Franco-Prussian War resulted after the fact in a politically unified German Empire, the fulfilled dream of German nationalists throughout the nineteenth century.[83] After 1871, the German Empire became the strongest land power in Europe, a development that caused diplomatic anxiety across Europe and helped to bring on the Great War. Even within Germany, however, beneath the surface of a monolithic Prussian military state, stark cultural divisions remained.

In religious terms for Central Europe, the confessional cleft between Catholics and Protestants remained strong. Protestant field chaplains and pastors on the homefront interpreted the war's quick and wildly

---

[82] István Deák, *Beyond Nationalism: A Social and Political History of the Habsburg Officer Corps, 1848–1918* (Oxford: Oxford University Press, 1990); Gunther E. Rothenberg, "The Shield of the Dynasty: Reflections on the Habsburg Army, 1649–1918," *Austrian History Yearbook* 32 (2001): 169–206.

[83] Geoffrey Wawro, *The Franco-Prussian War: The German Conquest of France in 1870–1871* (Cambridge: Cambridge University Press, 2003).

successful outcome in light of chosen-people nationalism. It was a mani-
festation of exclusive divine favor for a united German led by Protestant
Prussia. Although Germans united ideologically to denounce France's
legacy of republic secularism, the war's legacy highlighted many German regions squabbling among themselves about what the war meant.
Catholic Bavaria, in particular, was afraid that German Catholics would
be overwhelmed in a Protestant-dominated German Empire. Indeed,
German Catholic chaplains and soldiers from disparate German regions
stressed points of commonality with the Catholic French believers over
those with Protestant Prussian counterparts.[84]

Conclusion

In Central Europe in 1914, most Catholics came from rural agrarian
backgrounds and lived their lives in small traditional communities dominated by patriarchal families and clerical hierarchies as figures of official
authority. Although they shared liturgies and theologies of a common
Church seated in Rome, local customs and interpretations prevailed. For
most Catholics, outside of one's immediate surroundings, universalism
was an ideal at best. The idealized world of the rural village contained
a great measure of truth, but it was far from the final statement on
Catholic life in Central Europe. Especially viewed in terms of regions,
some Central European Catholics in industrial areas from Rhineland-
Westphalia, Silesia, and Bohemia became involved in the theory and
practice of advancing industrial modernity.

On the eve of the Great War, there were hints of larger developing imagined communities outside of local identities. In Austria-Hungary, vigorous national movements, dominated by new generations of increasingly
activist political priests, tried to reconcile nascent nationalist awakenings
with both imperial loyalty and Catholic universalism. The experience of
the Austro-Prussian war highlighted the relative backwardness of Habsburg society compared to its rising counterpart, the German national
state of which Protestant Prussia was the driving force.

Germany also was a fragmented imperial monarchy seeking means
to solidify its legitimacy as a great power. In Germany, the persecutions of Catholics during the *Kulturkampf* had formed Catholic political

---

[84] Rak, *Krieg, Nation und Konfession*, 398–406. For the vast importance of the chosen-
people theme in German nationalism, and its Protestant flavor, see Hartmut Lehmann,
"'God Our Old Ally': The Chosen People Theme in Late Nineteenth- and Early
Twentieth-Century German Nationalism," in *Many Are Chosen: Divine Election and
Western Nationalism*, ed. William R. Hutchinson and Hartmut Lehmann (Minneapolis,
MN: Fortress Press, 1994), 85–113.

solidarities in a defensive milieu hostile to many modern developments and to those of the encroaching industrial state. Facing discrimination made Catholic identity a viable political issue. Catholics had successfully outlasted Otto von Bismarck's official efforts at dismantling the primacy of Catholics' transnational religious affiliations. However, deep mutual suspicions reigned on both sides. The experiences of the Austro-Prussian and the Franco-Prussian conflicts showed that many German Catholics were starting to identify more with an exclusionary nationalism than were their counterparts in the Austro-Hungarian Empire. On the whole, in 1914, many Catholics' worldviews were strongly influenced by local conditions and transnational practices, rather than by loyalty to the nation.

In a largely agrarian world of rural Catholicism, when the war broke out, political considerations and ideals remained of low importance to fundamental ways of everyday life. Recent works have cast doubt on the extent of cheering crowds embracing a jubilant "Spirit of 1914," a cultural snapshot that fits well with a tragic vision of a short war.[85] For many rural Catholics in Central Europe, the mood was decidedly different. The declarations of war and the consequent mobilization orders in late-summer 1914 threatened the upcoming harvests. Far from joyful jingoism, Catholics saw the outbreak of the war in decidedly pessimistic terms. In autumn 1914, peasants were concerned about bringing in the annual harvest, and they worried about how the war would disrupt family life and agrarian rhythms.[86] As a child, Maria Gremel, a domestic servant on a farm in Lower Austria, remembered crying with the village children over the departure of their beloved brown horses, now requisitioned for military service. Combined with the absence of male laborers serving at the front, this made the necessary farm work much more difficult for those who remained behind. Gremel noted, "In farm households, one sensed the absence of the strongest laborers even more."[87] To many Catholics, war was another cyclical plague, redolent of the sinful human condition; it was not cause for celebration.

[85] Jeffrey Verhey, *The Spirit of 1914: Militarism, Myth, and Mobilization in Germany* (Cambridge: Cambridge University Press, 2000).

[86] Gunda Barth-Scalmani, "'Kriegsbriefe'. Kommunikation zwischen Klerus und Kirchenvolk im ersten Kriegsherbst 1914 im Spannungsfeld von Patriotismus und Seelsorge," in *Tirol – Österreich – Italien. Festschrift für Josef Riedmann zum 65. Geburtstag*, ed. Klaus Brandstätter and Julia Hörmann (Innsbruck: Wagner, 2005), 67–76; Ziemann, *Front und Heimat*, 39–54.

[87] Maria Gremel, *Mit neun Jahren im Dienst. Mein Leben im Stübl und am Bauernhof 1900–1930*, ed. Michael Mitterauer, *Damit es nicht verlorengeht* (Vienna: Böhlau, 1983), 210–12.

In contrast to the avant garde optimism about the war as joyful release from stasis, the dolorous Catholic vision of war proved more accurate in the long term. The main sources of labor were marching off to the killing fields. The war would shake pre-war norms on a fundamental level.

2   Theology and catastrophe

The theological story of the twentieth century has focused on Protestant Christianity, with 1914 as an epic marker of divide. The newest, most radical developments in Protestant theology in Central Europe articulated a fundamental break with the war years. Most famously, the Dialectical Theology of Karl Barth reacted against the October 1914 declaration of nintey-three prominent German intellectuals supporting Germany's cause, who included Adolf von Harnack and Wilhelm Herrmann, Barth's former teachers. For Barth, an entire tradition of theology culminating in idealistic liberal Protestantism died in the early days of the Great War, poisoned by the jingoistic "Spirit of 1914." One could also point to the theology of Paul Tillich, who served as a German army chaplain and quickly became disillusioned, as another Protestant repudiation of the Great War.[1]

Catholic theology, however, took a completely different course during and after the war, a delayed modernity that would only flourish in the post-1945 era, indeed during the Second Vatican Council of 1962–65. Instead of a radical break with the events of 1914–18, Catholic thought either bypassed the war years by continuing pre-war developments or articulated new theologies that did not repudiate the war. Previous histories of Catholic theology in Central Europe have focused on the aggressive war theology of the elite clerics, foremost among them the bishops, often showing much blend between Protestants and Catholics in loyal service to the aims of state.[2] In contrast to what Friedrich Wilhelm Graf has termed a "war generation" of Protestant university theologians,[3] Catholic theology showed much more continuity with the war, relativizing and minimizing the war's newness.

---

[1] H. Jackson Forstman, *Christian Faith in Dark Times: Theological Conflicts in the Shadow of Hitler* (Louisville, KY: Westminster/John Knox Press, 1992).

[2] Achleitner, *Gott im Krieg*; Hammer, *Deutsche Kriegstheologie*; Missalla, *"Gott mit uns"*; Pressel, *Die Kriegspredigt*.

[3] Friedrich Wilhelm Graf, *Der heilige Zeitgeist: Studien zur Ideengeschichte der protestantischen Theologie in der Weimarer Republik* (Tübingen: Mohr Siebeck, 2011), 1–110.

Viewed transnationally and comparatively at the episcopal level, this chapter shows that Catholic theology did not fit standard frames of disillusionment associated with a fundamental break of thought in 1914. The chapter develops lines of episcopal thought beyond the war years, sketching transnational lines of Central and Eastern European theological development beyond German-speaking regions. Going below the episcopal level, however, it also recovers a sense of "little theologies": the personalized, everyday theologies of ordinary participants, including military chaplains (stereotypical fire-breathers), soldiers, and civilians, trying to make sense of the war. While exploring new issues raised by the war, ordinary Catholic men and women largely understood the conflict in terms of their traditional worldviews, adapted to new conditions. New theological developments were already in formation, but these would come into full fruition only in the course of the Second Vatican Council. This chapter sketches these developments in sharp relief by focusing on three figures of great influence for the Second Vatican Council: Max Scheler, Romano Guardini, and Karl Adam.

Just war and the bishops

The overwhelming majority of German and Austrian bishops were prominent public-sphere advocates of just-war theology. The majority of religious theology in the public sphere during the Great War remained cloaked in the language of neo-scholasticism. Public theology fixated on the original principles and the justness of the cause of going to war. Conduct in war was of decidedly lesser importance, relative to the original postulate of belief in a just war of defense against aggression. The concept of just-war theory remained essential for the official theological understandings of the war. While the origins of Christianity in antiquity were rooted in anti-establishment pacifism, just-war theory developed after the accession of Constantine in AD 312 as the Catholic Church became a socially dominant institution. Drawing especially on the critiques of Saint Augustine and Saint Thomas Aquinas, just-war thinking had two main components: *jus ad bellum* (the right to war) and *jus in bello* (law in war). On the eve of the Great War, *jus in bello* had two basic principles: non-combatant immunity and proportionality of the means of making war. However, while the First World War was a huge milestone in the application of the principles of *jus in bello* to modern industrial warfare, the majority of scholarly and theological work throughout the previous centuries had focused on the nature of *jus ad bellum*. The basic principles here involved legitimate authority, just cause, right intention, reasonable hope of success, probability of a good outcome relative to the means of waging war, and the use of war as a means of last resort.[4]

After the seemingly divine mandate of a Protestant-led Prussia-dominated empire in 1871, the Great War presented German Catholics an opportunity to demonstrate their loyalty and sacrifice to the new nation conceived in the Franco-Prussian War. The bishops viewed the Great War as a patriotic test of belief and their public proclamations tended to overcompensate for years of real and perceived discriminated minority status. The Austro-Hungarian bishops saw the war largely in terms of dynastic honor, with religious means mobilized in defense of the threat against the House of Habsburg. As the bishops and prominent clerics declared their service to their state, they presented a public profession of faith in the state's war aims. Largely upholding traditional theologies, this left very little room for nuance.

The "Spirit of 1914" encompassed a theology of short-war illusions, demonstrating united devotion to victory.[5] Professor Joseph Mausbach wrote of the heady atmosphere of the early autumn days of 1914, saying that the declaration of war was "no terrible day and not an hour of darkness; it is a great day, a day of judgment, a day of the Lord."[6] Catholic newspapers like *Kölnische Volkszeitung* portrayed a romanticized atmosphere of the "Spirit of 1914," with priests accompanying throngs of dutiful soldiers leaving for the front, blessing them in front of cheering crowds while *"Deutschland über alles"* blared everywhere.[7]

Overall, German Catholics proved that they were caught up in a "delirium of nationalism." They saw the war as a "patriotic test of faith," integrating their loyalty to the state, especially after the *Kulturkampf*.[8] Like Protestant journals such as *Christliche Welt* and *Evangelische Freiheit*, the Catholic journal *Hochland*, under the editorship of Professor Carl Muth, devoted itself to religiously framed issues of intellectual culture, marking the war through chronicles from selected dispatches from the front lines. In the case of *Hochland*, these came from the military chaplain Balthasar Poertner, who wrote that, "God is with us and our just cause."[9]

---

[4] Achleitner, *Gott im Krieg*, 16–26; Hammer, *Deutsche Kriegstheologie*, 73–85. For an excellent overview, see Lloyd Steffen, "Religion and Violence in Christian Traditions," in Juergensmeyer et al., *Oxford Handbook of Religion and Violence*, 100–25.

[5] Verhey, *The Spirit of 1914*.

[6] Joseph Mausbach, "Vom gerechten Kriege und seinen Wirkungen. Zeitgemäßige Gedanken," *Hochland* 12 (October 1914): 1.

[7] *Kölnische Volkszeitung*, Morgenausgabe Nr. 817 (18.9.1914), cited in Missalla, *"Gott mit uns,"* 13.

[8] Hammer, *Deutsche Kriegstheologie*, 73–4.

[9] Balthasar Poertner, "Briefe eines Feldgeistlichen vom Kriegsschauplatz an den Herausgeber des Hochland," *Hochland* 12 (October 1914): 235. Poertner's series of articles

Compared to the bellicosity of German Protestant journals, Carl Muth's editorial line in *Hochland* was more reserved, but it ended up supporting the German cause anyway. Muth blended the sacrifice of soldiers with the sacrifice of Christ: "Christ and the warrior belong uneasily together. Hence, Christ can bless the warrior and a warring nation, but never war itself. Because Christ wants peace and not war. But as he sacrificed himself in order to bring reconciliation to men, so he blesses anyone who makes his life a sacrifice for the purpose of peace."[10]

According to their confident proclamations that God was on their side, religious leaders believed that they were fighting a just war of defense against aggression. In Austria-Hungary, Christian voices, especially that of the Archbishop of Vienna, Cardinal Friedrich Gustav Piffl, focused on the events in Sarajevo as an attack on the honor of the Habsburg monarchy deserving retribution. Thus, Great Powers who supported Serbia, or rather did not advocate the harsh punishments demanded by Habsburg officials, were seen in Habsburg circles as condoning the overthrow of divine order. The main Christian imperial daily newspaper, *Reichspost*, declared, "Never was a war begun for a more righteous cause, than that for which Austria now stands up."[11] As the administrative aide to the elderly Cardinal Franziskus von Bettinger, the titular head of Bavarian chaplaincy, Michael von Faulhaber, Bishop of Speyer and, after 1917, Bishop of Munich-Freising, deeply immersed himself in the war effort. Faulhaber declared in a sermon of 1915, republished in 1918, that the war was a "textbook example of a just war."[12] Faulhaber's personal odyssey through the war began with hypernationalistic fervor, developed into disillusionment with defeat and a turn toward a stab-in-the-back mentality, and ended in renewed devotion to Bavaria. Faulhaber developed a complicated relationship to the emerging Nazi movement, at first sharply criticizing the Weimar Republic and then moving toward partial opposition of the Nazi regime.[13]

The Apostolic Field Vicar of Austria-Hungary, Bishop Emmerich Bjelik, sent the Habsburg troops off to war with the proclamation of a pastoral letter that summed up much of the foundational theology of

continued throughout the war, and he served with devotion to the German cause, eventually earning the Iron Cross.
[10] Carl Muth, "Christus und der Krieger," *Hochland* 13, no. 1 (October 1915): 105ff., quoted in Hammer, *Deutsche Kriegstheologie*, 268.
[11] *Reichspost*, July 28, 1914, p. 1; Achleitner, *Gott im Krieg*, 262–9.
[12] Michael von Faulhaber, *Waffen des Lichtes. Gesammelte Kriegsreden*, 5th edn. (Freiburg im Breisgau: Herder, 1918), 132.
[13] Johann Klier, *Von der Kriegspredigt zum Friedensappell: Erzbischof Michael von Faulhaber und der Erste Weltkrieg: ein Beitrag zur Geschichte der deutschen katholischen Militärseelsorge* (Munich: Kommissionsverlag UNI-Druck, 1991).

the war. The letter, issued on July 30, 1914, demonstrated the perceived need to defend a threatened natural order: something that was common to all sides in the war. Bjelik wrote that, "Our struggle is a holy, just struggle for holy justice, for holy order. It is essential for the defense of the Fatherland, for the defense of our goods. It is essential for the securing of our own borders. Truly, it is a holy struggle for God's sake!" He firmly emphasized his assertion of a providential God, "This enterprise is begun with God; His omnipotence will finish it." Bjelik wrote that citizens of the Fatherland had a holy duty to defend the patrimony given to them by God: "The spirit of death-defying love of the Fatherland must animate you; because God has given you the Fatherland, it is God's will that you defend it, God's will that you mobilize your last breath for it, mobilize your last ounce of strength for it . . . " He then wrote that God would demand a reckoning (*Rechenschaft*) to see that the men were fulfilling the "duties of their holy call to battle." In this reckoning, Bjelik outlined two ways through which the believing solider could ease his conscience: "candid confession and dignified receiving of holy communion." He closed with a deeply enthusiastic call to battle:

Lord of armies, allotter of battles, stand by us! We place our hope in you! Hear our prayers, bless our weapons and give us victory! Give us courage and valor . . . And now, let us go! Forward in the name of God! Almighty God be our army! Let us go forth with full trust in the protection of heaven and in the support of the Holy Virgin against the enemy!

Loyal, dear soldiers, be manly and undismayed . . . On to battle and to victory! We will not flee! Either we triumph, or there on the field of battle will be our graveyard: we die with God for the throne and the Fatherland! The blessing of the triune God be with you. Amen.[14]

Many military chaplains, at least post-war, would deny that there had been a blessing of weapons, calling this a vicious rumor of the "enemies of the Church." Statements like Bjelik's opening proclamation, however, show that the Church princes themselves were wrong and had helped to confuse the issue. Writing in a post-war collection, former chaplain Viktor Lipusch vehemently denied that a blessing of weapons had taken place, invoking the authority of the then-current military vicar of Austria, Ferdinand Pawlikowski: "in Austria during the war neither a demand for blessing weapons was expressed, nor was a church blessing of weapons dispensed." Lipusch wrote that the confusion was likely due to misremembered practices of the Middle Ages and an inability to differentiate between the blessing of troops departing for the field and the actual

---

[14] Quoted in Ham, "Von den Anfängen der Militärseelsorge," 72–4.

blessing of weapons. Bishop Bjelik's proclamation, however, shows the slippage between the two categories: "Hear our prayers, bless our weapons and give us victory!"[15] Such scenes happened at both the center and the margins of the Catholic war effort. In August 1914, for instance, in no less a place that St. Stephan's Cathedral in Vienna, Professor Justin Bodnitz gave a fiery sermon in Hungarian before carrying out what *Reichspost* termed an official blessing of soldiers' weapons. Bodnitz conducted the services in concert with Apostolic Field Vicar Bjelik, who understood Hungarian. Thus, both men helped to validate the concept of a just war and begged for the blessing of departing troops' weapons.[16] Prominent Catholic theologians in Central Europe immersed themselves in the joyous frenzies of the war's initial public outpourings of communal loyalty. Numerous bishops and priests took part in blessing the troops marching off to war. Sometimes literally blessing the weapons of war, the clerics contributed heavily to the propaganda war of words.

For many critics of the Church's actions in the war, all its hypocrisy was encapsulated in the blessing of weapons: how could a religion advocate "peace on Earth, goodwill toward men" (Luke 2:14) and at the same time bless weapons whose ultimate purpose was the killing of human beings? Bishop Bjelik's confusion lent strength to the arguments of the critics of the Church. For many skeptics and non-believers, this highlighted the Church's moral bankruptcy as a voice for peace, and reaffirmed doubt in organized religion's efforts to promote the same. Whenever this issue of the blessing of weapons arose, the Church defended itself by pointing to a long tradition of just-war thinking promulgated by some of the Church's greatest theologians, foremost among them Augustine and Aquinas. In this tradition, conflict was seen as an unavoidable, though regrettable, part of human existence, directly stemming from the fallen condition of mankind through original sin; earthly life was necessarily messy and imperfect. On the specific issue of the blessing of weapons, chaplains adopted the casuistic rationale that weapons, as material instruments, were merely tools; as such, when chaplains invoked God's blessing on the weapons, this was no different than the blessing of a blacksmith's anvil or a baker's yeast, and did not advocate God's killing of the enemy. When pressed further, the chaplains clung to the rationale that it was God, not the chaplain, who was actually blessing the weapon.[17] In reality, however, the blessing of weapons was too closely associated with the highly charged

---

[15] See Viktor Lipusch, ed., *Österreich-Ungarns katholische Militärseelsorge im Weltkriege* (Vienna: Verlag für Militär- und Fachliteratur Amon Franz Göth, 1938), 100.
[16] "Das Stefansfest in Wien," *Reichspost*, August 21, 1914, p. 5.
[17] Vogt, *Religion im Militär*, 575–8.

war theology to be morally neutral. Weapons were not mere tools; they were explicitly designed for the taking of human life.[18]

The bishops' aggressive war theology continued throughout the conflict. It was fire-breathing fury proclaimed from the safety of the homefront, forming one of the most repellent aspects of men of Christian action during the war. It struck contemporary observers as hypocrisy, especially with the Church–state prohibitions on ordained Catholic priests carrying arms: they were essentially preaching that other men should fight and die for the cause.

War theology showed continuity during the war. In the war's closing days, the Austrian bishops held to the belief that God was on their side and that the Austro-Hungarian monarchy was a divinely-ordained polity, committed to holding together a wide variety of peoples. In an August 1918 pastoral letter, they wrote:

The war, not wanted by God but allowed, is in the hand of God a means of punishment and judgment over peoples whose destiny now perhaps for centuries will be determined. The horror of the war and the sufferings of the innocent will purposefully serve to separate us inwardly from this Earth with its darkness and contradictions and force us fully into the Arms of God. And the Gospel of Peace enters in our realm in order to bring inner peace and goes out into the lands of our enemies in order to vanquish the un-Christian hatred between peoples.

We do not have cause to hesitate. Our empire has hitherto enjoyed a special custody of Divine Providence. Think only on the dangers in which we hovered over the superiority of our enemies and which are now happily averted. This fills us with joyous hope for the future. Austria has a providential task to fulfill as a Catholic superpower in the heart of Europe and as the Fatherland of the League of Peoples (*Völkermacht*) that it houses. *Austria's power rests in the unity of its peoples and this rests in Catholic belief.* For us there is therefore only one serious danger: the decline of Catholic belief.[19]

There, were, however, distinctions between the clerics' public theologies and their more private doubts and examinations of the developing nature of the war. There are indications in their private correspondence that bishops were not blind to the new realities of war. Even Bishop Emmerich Bjelik, the Austro-Hungarian Field-Vicar, who had so enthusiastically sent off troops in the heady days of autumn 1914, began to understand that the changing nature of war posed new conceptual difficulties for its

---

[18] John Howard Yoder, *When War Is Unjust: Being Honest in Just-War Thinking* (Minneapolis, MN: Augsburg, 1984).

[19] EAW, Bischofskonferenzen, 11/2: 1917–18. Also found in ÖStAKA, AFV, Ktn. 204, Hirtenbrief der Erzbischöfe und Bischöfe Oesterreichs (Wien: Selbstverlag des Erzbischöflichen Sekretariates. Buchdruckerei "Reichspost," 1918), p. 16. Italics in original.

participants. In a March 1918 reflection on the need for "Inner Reform in the Army," Bjelik touched on Great War tropes about the difficulties of poison gas and static trench warfare, which posed a conceptual stumbling block to notions of discernible divine favor through quick victory. In contrast to the clear-cut campaigns of previous centuries, the endurance of artillery bombardment for lengthy time periods caused frustration and doubt among the soldiers. Bjelik wrote that, "Modern war has developed the necessity of holding out for days under the strongest artillery fire ('barrage'), that places especially high demands on nerves and will." In the static conditions of trench warfare, soldiers lived under the "force of holding out for months by the most primitive ways of life many times over, with the comfortless monotony of battle and work."[20] The new conditions of war were causing reappraisals of inner reform.

Though it was a prominent motif from the start, as the war dragged on public theology increasingly focused on the war as punishment, with the corresponding need for atonement. The pastoral letter of the German bishops, published in *Stimmen der Zeit* in 1915, identified the "primary task of the war" to be "repentance and atonement." The bishops declared that Germany was "not guilty for the outbreak of the war" but that the war nonetheless "revealed a deep guilt" on a social level: the need to combat the "modern, anti-Christian, non-religious culture of the spirit." Drawing on generic irrational diatribes against modernity, including the "most damaging outgrowths of women's fashion," the bishops' letter characterized modern culture as an "un-Christian, un-German, and unhealthy culture of superficiality" full of "inner decay." According to the bishops, the soldiers going off to war had provided a good example of the necessary return to repentance and atonement, leading to a change of public opinion that was sweeping through all of Germany.[21] In a Christmas 1916 pastoral letter, the Austrian bishops wrote that the war was God's judgment of punishment for collective sins. The war showed that the "fury of God now revealed itself from heaven about all godlessness and wrongfulness in man."[22]

As the quick-victory illusion faded, the bishops reframed their message. In the new interpretation, God had not wanted the war, but let it continue as a consequence of the need for deeper social change. In a pastoral letter for the Feast of Epiphany 1916, the Bishop of St. Pölten, Johannes Rößler, wrote that, "God does not make war; man does

---

[20] DAG, Nachlaß von Bischof Dr. Ferdinand Pawlikowski, Militärvikariat, Ktn. 1, Schachtel I, Heft 1: Gutachten des Apostolischen Feldvikars Emmerich Bjelik über die Schrift "Die innere Reform der Armee," pp. 2, 11–13.

[21] *Stimmen der Zeit* 91 (1915): 182–3, quoted in Hammer, *Deutsche Kriegstheologie*, 273.

[22] Quoted in Achleitner, *Gott im Krieg*, 16.

that . . . But God lets the war continue. Therefore, God lets the war continue, because it is a great means for the fulfillment of his plans in the
education of humanity."[23] Theologies of repentance allowed religious
believers to more easily deal with the stagnation and disappearance of
the short-war illusion. Protracted struggle reflected the supposed need
for deep-seated social change.

The bishops' public rhetoric remained largely in full force through the
end of the war. Even as critically observant religious men at the front
witnessed the senseless slaughter and began to question the justness of
the cause, the bishops remained fully convinced of the need to keep
fighting. In their All Saints' Day pastoral letter of November 1, 1917,
the bishops of Germany stressed their loyalty to "our dynasties and our
monarchical constitution." More ominously, they wrote of the war as a
contest of spiritual wills, in which inner enemies would sap the strength
of their side. They wrote, "We will always stand ready to protect the altar
as well as the throne against outer and inner enemies, against powers
of upheaval that want to establish a dreamed future state on the ruins
of the existing society, who have sworn themselves to the downfall of
the altar and throne." Grounding themselves in Romans 13:1–5, the
bishops declared that all authority stemmed from God and that therefore they were obliged to treat Kaiser Wilhelm with "unshakeable loyalty and sacrificial devotion." To this mindset, offers of peace were in
fact a form of betrayal. The bishops wrote that they regarded a peace
proposal as a "burning dishonor" that one had to "risk to offer peace
as a Judas-wage [*Judaslohn*] for breaking an oath and treachery to the
Kaiser."[24]

The theological implications of the stab-in-the back myth related to
religious nationalism also highlighted different responses to imperial collapse in Germany and Austria-Hungary. Here, the role of the Protestant
milieu was the dominant force in the religiously-tempered version of the
myth. The comparison between Austria and Germany was instructive.
Immediately after the war, the Austrian Catholic bishops and leading
members of the clergy accepted the radically-changed political circumstances much more readily than did their German Catholic counterparts,
who were more in line with German national Protestantism.[25] Despite

---

[23] Quoted in Achleitner, *Gott im Krieg*, 19.

[24] Reprinted in Max Meinertz and Hermann Sacher, eds., *Deutschland und der Katholizismus: Gedanken zur Neugestaltung des Deutschen Geistes- und Gesellschaftslebens*, 2 vols.
(Freiburg im Breisgau: Herder, 1918), 1:429ff.

[25] In his thorough study of the *Dolchstoss* phenomenon, Boris Barth has noted the central
role of the Protestant Church as a social–moral milieu for the "origin, dissemination,
and reception" of the *Dolchstoss* myth and other myths rationalizing German defeat.

their avowed preference for monarchist hierarchy as supposedly more organically democratic, the Austrian bishops nonetheless supported the legitimacy of the fledgling republic. On its first anniversary, the new Austrian First Republic was officially recognized by the Holy See, eventually setting aside the famous Concordat of 1855.[26]

Leading Austrian Catholics, including Cardinal Friedrich Gustav Piffl of Vienna, argued that Kaiser Karl's renunciation of his participation in the affairs of state enabled a transfer of loyalties from the monarchy to the new democratic republic. On the day of the First Republic's founding, drawing on Piffl's public pronouncements, the preeminent Catholic paper *Reichspost* championed the new republic in words that could scarcely have been more different from the political sentiments of Wilhelmine Protestants or their Catholic comrades. On November 12, 1918, a *Reichspost* editorial declared that, "For the Christian peoples of German Austria, the foundations are clearly indicated," and that, "no one would be a lesser Catholic" for believing in "the republican form of state that comes about through legal means." The editorial conveniently left open the possibility that a democracy could choose to constitute itself in forms other than that of a republic, arguing that Catholics would be "loyal to the lawfully achieved order" in which the "legal forms of democracy remained defended." The article closed by urging Austrian Catholics to display, "calm, patience, and loyal tolerance in face of convictions that were not [their] own."[27]

After the fall of the Habsburg monarchy, the shattering of the throne-and-altar alliance was less traumatizing for Austrian Catholics than grand narratives of Habsburg history indicate. The Catholic natural-law philosophy of the universal magisterium, which did not sanctify any one form of government, allowed Catholics to transfer their political allegiances from one polity to another, as long as it was legitimately formed. Thus, Austrian Catholics could keep their options open for transferring loyalty from the new republic to other, more authoritarian forms of state, such as the clerico-fascist Dollfuß-Schuschnigg regime that would emerge in interwar Austria.[28] However, as attempts to merge into a

---

Boris Barth, *Dolchstoßlegenden und politische Desintegration: Das Trauma der deutschen Niederlage im Ersten Weltkrieg* (Düsseldorf: Droste, 2003), 150–71, 340–59; quote from 555.

[26] Maximilian Liebmann, "Von der Dominanz,", 361–456, esp. 393–7; Karl R. Stadler, "Die Gründung der Republik," in *Kirche in Österreich, 1918–1965*, ed. Erika Weinzierl and Ferdinand Klostermann, 2 vols. (Munich: Herold, 1966–67), 1:72.

[27] "Große Entscheidungen," *Reichspost*, November 12, 1918.

[28] Although the German Catholic bishops were heavily skeptical about the Weimar Republic from the outset, there were elements of Catholic transnational philosophy on natural law and state governments that were also apparent in Germany. See, for example,

German-Austria proved politically impossible and interwar economic uncertainty increased, Austrian Catholics began to acquiesce to a kind of stab-in-the-back myth related to pan-German resentments.[29]

Springtime of the nations

The fall of the Habsburg monarchy gave a narrative end point to not only the course of the dynasty but also the Great War. However, this focus on decline and fall did not fit the theological conceptions of many Central European Catholics from all social classes; it can perhaps best be seen through the public rhetoric of the bishops. For many religiously-inspired nationalist movements that had sought greater autonomy in the framework of the Austro-Hungarian state, 1918 was a moment of freedom and opportunity, the founding of new states.

The Hungarian bishop Ottokár Prohászka, for instance, continued his wartime philosophy directly into the interwar period. He looked on the war as an opportunity for organic renewal, with the Church not discredited by the chaos and carnage of 1914–18, but instead serving as a reminder of humanity's fallibility in comparison to the City of God. In Prohászka's conception, although flawed, the Church was the best guarantor of peace and comfort in dark times.[30] Prohászka was one of the nationalist leaders of the reform wing of the Hungarian Catholic Church. In his unpublished pastoral letter of March 1919, he supported social revolution, continuing a trend from the last years of the war, when lower clergy members had made sharp critiques of the Hungarian Church's aristocracy. Prohászka remained a staunch supporter of Admiral Miklós Horthy and nationalist consolidations.[31] In religious terms, this increasingly exclusionary nationalism in a new political framework in Hungary (and elsewhere in East-Central Europe) strongly contributed to changing

Peter Lippert, "Klerus, Krieg, und Umsturz," *Stimmen der Zeit* 97 (1919): 84: "Die Regierungsformen der Staaten, die Wirtschaftssysteme, die Bedingungen der Produktion und der Güterverteilung sind an sich bedeutungslos für die Ziele und Aufgabe des Christentums, also auch bedeutungslos für den Priester und Seelsorger."

[29] Patrick J. Houlihan, "Was There an Austrian Stab-in-the-Back Myth? Postwar Military Interpretations of Defeat," in *From Empire to Republic: Post-World War I Austria*, ed. Günter Bischof, Fritz Plasser, and Peter Berger, *Contemporary Austrian Studies* (New Orleans, LA: University of New Orleans Press, 2010), 67–89.

[30] Bettina Reichmann, "Die Rolle des ungarischen Bischofs Ottokár Prohászka im Ersten Weltkrieg," in *Geistliche im Krieg*, ed. Franz Brendle and Anton Schindling (Münster: Aschendorff Verlag, 2009), 291–311.

[31] Jerzy Kłoczowski, "Katholiken und Protestanten in Ostmitteleuropa," in *Die Geschichte des Christentums: Religion, Politik, Kultur*, vol. 12: *Erster und Zweiter Weltkrieg: Demokratien und totalitäre Systeme (1914–1958)*, ed. Jean-Marie Mayeur and Kurt Meier (Freiburg im Breisgau: Herder, 1992), 878. Cf. A. Schütz, "Otto Prohaszka. Ein großer Bischof der Gegenwart," *Hochland* 28 (1930/31).

Figure 1 Honvéd Chapel (Lipusch)
"Heroic patriotic devotion under the patronage of the Virgin Mary can be seen in the altar picture of Saint Johann Kapistran, patron saint of the Hungarian Honvéd, painted by Merész Gyula."

mindsets, moving latent Catholic anti-Semitism into genocidal complicity during the Second World War.[32]

---

[32] Paul A. Hanebrink, *In Defense of Christian Hungary: Religion, Nationalism, and Anti-semitism, 1890–1944* (Ithaca, NY: Cornell University Press, 2006).

Furthermore, one could point to the seminaries of Poland, Croatia, Slovakia, and Hungary, where clergy members continued to express the pre-war ideological belief that Catholics could be both national and universal.[33] New generations of activist priests, often from the middle and peasant classes, took assertive leadership roles and attempted to enact major religious reforms in the new states. František Kordač, Archbishop of Prague from 1919 to 1931, was a symbolic figure in this process. Kordač was the first Bohemian primate who was not of noble origin, and he was a member of the Czechoslovak People's Party, participating in the Revolutionary National Assembly in 1918–20. Nevertheless, while he was a leader of Czech Catholicism, he was in a precarious position in the new Czechoslovak state, which was largely Protestant culturally and sought to enact wide-ranging separation of Church and state. Thus, Kordač both represented a movement and was responsible for reining in its excesses.

In the immediate post-war period in December 1918, the Czech bishops from the Prague diocese reflected clearly the profound new reorientation of public loyalties of bishops everywhere. They interpreted the war and the dissolution of the Habsburg monarchy as a divinely-ordained action that provided a blank slate for social regeneration in a new state framework. The bishops wrote that, "Insofar as we behold the hand of Divine Providence in the fortunes of the nations, we accept with thankfulness and devotion what Providence has decided, and we place in it the hope of the further auspicious development of our Fatherland under the powerful protection of the Lord ... Yes, we want and will love, also in its new form, our Fatherland, with all our soul and in harmony and justice, living with all our fellow citizens; and we will stand by the lawfully-proclaimed government with requisite attention and devotion to sacrifice, just as divine and human law demand. In this respect will no shadow fall on our blank slate."[34]

Further into the new Czechoslovak state outside of Prague, new religiously-based political movements were gaining strength. Perhaps most ominously, Father Jozef Tiso, who briefly served as a military chaplain in Austria-Hungary during the First World War, became the leader of the Slovak People's Party in its drive for a separate Slovak state. The Slovak Republic of 1939–45 became a satellite state of Nazi Germany, and Catholic anti-Semitism contributed strongly to the popular opinion that enabled the genocide of Slovak Jews. At the rank of captain,

---

[33] Gottsmann, *Rom und die nationalen Katholizismen*; Klieber, "Soziale Integration durch Religion?", 743–81.

[34] DASP (St. Pölten) XIII, Ktn. 5 (Rössler): Bischofskonferenzen, 1895–1919 (HD 03/20), "Die Bischöfe der Prager Kirchenprovinz," announcement of December 1918.

Father Tiso served as a military chaplain in the 71st Infantry Regiment of the k.u.k. Army, stationed on the Eastern Front in Galicia during the Great War's opening phase. Tiso's war diary describes the "overwhelming" horrors of war, including bodily disfigurement, mass graves of soldiers, and atrocities against civilians. Tiso quickly transferred out of front-line service and climbed the Church hierarchy. Speaking both languages and not easily categorized as either "Slovak" or "Hungarian" in the Austro-Hungarian Dual Monarchy, the category of "national indifference" fit Tiso and his milieu well. In terms of locally-based religious ministry, as Tiso's biographer notes, "Virtually all of Tiso's actions before 1917 can be understood as defending Catholicism and the Hungarian state." The shifting political realities in the late phase of the war and the immediate post-war period showed that Central European Catholics could keep their religious affiliation while transfering their political loyalties to new states and new nations. After 1917, Tiso saw his ministry in much more political terms. He felt a duty to reinvigorate spiritually the priesthood, which would serve as a vanguard for coming democratic political upheavals. Tiso welcomed the political realignments and turned to authoritarianism to harness the new mass politics.[35]

Similarly, in Croatia, Catholic religion was an essential force in ethnonational politics in the newly created state of Yugoslavia and its cleavages between Catholicism, Islam, and Orthodoxy. Eventually, this would culminate in the ethnic cleansings of the Second World War, and it continued even after the dissolution of Yugoslavia in the 1990s. Ante Pavelić created the infamous Ustaša in 1929, which saw the emergence of the Croatian nation in the aftermath of the Great War as a divinely-willed opportunity. The founding principles of the Ustaša were built on exclusion of Orthodox and Muslim elements in Balkan society, with the declaration that, "The Croatian nation belongs to Western culture and to Western civilization," and that anyone not descended from a "peasant family is not a Croat at all, but a foreign immigrant." During the Second World War, the primate of Croatia, Archbishop Alojzije Stepinac, saw "the hand of God at work" in the birth of the Croatian nation.[36]

In Polish Catholicism, the Great War was also a moment of rebirth and awakening. A conscious program to build a Catholic intelligentsia, a "weak point of Polish Catholicism," began at the University of Lublin in autumn 1918 under the influence of the Rector, Idzi Radziszewski. In the new Polish state, Josef Piłsudski's government celebrated the opening

---

[35] James Mace Ward, *Priest, Politician, Collaborator: Jozef Tiso and the Making of Fascist Slovakia* (Ithaca, NY: Cornell University Press, 2013), 31–8; quote from 37.

[36] Quoted in Michael Burleigh, *Sacred Causes: The Clash of Religion and Politics from the Great War to the War on Terror* (New York: HarperCollins, 2007), 262–3.

of parliament in 1919 with a celebratory Mass in the Cathedral in War-saw, full of old Polish traditional symbolism. Although the new Polish constitution theoretically contained provisions of religious freedom for other confessions, Article 114 declared that, "the Catholic confession as the religion of the overwhelming majority of the people takes first place among all equal confessions." This privileged position continued in interwar Poland, reinforced by the Concordat of 1925. The Concor-dat benefitted from the anti-Bolshevik sympathies of Achille Ratti, the papal nuncio in Warsaw from 1919 to 1921, who had witnessed the Polish–Soviet War and would become Pope Pius XI.[37]

As the Habsburg monarchy crumbled, its bishops transferred their loyalty to new political frameworks. In the case of Slovenia, Austrian bishops released an October 1918 pastoral letter begging for unity. In his interpretation of the letter, however, the Prince-Bishop of Ljubljana, Anton Jeglič, gave his priests local political autonomy to adjust to the revolutionary situation: "The priests are allowed to select and read out the paragraphs which they believe are appropriate with regard to the general mood pervading the society." Addressing a throng of demonstrators in Ljubljana on October 29, 1918, Jeglič was not full of doom and gloom at the fall of the monarchy. He radiated optimism, believing in God's providence for the emerging Slovenian nation, and addressed the crowd with the following words: "Lift up your heads, for your redeption is near. Yes, what we have all wholeheartedly and justly wanted is being fulfilled; the time is coming when we shall be on our own in the beautiful Yugoslavia . . . "[38]

Like the Austrian bishops, the public theology stressed Catholic natural-law philosophy, obedience to authority, and acceptance of new state frameworks. Loyalty to the Habsburg monarchy was a secondary concern, even for the bishops who had so vigorously defended the insti-tution during the war. New post-war political realities had emerged, and the bishops and members of the clergy adjusted disparately to new state contexts. In many cases, the Great War represented an opportunity for growth, not disillusionment, for Catholics could be both universal and national.

New theologies

Beyond the bishops, however, new theologies were already developing, which in Catholic circles represented largely an adaptation of tradition.

---

[37] Kłoczowski, "Katholiken und Protestanten," 879–81.
[38] Quoted in Pavlina Bobič, *War and Faith: The Catholic Church in Slovenia, 1914–1918* (Boston, MA: Brill, 2012), 238.

The newest, most radical developments in Protestant theology in Central Europe articulated a fundamental break with the war years. By contrast, Catholic theology took a completely different course during and after the war. Instead of a decisive break with the events of 1914–18, Catholic thought bypassed the war years by either continuing pre-war developments or articulating new theologies that did not repudiate the war. Three Catholic thinkers in particular highlight a spectrum of issues related to the Great War as a point of Catholic theological development: Max Scheler, Romano Guardini, and Karl Adam. The theologies of these three thinkers would reach their full implications only in the post-Second World War era, with particular influence on the Second Vatican Council of 1962–65.

Max Scheler had vigorously defended German *Kultur* throughout the war, most famously in his book *Der Genius des Krieges* (1916). His phenomenological approach to religion insisted on a "love community" (*Liebesgemeinschaft*) of solidarity and responsibility, with the Catholic Church as the "most expansive" form of collective persons. Scheler took note of the omnipresence of suffering after the First World War, referring to humanity being "drunk" with suffering, death, and tears, and calling for a human renewal. Scheler's publications on this theme were instructive. Most prominently, his supposed "post-war" work, *Upheaval of Values* (*Umsturz der Werte*), was published in a revised edition in 1919; in fact, as acknowledged in the preface, the revised edition contained essentially unaltered pre-1914 writings. Far from being an obscure theology professor in the Catholic ghetto, Scheler's phenomenological approach to religion found broad reception among his contemporaries in the interwar period, earning him high public praise from Martin Heidegger and José Ortega y Gasset. In 1926, Leon Trotsky invited Scheler to Moscow to give a series of lectures (which, alas, never took place) on the subject of "God and the State."[39] Perhaps most prominently for Catholic theology, for his second doctorate in philosophy in 1954, the future Pope Saint John Paul II would base his work on an analysis of Max Scheler's ethical system.

Like Eric Maria Remarque, Romano Guardini had also seen the horrors of war demonstrated in a hospital, when he served in Bavaria as a hospital chaplain; however, Guardini interpreted the suffering radically differently.[40] In his fundamental work of 1918, *The Spirit of the Liturgy*,

---

[39] For Scheler's comment on the war's suffering, see Max Scheler, *Gesammelte Werke* (Bern: Francke Verlag, 1954–), 5:103–4. For a biography of Scheler, see Manfred S. Frings, *The Mind of Max Scheler: The First Comprehensive Guide Based on the Complete Works* (Milwaukee, WI: Marquette University Press, 1997), 11–16.

[40] In a powerful scene in *All Quiet on the Western Front*, Paul Bäumer becomes disillusioned with Western civilization after seeing the aftermath of battlefield carnage in a hospital

Guardini stressed the need for civilization: "In all this is to be learned a really important lesson on liturgical practice. Religion needs civilization. By civilization we mean the essence of the most valuable products of man's creative, constructive, and organizing powers – works of art, science, social orders and the like. In the liturgy it is civilization's task to give durable form and expression to the treasure of truths, aims, and supernatural activity, which God has delivered to man by Revelation, to distill its quintessence, and to relate this to life in all its multiplicity."[41]

Guardini's work would inspire the interwar liturgical movement of youthful activism, reenergizing the Church. The historical interpretation of time here was quite different, stressing the success of the Church over a long period: "The fundamental conditions essential to the full expansion of spiritual life as it is lived in common are most clearly discernible in the devotional life of any great community which has spread its development over a long period of time. Its scheme of life has by then matured and developed its full value."[42] Guardini argued that the Catholic liturgy needed thought, not feeling, as the main motivator of prayer. Thus, he contrasted it with "popular devotions," which could express the local character of religion and the "changing demands of time, place and special circumstance," while the liturgy expressed the "fundamental laws – eternally and universally unchanging – which govern all genuine and healthy piety."[43]

Guardini drew a sharp distinction between Catholic and Protestant forms of liturgy, expressed in terms of individual and communal believers' relationships to God and each other. The Catholic Church was highly communal and was reinforced through hierarchical structures, dominated by priests administering sacraments. In Guardini's Catholic conception of the liturgy, he laid stress on the "united body of the faithful," which he equated with a Church with "lawful acts of worship" administered by priests. Repudiating liturgy as a form of individualized devotion for religious expression, Guardini wrote of the Catholic communalism of the liturgical movement, stating:

The primary and exclusive aim of the liturgy is not the expression of the individual's reverence and worship for God. It is not even concerned with the awakening,

---

(Erich Maria Remarque, *All Quiet on the Western Front*, trans. A. W. Wheen (Boston, MA: Little, Brown and Company, 1929), 263): "It must be all lies and of no account when the culture of a thousand years could not prevent this stream of blood being poured out, these torture chambers in their hundreds of thousands. A hospital alone shows what war is."

[41] Romano Guardini, *The Spirit of the Liturgy*, trans. Ada Lane (New York: Crossroad Publishing, 1998 [1918]), 33.

[42] Ibid., 18.   [43] Ibid., 20–2.

formation, and sanctification of the individual soul as such. Nor does the onus of liturgical action and prayer rest with the individual. It does not even rest with the collective groups, composed of numerous individuals, who periodically achieve a limited and intermittent unity in their capacity as the congregation of a church. The liturgical entity consists rather of the united body of the faithful as such – the Church – a body which infinitely outnumbers the mere congregation. The liturgy is the Church's public and lawful act of worship, and it is performed and conducted by the officials whom the Church herself has designated for the post – her priests. In the liturgy God is to be honored by the body of the faithful, and the latter is in its turn to derive sanctification from this act of worship. It is important that this objective nature of the liturgy should be fully understood. Here the Catholic conception of worship in common sharply differs from the Protestant, which is predominantly individualistic. The fact that the individual Catholic, by his absorption into the higher unity, finds liberty and discipline, originates in the twofold nature of man, who is both social and solitary.[44]

The importance of Guardini's concept of liturgy and theology would massively influence the architects of Vatican II, particularly Karl Rahner.[45]

Representing another Great War continuity was Karl Adam. In the prewar era, Adam had served as a religious tutor to the Bavarian royal family, the Wittelsbachs, representing a particularly personal connection with the Ancien Régime that would flower in the interwar period. Based on lectures composed in Tübingen in 1919–23, Adam's *Spirit of Catholicism* was published in 1924. He closed his work with an argument for the historical and institutional continuity of the Church as mother figure: "In her heart burns the ancient love. Out of her eyes shines the ancient faith. From her hands flow ever the ancient blessings. What would heaven be without God? What would the earth be without this Church? I believe in One Holy Catholic and Apostolic Church."[46]

Adam's theology and personal stances easily blended into his initial worship of Nazism as a guarantor of organic national community.[47] Drawing on the legacy of Romanticism, Adam's Catholic Tübingen School reacted strongly against modernity, idealizing the medieval era and its notion of the Catholic Church as an all-encompassing social unifier. In *The Spirit of Catholicism*, Adam wrote, "Just as the church by the compact unity and strength of its Christian faith gave the Middle Ages their inward unity and their strength of soul . . . so it alone is able in our modern day to introduce again amid the conflicting currents, the solvent forces and growing exhaustion of the West, a single lofty purpose, a constructive and effective religious power, a positive moral energy and

---

[44] Ibid., 19.   [45] McBrien, *Catholicism*, 493–9.

[46] Karl Adam, *The Spirit of Catholicism*, trans. Justin McCann (New York: Crossroad, 1997 [1924]), 228–9.

[47] Robert A. Krieg, *Catholic Theologians in Nazi Germany* (New York: Continuum, 2004).

a vitalizing enthusiasm."[48] In this mindset, while the medieval Church was the ideal, Nazism, which promised a return to unified community, could be seen as a force for regeneration and moral uplift. This mode of thought drew on a wealth of reactionary writings, especially the condemnations of modernist liberalism, atheism, and materialism found in the works of Pope Pius IX and Pope Saint Pius X, but also such thinkers as Joseph Lortz and Oswald Spengler.[49]

Everyday theologies

One of the most understudied areas of Great War religiosity is the everyday theology of common citizens. Beyond the writings of prominent members of the clergy, millions of people struggled to understand the unfolding events of the world war and tried to make sense of what was happening to them. In their letters, diaries, and memoirs, they left behind claims about how their religious views helped them endure the conflict.

Gendered representations of religion could make an enormous difference in coping with the stagnation of the war. The masculine-gendered chosen-people Protestantism, especially in its German variant, was not consoling when victory seemed more distant. It was the stereotypically feminine religion of Catholicism that offered homefront connections, with the Virgin Mary, as the ultimate symbolic unifier of human and divine realms, of homefront and battlefront, linking soldiers to a family-based sense of community. As Annette Becker has argued, it was in the trenches that soldiers rediscovered women's religion.[50] One German soldier near St. Quentin in 1914 wrote that whenever he prayed to his rosary, "I knew for certain that a mother's eye was watching over me and not only me but also over my wife and my seven children and that, if I should fall, that my family will bear no cross greater than she can carry." The soldier continued, "The thought about family is actually the chief concern; if one falls oneself, that doesn't come into question so much."[51] Such statements by soldiers not only invoked the Virgin Mary as a direct protector but also made the symbolic connection between their own wives and the Mother of God. If Mary could mourn the fallen Jesus and live in consoling Christian hope, certainly one's own wife would be able to console one's family and mourn one's death, enabling one to carry on in the hope of resurrection and reunification, too.

---

[48] Adam, *The Spirit of Catholicism*, 95.   [49] Krieg, *Catholic Theologians*, 88.
[50] Becker, "Faith, Ideologies," 241.
[51] N. N., Letter of November 1914, "Im Felde bei St.-Quentin," quoted in Georg Pfeilschifter, ed., *Feldbriefe katholischer Soldaten*, 3 vols. (Freiburg im Breisgau: Herder, 1918), 1:110–11.

The homefront, however, was not always a blessed isle of theological repose and comfort. The war also saw religious women adopt soldierly discourses, such as Andrea Hartl of Graz, who in her diary referred to her "trust in prayer as a weapon."[52] Especially among those who did not have to face combat or who did not have loved ones who were killed or wounded, the war could also sharpen ideological attitudes. This often reinforced the idea of militant Christianity, in which peace would only occur through victory.[53]

During the heat of battle, despite the prayers of believers, many were hit by bullets and shells. Sometimes bodies were obliterated by explosions or simply submerged in the morass of mud and never seen again. Bodily destruction was rampant. And all religions did not cope in the same way. Despite the idea of the wounded national fighter as an *imitatio Christi*, there are indications, for instance, that Catholic congregations had difficulty accepting wounded priests as consecrators at Mass. This was actually in accordance with Canon Law, a Catholic theology of the body, and an anthropological symbolism of the priest at Mass. According to these beliefs, a priest should be "unblemished" like Christ, and wounded priests formed imperfect symbolic representations.[54] Unlike their Catholic counterparts, Protestant congregations could more easily make the conceptual leap that wounded pastors were the highest examples of Christian devotion in battle. "National ecumenism" was not a catch-all term for the religion of war and peace, even within a particular religious tradition.[55]

---

[52] Dokumentationsarchiv Lebensgeschichtlicher Aufzeichnungen (Vienna). Andrea Hartl Tagebuch, "Vertrauen in Gebet als Waffe."

[53] Christian Pesch, "Wann wird unser Gebet erhört?", *Stimmen der Zeit* 93 (1917): 361–76.

[54] Sabine Kienitz, "Weihehindernisse: Kriegsversehrung und katholische Geistlichkeit im Ersten Weltkrieg," in *KriegsVolksKunde: Zur Erfahrungsbindung durch Symbolbildung*, ed. Gottfried Korff (Tübingen: Tübinger Verein für Volkskunde, 2005), 51–84. For the Canon Law provisions, Canons 968 and 984, see Peters, *The 1917 or Pio-Benedictine Code*, 336, 341.

[55] Recent studies of the Orthodox Jewish community in Frankfurt clustered around Rabbi Selig Schachnowitz, for instance, have cautioned against a singular German Jewish experience of the war, especially when looking at Orthodox Jews on the one hand and Liberal Jews on the other. Letters from the front reveal that for Orthodox German Jews, the topos of a newly-forged German *Volksgemeinschaft* during the Great War did not exist in their conceptualization of their own belief. Instead, Orthodox Jews blended a specifically "German-Jewish community of fate [*Schicksalsgemeinschaft*]" with much more traditional interpretations of both war in general and German war ideology in particular. In further research, one should also examine cross-confessional religious comparisons of the ritual and material affinities between Catholic, Eastern Orthodox, and Orthodox Jewish experiences of war. See Margit Schad, "Die bedrohten 'Gottesgüter' in die neue 'deutsche' Zeit retten. Selig Schachnowitz und die orthodoxe jüdische Kriegsdeutung in Frankfurt am Main 1914–1918," in Brendle and Schindling, *Geistliche im Krieg*, 265–89.

Soldiers who had to experience the daily horrors of battle often used their faith to cope. Their diaries and memoirs testify to their religious belief as an essential component of their worldview. They simply endured because of their belief. Hans Haugeneder, a k.u.k. soldier in the 70th Infantry Regiment, served on the Eastern Front, participated in the invasion of Romania, and then fought on the Italian Front in several battles along the Isonzo River. His diary reflections record frequent trips into hellish battles and his ultimate inability to represent the events: "What now follows, I can't form into words; even Satan's pen cannot spryly portray it with devilish color."[56] The effects of battle, viewed through the hospital as a focal point of suffering, caused much theological reflection. For Haugeneder, "The whole terrors of war are reflected never more frightfully true than in these places of suffering, where all everything is unified in horror and misery."[57] Yet, for the religious believer, there was a special reserve of hope, even as Haugeneder found himself confined in an epidemic ward: "'New life blooms again out of the ruins.' You strong faith in Life's eternal Spring [*Lebensfrühling*], you evergreen hope in the future!"[58]

In the closing days of the war, as the Habsburg state was crumbling, Haugeneder made his way back home to Salzburg, passing through Budapest. He saw the grim, depressing reality of the war in Central Europe: hungry, waif-like people waiting for meager allotments of food or aimlessly wandering about the streets. This social deprivation on a massive scale led Haugeneder to deeply emotional theological reflections on the nature of war and society. The shades of people on the streets caused him to wonder, "Is such a state of Being still human, overall worthy of existence?" When he saw such scenes, he was "overcome every time with a form of doubt in human and divine justice": doubts about human justice because of the "decided indifference regarding such burning questions of charity," especially because those blessed with good fortune seemed to exhibit "indolence and spiritual brutality" about helping those in need; doubts about divine justice because he could not see how "the Creator of all creatures" could allow such a situation of "degradation and disparity." In Haugeneder's religiously-based worldview, the question of human existence could largely be reduced to a single point: "That is now the tender point, the silent boundary-post on which so many answers depend, that stands contemplating and that divides humanity into two big groups: the believers in the hereafter and the deniers in

---

[56] Hans Haugeneder, *Gestern noch auf stolzen Rossen. Tagebuch eines Kriegsteilnehmers 1916–1918*, ed. Anna Kautsky (Vienna: Hermagoras/Mohorjeva, 2010), 93–7; quote from 93.
[57] Ibid., 111.   [58] Ibid., 111, 114.

the hereafter." Working through his doubt, using his empirical senses to reflect on the condition of war, Haugeneder's religious convictions influenced his appraisal of the question of human existence: "If justice was not done to these creatures already on Earth, so must it be done to them in greater measure beyond, there in Eternity."[59]

Religious beliefs also informed the social and political upheavals that would occur in the interwar period. Haugeneder complained bitterly about the false heroism of the homefront, and yet maintained the belief that peace would come. It would be the duties of "true soldiers, when they returned as civilians" to combat the luxurious jingoism spouted by those in safety on the homefront, to "wage a fierce war" to enforce the peace against the civilian "scoundrels" (*Halunken*).[60]

Religious women keenly noted how the war affected their lives, but it was not a moment of shattering breakage, a disillusionment with the pre-war era; rather, it was a depressing episode in the continuities of human existence. Maria Gremel, a farm worker in a poor peasant household in Styria, was around fourteen years old when the war began. She recalled in her memoirs the depressed mood in rural areas, where the loss of men and horses was keenly felt by farmers. Harvesting times were delineated by saints' days, with the especially difficult grain-cutting occuring between July 26 (Saint Ann's Day) and September 8 (the birth of the Virgin Mary). During the war, the state attempted to enforce production quotas from rural households, which put rural producers at a comparative advantage over city dwellers. However, this led to restrictions on farm lifestyles, as the state imposed bans on the slaughter of excess animals and production quotas on staples like grains and milk. In such an environment, a vibrant black market emerged, especially as urban populations traded luxury goods for food. Accusations and denunciations became increasingly widespread through the course of the war.[61]

The March 25, 1918 death of a local child provided an opportunity for the village to display different ways of grieving. The child's godmother was inconsolable, asking how God could take away such a small child. The mother, however, received comfort from Gremel, who stressed the connections between family and faith, especially during wartime. Gremel told her, "She now had a little Angel in Heaven, who would plead for the father to come home again." Apparently, this reassured the mother, for "She took comfort and realized that she had to be there for the

---

[59] Ibid., 125–6.

[60] Ibid., 81, 99. For the concept of veterans fighting for peace in the interwar period, see Benjamin Ziemann, *Contested Commemorations: Republican War Veterans and Weimar Political Culture* (Cambridge: Cambridge University Press, 2013).

[61] Gremel, *Mit neun Jahren im Dienst*, 211–28.

other two children if the father was already absent." Theologically, this provoked Gremel to reflect that humanity had a wide variety of responses to adversity, and her faith was a guiding light in her life. This was not, however, a naïvely optimistic belief structure: Gremel's faith was founded in a sense of determination that dealt well with the Great War as one episode among many: "Every human reacts totally differently to difficult suffering. One can curse everything, one can resign oneself; it leads to nothing. The only thing that helps us is only when we also accept the harshest blows of Fate and endure them. Because life goes on."[62]

Gremel's personal theological worldview centered not on the war, but on her unplanned pregnancy shortly after its end, which was to be the formative event of her life. She was courted by several local suitors, including one, Karl, who had fought on the Piave Front, from where he had corresponded with Gremel, asking her to pray for his safe return. Despite warnings from her recently-deceased mother that a young woman should protect her virginity, as Gremel recounted, "He took me, and I gave myself to him." She immediately regretted the act, which resulted in a pregnancy out of wedlock in 1921: "What is such a short span of lust, compared to the lifelong consequences." Her reflections demonstrated a frustration with traditional gender roles and the burdens of female sexuality in traditional society: "Even in the nice times of youth, I had to think: 'If only I weren't born a woman!' A boy keeps his reputation, his honor, nothing is shaken by him. For a girl, the least that happens is that it goes around that she is a slut. No one says anything about the man." In her own opinion, her views on sexuality in conservative villages were grounded in reality. Before one Sunday Mass, she was confronted in a barn by Karl's mother, who called her a "slut" and exclaimed, "Who knows where you've been whoring around!" She forcefully intervened to prevent a marriage, using religion as a moral cudgel: "You don't want to go to church with my son and shame yourself as if he were your man. You don't have anything to do in church, you only want to carry in your shame so that everyone can see it!" Karl was working beside them in the barn as they had this conversation, but he said nothing. Karl and Maria parted ways, never to speak again, although Karl and his mother continued to see Maria and her child in church. Yet Maria Gremel's fears regarding her reception within the village community were unfounded. After the dramatic confrontation with Karl's mother, the rest of the village treated Maria relatively well for the rest of her life, not saying a bad word to her or her child.[63] The daily rhythms and patterns of Central European Catholic

---

[62] Ibid., 235–6.   [63] Ibid., 245–54.

communal life, especially in traditional rural communities, contained relationships rooted in locally-focused existence.

At the end of the war, local Catholic communities reinforced everyday religious life and belief as a form of continuity. Religious life, especially in rural villages, continued to provide a major part of believers' worldviews. Religion was a stabilizing factor for the bitter post-war years, which reflected both the solidity of the pre-1914 agricultural world and a constructed nostalgia for that world, which shifted rapidly in the post-1945 era. Felix Nöbauer, a poor farm worker living in Sankt Willibald in Bubenberg, and later in Antlangkirchen during the interwar period, described a vibrant Catholic village life that began at home with "very strongly religious parents" who took him to Mass on every Sunday and holy day, creating a "peasant world that was a closed society on the points of religion and church visits." Nöbauer described that kind of religious obligation as "self-evident in those days, and in our village, no one was exempted from this duty." There were organized religious groups for boys and girls, women, and men, and for different professions and occupations, reflecting "religious life in full bloom." But these were not simple memories of good times: strong, harsh, theological discipline was also a part of this world, especially as a tool of moral renewal and social regeneration in the aftermath of the war. Recollecting his attraction to his girlfriend, Nöbauer recalled that, "Yes, from the pulpit in those days, Hell was spoken of more frequently. But I believe that was not entirely wrong. It is important for man to comprehend the sense of life and to achieve happily the last goal. Otherwise life would be senseless! A holy fear of eternal ruin in Hell is good for man. This belief and conviction have helped me overcome many cliffs and dangers of life."[64]

Catholic anti-Semitism

Anti-Semitism was a deeply ingrained part of the Central European Catholic worldview in the pre-1914 era. The Great War sharpened the traditional religiously-based Catholic anti-Semitism. As John Connelly has argued, it was only after the Second World War, indeed after the Second Vatican Council, that Catholic attitudes toward Jews began to shift from hostility toward ecumenical embrace.[65] At the end of the Great War,

---

[64] Ortmayr, *Knechte*, 177–233.

[65] John Connelly, *From Enemy to Brother: The Revolution in Catholic Teaching on the Jews, 1933–1965* (Cambridge, MA: Harvard University Press, 2012). As Connelly notes, this was largely due to the efforts of several key Jewish converts to Catholicism, who helped to reformulate ecumenical thinking in preparation for the Second Vatican Council.

such hostility was only too apparent. Apostolic Field-Vicar Emerich Bjelik bemoaned the lax morals and falling away of religious customs among the youth. He attributed this to the bad example of educators, specifically targeting Jews: "Therefore, unsuitable teachers, the Jewish element, of lapsed belief and thus giving a bad example, should be removed from teaching positions by this fact alone."[66]

For many Central European Catholics, Judaism became a catch-all complaint for secularizing influence, lax morality, and socio-economic disorder, often contrasted with an idealized nostalgic and delusional vision of a pre-war harmonious corporate society. For instance, a 1925 pamphlet of "Lessons and Instructions of the Austrian Bishops Concerning Social Questions of the Present" argued that the war had disrupted traditional society, introducing disorder on a massive scale. A draft version of the pamphlet categorized this as "Jewish spirit," which someone altered in the final printed version to "corrupting spirit" (verderblichen Geist).[67]

The Catholics of Central Europe retained many pre-war prejudices, which were accentuated by the social disruptions caused by the loss of the Great War. Nostalgically looking to the pre-war years as an idealized version of social harmony, many local Catholics reacted against perceived "outsiders." Anyone who threatened the organic corporate vision of society could be deemed a threat. Reflecting on her life in Kirchschlag, Styria, Maria Gremel voiced prejudices against "Gypsies" (Zigeuner), expressing her "distrust" of them. They nonetheless aroused "curiosity" in village, especially regarding their vastly different lifestyle. Gremel commented in particular on their rootlessness in contrast to settled village life, which led her to characterize the "Gypsies" as follows: "They are their own nation and even have a king." Immediately contradicting herself on the issue of rootlessness, however, she wrote of established "real Gypsy villages" (richtige Zigeunerdörfer) in nearby regions of Hungary. Complaining about a supposed "Gypsy" lack of work ethic that gave rise to theft, she reflected that, "Even Hitler could not incorporate them into being regular workers. How it is now in those [villages in Hungary], I do not know any more. It has been 50 years since I last saw them, and I have not heard anything more about them."[68] Writing in retrospect, Gremel's reflections

---

[66] DAG, Nachlaß von Bischof Dr. Ferdinand Pawlikowski, Militärvikariat, Ktn. 1, Schachtel I, Heft 1: Gutachten des Apostolischen Feldvikars Emmerich Bjelik über die Schrift "Die innere Reform der Armee," p. 2.

[67] DASP (St. Pölten): XIII, Ktn. 5 (Rössler): Bischofkonferenzen, 1895–1919 (HD 03/20), Pamphlet, "Lehren und Weisungen der österreichischen Bischöfe über soziale Fragen der Gegenwart" (1925).

[68] Gremel, Mit neun Jahren im Dienst, 100–6.

ominously refused to recognize the human carnage that such prejudice had helped to cause in the twentieth century.

The Great War exacerbated latent Catholic anti-Semitism in both rural and urban contexts, with slight differences of emphasis. Especially in metropolitan areas, which were starving by the end of the war, hungry people vented their food-supply problems at Jews. High-ranking officials such as the Christian Social Mayor Richard Weiskirchner of Vienna stoked fears of the influx of Eastern Galician refugees fleeing the advancing Russian Armies by denouncing the figure of the "Polish Jew" who lingered in coffeehouses before emerging to conduct black-market profiteering, selling prized foodstuffs like butter. Helping to reinforce such anti-Semitic code phrases as "refugees from the East" and lingering "men in coffeehouses," the Habsburg Empire's largest Catholic newspaper, *Reichspost*, enthusiastically printed lists of people punished for black-marketeering in food. Prominently featuring people with Jewish surnames, the list of violators often included the designation "Galicia," thus linking food crime to Eastern Jewish refugees.[69]

Christian fear-mongers also lamented the perceived decline of rigid social mores, especially through lax sexual codes.[70] Particularly at prominent sites of urban sociability such as coffeehouses, theaters, and cinemas, Jews became scapegoats for the corruption of wartime Christian society, undermining the steadfast dedication and sacrifice necessary for ultimate victory. In 1916, a group of Viennese women wrote to Mayor Weiskirchner, identifying themselves as "We Viennese Christian Business-wives" and demanding to know why their husbands were serving in combat while "all these young people and Jews . . . loiter at night in the coffeehouses."[71]

Among rural Catholics, who were better fed on the whole than those in the larger metropolitan areas, the war nonetheless aggravated traditional anti-Semitism, leading to anti-capitalist critiques; these also resonated with thousands of Catholic workers in the industrial regions of Central Europe, especially western Germany and Bohemia. Demonized scare-figures such as the "profiteering Jew" (*Wucherjude*) and "bloodsucker" (*Volksaussauger*) became part of a conspiracy of "financially powerful men behind the scenes," in the words of one municipal official from Freiburg. Overall, as a Freiburg soldier noted in June 1918, "One encounters great war-weariness everywhere, which ends in the pessimistic tone: 'the war will only end when the Jews have filled all their sacks.'"[72] As the war lengthened, frustration over the uncertain outcome turned into anti-capitalist sentiment. In Germany, nationalist social cohesion fragmented

---

[69] Healy, *Vienna*, 67. [70] Grabinski, *Weltkrieg und Sittlichkeit*, 137–210.
[71] Quoted in Healy, *Vienna*, 269. [72] Quoted in Chickering, *The Great War*, 498.

as Bavarian Catholics explained the war in terms of their unwilling sacrifice for "Prussia and big capitalists."[73] Interwar economic fluctuations compounded the uncertainty and aggravated the anti-Semitic stereotypes that the war had fostered.

Conclusion

Catholic war theology operated on a time scale that emphasized deep historical continuities of experience, placing the Great War as one episode in the panoply of disasters appropriate to the fallen human condition. Throughout the history of the Church and beyond the Great War, Catholic theologians framed their arguments in ancient and medieval justifications for the use of force and obedience to the state, drawing foremost on the doctors of the Church, Saint Augustine and Saint Thomas Aquinas.[74] This deeply historical view of the Church meant that Central European Catholics had witnessed epoch historical shifts, some calamitous, and had seen the Church adapt its tradition to face new challenges: the fall of the Roman Empire, the decline of medieval Christendom, the Reformation and the emergence of the early modern state, the intellectual ferment of the Enlightenment, and the rise of modern science and the European state system after the French Revolution. By contrast, what gave so much power to a religiously-tinged Protestant German *Sonderweg* was the retrospective plausibility of a unilinear narrative of German nationhood as a world-historical event of ever-increasing German victories and consolidation, beginning with Martin Luther and ending with Kaiser Wilhelm II as *summus episcopus* of the German Empire.[75]

Viewed transnationally, the Catholic theological history of the Great War showed that the elements of the nation-state were vastly important, framed in a wide variety of new state contexts that emerged in the aftermath of 1918–19. The brilliantly devastating satires of priesthood during the war by such authors as Karl Kraus and Jaroslav Hašek did not recognize that the interwar years were a period of pan-European Catholic flourishing, even among peoples whose states had lost the war. Annual ordinations for the priesthood in Germany rose dramatically, actually exceeding their pre-war levels in a few short years. By 1923, the number of new priests for the whole of Germany was eighteen percent higher than in 1914. This figure is even more significant when one takes into account

---

[73] Ziemann, *Front und Heimat*, 265–89.
[74] Hammer, *Deutsche Kriegstheologie*, 79. See also John Eppstein, *The Catholic Tradition of the Law of Nations* (Washington, DC: Carnegie Endowment for International Peace, published by the Catholic Association for International Peace, 1935).
[75] Williamson, "A Religious Sonderweg?"

the post-war territorial losses of Alsace-Lorraine and Prussia, which were both heavily Catholic areas of the German Empire.[76] Overall, vital new religious movements with varying degrees of direct Church control, such as the youth movement and the liturgical movement, demonstrated a Central European Catholicism that was not devastated by the war, but coping rather well and poised for a period of interwar renewal and growth.

In contrast to Protestant theology, which, on the whole, viewed the events of 1914–18 as a radical break, Catholic theology developed with more continuities of Church tradition. As demonstrated by theologians such as Scheler, Guardini, and Adam, a few seeds of new thought were developing as a result of the Great War, but these would take root only in the post-Second World War period, and indeed only after the Second Vatican Council of 1962–65. Ominously, Catholic anti-Semitism remained deeply in place in the theologies and worldviews of many Catholics, both clergy and laity, elite clerics and everyday lay believers. This hardening of hearts would contribute to the genocides of the Second World War.

As can be seen through the everyday theologies of Catholics who lived through the Great War and grew up in its aftermath, traditional worldviews remained strong and powerful influences on religious life in the interwar period and beyond. Nostalgically viewed and constructed in retrospect, especially after the even greater disruptions of the Second World War, Catholic belief structures nonetheless remained a strong source of orientation for the everyday lives of religious believers, providing a comfort and coping mechanism of fundamental power.

---

[76] Erwin Gatz, ed., *Der Diözesanklerus*, vol. 4: *Geschichte des kirchlichen Lebens in den deutschsprachigen Ländern seit dem Ende des 18. Jahrhunderts: Die Katholische Kirche* (Freiburg: Herder, 1995), 438. Based on statistics compiled in Erwin Gatz, ed., *Priester-ausbildungsstätten der deutschsprachigen Länder zwischen Aufklärung und zweitem Vatikanischem Konzil: mit Weihestatistiken der deutschsprachigen Diözesen* (Freiburg im Breisgau: Herder, 1994), 241–79. The numbers peaked at around 780 new ordinations annually, compared to around 660 in 1914.

3   The limits of religious authority: military chaplaincy and the bounds of clericalism

Moving forward into battle, the soldiers heard the sounds of their impending rendezvous. Booming artillery rounds punctuated the ever-increasing din of rifle and machine-gun fire. The troops marched in formation closer to the front line near Mühlhausen. A courier arrived from the commanding officer, and the battalion leader shouted out, "Herr Priest, it's serious: do your duty!" The military chaplain, a purple stola over his uniform, stepped to the head of each company. In his diary, he noted that his nerves trembled and his heart beat rapidly as he intoned as loudly and as confidently as he could muster: "Dear comrades! An earnest hour has arrived for you. Reconcile with your Lord God, repent with all your heart all the sins of your life and say: O God, be merciful to me, a poor sinner! Each man must do his duty at his post. I now give you absolution: I absolve you of all of your sins in the name of the Father, and of the Son, and of the Holy Spirit. Amen." The orders went out and the regiment went into action, the priest moving forward into a hail of bullets and shrapnel. Regardless of his intent to advance with the troops, he quickly became occupied ministering to the wounded and dying. From the very beginning of the Great War, industrial warfare strained the Catholic Church's resources at the front line.[1]

Near the end of the war, the Church still struggled to understand the conflict and to allocate its resources to the men at the front. In a 1918 position paper entitled "Inner Reform of the Army," the leader of Austro-Hungarian military chaplaincy reflected, "Modern war had developed the necessity of holding out for days under the heaviest artillery fire . . . that placed especially high demands on nerves and willpower." The chaplains' chief reflected that, "new forms of battle," especially the "so-called stationary struggle [*Stellungskampf*]" caused an "inconsolable monotony of battle and work" in the "extremely primitive forms of life." This type of warfare, over sustained periods of time, "unleashed an attritional and

---

[1] EAF, NL 44 (Jakob Ebner Tagebuch), entry of August 19, 1914, pp. 15–16.

demoralized effect on the troops."[2] Despite being depicted as military authorities fixated on matters of spirit in a war that became about brute material facts, some high-ranking military chaplains at the highest levels recognized that metaphysical will was intimately related to material conditions on the ground. Then, and ever after, the question remained: How could tradition adapt and cope with the new forms of industrial warfare?

Since Roman times, Christian military chaplaincy has formed a nexus of Church–state authority, representing both universal aspirations and local particularities. It is the Catholic Church's official support system for the provision of sacramental rites to Catholic soldiers. Believers have long had to reconcile the need to serve two masters during time of war.[3]

During medieval and early modern history, chaplaincy was an ephemeral phenomenon, paralleling the short military campaigns of the time. This changed during the nineteenth century, when state structures became more permanent. Chaplaincies became parts of standing armies, entwined in military bureaucracies. At the outset of the Great War, Catholic chaplaincies remained structured according to nineteenth-century regulations. Consequently, in both Germany and Austria-Hungary, Catholic chaplaincies had to confront the new circumstances of industrial warfare using impromptu methods.[4]

The numbers of chaplains who served, and the numbers killed, outline some of the major administrative issues. Drawing on the German figures, for example, of the 1441 official chaplains who served with the Prussian Army (not including Bavaria), eight were killed in battle and eight died of sickness or directly war-related diseases. Of the 986 chaplains who served at the front or in staging areas, 383 were members of religious orders. The official statistics only go so far, however, as an array of novitiates, lay brothers and sisters, and consecrated clergy members in unofficial capacities helped to supplement official pastoral care.[5] A highly sympathetic study compiled by a former chaplain lists 3077 Habsburg chaplains, of whom 54 died during the conflict.[6] For both Germany and Austria-Hungary, the number of chaplains and military religious caregivers was hazy and indeterminate at best. Nonetheless, the

[2] DAG, NL Bischof Dr. Ferdinand Pawlikowski, Militärvikariat, Ktn. 1, Schachtel 1, Heft 1: Emmerich Bjelik, "Die innere Reform der Armee" (1918), p. 2.
[3] Doris L. Bergen, ed., *The Sword of the Lord: Military Chaplains from the First to the Twenty-First Century* (South Bend, IN: University of Notre Dame Press, 2004).
[4] Houlihan, "Clergy in the Trenches."
[5] Wollasch, *Militärseelsorge im Ersten Weltkrieg*, lxxii.
[6] Lipusch, *Österreich-Ungarns katholische Militärseelsorge*, 58–78. By contrast, the latest German research, conducted by a team of archivists, admits that the German Catholic chaplaincy possesses "no systematic results of personnel from the time before 1918." See Brandt and Häger, *Biographisches Lexikon*, xii–xiii.

numbers killed and wounded during the conflict represent a difference between Austro-Hungarian Catholic centralization and German federal fragmentation, as this chapter will explore.

In his role as a state-sponsored clergyman ministering to troops, the Catholic priest as a military chaplain and intermediary authority figure was a key locus for determining the limits of the adaptation of Catholic tradition on the battlefield. In accordance with both Church and state regulations, the military chaplain was the designated representative of the clerical hierarchy of the Catholic universal magisterium legally empowered to minister rites to Catholic soldiers in battle. Consequently, the military chaplain was the Catholic soldier's final and often tenuous connection to the Church's network of pastoral care on the homefront, ultimately centered on the spiritual authority of the Vatican.

In terms of receiving official religious rites, the Catholic soldier's religious life depended on his military chaplain, who could consecrate communion, anoint the sick, and bury the dead. Perhaps most important for the soldier was the rite of reconciliation. Through the practice of confession and absolution, the chaplain as priest was designated to forgive sins so that a penitent soldier could die believing himself in a state of grace that would save his soul and gain him admission to Heaven. Given the extreme lethality of combat during the Great War, dying with a clear conscience became of utmost importance for the Catholic believer. Although a diffuse religiosity permeated many aspects of soldierly life, Catholic sacraments depended on military chaplains for their administration.

Thus, for a study of Catholicism during the Great War, it is essential to focus on the figure of the priest, and Catholic battlefront religion must confront the figure of the military chaplain. Scholars have debated the extent to which, during the nineteenth century – a century of increasing Catholic conservative opposition to industrial modernity – Catholic priests controlled their communities. Perhaps most pointedly, Olaf Blaschke argues that the priest was a "manager" of the Catholic milieu, directing religious impulses through clerical channels.[7] Yet, the Central European Catholic priest in wartime remains curiously understudied.[8] The Catholic priest in the role of military chaplain (who was thus imbued with additional authority in his role as an officer) represents a test case for how Catholic priests were able to shape the religious behaviors of lay believers.

Most studies of Central European Catholic chaplaincy during the Great War have focused on Germany and have declared that chaplaincy

[7] Blaschke, "Die Kolonialisierung der Laienwelt."
[8] Gatz, Der Diözesanklerus, 144. See also Erwin Gatz, Die Katholische Kirche in Deutschland im 20. Jahrhundert (Freiburg: Herder, 2009), 55–66.

was reactive and largely ineffectual in coping with the strains of modern warfare.[9] Studies of Catholic chaplaincy in Austria, although much less historiographically developed, present a similar story of large-scale institutional failure to adjust to mass industrial war.[10] Yet, studies of chaplaincy often do not examine the experiences of the Central Powers together, which can provide striking points of comparison and contrast.

This chapter argues that Catholic chaplaincy in Austria-Hungary was structurally better suited to providing a centralized system of pastoral care, which was more efficient than its counterparts in Germany. In several fundamental ways, such as pastoral reporting, field manuals, and overall leadership, Catholic chaplaincy in Germany foundered on the federal Church–state accords in the Wilhelmine Reich. Contrary to stereotypes of Habsburg sloppiness compared to Hohenzollern efficiency, Catholic chaplaincy in Austria-Hungary was more stable and yet more responsive to the new challenges of war.

The chapter begins by examining the devastating literary modernist portrayal of chaplaincy, which influenced historical studies of religion during the war. More recent cultural histories of religious behavior during the war have tended to subsume chaplaincy under the heading of "morale and consent," with Austria-Hungary representing a particular case of centrifugally nationalist instability and inefficiency.[11] The chapter then moves on to study military chaplaincy in the respective imperial contexts of the losing powers.

Outlining systemic hierarchies of chaplaincy and military dynamics puts contingent focus on the military priests designated by the Catholic Church to serve the needs of soldiers. As this chapter argues, Catholic chaplains as managers of the battlefield milieu were not in control of events and could not by themselves significantly alter soldiers' religious behavior. Although they were officers in an administrative sense, Catholic chaplains remained priests first, largely outside of the military hierarchy. Religious pastoral care at the battlefront was heavily dependent on the local conditions decided by junior officers below the division level. Previous studies of military religion have not accounted for unit dynamics and the particularities of different geographies of combat. Chaplaincy was heavily dependent on what officers would permit based on the military

---

[9] Above all, see Ziemann, "Katholische Religiosität," 113–36.
[10] Ham, "Von den Anfängen der Militärseelsorge," 13–98.
[11] Mark Cornwall, *The Undermining of Austria-Hungary: The Battle for Hearts and Minds* (New York: St. Martin's Press, 2000); Richard G. Plaschka, "Contradicting Ideologies: The Pressure of Ideological Conflicts in the Austro-Hungarian Army of World War I," in *The Habsburg Empire in World War I: Essays on the Intellectual, Military, Political, and Economic Aspects of the Habsburg War Effort*, ed. Robert A. Kann, Béla K. Király, and Paula S. Fichtner (New York: Columbia University Press, 1977), 105–19.

conditions of the front. This chapter thus explores disparate micro-level conditions on the archetypal Western Front, as compared with other fronts. In elaborating local and regional elements, the heavily Catholic and agrarian region of Tyrol serves as a particular case study, highlighting the plurality of identities and loyalties.

Although they were comparatively weak managers, because of their social position, Catholic chaplains were nonetheless valuable historical actors, due to their liminal social status and the kinds of records they created. While making appropriate generalizations about the nature of Catholic chaplaincy, the overall argument of this chapter underscores the paramount importance of micro-level detail and variability, in line with a view of a pluralized conception of religion that did not depend on a final outcome of victory. Simply because of the written records they left behind, Catholic chaplains recorded public military religiosity that would be otherwise lost to history.[12] Too often dismissed as an epiphenomenal superfluity, especially for the losing powers, the Catholic military chaplains documented personalized, local religious behaviors that do not fit convenient narratives of disillusionment, loss, and consequent irrelevance.

The literary modernist frame

The literary modernist portrayal of chaplaincy has interpreted religious belief during the Great War as a vestige of the old order, complicit in legitimizing the slaughter and yet radically out of place in the new jarring circumstances of industrial warfare centered on material reality, not metaphysics. As state-sponsored clergy members in positions of hierarchical authority, chaplains drew particular ire from authors. Contemporary observers clearly recognized this at the time, and chaplaincies attempted to defend themselves against modernist writers. A 1928 Munich stage adaptation of Jaroslav Hašek's novel *The Good Soldier Schweik* aroused a storm of controversy among those with sentimental affection for the Habsburg monarchy, especially since the production planned to come to the Volkstheater in Vienna. Ferdinand Pawlikowski, the Prince-Bishop of Graz-Seckau and a former high administrator of Habsburg military chaplaincy during the war, was then the head of chaplaincy for the Austrian successor state. Incensed about the play, he wrote in 1928 to the Austrian Chancellor, Monsignor Ignaz Seipel, in a futile attempt to halt its performance:

---

[12] Becker, "Faith, Ideologies," 241.

If the drama remains true to the thrust of the work, the performance must be deemed a scandal...It is a dirty denigration, slur, and accusation of all levels of the old Austria. In the most trivial manner, the officer class, military chaplaincy, doctors, police, gendarmes, and surely also the House of Habsburg including its family members, are dragged through the mud, nobility is damned and the cloisters portrayed as houses of ill-repute. In this work, every military chaplain is depicted as a dirty dog, daily and at every opportunity a drunkard, and only devoted to blasphemy...Against a contemporary denigration and insult of chaplains in war, I must protest.[13]

Pawlikowski was right to fear Hašek's novel and its staged version. In the novel, Hašek comments generally on war: "Preparations for the slaughter of human beings have always been made in the name of God or of some alleged higher being which mankind has, in its imaginativeness, devised and created." He goes on to condemn the First World War specifically, in unambiguous terms: "The shambles of the World War would have been incomplete without the blessings of the clergy. The chaplains of all armies prayed and celebrated mass for the victory of the side whose bread they ate...Throughout Europe, men went to the shambles like cattle, whither they were driven by butchers, who included not only emperors, kings, and other potentates, but also priests of all denominations."[14] The brilliant satirist Karl Kraus, in his epic apocalyptic drama *The Last Days of Humanity*, raised the critical ire further by portraying the monarchy's chaplains as direct participants in the violence that they preached.[15] Kraus's literary portrayal was not a work of pure fiction: ultimately, some chaplains did actually kill enemy soldiers, thus flagrantly violating the laws of both Church and state.[16]

Yet even some literary modernists recognized the need to differentiate between religious experiences of war. In one of the most famous war memoirs, *Good-Bye to All That*, Robert Graves vividly writes of the contrast between Catholic and Anglican chaplains in the English Army. Graves, no cheerleader of religion during the Great War, says, "Hardly one soldier in a hundred was inspired by religious feeling of even the crudest kind. It would have been difficult to remain religious in the

---

[13] Diözesanarchiv Graz, Nachlaß von Bischof Dr. Ferdinand Pawlikowski (Militärvikariat) Karton 5, Heft 83: Letter from Pawlikowski to Seipel, October 24, 1928.

[14] Jaroslav Hašek, *The Good Soldier Schweik*, trans. Paul Selver (New York: Frederick Ungar Publishing Co., 1930), 116–17.

[15] Karl Kraus, *Schriften*, vol. 10: *Die letzten Tage der Menschheit. Tragödie in fünf Akten mit Vorspiel und Epilog* (Frankfurt a.M.: Suhrkamp, 1986), esp. act II, scenes 6–7.

[16] Patrick J. Houlihan, "Imperial Frameworks of Religion: Catholic Military Chaplains of Germany and Austria-Hungary during the First World War," *First World War Studies* 3 (2012): 172. Accessible at http://dx.doi.org/10.1080/19475020.2012.728739 (last accessed October 31, 2014).

trenches even if one had survived the irreligion of the training battalion at home."[17] Nevertheless, Graves comments that Catholic chaplains in the British forces were both more effective and much more beloved by the troops than their Anglican counterparts, a sentiment echoed by the memoirs of other English officers. Graves writes:

For Anglican regimental chaplains we had little respect... [They were] under orders to avoid getting mixed up with the fighting and stay behind with the transport. Soldiers could hardly respect a chaplain who obeyed these orders, and yet not one in fifty seemed sorry to obey them... The colonel in one battalion I served with got rid of four new Anglican chaplains in four months; finally he applied for a Roman Catholic, alleging a change of faith in the men under his command. For Roman Catholic chaplains were not only permitted to visit posts of danger, but definitely enjoyed to be wherever fighting was, so that they could give extreme unction to the dying. And we never heard of one who failed to do all that was expected of him and more.[18]

Graves's fellow officer, Guy Chapman, provides an even more blunt contrast between the Anglican and Catholic experiences of military chaplaincy, although he underscores the difference between a generic operating order and a practical implementation by individual chaplains. Chapman writes in his memoirs, "[O]ur bluff Anglicans... had nothing to offer but the consolation the next man could give you, and a less fortifying one. The Church of Rome sent a man into action mentally and spiritually cleaned. The Church of England could only offer you a cigarette. The Church of Rome, experienced in propaganda, sent its priests into the line. The Church of England forbade theirs forward of Brigade Headquarters, and though many, realizing the fatal blunder of such an order, came just the same, the publication of that injunction had its effect."[19]

Although further studies of Protestant piety at the battlefront are warranted,[20] contemporary Protestant chaplains in Central Europe

---

[17] Robert Graves, *Good-Bye to All That* (New York: Anchor Books, 1998), 189. This view has been stridently challenged by Snape, *God and the British Soldier*, which argues for a concept of a "diffusive Christianity" that permeated the British Armed Forces during the era of the world wars.

[18] Graves, *Good-Bye to All That*, 189–90.Cf. John Ellis, *Eye-Deep in Hell: Trench Warfare in World War I* (Baltimore, MD: Johns Hopkins University Press, 1989), 156.

[19] Snape, *God and the British Soldier*, 84.

[20] The official Protestant histories of military chaplaincy mirror their Catholic counterparts insofar as they testify to relegation of the First World War to the status of one chapter of a continual historical mission under difficult circumstances. See Martin Schian, *Die Arbeit der evangelischen Kirche im Felde: Die deutsche evangelische Kirche im Weltkriege* (Berlin: E. S. Mittler & Sohn, 1921). The situtation of Austro-Hungarian Protestants can be approached through Julius Hanak, "Die evangelische Militärseelsorge im alten Österreich unter besonderer Berücksichtigung ihrer Eingliederung in den kirchlichen

acknowledged that their social position was fundamentally different to that of their Catholic counterparts. In the middle of the war, chaplain Adolf Risch, for instance, wrote:

In my judgment, the visitation of the troops in the trenches can only be an exception for the Protestant military chaplain. We Protestants affirm that the "administration of rites for the dying" ["*die Versehung der Sterbenden*"], that for the Catholic military chaplains is a duty and that forces them to go in the trenches, is not a prerequisite for beatification [*Bedingung zur Seligkeit*]. For Christian encouragement in the trenches, it would be sufficient in most cases if a religious paper from home would fly into the trenches on a weekly basis.[21]

In the twentieth-century age of atrocity, the figure of the chaplain in literature seems ludicrously superfluous at best and flagrantly hypocritical at worst. One should not equate literature with history, but one should also recognize how greatly literary perceptions, especially of an anti-war mindset, and often drawing on the memoirs of disillusioned middle-class former combatants, have helped to frame religious interpretations of the Great War with regard to military chaplaincy.[22]

Imperial frameworks of military chaplaincy in Austria-Hungary and Germany, ca. 1867–1918

Who was a Catholic chaplain? At first glance, the role was rather straight-forward, and was similar in Austria-Hungary and in Germany, but a more thorough examination reveals marked contrasts. The military chaplaincies had structurally different histories based on the relative position of Catholicism as a unifying factor within the imperial frameworks of military religion.

In Austria-Hungary, on the eve of the Great War, Catholic chaplains had to be ordained priests not more than 40 years old and in good health, with evidence of success in theological studies, three years of pastoral experience, and an "impeccable" personal life. Chaplains also agreed to swear an oath of loyalty to the monarchy.[23] The Apostolic

---

Verband" (Ph.D. dissertation, University of Vienna, 1970) or, more briefly, Ham, "Von den Anfängen der Militärseelsorge," 92–4.

21 Adolf Risch, "Mehr Einheitlichkeit in den deutschen evangelischen Landeskirchen," *Korrespondenz-Blatt für die Evang. Konferenz in Baden und die kirchlich-positive Vereinigung im Großherzogtum Hessen* 11 (1916), quoted in Wollasch, *Militärseelsorge im Ersten Weltkrieg*, lxxvii.

22 For a seminal example of the emergence of irony and the futility of struggle, at least for Britain, see Fussell, *The Great War and Modern Memory*.

23 Emmerich Bjelik, *Handbuch für die k.u.k. katholische Militärgeistlichkeit* (Vienna: Selbstverlag des Apostolischen Feldvikariats, 1905), 10–11. Austro-Hungarian chaplains also had to prove citizenship in the k.u.k. monarchy and demonstrate knowledge of

Field Vicar of Austria-Hungary, Emmerich Bjelik, conceptualized the military chaplains as a corps of young, fit, and active men. This would change during the war, as the preference for younger chaplains caused problems: as casualties mounted, more levies of older men were drafted to fill the manpower requirements, resulting in situations where twenty-year-old chaplains were preaching to middle-aged servicemen about the necessities of duty and virtue.[24]

During the war, this created problems with the dioceses on the home-front, which suffered an increasing shortage of younger clerics as the war dragged on. The Bishop of Pecs, for instance, wrote to Bjelik to complain that he had only ten to twelve "old, sick priests" in his diocese while forty served as military chaplains. Bjelik acknowledged that this was a problem that the Army was well aware of, but he informed the bishop that the problem was systemic and that other dioceses were making greater sacrifices.[25]

The institutional origins of military chaplaincy in the Habsburg lands date back to the early modern era. Chaplaincy was heavily influenced by the Baroque Catholicism of the Counter-Reformation, creating a throne-and-altar alliance that persisted until 1918.[26] The collective sociology of the chaplains reveals the influences of Josephinism and its liberal legacy. In the early modern era, Catholic chaplaincy in the Habsburg monarchy remained dominated by religious orders, particularly the Jesuits. During the course of the nineteenth century, it underwent a dramatic change in the relative numbers of priests from religious orders versus diocesan priests. In 1782, the 151 Habsburg military chaplains consisted of 107 priests of the order and 44 diocesan priests. By 1901, the situation had reversed completely: the chaplaincy consisted of 134 diocesan priests and only 4 priests from religious orders. This reflected the Josephinist desire to streamline Catholic monastic orders based on their utility to the state, with many monasteries being closed. It was the diocesan clergy,

German plus one other language of command in the military. Aside from the language requirements, German chaplains had to meet similar criteria, although these varied by federal state. Cf. Franz Albert, *Handbuch für die katholischen Feldgeistlichen des Preußischen Heeres* (Vilnius: Verlag der 10. Armee, 1918), 1–27.

24 ÖStAKA, LVM 1915: Ktn, 2383, Nr. 3268–15 (AFV 6737) AFV to MLV. Bjelik pleaded for better oversight of priests' qualifications in order to avoid complaints of unqualified older priests preaching to the troops while younger priests sat idle on the home front.

25 ÖStAKA, AFV, Ktn. 247, copy of KM, Abt. 9, Nr. 16594. As a gesture of conciliation, Bjelik sent three chaplains home to Pecs. The military, for its part, expressed to the church its desire to draft only the "most unavoidably necessary" clergy as military chaplains and was keen that this would not "burden individual dioceses in unequal measure." See ÖStAKA, AFV, Ktn. 247, copy of KM Abt. 9, Nr. 20004.

26 For an overview of Habsburg military chaplaincy, see Ham, "Von den Anfängen der Militärseelsorge," 13–98.

supposedly closest to the people "in the real world," that came to dominate state-sponsored religious activity, which included military chaplaincy.[27]

In the Habsburg monarchy, however, the throne-and-altar alliance centered on the Habsburg court in Vienna provided a key element of centripetal ideological support for Catholics in Habsburg lands. During the nineteenth century, various nationalist movements began to gain strength, although their influence among most Habsburg citizens prior to 1917–18 was often exaggerated in light of the monarchy's eventual collapse. Overarching transnational elements of practical and symbolic unification, such as the Church and the military, remained key pillars of the Habsburg dynasty.[28] During times of war, all Austro-Hungarian Catholic chaplains fell under the authority of the Apostolic Field Vicariate in Vienna, with streamlined methods for identifying chaplains and their duties.

As in Austria-Hungary, German chaplains were ordained priests designated as non-combatants, a separate liminal caste. In Germany, however, Catholic chaplains were part of an empire, in which religious issues became fragmented by the various Church–state regulations of disparate military bureaucracies. Although unification under Prussian leadership had been a goal of the Wilhelmine chaplaincies, on the eve of the Great War, German Catholic chaplaincy remained federally fragmented. The basic question of who was considered a German chaplain proved to be confusing – a fitting symbol of the fundamental institutional chaos of German chaplaincy. German Catholic chaplaincy contained several ambiguous categories of chaplain, each holding different bureaucratic identities, rights, duties, and benefits. These difficulties multiplied because each federal state in the German Empire retained different Church–state accords, with no less than six different kinds of chaplain in Bavaria alone. Attached at the division level as members of disparate federal army contingents in the German Empire, Catholic chaplains were subject to a variety of Church–state accords negotiated with each German state by the Holy See. Theoretically, German Catholic chaplaincy during wartime fell under the centralizing authority of the Prussian *Feldpropst*, Heinrich Joeppen.[29] But in practice, the situation was much more complicated.

---

[27] Ibid., 53.
[28] Adam Wandruszka and Peter Urbanitsch, eds., *Die Habsburgermonarchie 1848–1918*, vol. 4: *Die Konfessionen* (Vienna: Verlag der Österreichischen Akademie der Wissenschaften, 1985) and vol. 5: *Die bewaffnete Macht* (Vienna: Verlag der Österreichischen Akademie der Wissenschaften, 1987).
[29] Vogt, *Religion im Militär*, 455–648.

During the Great War, German centrifugal tendencies became exacerbated. Institutional chaos reigned with regard to German chaplains' identities, rights, and duties. Even such a basic task as organizing a common Catholic field manual proved troublesome. Not until summer 1918 did Catholic authorities issue a field manual for Prussian Catholic chaplains, which was largely based on the experiences of one Eastern Front chaplain, Franz Albert of the 10th Army in Vilnius, and this manual did not have time to find widespread usage in the German Army as a whole.[30] Further underscoring the fragmentation of the German Catholic war effort, the Prussian War Ministry disparaged even this late attempt at a common pastoral aid as something that would hold "no special interest for Bavarian military chaplains" because the handbook was designed for "*Prussian* chaplains."[31] On a pan-European level, Vatican attempts at providing coordination of religious duties in wartime proved of limited value, as the decrees of the Holy See had to be filtered through imperial, national, and federal contexts.[32]

Such structural confusion helped reinforce the nature of chaplaincy as worked out at a local level, based on shifting needs. Confusion and uncertainty reigned, leading to much improvisation and individual adaptation, as was recognized by senior commanders. For instance, the commanding general of the staging area of the German 6th Army *Oberkommando* wrote in January 1918 that military chaplains "are subordinate to, on the one hand their military, and on the other hand, their church laws. The double subordination places high demands on the discretion of the clergy, since it is in many cases difficult to separate sharply the boundaries between military and pure church activities [*rein kirchlichen Angelegenheiten*]."[33]

The leadership of the Catholic chaplaincies offered striking contrasts in the state networks of effective military religious ministry. Emmerich Bjelik, the commander of the Apostolic Field Vicariate of the Habsburg Army, provided more responsive leadership in military religious ministry than his German Catholic counterpart: firmly centralized, yet attuned to local particularities. Born in Illava in 1860, in what would become the Hungarian half of the monarchy, after his ordination, Bjelik joined the military chaplaincy as a chaplain in the reserve in 1883. Working his way up through the ranks, he became second-in-command

---

[30] Albert, *Handbuch*.

[31] BHStA, Abt. IV, MKr. 13852, p. 184: Nr. 246457a, KBKM, Ausschnitt aus dem preußischen Armee-Verordnungsblatt Nr. 45, August 31, 1918, p. 502. Emphasis in original.

[32] ASV, Seg. di Stato, Guerra 1914–1918, Fasc. 474, p. 11r–12v: "Facultates et declarationes pro sacerdotibus durante bello," June 24, 1915.

[33] BHStA, Abt. IV (Kriegsarchiv), Bd. 13850, p. 299: 31.1.1918, Etappen-Inspektion 6. Armee, IId. Nr. 142 pers. an das Armee-Oberkommando 6.

(*Feldkonsistorialdirektor*) in 1908 and overall commander, the Apostolic Field Vicar (*Apostolischer Feldvikar*), in 1911.[34]

Bjelik was intimately familiar with the history of the institution of chaplaincy, as well as its practical requirements. He quite literally wrote the book on Habsburg chaplaincy – two books, in fact: the first, a history of chaplaincy in the Habsburg lands since their inception, and the second, a detailed, thematically-organized handbook of the mundane day-to-day essentials required of military chaplains in the line of duty. This handbook, written in 1905, would serve as a central organizing administrative rulebook when war began.[35] Bjelik ultimately gave more responsive pastoral care than his German counterparts in terms of assessing the changing requirements of the war. During the Great War, Bjelik personally visited the fronts early and often, which gave him an informed view of actual conditions facing chaplains and soldiers.

In comparison to the command of the Habsburg chaplaincy offered by Bjelik, Heinrich Joeppen, the head of Catholic chaplaincy in Prussia, or *Feldpropst*, did much more poorly in supervising soldiers' religious lives in terms of providing a personal assessment of their shifting needs during the war. Joeppen was born in 1853 in Hüls in the province of Niederrhein and became ordained in 1875 in Osnabrück. The May Laws of the *Kulturkampf* temporarily prevented him from finding a position in the diocese of Münster, so he studied in Munich, completing a doctorate in 1887. In 1894, Joeppen became a military chaplain in the garrison town of Wesel, and he began to work his way up through the ranks, becoming a divisional chaplain in 1908 and head of chaplaincy in Breslau in 1910. Named a titular bishop of Ciasmo by Pope Saint Pius X, Joeppen became *Feldpropst* of the Prussian Army and German Navy on January 13, 1914.[36]

Fundamentally, Joeppen's shortcomings as *Feldpropst* stemmed from his lack of experience of the religious life at the front. During the entire war, Joeppen made only two visits to the areas where German troops were fighting, for the most part choosing to remain in Berlin in his seat as *Feldpropst*.[37] His first, to the Eastern Front, took place in February 1916. His second and final visit, this time to the Western Front, occurred in

---

[34] Gatz, *Die Bischöfe der deutschsprachigen Länder*, 54.
[35] Bielik, *Geschichte der k.u.k. Militärseelsorge* and Emmerich Bjelik, *Handbuch*. Bjelik's first and last names had various spellings in official correspondence, although "Emmerich Bjelik" predominates. Since this is the version he used in personal correspondence, I will follow it here.
[36] Erwin Gatz, ed., *Die Bischöfe der deutschsprachigen Länder 1785/1803 bis 1945: Ein biographisches Lexikon* (Berlin: Duncker und Humblot, 1983), 353.
[37] Joeppen's decision to remain in Berlin for most of the conflict was in keeping with the traditions of the Prussian *Feldpropstei*. It nonetheless remains an example of inattention to the drastically changing nature of modern war and its corresponding pastoral requirements.

late September 1918, mere weeks before the Armistice. Thus, the head of German chaplaincy first visited the war's decisive theater at a time when even delusional militarists like Erich Ludendorff admitted that Germany had lost the war. Even then, Joeppen stayed in rear areas away from the front and did not participate in the religious life of the common soldiers. Instead, Joeppen confined himself to holding conferences with groups of chaplains, trying to assess the overall religious mood of the troops, which, at this late date in the war, the chaplains collectively agreed to be extremely depressed. Acknowledging the pessimistic mood, *Feldpropst* Joeppen's only advice was to tell his chaplains to use their sermons to remind the soldiers of "their duty to continue to fight," cautioning that this should be done "in a discrete, not too frequent form" in order not to inflame the extant animosities.[38]

At first glance, a purely quantitative assessment of chaplaincy might seem to lend strength to the claim that the chaplains were either an epiphenomenal superfluity or else simply unable to perform a responsive and comprehensive pastoral ministry. While true in certain cases, such a wholesale judgment obscures important regional and local differences and peculiarities of place. Certainly, at times there was an acute shortage of chaplains, and the quantitative deficit was in some cases quite staggering. As Benjamin Ziemann has calculated, in the Bavarian Army of 1915, where the contingent was nearly seventy percent Catholic, one priest was responsible for approximately 1600 soldiers – compared to 665 peacetime parishioners, who had been practically stationary.[39] At the beginning of 1915, the number of Bavarian military chaplains at the front was 170; by 1917, this had increased to only 189. During the same period, the Bavarian Army had enlarged from 380 000 to 530 000 men.[40]

In the age of mass mobilization, Austria-Hungary did much better than Germany in providing chaplains for its troops. Every division of the Austro-Hungarian Army had a range of twelve to twenty-six Catholic chaplains, whereas many Prussian divisions had a single official Catholic chaplain (as well as one Protestant chaplain), perhaps supplemented by more ad hoc arrangements. Bavaria provided a middle ground by

---

[38] BA-MA, PH 32/391: Bericht, September 24, 1918, Konferenz in Brüssel. For the chaplains' overall pessimism at the end, see BA-MA, PH 32/391: Protokoll über die Konferenz des Hochw. Herrn Feldpropstes der Armee, Dr. Joeppen mit den Oberpfarrern und Feldgeistlichen der 1., 3., u. 7. Armee am September 18, 1918 in Charleville, pp. 1–2.

[39] K. Statistisches Landesamt, ed., *Bayerns Entwicklung nach den Ergebnissen der amtlichen Statistik seit 1840* (Munich: Lindauer, 1915), 1, 100.

[40] Benjamin Ziemann, "Katholische Religiosität," 119–20.

supplying around three or four chaplains per division. Comparative analysis demonstrates that Tyrolean units actually received special religious decrees from the Habsburg Army: in contrast to the one Catholic chaplain attached to some Prussian divisions, Tyroleans had a minimum of one chaplain per battalion.[41] Thus, locally-mustered Tyrolean units were thickly seeded with Catholic chaplains, representing an increased attention to local religiosity in a firmly devout Catholic region.

Catholic services at the front

The sacramental nature of Catholicism meant that Catholic priests had to administer rites to the troops, which necessitated that they stay at the front and in forward staging areas, in among the fighting men. In the most extreme cases, chaplains bore arms, in flagrant contradiction of Church and state law. Furthermore, as massive industrial armies fought on huge battlefields, a network of Catholic lay brothers and sisters, as well as priests who were not officially chaplains, supplemented the official priestly presence as military chaplains. Catholic sacramentality necessitated close contact with the troops whenever possible.

Catholic religious services at the battlefront ranged from simple, rather informal gatherings of men for group prayers or meditation to highly ritualized, elaborate field Masses. In this range of services, chaplains had varying degrees of control, but of course all Masses required the presence of a Catholic priest. When high-ranking religious dignitaries, such as the Apostolic Field Vicar of the Austro-Hungarian Armed Forces, Emmerich Bjelik, visited the front, the field Masses numbered thousands of participants, often including high-ranking officers.[42] Most religious services, however, were considerably smaller.

Regarding participation requirements, the official military line provided a base minimum of opportunity for communal worship, which was supplemented by more informal, spontaneously-chosen outlets. While these informal prayer services were not mandatory, Catholic military men in both armies had a theoretical scale of religious obligations mandated by the military. According to these regulations, Catholic servicemen were required to attend Mass on Christmas and Easter, in addition to as many of the civilian days of obligation (Pentecost, Ascension, Assumption, Corpus Christi, All Saints, All Souls, and Immaculate Conception being

---

[41] Ham, "Von den Anfängen der Militärseelsorge," 76–7. Cf. *Pastoralblatt für die k.u.k. Katholische Militär- und Marinegeistlichkeit Nr.* 1 (1917), p. 24.

[42] "Römisch-katholischer Gottesdienst in Belgrad," *Reichspost*, April 4, 1916, p. 7; "Feldmesse in Cetinje," *Reichspost*, April 16, 1916, p. 8.

the most prominent) as battlefield conditions would permit. At the very least, men were supposed to be able to attend services in "off-duty hours" (*Dienstfreie Zeiten*), at least once per month; this was already a diminution of pre-war regulations, which required attendance at every Sunday religious service.[43]

Officially, the troops' attendance at religious services was a military duty, as part of a state effort to show a united, disciplined body of troops in high morale. In practical terms, this took the form of a standing order to attend Church services, issued at the army, corps, and division levels. The loophole in all of these orders, however, was the exception of "military necessity" or "conditions of the front," which was meant to prevent troops wandering off to religious services when they were needed for battle operations.[44] In practice, local commanding officers at brigade, regiment, battalion, and company levels exercised wide degrees of latitude in interpreting what was a "military necessity." This was a jurisdictional chaos that lent itself to abuse and distortion by both officers and rank-and-file troops. Unless persistently challenged by appeals to higher authority, officers could claim that soldiers were always needed at the front and could not be released for services; it was nearly impossible for soldiers to claim otherwise. On the other hand, the idea of an unaccommodating officer provided a plausible excuse for rank-and-file troops who wanted to shirk attendance at Mass, which chaplains usually did not have the time or means to double-check.

The best means of ensuring troops attended religious services on a regular basis was a pious officer, especially a senior unit commander, who would accompany his men and set an example of good behavior, in obedience to the chaplains' performance of the religious rites. In the words of one division chaplain, "Wherever the officer is somewhat interested in the religious requirements of the troops, everything works."[45] Some

---

[43] See, e.g., ÖStAKA, AFV, Ktn. 231: Pastoralberichte, December 1917, for IR 25, IR 67, IR 84, IR 85. For pre-war decrees on religious service obligations, see Bjelik, *Handbuch*, 156–8.

[44] For Germany, see BHStA, Abt.IV (Kriegsarchiv), 5. Bayerische Res. Division, Bd. 68, Akt. 10. For a relevant act from the Prussian War Ministry, see KM Nr. M. 7519/16.C4: "Nach den Vorschriften der katholischen Kirche ist jeder katholische Christ streng verpflichtet, an den Sonntagen und gebotenen Feiertagen eine heilige Messe zu hören, falls nicht wichtige Gründe ihn daran hindern." Cf. BA-MA PH 2/24, "Teilnahme an dienstlich angeordneten Gottesdienste im Felde," June 15, 1917.

[45] BA-MA, PH 32/107: Tätigkeitsbericht June–July 1917, Divisionsgeistlicher Schindel. Numerous examples are found in BA-MA, PH 32/115–145, 607–611, e.g., PH 32/115, "Tätigkeitsbericht über die Ausübung der Seelsorge im Bereich des Militärgouvernements Lodz" von Pfarrern Brettle und Tabelion. For Austria-Hungary, see the examples in ÖStAKA, AFV, Ktn. 215–46.

chaplains specifically called out their officers by name to praise them, such as chaplain Leo Mauko of the Austro-Hungarian Army, who wrote, "My work was made easier through the good example of the officers and especially through the good example of our commander, Herr Lieutenant Colonel von Kautecky."[46] As a corporate body, the Habsburg chaplaincy quickly recognized the importance of high-ranking officer support – even printing and publicizing a testimonial collection during the war from some of the top army commanders.[47]

Chaplains were officially commissioned officers, but by and large did not choose to exercise this authority, instead relying on professional officers to enforce their decrees. Chaplain Jakob Ebner, of the 1st *Badische Leibgrenadier* Regiment, wrote in laconic and resigned fashion in his diary of a typically laid-back approach, which also testifies to the difficulties of ministering to far-flung artillery units: "Today [October 19, 1916], I order the light munitions company of Field Artillery Regiment No. 65 to confession and communion. One single man comes." Although empowered as an officer, Ebner took no disciplinary action against the rest of the unit and merely proceeded in his duties in a priestly manner.[48] Similarly, Bruno Spitzl, a chaplain of the k.u.k. 49th Regiment, demonstrated the extent to which chaplains relied on other officers to enforce military regulations regarding even flagrant transgression of Church laws. Upon discovering a plundered Italian church in Venzone where Austro-Hungarian troops were busily desecrating the altar, traipsing around in priestly vestments, and stealing valuables, Spitzl's initial reaction was merely to order them to leave the Church. Only afterward did he think to try to pursue an investigation with regard to punishing the guilty parties, for which he required the assistance of a junior officer, and which ultimately came to no avail.[49]

For purposes of attendance at religious services, it was important to differentiate between types of units and areas of combat. Services at the foremost line, directly in the trenches opposing the enemy, were a chaplain's supreme portrait of devotion, but were held less often. The sacramental requirements of the Catholic faith necessitated pastoral contact between priests and lay believers. Supplementing this when possible, priestly contact at the front most often included distribution of

---

[46] ÖStAKA, AFV, Ktn. 246: Pastoralbericht Feldkurat Leo Mauko, Baon 14 (1918).
[47] Emmerich Bjelik, ed., *Ruhmesblätter der k. u. k. Militär- und Marinegeistlichkeit aus dem Weltkrieg 1914–17* (Vienna: Verlag des k.u.k. Feldvikariates, 1917).
[48] EAF, NL 44 (Jakob Ebner Tagebuch): Entry of October 19, 1916, p. 549.
[49] Bruno Spitzl, *Die Rainer: Als Feldkurat mit IR 59 im Weltkrieg*, 2nd edn. (Innsbruck: Tyrolia Verlag, 1938), 306–10.

communion and the handing out of small gifts from the homefront, such as religious literature, portraits of saints, religious medals, and food.

Masses usually occurred in staging areas away from the front lines. Due to confines of space, services held too far forward could only take place for a relatively limited number of men in a small area; the return on the time invested was miniscule in terms of the numbers of souls that could be ministered. Thus, although it did happen on scattered occasions, by and large, regular Mass "in the trenches" was an ideological construct, although the personal presence of priests in the trenches was real.[50] Writing to Bishop Michael von Faulhaber in 1917, Casimir Braun, a Capuchin division chaplain, outlined the difficulties of military ministry in the Western Front trenches: "None of our companies has a front length of less than 1000 meters, many however between 1200–1400 with an average of 120 souls per company." Braun wrote that his normal service was a sermon of eight to ten minutes, followed by three Lord's Prayers "for various circumstances," and then a blessing and a distribution of literature. Father Braun assiduously tried to maintain services in the trenches but found the conditions "extraordinarily difficult." If a religious service was impossible, Father Braun tried to substitute it by going to field posts and talking with soldiers individually, while also distributing religious literature every five or six days.[51] Some chaplains were not as devoted to maintaining that degree of front-line service.

For similar reasons of insufficient spiritual return on an investment of time and energy, religious services were also not held too far in rear areas. This meant that rear-area units, especially artillery crews, but also transportation and baggage units, often went for longer stretches of time without Mass than did infantry units.[52] Thus, most services were held in the staging areas slightly removed from the front lines. Overall, military ministry at the battlefront remained an extremely improvised affair, dependent on individual initiative and local conditions.

---

[50] Matthias Höhler, *Die Kapelle im Schützengraben. Sonntagsfeier in der Front* (Mainz: Kirchheim, 1914).

[51] EAM, NL Faulhaber, Ktn. 6777: Letter, March 3, 1917 from P. Casimir Braun to Faulhaber.

[52] BA-MA, PH 32/17: July 31, 1915 Letter from Kühne to Divisionspfarrer Krause, 25. Infanterie Div. near St. Quentin. For confusion about the feasibility of pastoration to field and heavy artillery in rear areas, see BA-MA, PH 32/390: Bericht über die Konferenz der katholischen Feldgeistlichen der 2. Armee und Etappe am 9. November 1916 im Rathaussaale der Stadt St. Quentin. Feldoberpfarrer Middendorf, head of chaplaincy on the Western Front, eventually declared, "Da nach dem Gehörten eine einheitliche Regelung der Seelsorge für die Artillerie nicht möglich zu sein scheint, muss ein jeder tun, was er selbst bei den gegebenen Verhältnisssen für notwendig und zweckdienlich erachtet." See also EAF, NL 44 (Jakob Ebner Tagebuch), pp. 467–75.

Figure 2 Mass in the trenches (Lipusch)
"The field Mass in the forward positions was a highpoint of symbolic sacramental attention from priests serving with the troops."

Commonalities of Catholic ministry

Catholic military chaplains ministered to their soldiers in three main sacraments: communion, confession, and extreme unction. Catholic practices revolving around the issuance of communion had to adapt to the new circumstances of war. Pre-war Catholicism only distributed holy communion during the celebration of Mass, the Mass itself being the symbolic representation of the Last Supper. Even this reception of holy communion occurred more infrequently than for many post-Vatican II lay Catholics. Due to the exigencies of war, however, soldiers were often threatened with death, and it was often not possible to hold a complete Mass. Therefore, military chaplains quite regularly distributed communion during any kind of religious service, not necessarily a Mass.[53] Since confession and communion were the two foundational sacraments used to ease a Catholic soldier's conscience, the simplest form of religious service at the battlefront often consisted of hearing confessions and then issuing communion.[54]

---

[53] EAF, NL 44 (Jakob Ebner Tagebuch), p. 473. This was part of Ebner's report given at the conference of Catholic chaplains of the 3rd Army in Charleville on February 3, 1916.
[54] Ibid., 549.

The possibility of mass death brought a sense of extreme urgency to Catholic soldiers, who believed that if they were killed, they would go to Heaven only if a priest had absolved their sins through the sacrament of confession. Consequently, the practice of the sacrament of reconciliation underwent a dramatic shift. Confession under the threat of death on the battlefield was no longer about coercion and manipulation of behavior. Instead, it became purely a means of soothing soldiers' consciences.[55] This was a development born of necessity. Priests as military chaplains, outnumbered when compared to peacetime ratios of clergy to parishioners, were extremely overstrained by the sheer number of soldiers looking to confess during time of war.

Chaplains responded to the problem of battlefield confession in two ways. The first was in keeping with other aspects of military chaplaincy: chaplains maximized the number of individual confessions by making themselves available to penitents whenever possible. They would often be available for confession after a specifically prescribed Mass time, which was ideally posted at communal notice boards, with the permission of the local commander.[56] Richard Hoffmann, a chaplain serving with the 1st Bavarian Infantry Division, wrote in his war diary that front-line units had regular Sunday services at a time determined by the commanding officer of the division in consultation with the divisional chaplains. These "voluntary religious services" (*freiwillige Gottesdienste*) offered the possibility for troops not engaged in battle to report to Mass to receive communion and penance. "In this way, the troops fighting on the front line were always given the opportunity to meet their religious needs [*religiöse Bedürfnisse*] during periods of rest."[57] Most chaplains did not explore the tension between "voluntary chosen" religious services and a "requirement" of military-religious duty.

Chaplains, however, were simply not available in great enough numbers to administer individual confessions to all soldiers, especially in proximity to a moderate-to-large offensive. In such instances, chaplains communally administered the sacrament of reconciliation and soothed consciences through the granting of general absolution.[58] This practice had been a feature in previous centuries of warfare, but general absolution

---

[55] BA-MA, PH 32/390: Militär-Pfarrer-Konferenz in Laon, 7. Armee, April 20, 1915: "Hauptaufgabe des Seelsorgers ist und bleibt, seiner Gemeinde die Gnade zu vermitteln, darum muss er stets darauf Bedacht sein, recht oft Gelegenheit zur hl. Beicht zu geben."

[56] Erzbischöflichesarchiv Freiburg B2–35/1: Seelsorge waehrend des Krieges, 1914–1916. Poster, "Katholischer Militär-Gottesdienst in Roeselare."

[57] BHStA, Abt. IV: 1. Bayerische Reserve Division, Bd. 100: Tagebuch, Richard Hoffmann, August 8, 1914–August 31, 1915. Entry from November 7, 1915 (sic), pp. 10–13.

[58] BA-MA, PH 32/476: Bericht über die Feldseelsorge in der 30. Infanterie Division im Monat August 1915, Divisionspfarrer Dr. Egon Schneider.

took on new significance during the sustained slaughter of the First World War, being used much more frequently.[59] Its relevance was discussed at many levels of the military religious hierarchy: Catholic military authorities debated just how often the general absolution could be dispensed before it began to diminish the value of individualized confession. In any event, in the age of mass armies, mass absolution became a Catholic necessity for troops at the battlefront.

Catholic chaplains were also forced close to the front in order to administer the sacrament of extreme unction to the dying. Both the published memoirs and the private reminiscences of Catholic chaplains focus heavily on the administration of last rites to dying soldiers, often in the midst of heavy battle.[60] In extreme cases when chaplains died in battle performing these duties, their fellow chaplains represented their deaths as sacrifice and imitation of Christ, such as when chaplain Franz Hämmerle of the k.u.k. 14th Infantry Regiment was killed by artillery shrapnel while administering holy communion and last rites to a badly wounded soldier near Monte di Val Vella,[61] or when Josef Vonavka, a chaplain with the k.u.k. 32nd Infantry Regiment, calmed Czech troops on the battlefield and gave the viaticum to a dying soldier wounded in an air attack before himself being killed by another aerial bomb.[62]

Overall, in order to earn the respect of men who were suffering the repeated threat of violent death, chaplains had to share that danger, or at least be perceived to share a symbolic part of that danger, and because of their sacramental presence, Catholic chaplains were keenly observed. Units that served at the front quickly lost respect for chaplains they regarded as "bullet-shy" (*Kugelscheu*). Jakob Bisson, a chaplain serving a field hospital behind the front lines, and thus prevented from going directly to the front, received criticism from battle-hardened troops when they attended his services in the staging areas. As the chaplain reported to Bishop von Faulhaber, the men complained, "You spoke well [from a place] where you never found yourself in the dangerous position of a fighting soldier." Chaplain Bisson acknowledged the justice of this criticism and yearned to go to the front. He begged Faulhaber to make some kind of mandatory standing order that all chaplains accompany men to the front lines in order to forestall such criticism in the future.[63]

---

[59] Bjelik, *Handbuch*, 5–6.
[60] See, e.g., EAF, NL 44 (Jakob Ebner Tagebuch), pp. 17–23
[61] Lipusch, *Österreich-Ungarns katholische Militärseelsorge*, 80, 581–3; Spitzl, *Die Rainer*, 269–71.
[62] ÖStAKA, AFV, Ktn. 278: Personalakten Vonavka.
[63] EAM, NL Faulhaber, Ktn. 6779/3, Letter, June 24, 1916, Jakob Bisson, Feldgeistlicher, Bayerische 2 Armeekorps, Feldlazarett 12, to Bishop Faulhaber.

Chaplains who did spend most of their time at the front often used the proximity to battlefield danger as a proof of faithfulness, an iteration of the belief that there are no atheists in foxholes. For believers, the closeness to death was a nearness to the divine presence that brought men back to God; in contrast, the rear areas were perceived to be hotbeds of corruption and temptation. In his monthly pastoral report, Chaplain Johann Rysavy wrote, "... I only want to say here that officers at the front and those close to death are more religious than those who find themselves far back [from combat] ... Forward at the front is the best job for us in the field." Similarly, the Austro-Hungarian chaplain Karl Egger wrote in his post-war memoir that the battlefield experience made "the hardest hearts open themselves to the Lord Jesus."[64]

Except in rare cases, chaplains loathed to admit in their official reports that they were afraid to go to the front. When they did, they were usually transferred to another post in the rear area; as there was such a shortage of chaplains, they were not dismissed from the service. Chaplain Andreas Farkas, for instance, who served with the Austro-Hungarian 25th Infantry Regiment on the Eastern Front, wrote in his monthly pastoral report for October 1915 that he had only said Mass once the entire month and had not gone to the front at all because "it is dangerous" and "I do not have the appropriate hero's courage [Heldenmuth]." After it became clear to the Austro-Hungarian Apostolic Field Vicariate that this was not an isolated occurrence, Farkas was quickly replaced.[65]

In contrast, chaplains who regularly subjected themselves to danger at the front received praise from their men and made a more inspiring and trustworthy example. As chaplain Josef Stříz of the k.u.k. 13th Landsturm Infantry Regiment succinctly put it, "The more often one visits the men in the trenches, the easier one wins their hearts."[66] This could take extreme forms, with chaplains sometimes accompanying their troops into battle and occasionally even participating in the killing of enemy troops, in clear contravention of international law. This provided an example of moral atrocity that would form the basis for negative post-war literary depictions of chaplains, as will be discussed later.[67]

---

[64] ÖStAKA, AFV, Ktn. 228: Pastoralbericht Johann Rysavy, Divisionspfarrer, 30. Infanterie Division, April 1917. Karl Egger, Seele im Sturm: Kriegserleben eines Feldgeistlichen (Innsbruck: F. Rauch, 1936), 35.

[65] ÖStAKA, AFV, Ktn. 215: Pastoralbericht für Oktober 1915.

[66] ÖStAKA, AFV, Ktn. 234: Pastoralbericht für Oktober 1916 (misfiled).

[67] Article 2 of the Geneva Convention of 1864 provided for the identification of chaplains as non-combatants. See http://avalon.law.yale.edu/19th_century/geneva04.asp (last accessed October 31, 2014).

Equipment

Catholic military chaplaincy required appropriate equipment, which meant providing sacred space and creating sacramental objects that were compact and mobile. Mass often had to be conducted in the field, which meant materials were relatively easy to transport, usually on horseback. The ideal solution was a field chapel or field altar (*Feldkapelle*, *Feldaltar*), which was basically a portable altar with a tabernacle for the veneration of the host, housed usually in a suitcase that the chaplain could carry by himself, but sometimes in a larger container that required at least two men to carry it (in which case, the field chapel was transported on the chaplain's horse, or occasionally in one of the few automobiles possessed by the various Catholic chaplaincies in the field). With the field chapel, chaplains could create sacred space when they were away from the conse-crated ground of a Catholic parish church. These *Feldkapellen* generally had wings that could unfold to give the impression of an altar. At the center was usually a crucifix or a picture of the crucifixion, which would further replicate the church setting. Included in the *Feldkapellen* were various paraphernalia necessary for Catholic services. Foremost among these were a Bible, a book containing the Mass parts and prayers to be read during the service, chalices to hold communion bread and wine, Mass candles, vials of holy water and incense, priestly vestments (most often the stola), a container of oil for the anointing of the sick, and cloths for cleaning the aforementioned pieces of equipment.[68]

In cases where *Feldkapellen* could not be procured, chaplains had to be more resourceful. If they were quartered near a town with a Catholic chapel, they could, of course, use military authority to req-uisition this. In occupied territories, if they did not at least consult the local enemy civilian clergy to create some kind of civilian–military com-promise, such appropriation could cause seething discontent among the occupied population.[69] In the event that no permanent sacred space was available, chaplains had to enlist the help of their troops to build some kind of semi-permanent altar. Such altars were usually wooden and were constructed at some remove from the front lines, at a fixed point where the men knew they could congregate for services.[70] With the support of local commanders, chaplains could turn temporary wooden altars into

---

[68] Bielik, *Geschichte der k.u.k. Militärseelsorge*, 251–6. For an example of a *Feldaltar*, see Rainer Rother, ed., *Der Weltkrieg 1914–1918: Ereignis und Erinnerung* (Wolfratshausen: Edition Minerva, 2004), 199–200.

[69] EAF, NL 16/1, Kriegstagebuch 1914–1918 von Feldgeistlicher Fridolin Weber, pp. 80–3.

[70] Bjelik, *Handbuch*, 11.

Figure 3 Field chapel, LIR 13 (Lipusch)
"Created to allow Mass to be held, this wooden chapel shows careful craftsmanship."

increasingly permanent field altars. Where battlefield positions were relatively static, the positions of these field altars often became fixed field chapels.[71]

---

[71] Spitzl, *Die Rainer*, 67–8, 82.

Chaplains were also equipped with various books of prayer issued by Church authorities with the approval of the respective army chaplaincies.[72] While Mass parts and most sacramental procedures were recited in Latin, some more idiosyncratic and informal prayers were also said in the vernacular. However, this posed a problem for chaplaincy in the multi-lingual Austro-Hungarian Empire. In an attempt to solve it, primarily for the sacrament of confession, but also for the other main sacraments, the k.u.k. Apostolic Field Vicariate issued a *"confessarius polyglottus"* in all languages of the monarchy, which meant that Austro-Hungarian chaplains sometimes absolved sins that they quite literally could not understand.[73]

Geographies of front experience

The unleashing of troops into battle on the Western Front was the archetypal representation of combat during the First World War. Chaplain Josef Menke, serving with the 5th Prussian Landwehr Division, wrote in his memoir a description of the events of the Verdun offensive that portrayed the reality of combat in highly-charged apocalyptic language: "From the heights of Béchamps, I saw the booming, boiling, roaring, sizzling, flaming battle. The earth shook to its depths, the underworld seethed with all its hellish power, the horsemen of the apocalypse in their blood-red cloaks attacked there, crushing every resistance under the hooves of their deathly steeds... Everywhere, in the plains and on the heights, triumphant Death unfurled its black flag."[74] The chaplains' most detailed and graphic descriptions of combat, however, stem from post-war reminiscences, largely self-serving in character. In his memoir, Menke, for instance, was keen to declare the futility of attacking enemy trenches, although no contemporaneous materials document his voicing any doubt to anyone during the war years. He wrote, post-war, that on the day of his unit's assault on the French positions early in the Verdun offensive, "it was clear to me, what an attack over open fields against crackling rifle muzzles or even against machine guns means. It is something egregiously terrible, something unspeakably difficult, a type of insane action [*Wahnsinnstat*]."[75]

---

[72] For an example for Catholic soldiers, see Katholisches Pfarramt in Cöln, *Vor Gott ein Kind, vor dem Feind ein Held. Gedanken, Gebete und Lieder zur Massenverbreitung unter die katholischen Mannschaften des Heeres und der Flotte* (Cologne: Bachem, 1915).
[73] Spitzl, *Die Rainer*, 131.
[74] Josef Menke, *Ohne Waffe: Das Kriegserlebnis eines Priesters*, 2nd edn. (Paderborn: Ferdinand Schöningh, 1930), 126–7; for Menke's full post-war account of his participation in the battle of Verdun, see pp. 122–84.
[75] Ibid., 136.

Compared to their official public memoirs and reminiscences, the letters and diaries of chaplains reveal a much more honest and doubtful contemporary appraisal of the war's course. Chaplains on the Western Front began to share their troops' increasing doubt about imminent victory and divine favor. Discussion of the archetypal battles of the Western Front brought out candid and pessimistic assessments from chaplains concerning the religious mood. A general shift of sentiment occurred on the Western Front in 1916, following the battles at Verdun and the Somme. One chaplain from the Rhineland, Dr. Friedrich Erxleben, of the 34th Infantry Division of the Prussian Army, wrote to Bishop Faulhaber of Speyer:

Here before Fleury-Thiannmoel it has become a bit quieter now. At the Somme there was a type of shell fire five times as strong as here, yet there was at least faith and shelter. Here, however, the troops lie four days and four nights under shell fire with the dead and wounded together, without any kind of protection against rain, cold, and enemy fire and without support of any kind. Because everything possible was given up on the Somme. People are in the strictest sense cannon fodder. [*Die Leute sind in sensu strictissimo Kanonenfutter.*] And it always occurs more frequently that the men avoid having to go through the barrage and having to go forward. The French are at least chivalrous, inasmuch as they do not shoot at the orderlies, who, from 7 until 8 each morning bear as much as possible the wounded and dead.[76]

Erxleben's letter highlights several important issues and shows that not all chaplains were insensitive fire-breathers. Most importantly, such letters underscore that the German will to advance to victory underwent diminishing returns as combat dragged on, seemingly without an end in sight.

Regarding military religion, one can make generalizations about the apparent decline of collective morale after the failed Western Front offensives of 1916.[77] Extant quantifiable records, such as those of communion reception, although sometimes sparse and problematic as an indicator of religiosity, seem to confirm the shift of sentiment. For instance, during Easter 1916, the chaplains of the 1st Bavarian *Landwehr* Division held 147 church services and distributed communion to a total of 10 240 men. One year later, during Easter 1917, only 62 services were held, with a communion distribution of 3535.[78]

---

[76] Archiv des Erzbistums München und Freising, NL Faulhaber, Ktn. 6777: Feldpostbrief, Erxleben an Faulhaber, 19[16]. Erxleben's post-war life is shrouded in mysterious circumstances. He was ordained in Trier in 1909 and was listed in the diocesan records until 1928, but information after that, including his date and place of death, is unknown. See Brandt and Häger, *Biographisches Lexikon*, 184.

[77] Ziemann, *Front und Heimat*, 250–2.

[78] BHSAKA, 1. Bay. Ldw. Div, Bd. 62, Akt. 4, Heft 3.

Concerning the collective outcome of the war, uncertainty and pessimism began to creep in around 1916. By the end of the war, in conferences with the chief of German chaplaincy, chaplains on the Western Front acknowledged the overall pessimism. The overall religious mood was much more grim when expressed in channels of military religious authority. Collective enthusiasm for the war vanished as it dragged on, and chaplains, even those who continued to believe in exclusive divine national favor, were eventually forced to admit this even at the highest levels. At a conference of chaplains of the 1st, 3rd, and 7th Armies in Charleville on September 18, 1918, led by the head of German Catholic chaplaincy, Heinrich Joeppen, one chaplain pointedly asked the conference members whether there were any way to "address the overall depressed mood of the troops." *Feldpropst* Joeppen acknowledged that the "mood overall was much less favorable." As a remedy, Joeppen recommended that his chaplains "fight on" by holding fast to the notion of "duty" enshrined in their sermons, although he thought this should be expressed in "discrete, not too-frequent form."[79] Even the head of Prussian Catholic chaplaincy recognized that by this stage of the war, the incessantly boisterous patriotic sermons were proving counterproductive.

Other fronts

In contrast to the fixed trench warfare and stationary sustained killing of the Western Front, the Eastern Front was characterized by a more fluid, territorial positioning, entailing more irregular battles of movement.[80] At an organizational level, this rendered the Eastern Front even more difficult than the west in terms of logistics. The fixed nature of trench warfare in the west at least provided chaplains there with a definitive topography of the ground in a relatively enclosed space. As discussed earlier, however, deficiencies in the number of chaplains serving, as well as the transportation difficulties in traveling the battlefront, meant that Western Front chaplains often conducted a highly ad hoc and irregular ministry.

On the Eastern Front, the logistical problems were even worse. With much more territory to cover and the greater movement of armies, chaplains were less able to provide regular ministry to their troops at fixed

---

[79] BA-MA, PH 32/391: Protokoll über die Konferenz des Hochw. Herrn Feldpropstes der Armee, Dr. Joeppen mit den Oberpfarrern und Feldgeistlichen der 1.3. u. 7. Armee am 18. Sept. in Charleville, pp. 1–2.

[80] Herwig, *First World War*; Manfried Rauchensteiner, *Der Tod des Doppeladlers: Österreich-Ungarn und der Erste Weltkrieg* (Graz: Verlag Styria, 1993); Norman Stone, *The Eastern Front, 1914–1917* (London: Penguin, 1975).

points or definitive times. One chaplain serving as the head of Catholic chaplaincy for the 224th Prussian Infantry Division complained of the "monstrously stretched thin" battle line, running 180 km from west to southeast, which he had to traverse on horseback in order to minister to his men.[81] This experience was typical in the east, and the military chaplains serving there were extremely defensive about complaints to that effect from outsiders.[82] During a conference of the 10th Army in Vilnius, the head of Prussian Catholic chaplaincy for the Eastern Front, *Feldoberpfarrer* Jung, opened the conference defensively by asserting, "The oft-expressed complaints about deficient ministry on the Eastern Front" were "often reflective of unfamiliarity with the eastern conditions." However, the chaplains' reports then largely underscored that the conditions made for strained logistics, which could easily be seen as deficient ministry.[83]

All of these problems may have seemed more "disillusioning" in religious terms than those in the west. Issues of combat experience and political outcome also provided an extreme contrast to the Western Front. The traditional nature of warfare in the east, in terms of rapid advances and retreats, huge territorial victories, and an extremely favorable political outcome for the Central Powers in the eastern campaign, made all of the irregular services seem more tolerable. Plus, in distinct contrast to those on the Western Front, Eastern Front chaplains were much more embedded with front-line units. On the Western Front, Mass in the trenches was largely an ideological construct. The physical confinement of the permanent trench system prevented chaplains from holding front-line Masses for more than a handful of men at a time; rear-area Masses were required for religious ministry to hundreds or thousands of troops at once. While chaplains faced the same trench confinements wherever a similar static warfare developed on the Eastern Front, nevertheless, the more fluid battle situations in the east made sure that chaplains were closer to the front-line actions of their units.

Eastern Front battles were more irregular, occuring over wider stretches of territory. Chaplains had to seize any opportunity they could to hold Mass for a large group of soldiers. Some chaplains, however, were

---

[81] BA-MA, PH 32/350: Tätigkeitsbericht, kath. Divisionspfarrer Jungkamp, 224 Inf. Div., March 7, 1918. The chaplain claimed that "daily operations" along the extended battlefront further hindered his ability to hold any church services at all.

[82] BA-MA, PH 32/389: Protokoll der Konferenz der kath. Feldgeistlichen der Heeresgruppe von Linsingen, December 12, 1916, in Kowel; BA-MA, PH 32/389: Bericht über die Konferenz der Katholischen Feldgeistlichen der 10. Armee, February 6, 1917, in Wilna.

[83] BA-MA, PH 32/389: Bericht über die Konferenz der Katholischen Feldgeistlichen der 10. Armee, February 6, 1917, in Wilna.

pedantic in the extreme, refusing to acknowledge that Eastern Front conditions necessitated a different type of pastoral care. One took to the pages of an Austrian journal for Catholic clergy in order to denounce his fellow chaplains who held Sunday Mass outside the hours when it was technically permitted by Church regulations (i.e., from one hour before sunrise until 1 p.m.).[84] Most chaplains, however, were more accommodating to the realities of the situation. Bruno Spitzl, for instance, normally held Sunday Mass four times per day, or six if he could find assistance from another chaplain.[85]

Chaplains on the Eastern Front also helped lend strength to one of the war's most pernicious myths: that the Central Powers had "won" in the east and had lost the war only because they had been stabbed in the back on the homefront. This myth was founded on the isolated experience of Eastern Front combat, culminating in the Russian capitulation at Brest-Litovsk and Bolshevik Russia's withdrawal from the war in 1918.[86] The "victory" in the east was divorced from the much more hopeless and interminable strategic situation on the Western Front. Many veterans of the campaign in the east clung eagerly to this belief, based on years of shared suffering during the war. Victory seemed all too apparent: Russian humiliation at Brest-Litovsk was followed by occupation and exploitation of the vast swaths of newly acquired territory by the armies of the Central Powers.[87]

As bearers of military religious authority, chaplains were only too eager to seize upon such perceptions of victory. Benedict Kreutz started his chaplaincy on the Western Front before serving in the east in Galicia. He eventually ended his war service in Finland, fighting communists. When news of the November 11 Armistice reached him, he headed home believing in the victory of the Central Powers. In his farewell letter to the head of chaplaincy in Helsinki, Kreutz exuberantly wrote, "Thanks be to God, who gave me the strength and health to serve the victorious German army at the front in priestly helpfulness . . ."[88]

Chaplains on other fronts also seized on the myth of the Central Powers' victory in the east. Often immersed in extremely difficult conditions for their own ministries, they were keen to appropriate the defeat and

---

[84] Anon., "Aus dem Felde!", *Korrespondenzblatt der katholischen Klerus Österreichs* 34, Nr. 18 (September 25, 1915): 559–61. The anonymous author claimed to speak "for many" when he wrote that "Gegen die Zelebration am Nachmittage auch im Felde müßten wir ernste Bedenken erheben."

[85] Spitzl, *Die Rainer*, 70.   [86] Barth, *Dolchstoßlegenden*.

[87] Vejas Gabriel Liulevicius, *War Land on the Eastern Front: Culture, National Identity, and German Occupation in World War I* (Cambridge: Cambridge University Press, 2000).

[88] BA-MA, PH 32/129, Letter from Kreutz to Feldpropst Helsingfors, December 12, 1918. Reprinted in Wollasch, *Militärseelsorge im Ersten Weltkrieg*, 166.

humbling of mighty Russia as evidence of the favor of Divine Providence. After months of acknowledgment of the depressed mood of the troops, some chaplains serving in the profoundly dismal conditions of the Western Front wrote that the victory against Russia had raised hopes of peace – even peace through victory.[89]

The desperately grasped interpretation of victory in the east even reached as far as chaplains in the Middle East, who, despite the difficult conditions there, nonetheless seized on the Eastern Front as evidence that the tide of the war had turned in their favor. For Easter 1918, chaplains in Mosul staged a triumphant "Easter and Victory Celebration" in the Chaldean Church. After opening with a "triumphal march" played by a Benedictine nun, the program interspersed Bible readings and sermons with such predictable German patriotic hymns as "Now Thank We All Our God" and "A Mighty Fortress Is Our God," and even Mozart's "Within These Hallowed Halls" from *The Magic Flute*. The program closed with a chorus of "Great God, We Praise Thee."[90]

Compared to the Western Front, where spirit and resolve were extremely attenuated by 1918, the Eastern Front presented a situation of much more variability, based on the different unit characteristics. Within a group of Austro-Hungarian regiments serving in the same region, reception of the Easter Sacrament in 1918 ranged from 900 men (the 42nd Infantry Regiment) to 2800 (the 92nd Infantry Regiment).[91] Serving in Galicia in 1917, the *Divisionspfarrer* of the 5th Prussian Reserve Division was an experienced chaplain who offered even-handed assessment of the successes and failures of chaplains both individually and corporately. He and his fellow ministers in the field decried always having to read the "radiant reports of successful ministry" from chaplains of other divisions. "For Heaven's sake," he wondered, why could some

---

[89] BA-MA, PH 32/266, Tätigkeitsbericht, February 8, 1918, Prof. Dr. Schneider, Kath. Gouvernementspfarramt für den Kreis Nivelles Provinz Hennegau. Schneider wrote, "Die vor allem infolge der Ernährungsschwierigkeiten sehr niedergedrückte Stimmung der Truppen wurde durch die militärischen Erfolge, durch den befriedigenden Ausfall der Ernte, durch den Zusammenbruch in Russland und die Aussicht auf Friedensmöglichkeiten gehoben." But Schneider was not simply naïvely swayed into believing another mood had overtaken the troops. He wrote of the socialist and pacifist elements, "Anderseits macht sich der ungünstige Einfluss unzufriedener Elemente hier und da bemerkbar." See also BA-MA, PH 32/265, Tätigkeitsbericht, Jan. und Feb. 1918, R. Gierlichs, Gouvernementspfarrer für die Provinz Antwerpen.
[90] BA-MA, PH32/261: Program, "Zur Erinnerung an die Oster- und Siegesgedankfeier 1918 in der Chaldäischen Kirche zu Mossul."
[91] ÖStAKA, AFV, Ktn. 240: Pastoralbericht for Infantry Regiments 42, 92 (April 1918). Two nearby regiments tended toward a higher participation figure: IR 29 (1739 men) and IR 94 (1955 men). Two others had participation figures at the lower end of the scale: IR 121 (1029 men) and IR 10 (1060 men).

chaplains not be "humble and small" in their assessments of effectiveness? He noted that military religiosity could be vastly different within different sub-units of his division. For instance, for Easter communion in 1917, five battalions of the 5th Prussian Reserve Division – he noted they were from the Rhineland, Westphalia, West Prussia, and Alsace – "came man for man," while "1/3 to 1/2" of the men from the remaining nine battalions – this time, from Berlin and Poland – attended.[92]

The Italian Front, with its harsh mountain warfare, represented a quantitatively and qualitatively different type of military ministry again. While chaplains were deeply embedded with particular units, as on the Eastern Front, on the Italian Front the relatively more stable geographical positions allowed them to provide a much more regular religious ministry to their troops. It was in this theater of combat that Tyrol presented a case of military chaplaincy negotiating Catholic soldiers' multiple loyalties even within a subregion, as mentioned earlier.

Regionalism

One must account for regional disparities even within Austria-Hungary, and the region of Tyrol presents an intriguing case of local and transnational comparison that highlights several issues associated with wartime religiosity. Within the Habsburg polity, the region of Tyrol had a reputation for ultraconservative Catholic piety and loyalty to the Habsburg monarchy, rooted in a pre-modern agrarian society that was suspicious and hostile toward the modern world. However, beyond stereotypes of homogeneous reactionary anti-modernism, Catholic religiosity in Tyrol had multiple layers, which sometimes conflicted with one another.[93] The leading regional history of Tyrolean Catholic wartime life argues that the Great War should not be seen in terms of the famed throne-and-altar alliance and instead reconceptualizes pastoral care in terms of disparate Church socio-political movements.[94]

At the level of episcopal leadership, Tyrol was torn between loyalty to Germany and to a more universalist conception of the Catholic Church. On the one side, the German national-loyalist movement was influenced by the Bishop and the Auxiliary Bishop of Brixen, Franz Egger (1912–18) and Sigmund Waitz (1913–21), respectively. On the other side was

---

[92] EAM, NL Faulhaber, Ktn. 6777: Letter, April 4, 1917, from Divisionspfarrer Sebastian to Cardinal Faulhaber.

[93] Laurence Cole, *"Für Gott, Kaiser und Vaterland": Nationale Identität der deutschsprachigen Bevölkerung Tirols 1860–1914* (Frankfurt: Campus, 2000).

[94] Matthias Rettenwander, *Der Krieg als Seelsorge: Katholische Kirche und Volksfrömmigkeit in Tirol im Ersten Weltkrieg* (Innsbruck: Universitätsverlag Wagner, 2006), 424–7.

the Bishop of Trent, Celestino Endrici (1904–40), whose more universalist conceptualization of Catholic loyalty was suspected of having Italian irredentist sympathies by the Habsburg high command, which took the drastic step of removing him from Trent and interning him in the Vienna Woods.[95] These two camps would rally diverging sentiments among Tyrolean Catholics. Loyalty was not a simple matter of Catholic obedience to the throne-and-altar alliance. Indeed, many Tyrolean soldiers perceived a lack of religious respect from the imperial Habsburg Army authorities.

Beyond the Church politics of the bishops, basic matters of Catholic practice were not straightforward, either. Indeed, the war years showed that centralizing movements of ultramontane piety such as the Eucharistic Movement and the cult of the Sacred Heart had difficulty making inroads against the wide variety of regional practices deeply entrenched as forms of Catholic peasant piety within various subgroups within Tyrol.[96] Furthermore, on the homefront, widespread discontent with the military requisition of Tyrolean church bells for metallurgical smelting caused Tyrolean citizens to practice forms of passive and active resistance against the state. In February 1915, Army Command tried to requisition bells from the Archdiocese of Salzburg for these purposes. Of thirty-eight parishes, only seven responded that they were ready to give up a bell. In the diocese of Trent, particularly in Italian areas, only very small bells with a diameter of 30–70 cm were offered up. Unsatisfied with the initial unresponsive calls for metal, the military took increasingly strong requisitioning measures, claiming around fifty to seventy-five percent of all bells. Local Catholics resisted these attempts at all turns, subverting the state whenever possible by offering inferior bells or other sources of material. The military attempts to requisition bells deeply affected rural communities, where bells were prominent markers of time and conveyors of news, and were even believed to ward off storms. In Alpine lands, where beloved cows answered to the individual sounds of their own bells and featured prominently in festivals, the state encroachments struck at the heart of local identity.[97] Thus, some Catholic citizens in Tyrol conceptualized the war's eventual outcome as a deserved punishment for the defunct Habsburg state.

Nevertheless, despite the war's unfavorable outcome (and, indeed, the loss of South Tyrol), the war represented an opportunity for the Catholic clergy as a corporate body. The Church fell far short during the war of the absolute control theorized by scholars of ultramontanism, as indicated

[95] See ibid., 116–76, 270–93.   [96] Ibid., 177–229.   [97] Ibid., 324–44.

by the milieu-manager model of clerical control.[98] But despite the war's loss, the Catholic clergy in Central Europe was poised to advance a social-caritative agenda that responded more to the needs of the population, instead of solely advocating the pre-war political agendas of the clerical hierarchy. With roots in the reformist impulses of *Rerum novarum*, the Great War opened up new possibilities for a Catholic third way between individualist and collectivist utopias.[99]

Seen through the war experience in Tyrol, Kraus and Hašek based their literary portrayals on actual events. As in other armies, some chaplains became "fighting padres," taking up arms and killing enemy troops – an action that violated both international and ecclesiastical law, as Catholic chaplains were designated non-combatants. The absurdity and outright hypocrisy of chaplains may have offended the sensibilities of modernist writers, but the Catholic priest was still a figure of respect in the post-war period. In the interwar era, and indeed even after the Second World War, former Tyrolean chaplains such as Josef Hosp and Matthias Ortner became lionized figures in the pantheon of militant Christian heroes.[100]

The regional experience of Tyrolean Catholics highlights several issues of military religiosity, its local dimensions, and the need for further historical contextualization. War on the Italian Front, long a forgotten theater of the conflict, represents an example of heightened ideological animosity, geographically extreme conditions, and little apparent gain or loss for the sacrifice incurred.[101] For Tyrolean Catholics, the battlefront was on their doorstep. Josef Hosp's unit, the *Standschützen Bataillon* Nr. 1 from Innsbruck, was a form of defensive militia, mobilized, based, and operating locally. Hosp, as a civilian pastor and indeed peacetime neighbor of many of the men he served with, was deeply imbricated in a community network with a local identity and strong bonds of homefront solidarity transposed to a battlefront environment. Hosp's regular, avid participation in the killing of enemy troops violated both Church and international law. His wartime activity is well documented, allowing one to examine the

---

[98] Houlihan, "Clergy in the Trenches."

[99] John W. Boyer, "Catholics, Christians, and the Challenges of Democracy: The Heritage of the Nineteenth Century," in *Christdemokratie in Europa in 20. Jahrhundert*, ed. Michael Gehler, Wolfram Kaiser, and Helmut Wohnaut (Vienna: Böhlau, 2001), 23–59; Wolfram Kaiser, *Christian Democracy and the Origins of European Union* (Cambridge: Cambridge University Press, 2007).

[100] See Joanna Bourke, *An Intimate History of Killing: Face to Face Killing in 20th Century Warfare* (New York: Basic Books, 1999), 256–93, esp. 73.

[101] A massive transnational cooperative has also yielded promising new results. See Hermann J. W. Kuprian and Oswald Überegger, eds., *Der Erste Weltkrieg im Alpenraum: Erfahrung, Deutung, Erinnerung/La Grande Guerra nell'arco alpino: esperienze e memoria* (Bozen: Athesia, 2006).

commitment of atrocities by a theoretically non-combatant chaplain. On several occasions throughout the war, Hosp killed enemy troops, shooting them with a sniper rifle; he referred to this as "blessing" the enemy soldiers. His declared reason for killing was that he had been left alone with no other recourse. Ensconced with this belief, he firmly wrote about the action that, "Reasonable men will judge me reasonably."[102] Indeed, a closer examination of Hosp's service record testifies to his volunteerism: he participated in many violent acts that were not part of a chaplain's duty. Due to his extensive knowledge of the mountain terrain, Hosp led patrols of scouts to reconnoiter enemy positions. He also volunteered to serve as an artillery spotter, and so was directly responsible for raining down shells upon the enemy.[103]

Hosp's men were only too happy to embrace the fighting chaplain. As the unit report proudly noted, "Battalion chaplain Hosp knew how to raise the spirits of the troops not only through his sermons, but also through the actions that he performed as an...always adventurous patroller."[104] Despite protests that eventually reached a Milan newspaper, Hosp was never disciplined or even admonished for his actions. In fact, he became widely admired in Tyrol, especially among former servicemen from the *Standschützen* units.[105]

This accorded well with the romanticized historical example of localized patriotism intertwined with religious sanction particular to the collective historical remembrance of Tyrol. During the Napoleonic Wars, the Tyrolean resistance made its leader, Andreas Hofer, into a local hero. Johann Haspinger, a Capuchin friar, second only to Hofer in the Tyrolean pantheon of heroes, was a military chaplain who served in Hofer's forces and explicitly led Tyrolean men into action against Napoleon. Thus, Friar Haspinger was a mythologized and idealized figure worthy of emulation for Tyrolean chaplains.[106] Tyrolean chaplains who emulated the

---

[102] "Kriegserinnerungen des Feldkuraten Josef Hosp," quoted in Oswald Ebner, *Kampf um die Sextner Rotwand* (Bozen: Athesia, 1978), 52.

[103] See Tiroler Landesarchiv (hereafter TLA), Tiroler Landesverteidigungsakten (hereafter TLVA), Standschützen Bataillon Innsbruck I, Fasz. I, "Bericht über die Expedition auf die Rotwand vom 16.–19. April 1916 vom Patrullenleiter, Feldkurat Josef Hosp," TLA, TLVA, Standschützen Bataillon Innsbruck I, Fasz. I, "Bericht über die Patrull auf den Elfer vom 24. u. 25. Juni 1915."

[104] TLA, TLVA, Standschützen Bataillon Innsbruck I, Fasz. I, "Tätigkeitsbericht über die Zeit vom 19.V.15 bis 10.V.16," p. 16.

[105] Helmut Golowitsch, *"Und kommt der Feind ins Land herein – ": Schützen verteidigen Tirol und Kärnten: Standschützen und Freiwillige Schützen 1915–1918* (Nürnberg: Buchdienst Südtirol E. Kienesberger, 1985); Anton von Mörl, *Die Standschützen im Weltkrieg* (Innsbruck: Tyrolia, 1934); Anton von Mörl, *Standschützen verteidigen Tirol, 1915–1918* (Innsbruck: Universitätsverlag Wagner, 1958).

[106] Lipusch, *Österreich-Ungarns katholische Militärseelsorge*, 25–9. Major General Hugo Kerchnawe, director of the Austrian Archives, wrote in Lipusch's volume that Haspinger was one of the "heroic priests of bygone times."

fighting friar offended the sensibilities of literary modernist writers, but their actions found warm reception in Tyrol.[107]

The decline of fire-breathing

Catholic military chaplains found their personal theology largely in line with service to the state. This is perhaps most pointedly demonstrated in the diaries of Ludwig Berg, the Catholic military chaplain stationed at the headquarters of Kaiser Wilhelm II. Berg's personal theology did not waver from his belief in the justness of the German cause in a war of defense against aggression.[108]

It is important to outline more personal theologies in relation to the public theologies of the bishops and elite clerics. Military chaplains at the front were the stereotypical fire-breathers of literature, in extreme cases subscribing to a theology of patriotic chauvinism of "Praise the Lord and pass the ammunition," in the words of a famous American Second World War song. These themes would be fundamental to chaplains' understanding of the ensuing conflict and would form the basis of exegesis to their soldiers. Chaplains during the First World War did not problematize this issue; they clung to the just-war tradition.

One of the more elegant sermons in this vein was delivered by Feldkurat and Divisionspfarrer Anton Dvorak of the 29th Infantry Division of the k.u.k. Army. Dvorak began, not by quoting scripture, as was often the case, but by quoting Schiller from *Die Braut von Messina*: "Life is not the highest of goods/higher than life stands duty." (*Das Leben ist der Güter höchstes nicht/höher als das Leben steht die Pflicht.*) Dvorak argued that, "The pains of a dying warrior are a type of martyrdom, his death a baptism of blood [*Bluttaufe*] that takes away the sins of his life."[109] This accorded well with the views of Aquinas on military duty directed toward God.[110]

---

[107] Another celebrated Tyrolean chaplain, Matthias Ortner, even received a *Festschrift* after the Second World War. Martin Wörgötter, *Unser Feldpater Ortner: Festgabe zum "goldenen" Priesterjubiläum unseres Feldpaters Matthias Ortner, Pfarrer in Aschau, Brixental* (Salzburg: Salzburger Druckerei, 1956).

[108] Betker and Kriele, *Pro fide et patria!*

[109] ÖStAKA, AFV, Ktn. 216: Allerseelenansprache 1915, Anton Dvorak, Feldkurat, 29th Infantry Division. For a comparative examination of the rhetoric of blood sacrifice of English and German Protestants in the military during the war, see Patrick Porter "Slaughter or Sacrifice? The Religious Rhetoric of Blood Sacrifice in the British and German Armies, 1914–1919" (D.Phil, University of Oxford, 2006).

[110] Article 124.5: "The good of one's country is paramount among human goods: yet the Divine good, which is the proper cause of martyrdom, is of more account than human good. Nevertheless, since human good may become Divine, for instance when it is referred to God, it follows that any human good in so far as it is referred to God, may be the cause of martyrdom." Translation from http://www.ccel.org/ccel/aquinas/summa.SS_Q124_A5.html (last accessed October 31, 2014).

Sermons of 1914 to mid-1916 tended to be full of the aggressive tone of the days of August 1914. A sermon from chaplain Viktor Varady of the military hospital at Nowe Miasto emphasized his belief in the unfolding of history – and the rightness of his cause. He argued that, "History teaches that only those peoples have reached the highpoint of their culture, whose sons are conscious of their calling to military service and who are ready at all times to sacrifice blood and treasure for their Fatherland." Similarly, Chaplain Melchior Zelenyi of the 26th Infantry Regiment of the k.u.k. 2nd Army wrote in his monthly pastoral report for November 1915 that some of the basic themes of his sermons were "The war can be only according to the will of God," "We should follow in the footsteps of our heroes," and "Our fallen soldiers are martyrs."[111]

The most infamous of the German theological formulations about the Great War was "God with us" (*Gott mit uns*), which emphasized the belief that "with us" implied that God was "on our side" and thus "not with our enemies."[112] Jakob Ebner, a chaplain serving with the 1st *Badsiche Leibgrenadierregiment*, directly addressed this theme in his sermons. Ebner pointed out the symbolic significance and deep associations that the very words carried; *Gott mit uns* was printed on German belt buckles and rifles. He reminded his listeners that, "God had been with them in so many dangers" and specifically mentioned successful actions, including Lanfroicourt, Chantas, and Senones, as well as further actions in the trenches. He then elaborated on an idea common to many members of the Catholic clergy: that the war was a tremendous opportunity to transcend the pre-war fall from religion associated with modern society. Ebner declared:

"God with us" has yet another entirely different meaning than only protection in distress and victory in the struggle. Some among us, in the bustle of modern life, liked to cover the soul with a cloak of fog, and the eye of the soul lost its view toward the Father in Heaven. The belief in your immortality and in eternal life was suffocated and oppressed under this dark fog. Then came the great, terrible war . . . The call to war was the best God-seeker [*Gott-Sucher*], the danger in the rain of bullets was the best God-finder [*Gott-Finder*]. From many soldiers' souls, the cloak of fog has lifted, and the belief in the dear Father in Heaven has risen like sunlight. And from the depths of the soul climbs aloft to Heaven: "Our Father who art in Heaven, O God, be merciful to me, a poor sinner, O my God, in You I believe, in You I hope, You I love with all my heart." Where the love of God is awakened, there blooms also the comradely love of one's brothers.[113]

---

[111] ÖStAKA, AFV, Ktn. 216: Pastoral Report, November 1915, Epidemie Spital Nowe Miasto; November 1915, Infantry Regiment 26.

[112] Missalla, *"Gott mit uns."*

[113] EAF, NL 44 (Jakob Ebner Tagebuch), pp. 87–90; quote from p. 88.

In this theological formulation, the outbreak of war was an admonition to abandon pre-war selfishness and return to an idealized social order that was closer to God. As one abandoned the fragmenting individualism of hectic modern life, one cast aside egoism and returned toward an altruism more in line with communal obligations and oriented toward a community fulfilling God's will. This was a powerful belief that existed on the homefront as well as the battlefront.

Although dating of such trends is necessarily imprecise, the great offensives of 1916 on both the Western and Eastern Fronts were the events that helped cause the shift of sentiment. As the war dragged on, military chaplains noticed that incessant hurrah patriotism was having a counterproductive effect. One chaplain from the Austro-Hungarian Army specifically complained that the longer the war continued, the more divided he felt between giving the required "apologetic lectures" in public and having to provide more realistic personalized defenses in private conversations with individuals.[114] After the enormous bloodletting of the 1916 offensives, an increasing number of sermons dwelt on more existential themes, such as "Is there a God?" and "Is there a hereafter?"[115] Jakob Ebner, who had earlier declared his belief in "*Gott mit uns*," began to be plagued by doubt. In December 1916, after attending a conference of Western Front chaplains, Ebner berated some of his fellows who were still adamant about Germany's God-ordained triumph: "Then where are the conquered and the victors? Just come to us at the Somme [and figure it out]!" After receiving furlough to visit his hometown in March 1917, Ebner preached a sermon and taught catechism classes, before making a round of visits to friends and relatives. Everybody wanted to know his evaluation of the war. In his diary, he noted, "Many questions about the war. I cannot answer most of them myself. Many question marks for me, too."[116]

Sermons also began to focus explicitly on the longing for peace. This was not a strictly pacific shift, however; most chaplains would continue to offer sermons about duty, in which they referred to the classic Biblical dilemma of state authority: "Render therefore unto Caesar those things that are Caesar's and unto God those things that are God's" (Matthew 22:21), ultimately emphasizing the virtue of loyalty to the state and the justness of the cause. Nevertheless, compared to the bellicose rhetoric of

---

114 ÖStAKA: AFV, Ktn. 227: Pastoralbericht, February 1917, 90th Infantry Regiment, Pfarrer Djzielcki.

115 ÖStAKA, AFV, Ktn. 233: Pastoralbericht for September 1917, Feldjägerbataillons Nr. 19.

116 EAF, NL 44 (Jakob Ebner Tagebuch), pp. 576, 604 (December 13, 1916; March 4, 1917).

the early war years, chaplains interjected themes of peace and friendship on an individual and collective level. Bruno Spitzl of the k.u.k. 59th Infantry Regiment, for instance, gave sermons whose themes were "Love of God and altruism [*Nächstenliebe*]: two poles of Christian faith" and "God's offer of peace."[117]

In many cases, the chaplains' sermons became much less dogmatic, transcending confessional bounds by approaching universal existential themes. Such sermons could bring disapproval from higher authorities, and here one can observe an ideological split between military religious authorities and the deeds of chaplains on the battlefield.

The complicated social position of a chaplain had to take account of numerous and conflicting loyalties, as exemplified by the position of Michael Buchberger, the *Domkapitular* of Munich-Freising and the administrative factotum of Bavarian chaplaincy during the Great War. Buchberger visited the front numerous times to assess the situation there and report to his superior, Cardinal *Feldpropst* Franziskus von Bettinger, on the everyday conditions.[118] Although his officially published book was highly valedictory of the Bavarian war effort, Buchberger was much more realistic in private correspondence. In 1915, he wrote to Bishop Michael von Faulhaber, later Cardinal and *Feldpropst*, testifying to the war's overwhelming dimensions. Buchberger described units going for "week- and even month-long" periods without the opportunity to hear Mass or receive communion. Because of the prohibition against members of the Catholic clergy holding evening Mass, chaplains were forced into desperate straits. Some held illegal evening services in secret. Others skipped morning and midday meals for months on end in order to hold as many Masses as possible in the mornings. Buchberger acknowledged the reality of the situation: "The war has taken on a form that in the year 1890 no one could have thought of."[119]

Nevertheless, in his official capacity, Buchberger had to uphold chaplaincy's line of perseverance and duty. But there were hints that chaplains were doing precisely the same thing as him at the front: espousing more personalized contingent views in their sermons, even sometimes against the wishes of Catholic troops, who demanded more traditional religious

---

[117] ÖStAKA, AFV, Ktn. 232: Pastoralbericht for August 1917, IR 59. Cf. Spitzl, *Die Rainer*.

[118] Michael Buchberger, *Die bayerischen Feldseelsorge im Weltkrieg* (Munich: Jos. Köselische Buchandlung, 1916).

[119] EAM, NL Faulhaber, 6779/3: Letter, Buchberger to Faulhaber, June 22, 1915. He pleaded with Faulhaber to obtain official permission from the Holy See to hold multiple Masses per day, although he acknowledged this would be difficult due to the strict regulation of correspondence following Italy's entry into the war.

behavior. In late November 1917, Buchberger wrote an official letter berating the divisional chaplains of the Bavarian Army because "One often hears the complaint that the sermons are insufficiently religious [*zu wenig religiös*] and deal with the conditions of the moment and contemporary questions [*Zeitlage und Zeitfragen*], rather than stabilize the troops' belief, fill them with Christian hope and Christian trust, lead them to the source of mercy of the Church, and thus encourage them to a willingly sacrificial perseverance in the loyal fulfillment of duty."[120] Buchberger's claim that chaplains' sermons were "insufficiently religious" and dealt with "contemporary questions" does not fit with stereotypes of chaplains as reactionary fire-breathers. It also reveals that, even deep into the war, some Catholic soldiers wanted chaplains to be more traditionalist. All of this indicates the need to look locally, and whenever possible, on a personal level, to assess properly the many dimensions of religion during the war.

Conclusion

The study of military chaplains highlights the inadequacies of the milieu-manager thesis as a description of military priests. Even more than their clerical counterparts on the homefront, Catholic chaplains were state-sponsored authority figures, commissioned as officers in the military hierarchy. Despite such authority, however, chaplains could not compel men to be religious or religiously observant in the public sphere. As "milieu managers" of the battlefront, chaplains could only attempt to channel the outpouring of spiritual energy, but they were overwhelmed: the experience of the Great War showed spirituality escaping the boundaries of clerical channels.[121] As a result, diffuse religiosity emerged in the interwar period, drawing on traditional symbols, texts, images, and practices, but in a radically new context. During this time, and primed for a surge in the post-1945 era, individual lay Catholics asserted their agency to practice their beliefs as they saw fit. While such assertion had taken place in previous eras, the Great War was a watershed moment for individual Catholic empowerment, viewed in terms of the Church's declining corporate control over believers.

Nevertheless, the study of chaplains in their attempt to cope with the overflow of this religious energy can help to illuminate the spectrum of

---

[120] ABF (Archiv der Bayerischen Franzsikaner), PA I: 1589, Letter from Dr. M. Buchberger, "an die H.H. Divisionspfarrer u. Etappenpfarrer der bayer. Armee, betr. Feldseelsorge," November 27, 1917.
[121] Blaschke, "Die Kolonialisierung der Laienwelt"; McLeod, *Religion and the People*, 94–5.

belief and disbelief that existed during the conflict. Although the direct agency of the chaplains was severely limited, their ambiguous social position can help to give a cultural history of religiosity at the battlefront that restores the plurality of narratives and the fundamental subjectivity that are crucial to religious studies. Evidence of religious behavior poses a fundamental question of historical representation,[122] and chaplains as historical actors left behind valuable written records of public religiosity that would otherwise be lost to history. Fundamentally, the comparative examination of Catholic military chaplaincy in Germany and Austria-Hungary shows ways in which the centralized Catholic chaplaincy in the archaic, ramshackle Habsburg Empire held together better during the war than did Catholic chaplaincy in Germany, which foundered on federalism of the Wilhelmine Empire.

Military chaplains were not merely the fire-breathing zealots of literature; they were much more interesting than that. On the whole, Catholic chaplains were unable to contain the flow of spiritual energy that poured out during the Great War, demonstrating the limits of hierarchical authority. Because of the records they left behind, however, they form an invaluable source on public religiosity and the conflicting identities and loyalties felt by Central European Catholics. Religion during the First World War, as ever, was about personal subjectivity and belief. With chaplains unable to provide adequate spiritual comfort on a mass scale, the next chapter examines how Catholic soldiers themselves coped, using an improvised form of religion that was somewhere between magic, superstition, and dogma.

[122] Becker, "Faith, Ideologies," 241.

4   Faith in the trenches: Catholic battlefield piety during the Great War

In the early phase of the war, Constantin Schneider, an Austro-Hungarian infantry officer with the 8th Division, 4th Army, noted in his diary a brief religious scene that made a strong impression in his memory. After the division's "baptism of fire" near the town of Belz in Galicia in August 1914, Schneider observed a group of Austro-Hungarian soldiers praying together: "On a tree near a small meadow hung a squalid picture of a saint. Here the men crowded together and murmured prayers. Since the first battle, did the men become God-fearing, or from belief did a secret power actually spring forth that was more powerful than death?"[1] Schneider never answered the question, but he touched on important parts of religious faith: for some soldiers, the experience of battle and its brush with existential chaos made them discover (or rediscover) religious feelings. In many instances, soldiers' preexisting religious faith helped them to cope with the horrors of battle. Schneider did not mention, however, that combat also caused soldiers to abandon their religious faith – a subject that for many Great War histories is the sole way of representing religious believers' reactions to industrial warfare.

Much ink has already been spilled on the topic of disenchantment. Contrary to believers' stereotypes about the rush to religion during time of war, there certainly were atheists in foxholes, and moreover, it was precisely the encounter with industrialized mass carnage that made some religious believers abandon their religious faith. The archetypal hellish landscape of the Western Front served as the potent symbol of a loss of faith, the shattered illusions of the pre-1914 world. The English artist Paul Nash succinctly described his impressions of the trench setting: "No pen or drawing can convey this country – the normal setting of the battles taking place day and night, month after month. Evil and the incarnate fiend alone can be master of this war, and no glimmer of God's hand

---

[1] Constantin Schneider, *Die Kriegserinnerungen 1914–1919*, ed. Oskar Dohle, *Veröffentlichungen der Kommission für Neuere Geschichte Österreichs* (Vienna: Böhlau, 2003), 59.

is seen anywhere . . . It is unspeakable, godless, hopeless."[2] This chapter, however, will focus on areas where enchantment persisted in the midst of the hellish battlefield.

Influential histories of the First World War since the cultural turn have rightly noted the outpouring of spirituality that occurred during the conflict. However, this spirituality is usually classified under the heading of "spiritualism" or "superstition," often to highlight a return to primitivism.[3] This notion of spirituality represents a form of personal devotion, a "privatization of divine help" beyond the official efforts of organized religion and military chaplaincy.[4] A notion of privatized primitivism, however, creates unnecessarily artificial conceptual boundaries – boundaries that were, in many cases, unknown to contemporary religious believers. There was a wide spectrum of belief and disbelief, and categories were often blurry. Most often, soldiers found themselves between the extremes of atheism and official dogma. Consequently, analyses of religion during the Great War must seek to recapture what faith and belief meant to the people of the time, moving beyond dichotomies of organized versus popular religion and progressive atheism versus archaic belief.

This chapter studies how Catholic soldiers coped with the existential chaos posed by the new battlefield conditions of the Great War. By focusing on an ecumenical sameness of religion during the war, viewed largely through the writings of clerical elites in service of the state, often at the homefront, previous histories have given a limited picture of religious life at the battlefront. In fact, not all religions coped equally well with the new circumstances of trench warfare: some Christian denominations fared better than others.

The stereotypically archaic religion of Catholicism adjusted comparatively well to the new conditions of modern war. In fact, this occurred precisely for many of the reasons for which outside observers condemned Catholicism as a superstitious relic of a bygone era. Catholic battlefield religiosity was surprisingly resilient in modern conflict, affecting how scholars view religious practice at the most destructive sites of battlefield violence during the Great War. The micro-level Catholic experience of

[2] Quoted in Ellis, *Eye-Deep in Hell*, 9.
[3] For spiritualism, see Winter, *Sites of Memory*, 64–77. For superstition, see David Stevenson, *Cataclysm: The First World War as Political Tragedy* (New York: Basic Books, 2004), 175.
[4] For the "privatization of divine help," see Peter Knoch, "Erleben und Nacherleben. Das Kriegserlebnis im Augenzeugenbericht und im Geschichtsunterricht," in *Keiner fühlt sich hier mehr als Mensch. Erlebnis und Wirkung des Ersten Weltkriegs*, ed. Gerhard Hirschfeld, Gerd Krumeich, and Irina Renz (Essen: Klartext, 1993), 209 and Watson, *Enduring the Great War*, 95.

battle addresses the pan-European Catholic experience of the twentieth century, comparing it with the standard cultural histories of the Great War. Instead of the disenchantment and loss associated with secularization theory and literary modernism, this chapter highlights the coping mechanisms of ordinary people from the losing powers at the most disillusioning sites of destructive violence.

One should begin with the critics. According to some of its harshest, the Catholic religion was "stupid," "backward," "medieval," "superstitious," "feminine," and, perhaps most pointedly for Central Europe, "un-German."[5] As with some stereotypes, however, anti-Catholic critiques contained an element of truth. While intended as terms of scorn, the generalized stereotypes of Catholicism pointed to important reasons for why and how it coped with battlefield destruction.

On a continuum of belief between superstition and dogma, Catholic practices lay closer to more archaic forms of superstition, incorporating elements of popular folk piety more readily than did the ideal type of Protestant faith through belief alone. Catholic tradition adapted to the realities of modern combat, providing comfort to Catholic believers in a variety of quasi-official outlets – and even in some that the official Church denounced as "superstitious." Catholicism lay on an advantageous middle ground of the belief spectrum, incorporating large swathes of superstition, popular piety, and Christian doctrine in a holistic repertoire of concrete practices. This selective adaptation of tradition gave believers both individual agency and collective identity.

As a religious confession based on sacramental practices and spiritual intercession, Catholicism weathered the chaotic environment of battle with tangible spiritual comfort mechanisms, such as relics, devotional pictures, scapulars, rosaries, and amulets. In the heat of battle, mere words provided little comfort to the religious soldier enduring artillery shelling or poison gas attacks. Catholic tradition had a wider repertoire of comfort mechanisms available to soldiers. The Protestant view of the ultimate reliance on individual faith, heavily emphasizing the word of God as recorded in the Bible, meant that Protestant soldiers found less religious sanction for material objects that could help focus belief. In the wide and blurry spectrum of Christian religiosity, there was certainly some overlap between the beliefs and practices of Catholics and

---

[5] Such descriptions served the self-conceptualizations of the patriarchal, bourgeois ideology that emerged in nineteenth-century Europe, as well as a socialist view of the political order. For the centrality of anti-Catholicism to Central European liberalism, see Gross, *War against Catholicism*, 22. A vivid overview of the anti-religious identity claimed by liberals and socialists on a pan-European level can be seen in Burleigh, *Earthly Powers*.

Protestants. However, as contemporary observers noted, Protestant soldiers had much more difficulty accepting "magical" and "superstitious" objects as part of their Christian faith.[6] As Anettte Becker has noted, the religious "bric-a-brac" of spirituality and tangible objects at the front was especially suited to Catholicism.[7] Furthermore, as Philip Jenkins has recently written in a global overview, Catholicism attracted believers in the war, including non-Catholics, because its beliefs and practices incorporated the presence of the supernatural, as well as a charismatic power that could be altered through human interaction. Preexisting shrines and grottoes became sites of devotion, and religious places of worship received new spiritually-charged meaning, especially churches and religious sites that were damaged during battle – particularly those in the heavily Catholic regions of Belgium and northern France.[8]

Catholic communal links to the homefront were of vital importance in a spiritual network. Catholic aspects of intercession and sainthood reinforced Catholic beliefs in family social bonds and helped Catholic soldiers fight against creeping alienation and atomization. The feminine aspects of Catholic public piety, especially the cults of the saints and the Virgin Mary, helped console soldiers by appealing to the help of others, reconnecting with their families. Through feminine piety, Catholic soldiers retained ties to the homefront and the dolorous consolation of the archetypal grieving religious mother, thus helping to validate Christian notions of sacrifice. Beyond the comfort of the Pietà, the theoretical and practical internationalism of the Church helped reinforce the belief that the war was about natural sinfulness rooted in the human condition, something that crossed national borders. As the war lengthened without end in sight, the notion of a divinely-chosen German national Protestantism, with its militantly masculine-gendered overtones and their lack of consolation, seemed increasingly inadequate as a collective explanation for the war's stagnation.[9]

---

[6] Albert Hellwig, *Weltkrieg und Aberglaube: Erlebtes und Erlauschtes* (Leipzig: Wilhelm Heims, 1916), 24–5. More recently on this issue, see Christine Beil and Ralph Winkle, "'Primitive Religiosität' oder 'Krise der sittlichen Ordnung'? Wissenschaftsgeschichtliche Anmerkungen zur Aberglaubensforschung im Ersten Weltkrieg," in *KriegsVolksKunde. Zur Erfahrungsbindung durch Symbolbildung*, ed. Gottfried Korff (Tübingen: Tübinger Vereinigung für Volkskunde, 2005), 162–3.

[7] Becker, "Faith, Ideologies," 234–47. For a slightly modified view, see Gregory, "Beliefs and Religion," 435.

[8] Jenkins, *The Great and Holy War*, 118–24.

[9] One Protestant soldier in the trenches argued against "soft" and "weak" portrayals of Jesus, instead emphasizing the hard, masculine duty of soldiers, equating a "soldier's uniform," a "man's honor," and the "name of a Christian." See Anon., "Soldatische Froemmigkeit," *Der Champagne-Kamerad. Feldzeitung der 3. Armee. Beilage*, February 13, 1916,

Writers more sympathetic to the Catholic tradition have talked about the fundamentals of Catholic identity, especially regarding the core related principles of sacramentality and mediation and their link to an idea of magical object worship. The Catholic scholar Richard P. McBrien notes that, for the Catholic believer, "A sacrament not only signifies (as Protestants have historically emphasized); it also causes what it signifies. That is, God is not only present as an object of faith in the sacramental action; God actually achieves something in and through that action. Thus created realities not only contain, reflect, or embody the presence of God, they make that presence spiritually effective for those who avail themselves of these sacred realities." McBrien, however, immediately points to a danger of Catholicism long noticed by those outside the faith: "Just as the principle of sacramentality edges close to the brink of idolatry, so the principle of mediation moves one along the path toward magic."[10] Historically-rooted forms of Catholic devotional practice lay closer to the concept of primitive magic, which was an essential part of the flood of Great War spirituality.[11] The First World War trenches resounded with primitivism and magic, as soldiers turned to whatever outlets helped them cope with the terrors of combat and the chaos of the battlefield environment.[12] How did a predominantly peasant Catholic subculture experience the war between superstition and dogma?

This chapter considers the imperial dimensions of a conflict that, for all its retrospective importance to the cultural field of modernism, was fought predominantly by peasants. Broken down regionally, the war in Central Europe was fought by people from rural areas, whose everyday mentalities and worldviews were quite different than standard cultural histories of the war normally depict.[13] Important, path-breaking studies, most notably Benjamin Ziemann's work on Bavaria, have begun to

p. 1. Cf. Lt.d.L. Hoenninger "Gebet der deutschen Krieger!", *Der Schuetzengraben* Nr. 5 (1915): p. 20.

[10] See McBrien, *Catholicism*, 2–17; quotes from 11.

[11] Historical accounts of the relations between religion and magic point not only to key developments in Western society but also to the Great War's reversion to an earlier era. For a key interpretation of religion, magic, and history, see Keith Thomas, *Religion and the Decline of Magic: Studies in Popular Beliefs in Sixteenth- and Seventeenth-Century England* (New York: Scribner, 1971), 643.

[12] During the Great War, contemporary German observers studying the blurred boundaries between concepts like magic and religion argued that superstitious phenomena occurred more easily in backward, peasant nations without a sense of cultivated education; for a German author, this meant "Russia, the Balkan states, as well as Italy." See Hellwig, *Weltkrieg und Aberglaube*, 5–6.

[13] Although, here, too, historiographical attitudes are shifting. In examining the religious beliefs and practices of preeminent sites of urban modernism in the capital cities, Adrian Gregory and Annette Becker have noted the resilience of religious beliefs and practices throughout the war. See Gregory and Becker, "Religious Sites and Practices," 383–427.

explore questions of rural faith.[14] This chapter puts these questions at the imperial and local levels. Catholic soldiers from the losing powers coped with the pressures of the Great War better than the collective literary modernist imagination would have it, using their faith as a way of experiencing and understanding the war. This is how and why they did it.

A wide spectrum

Soldiers and their families invoked a wide variety of metaphysical spiritual means for two main purposes: to protect their lives and to harm the lives of their enemies.[15] The typical soldier's religious beliefs took on disparate forms during the First World War. Contemporary participants recognized the variability of mood even within individuals. Choosing to see humor in this, one German combatant commented, "We soldiers became at the time a comic type of man, quickly lighthearted, quickly devotional, *Simplicissimus* lying next to the New Testament." For others, of course, rapid changes of mood, as well as monotony, brought them to the brink of madness. Social scientific studies attempting to be concrete and systematic about possible expressions of metaphysical belief commented that the soldiers' souls were full of contradictions and could not be portrayed too generally.[16] Members of the military clergy, such as the Bavarian chaplain Balthasar Meier of the 5th Bavarian Reserve Infantry Regiment, commented on the waxing and waning of religiosity, especially before major actions. Meier noted that in his division, the number of Catholic soldiers going to confession was five times higher than normal during the Somme offensive of 1916. In times of "crisis and danger," as Meier put it, "faith [was] taken off the shelf." After the danger was over, religiosity was "banished to its former position."[17] This was precisely in line with mechanistic conceptions of rural faith, with its focus on public

---

[14] Ziemann's study emphasizes the connections between home front and battlefront, arguing that, rather a mythical Nazi "community of battle" formed by war experience at the front, Bavarian soldiers retained close regional ties to farm, family, and faith, which strongly included aspects of popular religion and superstition. See Ziemann, *Front und Heimat*.

[15] Hanns Bächtold, *Deutscher Soldatenbrauch und Soldatenglaube* (Strassburg: Tübner, 1917), 23.

[16] Paul Plaut, "Psychographie des Kriegers," in *Beiträge zur Psychologie des Krieges*, ed. William Stern and Otto Lipmann (Leipzig: Johann Ambrosius Barth, 1920), 70–110; quote from 75.

[17] EAM, Akten des Domkapitular Michael Buchberger, Pastoral Report of Chaplain Balthasar Meier, February 7, 1917.

piety as a "visible demonstration of faith" in which soldiers' answered prayers reinforced their belief in God.[18]

Even deep into the war, religious faith continued to be important for many soldiers in extreme existential situations. Some comparative numbers help to put things in perspective. An advanced study derived from a questionnaire given to soldiers by the *Institut für angewandte Psychologie* in Klein-Glienicke bei Potsdam, censored during the war, was generally skeptical about the idea of the persistence of religious belief during the war. Nonetheless, the study found that around one-third of the respondents mentioned receiving direct divine assistance that had saved their lives. In a study of the frequency of phrases in soldiers' correspondence, designed to gauge their values, mentions of "religion feelings" were in first place, before such categories as "memories of home," "social emotions," "fatalism," and "consideration of the degree of possible unpleasantness."[19]

Soldiers who fought in the First World War emphatically did not endure four long years in the trenches under sustained shell fire.[20] Units were shuffled between areas of heated combat and areas of quiet. Even under combat conditions, soldiers cycled between the front lines and places of recuperation behind the immediate danger zone. Perhaps most importantly for religious believers, new echelons were constantly being called up from the homefront, some of whom experienced battle for the first time only as the war was ending. Writing to the Apostolic Field Vicariate in April 1917, one Austro-Hungarian chaplain, Adalbert Bukowiec, offered a differentiated group portrait of Catholic piety, claiming substantial variety in religious observance between "the newly called-up" and

---

[18] Mooser, "Katholische Volksreligion," 156; Ziemann, *Front und Heimat*, 246–8.

[19] Walter Ludwig, "Beiträge zur Psychologie der Furcht im Kriege," in Stern and Lipmann, *Beiträge zur Psychologie*, 172. As Alexander Watson has recently observed, "Walter Ludwig's investigation of soldiers' coping strategies is probably the most sophisticated piece of psychological research to be undertaken on either side during the First World War." For a discussion of Ludwig's study, see Watson, *Enduring the Great War*, 236–7.

[20] Indeed, a profound study of soldiers' narratives of the war, and our myths about it, acknowledges the archetypal power of Western Front combat as meaningless hell, while at the same time cautioning against it: "[N]ot every day in every sector was the Inferno that is fixed in our imaginations. That hell is the war we remember because we want the First World War to be the worst, the cautionary example of war horror. And sometimes it was; but there were also times of ordinary war, when men performed their routine duties and nobody attacked and nobody died. Sometimes they felt moments of peace, enjoyed small pleasures, noticed and recorded a fine day, a sunset, as men at war always have. They saw and felt the horrors too; of course they did. But locally and intermittently. Nobody lived at that pitch continuously." Samuel Hynes, *The Soldiers' Tale: Bearing Witness to Modern War* (New York: Viking, 1997), 55.

the "long-serving," as well as between "peasants" and "city-dwellers."[21] The Swabian military chaplain Karl Lang, serving with the Bavarian 11th Infantry Division, emphasized the particularly strong religiosity of peasant farmers, as did Karl Egger, a Jesuit in the 2nd Tyrolean Kaiserjägerregiment.[22]

Deep into the war, some Catholic soldiers, especially those just being called up, earnestly believed in the exclusive justness of their cause and that the Divine Providence would lead them to victory. Writing to Bishop Michael von Faulhaber in 1916 after having seen combat numerous times already, Major Loibl of the 6th Bavarian Reserve Infantry believed that he was engaged in a "fight for peace for the most heavily opposed people" (in his mind, Germany), imploring, "God bless our weapons to that end!" Loibl begged God to be allowed the opportunity to face the enemy again.[23] Major Loibl's "Sprit of 1914" was well alive in 1916. But one must explore other soldiers' emotions, too, both individually and systemically.

More personalized accounts of religiosity reflected individual viewpoints that did not coincide with collective meanings of war experience. For Hans Haugeneder, an infantryman with the Austro-Hungarian 70th Infantry Regiment, something like the famed "Spirit of 1914" was still occurring in his regiment in mid-1916 as it went into battle on the Eastern Front, even as it entered areas where the devastating Brusilov Offensive had already begun. Haugeneder recalled joyously arriving on June 18, 1916, "for the first time on the battlefield!" after departing the train station with the "prayer before battle" and the accompaniment of hymns. He noted, "From all windows, flowers and greetings were showered upon us!" Only on July 10, 1916, did the 70th Regiment start making patrols against enemy positions and only on August 10 did they start encountering heavy Russian artillery fire.[24]

For many believing soldiers, even at the war's end, the accumulated suffering was read not as abandonment or futility, but rather as a cyclical form of atonement that testified to the nostalgic need for a return to

---

21 ÖStAKA, AFV, Ktn. 228: 1917 (IV), Pastoralbericht April 1917, Schützen Regiment 16. The chaplain claimed that both the long-standing servicemen and the city-dwellers were bad influences on neophytes, especially those from rural regions. In future studies of military religiosity, the chaplains' comments on structures of belief need to be explored on a micro-level, taking into account personal subjectivity and group dynamics.

22 ABA, NL Karl Lang, *Kriegschronik*, p. 113, quoted in Ziemann, *Front und Heimat*, 254. See also AASI Vienna, Autobiographie des P. Karl Egger, S.J., "Aus meinem Leben", pp. 48–63 and cf. Egger, *Seele im Sturm*.

23 EAM, NL Faulhaber, Ktn. 6777: Letter, April 8, 1916 from Major Loibl, 6. Bay. Res. Div.

24 Haugeneder, *Gestern noch auf stolzen Rossen*, 13–27.

an imagined more harmonious social order. In this myth of the eternal return, the Catholic Church would provide organic social stability in place of other organizations, which had proved a corrupt form of secular modernity.[25] From a military hospital in 1918, Max Peinkofer of the 13th Bavarian Reserve Infantry Regiment wrote to Bishop Michael von Faulhaber that, "should our people emerge refined from this test," it would be "necessary to return again to the old and only foundation of social harmony, of belief in God, of true labor, of simplicity, and of customary ways of life that are all outgrowths that a degenerate culture has sloughed off."[26] Notions of degenerate culture and the perceived need to return to a nostalgic world of purer values would resonate in interwar Central Europe among peoples from the losing powers.

Deep into the war, religious soldiers tended to vent their frustrations not at religion in general but at classes of authority figures, such as officers and the rich. The *Landsturm* soldier Michael Panni from Budweis, serving with the 45th Landsturm Infantry Regiment in the Austrian Army in Serbia and later Italy, aimed his frustrations at officers, particularly the major of his regiment. Suffering vicious campaigns, Panni decried meaningless drills and senselessly imposed authority. After one more seemingly insufferable task in July 1917, Panni cursed, "The Devil take the entire military, and the officers and their helpers especially!" Yet the condemnation of authority did not extend to religious authority figures – not even the chaplains who were so heavily associated with the military and the officers. For Panni, the dichotomy of religious belief and skepticism about military authority was encapsulated in the events surrounding a June 29, 1917 battlefield Mass. After the Mass, he received in the name of the Kaiser a silver second-class medal for bravery, upon which he commented, "I wasn't very pleased about it. For this purpose, I've experienced too many terrible things." Later, however, he wrote in his diary that he prayed deeply in earnest. Throughout his diary, his reasons for doing so highlight key themes that kept religious soldiers believing: the desire to see their families again and the desire for peace.[27] As long as he survived, the religious soldier clung to hope: a belief that he could survive the horrors of war to rejoin his family and see his homeland in peace again. Family and peace were powerful motivations not to lose

---

[25] See the war diary of Jakob Eberhard, quoted in Ziemann, *Front und Heimat*, 257.

[26] EAM, NL Faulhaber, Ktn. 6777: Letter, January 2, 1918, Max Peinkofer, Schulverweser aus Tittling bei Passau, Gefreiter im 13. bayr. Res. Inf. Regt., 1. Marsch.-Gew.-Komp., z.Z. Kriegslazarett 122, an Faulhaber.

[27] Michael Panni, *Das Tagebuch des Michael Panni. Kriegserlebnisse aus dem Ersten Weltkrieg*, ed. Peter Wendlandt (Rottenburg am Neckar: Mauer Verlag, 2009), 171–7.

faith – a theme that found vivid expression in army trench newspapers.[28] Other strong Catholic factors also aided the soldiers' strong desire for peace and a return to normalcy.

Organized churches/authorities

In contrast to the blatant power politics of one-sided throne-and-altar alliances of previous centuries, during the Great War the Vatican became a more impartial actor focused on humanitarian concerns and the search for peace. Although this was partially through the need to aid refugees and war victims, the new Vatican policy also happened in no small measure indirectly, resulting from the mutual suspicion of the warring powers.[29] Yet the Vatican's efforts and mere existence served as powerful transnational symbols of peace, which soldiers and civilians could aspire toward even in the darkest hours. Furthermore, the Catholic transnationalism showed a movement away from the August 1914 experiences of jingoism toward a more universal interpretation of war and the desire for peace. One can trace this not only through the evolution of public discourses in Catholic periodicals such as *Reichspost* and *Kölnische Volkszeitung*, but also through micro-level correspondence. For instance, the Austrian soldier Kurt Döhl, a farmer and later teacher and tailor from Tyrol, wrote in his diary of the heady days of the war's initial phase, when he was caught up in national hatred. Döhl railed against the French in particular: "O God, stand by us and save us from the un-humans[*Unmenschen*]. They are not worth pardon, they must be beaten down like wild animals." After facing the horrors of battle, however, Döhl's attitudes shifted, with the Catholic Church providing the means for reconciliation in the midst of war. Döhl wrote in his diary of the upcoming day of prayer decreed by the pope, February 7, 1915, copying the Vatican's words directly: "His Holiness Benedict XV, dejected by the view of the storm of war that smashes young life, throws families and cities into despair, and sucks the leading nations into its whirlwind . . . orders presently that in the whole Catholic world humble prayers be brought toward the Lord, in order to invoke from His mercy the desired peace." Döhl wrote that on this pan-European day

---

[28] "Crucifixus," *Der Champagne-Kamerad. Feldzeitung der 3. Armee* January 7, 1917, p. 2; "Heimkehr," *Der Champagne-Kamerad. Feldzeitung der 3. Armee* December 31, 1916, p. 2. For an overview of peasant longings for home, see Ziemann, *Front und Heimat*, 230–46.

[29] John F. Pollard, *The Unknown Pope: Benedict XV (1914–1922) and the Pursuit of Peace* (London: Geoffrey Chapman, 1999). See also Atkin and Tallett, *Priests, Prelates, and People*, 195–203. The substance of the Holy See's efforts will be explored more thoroughly in Chapter 6.

of Catholic prayer for peace, the ceremonies would consist of the 51st Psalm *Miserere mei Deus* (*da pacem*), a saying of the rosary, and a liturgy from the Roman Missal, to be followed by individual personal devotions of 40 hours of prayer.[30]

During the war, the Vatican also continued to try to tame popular religion, with limited success. Acknowledging the force of popular belief, Church authorities at the same time attempted to steer devotions toward hierarchically-approved channels, perhaps most famously in the case of the Marian apparitions at Fátima, Portugal, in 1917.[31] Especially given the rise of Marian apparitions on the battlefield, the Vatican approved specific forms of Marian devotion for Bavaria. Addressed to Cardinal von Bettinger of Munich, Benedict XV granted a special apostolic bless-ing to Bavaria acknowledging its special devotion to Mary, along with the injunction to "pray to Mary as the Mother of Peace."[32] The Church tried to retain explicit control over all devotionals by offering dispensa-tional blessings approved through the local Ordinaries of the combatant nations.[33] The Archdiocese of Vienna banned activities such as séances that gave more freedom to women as spiritual authority figures. Even approved Catholic cults like the Sacred Heart tried to limit the influence of female prophets and visionaries, such as the seventy-year-old Barbara Weigand from Schippach.[34] Female seers and stigmatics were especially threatening to the Catholic patriarchy, and Catholic women used their special status as a form of resistance, creating authority within patriarchal structures.[35]

As throughout much of European history, forms of popular devotion headed in directions that did not always agree with the Church's approved decrees. Faced with overwhelming evidence of folk piety outside of cleri-cal channels, Church authorities in Munich attempted to curtail the use

---

[30] Kurt Döhl, Dokumentationsarchiv Lebensgeschichtlicher Aufzeichnungen, Uni Wien, "Kleine Kronik vom verhängnisvollen Kriegsjahre 1914," Tagebuch, "Der Bettag am 7. Februar 1915," pp. 20–2.

[31] For a seminal study of the attempts to control the popular religiosity of Marian visions in Germany, see Blackbourn, *Marpingen*.

[32] *Acta Apostolicae Sedis*, 8:394.

[33] Anon., "Ablass für den Friedensgebet des Heiligen Vaters," *Wiener Diözesanblatt* (1915), 36–7. Cf. *Acta Apostolicae Sedis*, 7:66.

[34] Anon., "Spiritismus. Teilnahme an solchen Sitzungen verboten," *Wiener Diözesanblatt* (1917), 90; Claudia Schlager, *Kult und Krieg. Herz Jesu – Sacré Cœur – Christus Rex im deutsch-französischen Vergleich, 1914–1925* (Tübingen: Tübinger Vereinigung für Volks-kunde, 2011), 290–306. The subject of female religious authority will be explored in the next chapter.

[35] Anna Maria Zumholz, "Die Resistenz des katholischen Milieus: Seherinnen und Stig-matisierte in der ersten Hälfte des 20. Jahrhunderts," in *Wunderbare Erscheinungen. Frauen und katholische Frömmigkeit im 19. und 20. Jahrhundert*, ed. Irmtraud Götz von Olenhusen (Paderborn: Ferdinand Schöningh, 1995), 221–51.

of *Schutzbriefe* and "prayers with miraculous promises" (*Gebete mit wunderbaren Verheißungen*) by condemning these as "irrational superstitions" and shaming Bavarian Catholics into changing their behavior. The General Vicar of Munich-Freising wrote that, "Whenever Catholics spread such things, they sin not simply through superstition, but rather they also place their Church and Catholic soldiers in danger of mockery."[36] At least some Catholic soldiers harbored similar views about upholding collective dignity. Writing to the Archdiocesan Ordinary on Christmas Eve 1916, the *Gefreiter* Max Reitberger complained of chain letters (*Kettenbriefe*), also called snowball prayers (*Schneeballgebete*), arriving at the front from home, which promised that a good event would happen if the chain of recipients was not broken. Reitberger dismissed such letters as "superstition" and "frivolity," noting that they "brought forth only scoffing, not least because they make the worst possible impression on those of other faiths."[37] On the whole, however, chain letters continued to be sent as people clung to whatever hope and sense of good fortune they thought they could obtain through their own personal action.[38]

Even contemporaneous studies of superstition written from a Catholic perspective noted the cultural relativism and personal perspectives inherent in trying to classify superstition and religion.[39] At least in hindsight, the Jesuit Karl Egger, as a military chaplain and thus an enforcer of the Church's law at a micro-level on the battlefield, noted the difficulties of trying to distinguish "superstition" from "true faith."[40]

As seen in the previous chapter, in the age of industrial warfare the official representatives of organized religion at the battlefront, the military chaplains, could not provide adequate religious ministry to the vast numbers of soldiers. Accordingly, Catholic soldiers improvised their own forms of devotion with adapted Catholic elements of rural traditionalism. In the words of the German priest and Catholic polemicist Georg Pfeilschifter, Catholic soldiers led their own "prayers and services in order to replace the sacramental Mass of the Priest." Sometimes with the permission of their officers and sometimes on their own initiative, Catholic soldiers erected small chapels and Marian altars, similar to the local ones

---

[36] Anon., "Verbreitung von abergläubischen Gebeten und sekterischen Schriften betr.," *Amtsblatt für die Erzdiözese München und Freising* 1917, 30.

[37] EAM, Ordinariat, Kriegsseelsorge 1914–18, "Kriegsseelsorge in der Heimat," Letter, December 24, 1916, Gefr. Max Reitberger (Im Felde), an das Ordinariat M-F.

[38] Bächtold, *Deutscher Soldatenbrauch*, 22–3.

[39] Bruno Grabinski, *Neuere Mystik. Der Weltkrieg im Aberglauben und im Lichte der Prophetie* (Hildesheim: Franz Borgmeyer, 1916), 43.

[40] Egger, *Seele im Sturm*, 141–4.

Figure 4 Trench grotto (BfZ)
"Soldiers created their own forms of devotion, such as this grotto hol-
lowed out beneath the trenches."

found near roadsides across rural Europe. Especially in reserve positions
far from the front (and from staging areas in which military chaplains
could be found), the so-called "forest chapels" provided opportunities
for religious soldiers to exercise a form of devotion that was at once
individual and yet unmistakably Catholic.[41] Pfeilschifter was a Catholic
priest at the forefront of German Catholic ideological campaigns during
the war. He wrote from the standpoint of a convinced believer, trying
to demonstrate the justness of the German cause and the persistence
of German faith. His edited collections, despite polemical assumptions
combating French clergy on the persistence of faith, are nonetheless an
invaluable source of religiously-themed letters that would otherwise be
lost to history. These collections hint at ways in which believing Christian
soldiers exercised their faith as they saw fit.

[41] Georg Pfeilschifter, "Seelsorge und religiöses Leben im deutschen Heere," in *Deutsche
Kultur, Katholizismus und Weltkrieg: Eine Abwehr des Buches, La guerre allemande et le
catholicisme*, ed. Georg Pfeilschifter (Freiburg im Breisgau: Herder, 1915), 248f.

Connections with the home front

Although it may seem overly sentimental to the modern reader, early twentieth-century romanticism was found in many Great War love letters, which were also redolent with religious phrases. One should not underestimate the power of love to those who believed in it: across Europe, belief in a union of souls existed beyond the horrors of the trenches and defied death itself, helping both soldiers and civilians endure the war.[42] Even for the losing powers, religiously-themed love was not a simplistic unquestioned reflexive piety. As correspondence between husbands and wives demonstrates, subtle forms of faith and perseverance developed during the war, in spite of destruction and widespread discontent. In September 1916, the Tyrolean soldier Adolf Gabmair wrote home to his wife, Maria, affectionately calling her "sweet Moidl":

Now it's already the second time that I had to celebrate [the feast of the Assumption of the Virgin Mary] in the field. It is now half past eight o'clock in Tulfes, where the celebratory church service is and unfortunately, I cannot take part; I must just take part in my thoughts. Yet I hope that your immaculate prayer finds elevation to God that nothing really bad can happen to me!

In war, there is overall lying, stealing, robbing, breaking marriage bonds, delinquency, slander of customs! He that doesn't do it isn't worth much, so it appears! Dear Moidl! I must be more reserved. I went too far, but see one does that when the holy war became a robbers' war [*der heilige Krieg zu einem Räuberkrieg gekommen ist*]! Now we should know again to stop hoping for something new to begin; it began once and it also will one day cease – as God wants![43]

Even as the "holy war" turned sour, Gabmair's Catholic beliefs helped him to make sense of the events. His devotion to the Virgin Mary during the Feast of the Assumption not only connected him to the idealized feminine homefront piety of his wife but also reinforced the notion of Christian sacrifice, as the dolorous Virgin Mother grieved over Christ her son, and by extension, all the fighting, fallen soldiers. In any case, despite doubts about the course the war had taken for Austria-Hungary, Gabmair retained belief in a Divine Providence that would one day cause the war to end.

Homefront correspondence also traveled to the battlefront, revealing the facets of total war. Published in the newspaper *Armeeblatt*, Barbara Moskirchner wrote to her husband Johann of her struggles to keep the

---

[42] Martha Hanna, *Your Death Would Be Mine: Paul and Marie Pireaud in the Great War* (Cambridge, MA: Harvard University Press, 2006).

[43] TLA, TLVA, Fasz. II, Feldpostbrief, Adolf Gabmair an seine Frau, Maria, in Hall, 10. September 1916. See also F. F., "Briefe eines Okkupationsoldaten" *Hochland* 15 (1917): 206–14

family farm going alone: "In the beginning it burdened me a bit hard. But I thought to myself: grit your teeth, Barbara . . . I will do it with God's support alone. And so it was . . . My dearest [Johann], if you had seen me on the same day, how I ploughed the field for the winter crop." She continued with talk of religious devotion, reunion with her husband, and hope for victory: "My dearest [Johann], I have offered two thick wax candles to the altar of Mary, the Mother of God, that we will be able to drink the new wine with each other. Hale and victory on the battlefield! In passionate love, I remain in eternity your wife, Barbara."[44] In Barbara's mind, two main items stabilized the situation: her faith in God and her determination to hold out for her husband.

Religious women also adopted more masculine, hardened discourses of combat that emphasized the homefront as an arena of battle, albeit in the sense of communal contests of wills. Ways of speech emphasized soldierly virtues and military language. Andrea Hartl of Graz repeatedly referred to her "trust in prayer as a weapon." Hartl wrote in her diary of the absolute necessity of homefront belief: "So that all the victims would not be passed over, we too in the homeland are obliged with duty to hold out [*durchzuhalten*] despite all needs."[45] Periodical publications such as the Austro-Hungarian *Armeeblatt* asserted that civilians were "spiritual co-combatants" (*Geistige Mitkämpfer*) who would provide "moral reserves" to strengthen the cause of victory by reinforcing moral and ethical determination.[46] Even under the harsh occupation by the encroaching German military state, religious women such as Eugène Delahaye-Théry of Lille believed that the power of their faith was a moral weapon that could be used in their defense.[47]

Soldiers adapted personal elements of superstition and folk practice in the hope that this would preserve their lives. In so doing, they retained their connections to their families and returned to a sense of pre-war normalcy. Thus, superstition was bonded with a longing for home. Soldiers marched off to war longing for homefront connections, and it was rural

---

[44] "Barbara Moskirchner an den Korporal Johann Moskirchner," *Armeeblatt*, February 12, 1916, p. 5f.

[45] Andrea Hartl Tagebuch, Dokumentationsarchiv Lebensgeschichtlicher Aufzeichnungen, Uni Wien, 1914–1918.

[46] "Geistige Mitkaempfer,"*Armeeblatt*, March 4, 1916; "Moralische Reserven," *Armeeblatt*, January 8, 1916, p. 3f.

[47] For her diary of religious suffering under occupation, see Eugène Delahaye-Théry, *Les Cahiers Noirs. Notes quotidiennes écrites d'October 1914 à Novembre 1918 par une Lilloise sous l'occupation allemande* (Rennes: Éditions de la Province, 1934). For an overview of the religious dynamics of occupation, see Patrick J. Houlihan, "Local Catholicism as Transnational War Experience: Daily Religious Life in Occupied Northern France, 1914–1918," *Central European History* 45, no. 2 (2012): 233–67. Accessible at http://dx.doi.org/10.1017/S0008938912000040 (last accessed October 31, 2014).

peasant folk culture that provided strongly traditional ways of maintaining these bonds. These often drew on established Catholic motifs and practices, but also incorporated individual idiosyncrasies, some of which were directly forbidden by the official Church. For soldiers dropped for the first time into a world of strong masculine martial virtues apart from the world of domesticity, such traditions maintained ties to an idealized femininity and family on the homefront. These soldiers sometimes wore their mother's wedding ring on their right hand, or carried a lock of hair from their beloved. Other times they wore either yarn spun by a young girl or clothing or a homespun cross made out of such yarn. In certain instances, the demands could be quite specific, such as shirts spun by a seven-year-old girl, known as "emergency shirts" or "St. George shirts" in the Franco-Prussian War but now styled and mass-produced as "victory shirts." Such homefront objects could also be more literally and figuratively earthy, such as dirt from the home parish or teeth removed at midnight from the church graveyard, carried as a talisman of mortality and hopeful ties to homefront religiosity.[48] The exchange of these items between homefront and battle zone proceeded in both directions.

Requests for such items touched on folk beliefs that could be quite pointed in their demands. In July 1915, Minna Falkenhain wrote the following to her husband, then in Russia: "My dear, good husband and good-hearted father! Today I found out from an old woman that there's protection for you. I should always wear a few hairs from you. Please be so good and cut some from you and send them to me in a letter." The advice from the old woman was more explicit than one might first imagine. Frau Falkenhain specified, "[The hairs] however must be from below your stomach: you know, of course, from your genitals. [The hairs] must be approximately half a measure long. If I had already known that when you were here, it would have been better. Please cut some and send them to me."[49] Explicit intimacy revealed love and faith on a micro-level.

At the battlefront, the believing soldier felt cut off from his family network, and his imagination could run wild. At all hours of day and night, the superstitious soldiers saw events ripe for interpretation. Meeting someone from outside of the ordinary military routine, such as an old woman or young boy, could be interpreted as an omen of good or ill fortune. Interactions with animals provided other sources of premonition:

---

[48] Bächtold, *Deutscher Soldatenbrauch*, 11–12, 23.

[49] Letter of July 16, 1915, Minna Falkenhain to her husband, quoted in Frank Schumann, ed., *"Zieh Dich warm an!" Soldatenpost und Heimatbriefe aus zwei Weltkriegen. Chronik einer Familie* (Berlin: Neues Leben, 1989), 51–2. The Falkenhains were Protestants, but their folk practices typify a rural peasant culture that was, statistically speaking, a decisively Catholic majority in Central, Eastern, and Southern Europe.

while domesticated animals like dogs and cows could be a sign of good luck, a wild rabbit crossing one's path, a nearby howling fox, and especially the appearance of a raven could be ill omens of death, especially in the days preceding a major planned military action.[50]

Believers wore items into battle that both reminded them of their pre-war domestic connections and provided them with comfort in their new environment. Both Catholic and Protestant believers carried the Bible or short Biblical texts. The opening verses of the Gospel of John were a popular choice: "In the beginning was the Word, and the Word was with God, and the Word was God. / He was in the beginning with God. / All things came to be through him, and without him nothing came to be. What came to be through him was life, and this life was the light of the human race; / the light shines in the darkness, and the darkness has not overcome it." So too was the 91st Psalm, known as the "Soldier's Psalm" in many countries. This short psalm reads:

> You who dwell in the shelter of the Most High, who abide in the
>   shadow of the Almighty
> Say to the LORD, "My refuge and fortress, my God in whom I trust."
> God will rescue you from the fowler's snare, from the destroying
>   plague,
> Will shelter you with pinions, spread wings that you may take refuge;
> God's faithfulness is a protecting shield.
> You shall not fear the terror of the night nor the arrow that flies by day,
> Nor the pestilence that roams in darkness, nor the plague that ravages
>   at noon.
> Though a thousand fall at your side, ten thousand at your right hand,
>   near you it shall not come.
>   . . .
> No evil shall befall you, no affliction come near your tent.
> For God commands the angels to guard you in all your ways.
> With their hands they shall support you, lest you strike your foot
>   against a stone.
>   . . .
> All who call upon me I will answer; I will be with them in distress; I
>   will deliver them and give them honor.
> With length of days I will satisfy them and show them my saving
>   power.[51]

The power of the word of God was especially reinforced whenever the physical text prevented bullets or shrapnel from causing a soldier physical harm. Bibles were often carried in pockets directly over the heart, which

[50] Bächtold, *Deutscher Soldatenbrauch*, 13–14.
[51] Donald Senior and John J. Collins, eds., *The Catholic Study Bible*, 2nd edn. (New York: Oxford University Press, 2006), 749–50.

offered at least a few more layers of padding in a vital area. Verses were also placed inside a scapular and worn around the neck, or else carried inside a pocket so they would be easily reachable in times of distress.[52] Especially prominent in the cult of the Sacred Heart of Jesus, the scapular was an officially sanctioned Catholic amulet, consisting of a consecrated cloth pendant that brought protection to its wearer through indulgence of sins.[53]

Certainly, Biblical texts provided comfort to many Christian soldiers, but Catholic soldiers also had other options.

Hail Mary: intercession and sainthood

The figure of Christ on the battlefield, especially visiting dying soldiers or supervising a victorious battle scene, was a common Christian motif. Catholicism added further layers of belief, with patron saints and intercessory figures providing a plethora of protective agents that could be invoked in times of distress. This combated the atomizing anomie of industrial warfare, reinforcing to the soldier that he was bound up within a larger spiritual community of past, present, and future believers. With legions of angels in support, the intercessory culture also reinforced the bonds of family and the wish to return home.

Saint Joseph was a key figure for soldiers, due to his role as the spouse of Mary and foster father of Christ; he was the patron saint of fathers and of a happy death. Karl Döhl, an Austrian Catholic soldier from Tyrol, wrote in his diary a war prayer (*Kriegsgebet*) in which he declared, "St. Joseph, you special patron of the dying, go on the battlefields to the dying soldiers who must die alone and forgotten, comfort them, protect them, and lead them mercifully in the heavenly Fatherland."[54]

However, masculine piety had its limits, and it was especially here that Catholicism tapped into feminine reserves of religious comfort. As the mother of Jesus and a highly influential figure in a system of dolorous consolation, the Virgin Mary was the most frequently implored saint in the Catholic religious pantheon. One should underscore the Marian aspects as a special Catholic avenue of devotion. As the original mother of sorrow over the crucified Christ, to the Catholic imagination Mary represented a figure of immense comfort who was central to the Catholic belief system. She was frequently invoked by Catholic soldiers seeking the comforts of home and the mourning community of families in Christian belief.

---

[52] Bächtold, *Deutscher Soldatenbrauch*, 17.   [53] Schlager, *Kult und Krieg.*
[54] Karl Döhl, Dokumentationsarchiv Lebensgeschichtlicher Aufzeichnungen, 1914–1918, Uni Wien. Tagebuch, p. 21.

Figure 5 Christ and the dying soldier (Rudl)
"Christ and the saints were believed to intercede to comfort the dying."

Figure 6 Field-altar Madonna (Lipusch)
"The 'Kaiserjäger Madonna' by Lieutenant Emanuel Raffeiner demonstrated a localized devotion to the Virgin Mary This was especially
important for Tyrolean identity on a regimental level – in this case for
the 1st Tyrolean Kaiserjäger Regiment."

The gendered role of the Virgin Mary as a feminine protector of families was central to Marian devotion and of vital importance for Catholics seeking to understand the Great War. In the context of the war, this meant that Mary was the symbolic figure that united homefront and battlefront at a more human level, based on family relationships. Although the figure of Jesus Christ was of course central to Christian beliefs, the notion of Christ's partial divinity as an aspect of God could be a conceptual stumbling block for imploring believers. In contrast, Mary, as the pinnacle of the intercessory saint culture, provided a more accessible notion of a protector. Holy Mary, Mother of God, was fully human and yet in contact with the Divine Master of the Universe, represented through her son, Jesus Christ. The Mother of God was a powerful consoling figure for Catholic soldiers and their families, especially in the popular piety of rural regions in Central Europe.[55]

With the aid of tangible objects such as the rosary and scapular, Catholic soldiers sought the protection of the Virgin Mary, often by reciting the Hail Mary (Ave Maria) prayer: "Hail Mary, full of grace. The Lord is with You. Blessed are You among women, and blessed is the fruit of Your womb, Jesus. Holy Mary, Mother of God, pray for us sinners, now and at the hour of our death. Amen." Ritual aids to prayer such as the rosary prayer beads often had a practical aspect: they allowed the believer to pray during long winter nights and in darkness, especially when reading light was not available in the trenches.[56]

For some Catholics, it could be hard to pray to Mary, at least before the war. The battlefield violence, however, made even many aggressively masculine soldiers long for home and its motherly comforts. A forty-three-year-old farmer turned soldier wrote from his post at the front in the Vosges Mountains that, "Even some men and boys who before the war scoffed at the pious and the rosary hurried now again to church, visited the May devotions and before the picture of the Queen of May let the rosary glide through their fingers. Yes, the war is a hard, but for some a good school . . . " Such testimonials of the "return to religion" describe emotional scenes in which groups of bearded men openly wept with each other. Worship of Mary could even reconcile Protestants and Catholics: one Catholic lieutenant recalled an occasion in 1916 when a patrol of Protestant soldiers went on a special mission to rescue a picture of Mary

---

[55] Ziemann, *Front und Heimat*, 257–8. See Michael Mitterauer, "'Nur diskret ein Kreuzze-ichen.' Zu Formen des individuellen und gemeinschaftlichen Gebets in der Familie," in *Religion und Alltag. Interdisziplinäre Beiträge zu einer Sozialgeschichte des Katholizismus in lebensgeschichtlicher Aufzeichnungen*, ed. Andreas Heller, Therese Weber, and Olivia Wiebel-Fandel (Vienn: Böhlau, 1990), 181–8.
[56] Ziemann, *Front und Heimat*, 257.

from a damaged chapel threatening to collapse; they brought the picture
to the lieutenant and claimed it should be placed in the trenches: "We are
Protestants, but that is the picture of the mother of that God to whom
we also pray."[57] As Annette Becker has noted, to escape the terrors of
battle during the Great War, soldiers rediscovered women's religion and
the comforts of childhood.[58]

Marian devotions occurred throughout the calendar year but were particularly acute in the month of May. Symbolically primed at the beginning
of the year, the Feast of Mary, Mother of God took place every January 1.
The Feast of the Annunciation on March 25 (nine months before the
birth of Jesus) was another highlight. Throughout the year, soldiers at
the front lines dug grottos to Mary in the trenches, often adorning the
improvised niche altars with fresh flowers. For some soldiers, these grottos became oases where believers could gather to collect their thoughts
and spend a few minutes in repose, refreshing their minds before carrying
on with their duties.[59] Marian devotions surged in May, the "Month of
Mary," with Mary the "Queen of May" (*Maienkönigin*). During that time,
Catholic soldiers erected numerous May Altars devoted specifically to the
worship of statues and pictures of Mary, adorned with lily-of-the-valley
(*Maiglöckchen*) and sprigs of evergreen trees. During communal services,
German Catholic soldiers sang May songs to Mary and prayed the rosary
together.[60] To many Catholics, the Marian apparitions in Fátima, Portugal, that began in May 1917 signaled that the Mother of God heard the
suffering of war-torn Europe and was advocating for peace.[61]

The devotions to Mary continued through the rest of the year. Especially important for soldiers facing omnipresent death was the June 27
Feast of Our Lady of Perpetual Help, followed by the Feast of the
Assumption (i.e., Mary's ascension into Heaven) on August 15. The
more dolorous aspects of Marian worship were celebrated on September 15, the Feast of Our Lady of Sorrows. Finally, the Marian calendar

---

[57] Herr V., Letter of May 1915, "Hochvogesen," quoted in Georg Pfeilschifter, ed., *Feld-
briefe katholischer Soldaten*, 3 vols. (Freiburg im Breisgau: Herder, 1918), 1:112–13.
Echoing the sentiments of Kaiser Wilhelm II at the outbreak of the war, they continued,
"And in war, there are no parties . . . " For Protestant approaches to Marian worship,
see Dr. Lorenz Krapp, Letter of June 1916, quoted in Pfeilschifter, *Feldbriefe katholischer
Soldaten*, 1:114–18.

[58] Becker, "Faith, Ideologies," 241.

[59] Leander Schirlinger, letter of November 17, 1915, quoted in Pfeilschifter, *Feldbriefe
katholischer Soldaten*, 1:113–14. Schirlinger was a Benedictine lay brother writing to his
Prior.

[60] Herr V., Letter of May 1915, "Hochvogesen," quoted in Pfeilschifter, *Feldbriefe katholischer Soldaten*, 1:112–13.

[61] Blackbourn, *Marpingen*, 327–8.

came to its yearly conclusion with the December 8 Feast of the Immaculate Conception, the controversial anti-modernist dogma of Pope Pius IX declaring that Mary, and hence also Jesus Christ, was conceived without original sin. These were only some of the most significant Marian holy days. Catholic worship to Mary found ample days for devotion throughout the year.

The intercessory culture of Catholicism also provided a huge array of other saints whom believers could invoke to help them endure. Saints could be called upon for a variety of reasons. Some Catholics invoked a personal patron saint with whom they had identified since childhood. For some soldiers and their families, a local saint from home, such as Saint Nepomuk for regions of Austria and Bohemia, or a saint associated with family tradition, proved the best option. For others, saints associated with particular virtues or causes were the focus of prayer. More peculiar to the battlefield conditions of the Great War, Saint Sebastian, a patron saint of soldiers, usually depicted with his body bound and pierced with the arrows of Roman soldiers, was frequently invoked. The figure of Saint Sebastian also emphasized a Christian spiritual dimension that went beyond military authority. Saint Jude, the patron saint of hopeless causes, was another key figure. Certain groups of soldiers had their own particular saints; for example, Saint Barbara was associated with artillerymen and trench diggers: one trench bore the inscription, "St. Barbara, help us in need / Give us victory – and death to the enemy."[62] More ideologically national saints, such as Saint Michael for the Germans and Saint Wenceslas for the (Catholic) Czechs and Slovaks, also received increased devotion during the war. In such cases, a militant masculinity generally predominated. However, particularly in the case of Saint Michael, this masculinity could generate hostility among believers, when they perceived it as aggression directed toward a lost cause in the latter phases of the war.[63] There was certainly room for symbolic conceptual tension between the saintly associations of militancy and consolation, but as lived experience, what mattered most was the saints' symbolism in the minds of individual believers.

---

[62] Ernst Moritz Kronfeld, *Der Krieg im Aberglauben und Volksglauben kulturhistorische Beiträge* (München: Schmidt, 1915), 73.

[63] For a current table of patron saints, see http://www.catholic.org/saints/patron.php (last accessed October 31, 2014). For ideologically national uses of the saint cult, see Thomas Fliege, "'Mein Deutschland sei mein Engel Michael'. Sankt Michael als nationalreligiöser Mythos," in Korff, *Alliierte im Himmel*, 159–99; Cynthia J. Paces, "Religious Heroes for a Secular State: Commemorating Jan Hus and Saint Wenceslas in 1920s Czechoslovakia," in *Staging the Past: The Politics of Commemoration in Habsburg Central Europe, 1848 to the Present*, ed. Maria Bucur and Nancy M. Wingfield (West Lafayette, IN: Purdue University Press, 2001), 209–35.

Soldiers' Christian and quasi-religious prayers could also be invoked to harm the enemy. One Marian amulet bore the inscription, "If you wear this holy sign / every enemy will yield before you."[64] Chanting curses were designed to rob the opponent of their will and means of fighting. Similarly, blessed weapons could have a sign of the cross scratched or painted upon them, or could be touched with a piece of consecrated bread or even communion host to ensure a solid hit.[65] Most Catholic military chaplains denied that Church-sanctioned blessing of weapons by clergymen actually occurred, arguing that they were blessing the overarching cause, not the implements.[66] Some chaplains, however, were willing not only to bless weapons but even to participate in combat, taking up arms and killing enemy troops (see Chapter 3). In any event, widespread reports of the blessing of weapons continued, reflecting a popular consciousness that did not recognize the Church's distinction between means and ends.

The intercessory saint culture so prominent in Catholicism had a powerful attraction for those who believed in it: it helped them to deal with the suffering and chaos that the war unleashed and strengthened ties between homefront and battlefront, uniting soldiers and their families. Intercessory pleas continued to pour in to Vienna in 1918, even as the monarchy was collapsing, citizens were starving, and Austria-Hungary, the Catholic monarchy, was doomed to defeat and a place in the dustbin of history.[67] Folk practices continued to affirm belief in Divine Providence and saintly intercession for both individuals and their families. One example is the practices of the Judas Thaddäus cult of the Apostles, which dated to early modern times and experienced a surge in the nineteenth century, alongside the cult of the Sacred Heart. During and after the Great War, thousands of votive tablets left at the Kirche Am Hof and the Minoritenkloster in Alserstrasse, for example, contained imploring messages such as this one, written by an anonymous woman in 1918: "From extreme gratitude for Your intervention, through which my husband returned home from the war healthy. O, St. Anthony, please help us further."[68] Even though the throne had fallen, many Christian believers continued to uphold their faith after the war. Instead of focusing on the dead, one must look at the survivors. It is here that family histories shed light on religious belief structures, as many believing Christians did not care about the monarchy or a national or imperial cause; they were happy just to get their family members back alive.

---

[64] Kronfeld, *Der Krieg*, 73.   [65] Bächtold, *Deutscher Soldatenbrauch*, 25–7.
[66] Lipusch, *Österreich-Ungarns katholische Militärseelsorge*, 100.
[67] For a recent vivid portrait of Vienna's collapse, see Healy, *Vienna*.
[68] Herbert Nikitsch, "'... den unsern Jammer, der anders brennt.' Verortungen des Judas Thaddäus-Verehrung im Ersten Weltkrieg und 'in unserer Zeit,'" in Korff, *Alliierte im Himmel*, 238–9.

Regarding these family histories, some believers who had lost loved ones certainly found it more difficult to continue believing; for others, however, a Christian notion of heroic sacrifice was the only way to mourn the loss.[69] Many religious believers attributed their survival, or the survival of their loved ones, to divine intervention at a personal level, prompted by a Catholic notion of intercession and familial aid. At any rate, individual family histories suggest a plethora of individualized beliefs.

Individual practices

Many individual beliefs could be labeled "superstitious" according to certain viewpoints. One German soldier in the trenches, for example, realizing that it was the thirteenth day of the month, became convinced that he would be killed that day unless he sacrificed thirteen flies. He accomplished his goal, and, in his own mind at least, saved his life.[70] The military psychiatrist Ludwig Scholz observed numerous soldiers attempting to ward off bullets and shells by declaiming a variety of words and performing numerous actions.[71]

Even when dismissive of the idea of persisting religiosity at the battle-front, most military psychological studies agree that in the heat of battle, soldiers' personal rites were often explicitly Christian. Such studies report that the Lord's Prayer, the "Our Father," was the most commonly used form of protective prayer.[72] For the believing soldier, religious conviction provided a way of coping with the harsh pressures of combat. Especially in the face of omnipresent death, religion also provided a rationalization of why one survived. As in the case of the Austro-Hungarian soldier Michael Panni, the simple prayer "God protect me!" uttered in the heat of combat was a reflexive action for the believer that could turn into a post-battle explanation of survival as well as a hope for the future.[73]

In many cases, the believer's pre-war conception of God proved resilient, adapted to the new battlefield environment. For instance, the Grenadier Franz Meier wrote to an acquaintance at home that he had survived "some difficult hours" throughout the war due to what he attributed as "God's protection and help [that] was with me and my

---

[69] For the inescapability of religious motifs as cultural elements necessary for the mourning of the war's extensive losses by European society, see the classic example of Winter, *Sites of Memory*.

[70] Plaut, "Psychographie des Kriegers," 78–9.

[71] Ludwig Scholz, *Seelenleben des Soldaten an der Front: hinterlassene Aufzeichnungen des im Kriege gefallenen Nervenarztes* (Tübingen: J. C. B. Mohr, 1920), 180.

[72] Ludwig, "Beiträge zur Psychologie," 170–1; Plaut, "Psychographie des Kriegers," 74.

[73] Panni, *Das Tagebuch des Michael Panni*, 62.

comrades."[74] Especially when they came through a particularly harsh battle, soldiers attributed their survival to the persistence of divine favor. A sergeant major and Iron Cross-winner serving near Pozières wrote to his siblings, "Don't worry too much. The old, good God yet lives! What befalls me comes from Him."[75] Similarly, Gotthard Gruber wrote in his diary of long-term motivations as the primary factor putting him back into combat: "The thought which always put me personally back on my feet was that a God of Love stands behind everything."[76] In related circumstances, contemplating a 1916 transfer to the Somme, which had already acquired a reputation for carnage beyond the normal, Arthur Meier noted that, "even in this case, I trust in our omnipotent and all-loving God, who guides everything for the best."[77] Throughout the war, any singular instance of a near-miss of a bullet or shell could be interpreted as divine intervention, such as when Kurt Reiter wrote in his diary that, "the dear God mercifully protected me."[78]

In such cases, an ecumenical Christian faith animated the sentiments of the believers. One should not diminish the power of Protestantism to console, especially compared with the lack of alternatives available to the soldier with metaphysical beliefs. Yet, looking at many soldiers' testimonials, one can observe the extra measure of tangible consolation that Catholic beliefs could provide. On the eve of the opening of the Somme offensive, a nineteen-year-old bank official named Hans Fritz wrote that he was delivering messages to the foremost front lines because the communication cables had been cut. He declared that he did this "only through the assistance of the Most Holy Virgin. With the rosary tight in the hand, one goes through the rain of enemy shells." In his mind, however, Fritz's faith more easily enabled him to accept the possibility that he might be killed. Regarding his persistent survival, he wrote, "Whenever God's decision should be determined otherwise, now then ... I say to you hale and farewell! I'll see you again up there [in Heaven]! Do not forget me in prayer, and comfort my loved ones." On the first day of the Somme offensive, Fritz was badly wounded in action, and he died in a field hospital on July 6, 1916.[79]

[74] BA-MA, MSg 2/5800: Franz Meier, letter to Fräulein Dölker, March 19, 1917, quoted in Watson, *Enduring the Great War*, 95.

[75] Pfeilschifter, *Feldbriefe katholischer Soldaten*, 1:199, 211.

[76] DTA, 138a: Gotthard Gruber, diary, February 27, 1916, quoted in Watson, *Enduring the Great War*, 95.

[77] BA-MA, MSg 2/5799: Arthur Meier, letter to Oberpostsekretär Dölker, September 6, 1916, quoted in Watson, *Enduring the Great War*, 95.

[78] BA-MA, MSg 1/161: Kurt Reiter, diary, June 22, 1916, quoted in Watson, *Enduring the Great War*, 95.

[79] Pfeilschifter, *Feldbriefe katholischer Soldaten*, 1:195.

Other soldiers' letters similarly show faith in core Christian principles and yet also demonstrate how Catholic beliefs could provide an extra measure of comfort. While the battle of the Somme was still raging in August 1916, a German soldier who was a student of medicine wrote from near the Champagne region to the clergyman at his homefront parish, "In my breast pocket, I carry the picture of the crucified, the best example of the warrior. As Christ suffered innocently, so must we, as individuals innocent of the war, nonetheless we must patiently bear the difficulties and sufferings of the war, and should our death bring victory to the Fatherland, then he should require it of us and consequently lead us to the heavenly resurrection." The soldier then wrote that he also carried a second picture, a "'medallion of perpetual help' of our heavenly Mother. In its protection and shielding I have often trusted in the big battle. It will protect me and fortuitously lead me home." Emphasizing the power of his devotional pictures, the soldier underscored that, "In the thunder of cannons at La Boiselle, I felt so rightly the connection between God and Man. Without trust in our Lord God, man is nothing."[80]

Some believing soldiers cleaned up their descriptions of combat in order to protect the sensibilities of their loved ones on the homefront. This was not always the case, however, and religious war letters were far from a recitation of only good, heroic victories. Precisely by describing the horrors of war in detail, believing soldiers helped to reinforce their claims that religion could exist in the worst possible circumstances imaginable. Shortly before the early-November celebrations of All Saints and All Souls, in an October 30, 1916 letter to the editors of a major German Catholic daily newspaper, a lieutenant on the Western Front noted that:

We came out of the "hell" of the Somme. There were days that, like earthquakes, nature ransacked human life... Screaming shells harshly whipped the patient Earth just as they did the uncovered bodies of men; we cowered lethargically with glazed eyes in dugout shelters, the shell hits made us reel; with nerves close to rupturing, we surged forward over open fields through merciless fragments of iron – this was not life anymore, no certain gain, an act of free will; it was spiritless existence [*geistloses Vorhandensein*].

. . .

And suddenly there stood a sunny autumn morning in the window. We went to church. Head-to-head, soldiers filled the house of God. The priest spoke and stirred up thoughts that we wanted to send to heaven when the horror was around us, when we felt rootless and dead to life. There was one power that stood by us, a spirit that protected us in unspeakable need. That flames up like the sun after the night. Devotion and trust in the Father in Heaven pulled the souls of the

[80] Ibid., 1:192–4.

graciously ransomed [*Preisgegebenen*]. They spoke to Him like pleading children. A soft cloak of protection [*Geborgensein*] wrapped around them all, they prayed to their God, not to Him who controlled nature in its great glory, who speaks as powerful Lord with lightning and thunder, storm and hail – but rather to the mild, benevolent God who tenderly feeds His children . . . [81]

There was most certainly faith in the trenches, even in the midst of slaughter. Writing from the Somme in late September 1916, an Iron Cross-winning lieutenant told his siblings of the fight for the village of Thiepval, which German forces "lost, but not through our fault," because the writer's own 77th Regiment had performed valiantly. Nevertheless, the lieutenant told his siblings that the regiment entered the fight with 612 men, of whom 12 were officers, and left with only 134 soldiers and 3 officers surviving. Instead of sanitizing his reports for his audience on the homefront, he told of being attacked by the first combat deployment of British tanks in grim detail, describing the tanks as "gigantic auto-mobiles without wheels, each equipped with six machine guns and two artillery pieces, heavily armored and flat completely around." Surviving the conflict, he reflected, "The old God yet lives, there exist miracles yet today."[82] Given that the lieutenant described his battle scenes with such vivid detail of mechanized warfare, it would have been comparatively easy for him to take the next step and question the existence of God in such an industrialized landscape of death. Yet he did not. While one cannot discern the ultimate motivations in the lieutenant's soul, one can state that either for him, for his audience on the homefront, or for everyone involved, religious belief in the continued existence of God remained a source of consolation. It was also a convenient narrative device to illumi-nate one's own survival. Those who discount miracles must nonetheless acknowledge that some people do believe in them, and live their lives based on this belief.

Amulets and talismans

As visual testimonials of their belief in the intercessory saint culture, Catholic soldiers wore a wide variety of medallions, amulets, and tal-ismans. As Benjamin Ziemann has noted, these objects reveal a mech-anistic understanding of religion, with the act of demonstrating loyalty

---

[81] *Kölnische Volkszeitung*, Nr. 874, October 30, 1916, quoted in Pfeilschifter, *Feldbriefe katholischer Soldaten*, 1:213–14.
[82] Ibid., 1:204–11.

to God through a material object causing the believer to expect protection from the deity.[83] The Catholic Church sanctioned some of these objects, such as the scapular for the cult of the Sacred Heart of Jesus.[84] The Church also tried to set limits to superstitious behavior, from the Holy See down to micro-level rural parishes such as Neuhofen, Bavaria. There, the village priest complained from the pulpit in 1915 about superstitious forms of prayer letters, and was met with "hate and persecution" from the village community after reproaching a farmer's wife who passed out superstitious letters to all departing soldiers.[85] Religious believers adapted their own practices and specialized forms of devotion.

Local customs provided pre-war connections to the homefront and adjusted to the new circumstances of war. Grounded in folk traditions, these forms of belief proved resilient to battlefield conditions. One example, "little lucky rings" (*Glücksringlein*) from the heavily-Catholic peasant region of Tyrol, were worn by people of all ages, even being placed with newborn children in the cradle. The little lucky rings followed a child through major rites of passage in life, such as baptism, confirmation, and marriage, but could also be given as special presents at other occasions, such as festivals and birthdays. At the first Tyrolian State Exhibition in 1893, the rings were described as follows: "Better than gold and gems / This little ring brings happiness . . . A ring of happiness is a true treasure / Yet mark you thereby this sentence: / Don't place in a ring alone / The hope for the future / Only when to your type of essence / The good power of the ring pairs up / Will the effort richly reward you / The magic that lives in the little happy ring." Such instances of folk piety could be adopted by official organizations of state. The Austrian War Assistance Bureau of the Ministry of the Interior managed to adapt the tradition and turn a profit. Through the initiative of the Mayor of Vienna, who organized the jewelers and metalworkers for the project, the ministry had thousands of rings made, at a price of two kronen per piece. Each ring bore the inscription "War Charm [*Kriegsglück*] 1914" and was enclosed in a small box inscribed with the phrase, "Through battle to victory, souvenir of the World War, 1914."[86]

War amulets were highly personalized as well as mass-produced. Devotional objects carried a wide variety of significance to those who carried

[83] Ziemann, *Front und Heimat*, 259–60.
[84] Norbert Busch, *Katholische Frömmigkeit und Moderne: Sozial- und Mentalitätsgeschichte des Herz-Jesu-Kultes in Deutschland zwischen Kulturkampf und Erstem Weltkrieg* (Gütersloh: Chr. Kaiser, 1997), 308–9.
[85] Neuhofen parish office, June 13, 1915, ABP, DekA II, Pfarrkirchen 12/I, quoted in Ziemann, *Front und Heimat*, 259.
[86] Kronfeld, *Der Krieg*, 62–3.

them. For soldiers at the front and their loved ones at home, a tangible object helped to reinforce the sense of connection between them. Soldiers carried pictures of loved ones, including wives and children, their betrothed and lovers, and their parents; sometimes these pictures included a lock of hair.[87]

As contemporary scholars of such phenomena recognized, it was incredibly difficult to attach generic labels to objects that held a wide variety of meaning based on personal beliefs, which could and did fluctuate during the war and in the course of a person's life. Some soldiers, for instance, carried pictures of family members merely as tokens of memory and were soothed by thoughts of distant connections; others, however, believed that such photos contained the protective power to ward off bodily injury and death. Furthermore, changes of belief occurred over the course of combat experience. Belief in a photo's talismanic qualities could develop after a soldier survived a few heated engagements, while a solider who believed in the power of talismans and was severely wounded could lose that belief.[88] In the latter case, however, the relationship was not always proportional. Histories of magic hold one possible explanation for this: once a person has held beliefs about spirituality that form a systemic worldview, exceptions to the rules of the system do not tend to invalidate it; instead, exceptions are explained in terms of the system itself.[89] For example, if a soldier carrying a talisman was struck and deeply wounded, he would often not lose belief in the value of talismans as such, but merely invent an explanation for why he had been wounded, such as having doubtful, impure, unfocused, or selfish thoughts immediately before the wound occurred. See, for example, the account of one German soldier who carried a protective charm called a *Schutzbrief* (discussed in the next section), was wounded and captured in battle, and yet maintained his belief in its effective power and blamed himself for his injury: "I carried it with me always and believed in it. But nonetheless, I was wounded and captured because one time during a battle I suddenly lost my faith for fifteen minutes."[90]

For soldiers, devotional objects also represented an aspect of the shared combat experience that helped define their brotherhood-in-arms. At an imperial level, amulets often referred to the supposedly unbreakable bonds between the Central Powers. The German-Austro-Hungarian blood brotherhood figured most commonly, with state-sponsored medals bearing rhymed verses such as "Indissoluble is this band / It stops all

[87] Hellwig, *Weltkrieg und Aberglaube*, 26–7.   [88] Ibid., 26–8.
[89] Thomas, *Religion and the Decline*, 641.
[90] Quoted in Bächtold, *Deutscher Soldatenbrauch*, 19.

enemies" and, after Turkey joined the war, "Faithful united / With the friend / Hand-in-hand / For the Fatherland." The themes of the state medallions tended toward bombast, written with such fervor as "Powder, lead, and iron / Will be my strength."[91]

At a more personal and more common level, fallen or wounded soldiers were remembered by their comrades, who carried tokens of military memory. Most commonly, these articles included pieces of their fellow soldier's uniform or a favored small possession, such as a harmonica. Sometimes they included more direct representations on what had caused the soldier's absence, such as bullets or bullet fragments and bits of shrapnel from the shells that had killed or wounded them.[92] Soldiers carried such objects to protect themselves, too. Anything that stopped a bullet or shell splinter could be appropriated as a supposed defense against further injury: coins, watches, ration boxes, cigarette cases, and especially Bibles.[93] Soldiers applied folk remedies such as ointments and herbs to cure a variety of ailments, including toothache and stomach cramps. For cutting wounds, folk practitioners recommended healing methods such as the application of spiderwebs, fresh cow dung, or urine. These methods of folk healing could easily overlap with Christian practices, especially when prayers were involved. To stanch blood flow, the folk remedy was to make the sign of the cross three times over the wound while chanting, "Happy is the wound, happy is the day, happy is the hour that Jesus Christ was born."[94] Such practices reinforced in soldiers' minds the idea of Christian sacrifice as a source of their personal suffering and eventual redemption. A perceived imitation of Christ was a powerful source of endurance for Christian believers.

Amulets could also be given to soldiers directly from their homefront relatives. One inscribed amulet from a beloved read, "Win honor and praise / And don't forget your sweetheart." Another took the form of a horseshoe, on which was written, "It brings you luck / Return healthy!"[95] Amulets and talismans contained a wide variety of symbols, incorporating Christian, pagan, and non-religious motifs in a metaphysical bricolage of comfort. Western Christian symbols included the cross, dove, fish (the "Jesus fish": the Greek spelling of "Jesus Christ" was similar to the word for "fish," which made it a symbol for early Christian communities), and lamb (i.e., the Lamb of God). More imperially-oriented symbols were the eagle for Germany and the double eagle for Austria-Hungary. Additionally, ethno-national motifs proved popular, such as runic symbols and

[91] Kronfeld, *Der Krieg*, 73–4. See also Ziemann, *Front und Heimat*, 260.
[92] Hellwig, *Weltkrieg und Aberglaube*, 26–7.   [93] Kronfeld, *Der Krieg*, 75.
[94] Bächtold, *Deutscher Soldatenbrauch*, 28–30.   [95] Kronfeld, *Der Krieg*, 74.

the hammer of Thor, as well as more pan-theistic representations, especially from the Middle East and Asia; besides various forms of hooked crosses, including the swastika, these included Egyptian motifs of resurrection such as the scarab beetle and the ankh cross.[96] Motifs associated with particular military units also became popular, such as the silver horn of the "Kopal-Jägers," Austro-Hungarian soldiers proud of their unit's performance in Radetzky's Army in 1848 and their bravery in the contemporary battles along the Nida River.[97]

Soldiers carried a wide variety of talismanic objects, most of which were perceived to bring good luck, such as four-leaf clovers and fish scales (especially of carp).[98] Conversely, carrying certain objects could also bring bad luck; this was tied to long-standing popular notions of vanity. Chief concerns in this regard were money or any precious metal, playing cards, musical instruments, mirrors, or anything that seemed to represent frivolity and thus indicate a lack of seriousness in believers about to die and meet the creator of the universe.[99]

Letters from Heaven

A more distinctly Catholic practice, especially common to soldiers from rural backgrounds, was the *Schutzbrief* (letter of protection) or *Himmelsbrief* (letter from Heaven), which was a letter from the area near the soldier's hometown that he took into battle in the belief it would ward off grievous injury. Such letters were often highly Christological, invoking Christ as personal patron and protector, imbuing a sense of local communal continuity that introduced magical elements regarding the objects' creation and usage. One such letter found its way back to the Bavarian military chaplaincy. Unsigned and undated, it claimed to be "sent from Heaven and found in Gollstein" in the year 1724. The *Schutzbrief* was then copied and given out for protection – not only in times of war, but it especially suited those purposes. Redolent with rural stylistics, the letter implored:

In the name of God, of the Father, and of the Holy Spirit. Just as Christ stood pacified in the olive garden [i.e., Gethsemane], so should all weapons be pacified. Whosoever carries this letter, nothing will harm him. Nothing will hit him; God will overpower the enemy's weapons so that [the bearer of this letter] need not fear thieves and murderers. Guns, rapiers, and pistols through Your command and through the death of Jesus Christ know to stand still, all visible and invisible

[96] Ibid., 40–2.   [97] Ibid., 79–80.   [98] Watson, *Enduring the Great War*, 95.
[99] Bächtold, *Deutscher Soldatenbrauch*, 24.

weapons. Through the command of the angel Michael and in the name of the Father, and of the Son, and of the Holy Spirit. Amen.[100]

Some *Schutzbriefe* and amulets were sold by hustlers trying to take advantage of Catholic believers, beginning almost immediately after the outbreak of hostilities. By mid-August 1914, newspapers were reporting that Berlin women were receiving the following card: "My dear gracious lady! Allow me to send you the enclosed little card. In our evil times we all pray for protection and help. A personal talisman of scientific, astrological calculation possesses the power to protect us and to keep evil away from us. Don't you, gracious lady, wear an amulet? . . . Amulets of gold, silver, stamped (at 30 and 20 marks) to wear as pendants and pins, in diffi-cult times for personal protection, after scientific-astrologic calculation – besides horoscope – after indication of date of birth, available within three days." In another instance, the Munich police warned of a scheme perpe-trated by a local self-described "natural healer" (*Heilkundiger*) operating in the Rosenheimerstrasse who was mass-printing and distributing papers described as "bullet-blessings" (*Kugelsegen*) that declared, "Secret! A blessing against all weapons and bullets." At 50 pfennigs apiece, the "healer" sold copies to numerous women, advising them to give them to their soldiers to keep in their uniforms.[101]

Fortune tellers also played on the fears of families anxious about their relatives in battle, in some cases earning themselves considerable sums of money. In one notable case in Munich in February 1915, a soothsayer caused a public outcry and earned a jail-term of six weeks for charging hundreds of women five marks a prophecy to make false predictions of their husbands being killed at the front or returning as cripples. Tarot card readers and phrenologists in Bremen and Frankfurt were similarly punished after accumulating too many false predictions.[102] While the analytical distinctions between religion and superstition remained blurry, treading too far toward blatant untruths, especially to make a profit, incurred social outrage and civil retribution.

---

[100] EAM, NL Faulhaber, Ktn. 6578: "Heil und Schutzbrief." The original reads, "Im Namen Gottes, des Vaters u. des Hl. Geistes. So wie Christus im Ölgarten stillstand, so sollen alle geschützte [sic] still stehen. Wer dieses bei sich trägt, dem wird nichts schaden. Es wird ihn nichts treffen, des Feindes Geschütze. Denselben wird Gott kräftigen, dahs er sich nicht fürchte vor Dieben und Mördern. Es soll Ihm nicht schaden Geschütz Degen u. Pistolen durch deinen Befehl u. durch den Tot Jesus Christus wissen still stehn, alle sichtbaren u. unsichtbaren Gewehre. Durch den Befehl des Engels Michael u. im Namen Gottes u. des Sohnes u. des Vaters u. des Hl. Geistes Amen."

[101] Grabinski, *Neuere Mystik*, 61–2.   [102] Hellwig, *Weltkrieg und Aberglaube*, 147–50.

For guardians of the Central European social order, the wave of superstition during the war was unsettling because of its liberating and uncontrolled aspects. Even the sympathetic chroniclers who held that superstition was a real phenomenon, instead of metaphysical nonsense or insanity, argued that this was because superstition was fundamentally feminine. One of the most prominent studies, for instance, claimed that, "in [women] overall, the sense of reason is less developed than fantasy and feeling," which made women more susceptible to listening to sooth-sayers, "doctors" of magic, and other tricksters.[103] Thus, when major studies noted the affinities between Catholicism and superstition, even from perspectives sympathetic to Catholicism, they drew upon stereo-types of Catholicism as strongly rooted in irrational feminine piety.[104] Into the post-war era of defeat, this conveniently merged with critiques of a dissolute, dissipated society corrupted by loss. In such conceptualiza-tions, women on the homefront bore a moral burden for being corrupted, in contrast to the fighting soldiers who had defended the homeland.[105] Contemporary studies of superstition bemoaned the destruction of social bonds, noting that the war had destroyed the foundations of customs.[106]

Beyond belief: incorporating doubt

There were certainly limits that strained and sometimes broke soldiers' religious beliefs, whether official or quasi-superstitious. Sometimes these were inescapably related to official dogma disseminated by military chap-lains. Especially in sustained situations of seemingly endless violence, proclamations of imminent victory and just war seemed increasingly hol-low as the war dragged on. Belief in Divine Providence could be absurd in the face of the slaughter at Verdun. Even the chaplain Karl Lang, witnessing the Verdun casualties at a hospital, asked, "Can there be a God?" and, after affirming that there was, demanded, "O Lord, increase my faith! You did not want any of this to happen!"[107] At other times, situational peer-pressure dynamics created social conformity among reli-gious believers. As Benjamin Ziemann has noted, demonstrably pious soldiers faced social shame from both religious doubters and "lapsed and half-hearted Catholics." One soldier reported to Bishop Michael von Faulhaber that the "filthy talk" of naysayers filled him with "scorn

---

[103] Ibid., 7–8.   [104] Grabinski, *Neuere Mystik*; Hellwig, *Weltkrieg und Aberglaube*, 24–5.
[105] Lisa M. Todd, "'The Soldier's Wife Who Ran Away with the Russian': Sexual Infideli-ties in World War I Germany," *Central European History* 44, No. 2 (2011): 257–78.
[106] Grabinski, *Weltkrieg und Sittlichkeit*, 137–66.
[107] ABA, NL Karl Lang, *Kriegschronik*, p. 36, quoted in Ziemann, *Front und Heimat*, 262.

and derision" but also motivated him to pray to the "Holy Archangel Michael" as a Defender of the Faith. The voices of the religious mockers and doubters tended to become stronger as the war dragged on.[108]

Nonetheless, the wide spectrum of belief and disbelief necessitates that scholars continue to examine religious behavior pluralistically and individualistically whenever possible. There were much more complicated modes of belief than standard Manichean depictions of hollow religious zealotry versus progressive disenchantment.

Conclusion

By looking at the most disillusioning sites of battlefield violence, this chapter has shown religious soldiers struggling with the limits of chaos. Now that homefront–battlefront distinctions have been blurred in studies of total war, the study of human relationships during the war shows that the homefront was a spiritual community in arms, trying not only to help the cause but also to protect loved ones. Catholic soldiers and their families coped and endured remarkably well.

What about those soldiers who endured the hellish combat and continued believing? They endured because Catholic beliefs and practices, stereotyped as "feminine," "superstitious," and "archaic," provided tangible comfort mechanisms that linked home and battle for soldiers and their families. In some cases overlapping with rural folk practices, Catholic beliefs, based on sacramentality and intercession, invoked spiritual aids to intervene for the believer. This helped the Catholic solider to believe that he was not alone, that he was linked with a larger community of faith. Even if the soldier was brutally killed in battle, the archetypal suffering mother, the Virgin Mary, provided the model of dolorous consolation, the Pietà. Such symbolism reinforced the notion that soldiers were dying for a Christian cause and would find resurrection and redemption. The Virgin Mary ensured that believing Catholic families would be comforted in their grief.

The combat of the Great War did not inherently transform soldiers into deeper metaphysical believers. Just the same, it did not turn them into unbelievers, either. Yet the disillusionment of disbelievers has become cultural shorthand for the futility of slaughter encapsulated by the Western Front. That story has been told before. The cultural history of the war needs to move beyond convenient narratives of modern secularization and disenchantment.

---

[108] Quoted in Ziemann, *Front und Heimat*, 261–5. See also Ziemann, "Katholische Religiosität," 116–36.

Instead of the Great War stereotypes of disillusioned modernism, interwar Central European Catholicism was renewed and energized by the war. The stereotypically rigid and anti-modern religion of Catholicism was remarkably adaptive to the contemporary needs of its believers at the most disillusioning sites of violence. The nihilism and personal anomie of combat did not bring comfort. In a world fundamentally changed by new forms of warfare, adapted ancient traditions and a larger sense of community, both local and universal, were forms of Catholic social cohesion.

5 The unquiet homefront

Catholic women and children experienced both positive and negative changes in their traditional roles during the war. Massive historiographical shifts in social and cultural histories of the First World War have demonstrated women's fundamental importance during the conflict.[1] The process of total war was already dramatically reordering pre-war conceptions of gender roles, creating a fundamental tension between traditional images and new expectations for both men and women in Central Europe. The war saw attempts both to challenge gender roles and to restore order.[2] Even in progressive nations like Weimar Germany and the United States where women gained the right to vote comparatively early as a direct result of the war, there was often a wide gap between the rhetoric and the practical reality of women's roles in the new social orders. As Erika Kuhlman has argued in a path-breaking transnational study, new public focus on human rights and equality did not correct unequal imbalances in gender relations. Through discourses on motherhood and female virtue, women were active agents in a process whereby "nations reinforced traditional, patriarchal relationships among men and women (in which masculinity remained privileged and femininity continued to be valued) by shunting women back to traditional

---

[1] Susan R. Grayzel, *Women and the First World War* (New York: Longman, 2002); Richard Wall and Jay Winter, eds., *The Upheaval of War: Family, Work, and Welfare in Europe, 1914–1918* (Cambridge: Cambridge University Press, 1988). More recently, see Ute Daniel, "Women," in *Brill's Encyclopedia of the First World War*, ed. Gerhard Hirschfeld, Gerd Krumeich, and Irina Renz (Boston, MA: Brill, 2012), 1:89–102. For a superb comparative overview that remains empirically grounded, see Catherine Rollet, "The Home and Family Life," in Winter and Robert, *Capital Cities at War* (Cambridge: Cambridge University Press, 2007), 315–53.

[2] Karen Hagemann and Stefanie Schüler-Springorum, eds., *Home/Front: The Military, War, and Gender in Twentieth-Century Germany* (Oxford: Berg, 2002); Nancy M. Wingfield and Maria Bucur, eds., *Gender and War in Twentieth-Century Eastern Europe* (Bloomington: Indiana University Press, 2006).

female employment and honoring women as mothers (and fallen soldiers as heroes)."[3]

While new generations of scholarship have blurred boundaries between homefront and battlefront, women's religious experience of the war, especially in defeated Central Europe, remains a comparatively unexplored aspect of the cultural history of the war. The historiography of gender in the Habsburg monarchy during the war, long neglected in comparison to other combatant states, has seen recent advances. As Christa Hämmerle has recently argued, multifaceted conceptions of gender reflect the all-encompassing social relations of the drive toward total war, thus illuminating changing identities during periods of immense upheaval and reform. Perhaps especially poignant in a dissolving ancient patriarchal monarchy that passed away during the war, gender roles and new social norms would become heated topics in the memory cultures of post-1918 Central Europe.[4]

As previous chapters have shown, Catholic women were involved in the process of total war, even in particularly gendered male environments of public theology and combat. This chapter, however, focuses more exclusively on Catholic women's experience of the Great War. Especially given the Catholic Church's views on sexuality, scholarship on the Great War must address religious women's sexuality as a marker of difference. Perennial issues such as prostitution, contraception, and family values became especially contentious issues in wartime. Fears of falling birthrates, the spread of vice on the battlefront and homefront, and perceptions of society-wide degeneration led established Church and state authorities to debate the use of repressive sanctions to remedy these apparent trends. Bent on increasing the productive capacities necessary for sustaining a victory in a totalizing war, the increasing power of the military state made religious women's issues especially controversial and important. Although the state tried to enforce largely bourgeois norms, repressive measures often highlighted the limits of its power.[5]

While their domestic-sphere responsibilities increased, women were also involved in the public-sphere war effort in three main areas: war relief, nursing, and industry. The first two were stereotypically "traditional" areas of women's work, but were nonetheless of increased

---

[3] Erika Kuhlman, *Reconstructing Patriarchy after the Great War: Women, Gender, and Postwar Reconciliation between Nations* (New York: Palgrave Macmillan, 2008), 3–4.

[4] Christa Hämmerle, *Heimat/Front: Geschlechtergeschichte/n des Ersten Weltkriegs in Österreich-Ungarn* (Vienna: Böhlau, 2014).

[5] Nancy M. Wingfield, "The Enemy Within: Regulating Prostitution and Controlling Venereal Disease in Cisleithanian Austria during the Great War," *Central European History* 46 (2013): 568–98.

importance in sustaining the state of war. Women's involvement in industry represented a more radical reordering of presuppositions about female contributions outside of the home.

This chapter argues that Catholic women's self-perception inclined them to embrace more conservative, traditional roles in comparative complacency, especially compared to socialist-oriented women. In the collapsing social truce of the *Burgfrieden*, historians have rightly given attention to the plight of working-class women and children, whom contemporaries first perceived as war victims and then, especially in the post-war period, as revolutionary, destabilizing agitators. Particularly in the urban capitals of Vienna and Berlin, the war caused women to become political actors with grievances against the patriarchal state, whose legitimacy they questioned when it could not provide basic foodstuff and other essential materials.[6] Across Central Europe, however, many Catholic women came from rural, peasant, traditionalist backgrounds, and while the war caused new emancipatory opportunities, such women adapted their religiously-based experiences in a more traditional manner, thus destabilizing pre-war norms much less than one would expect from master narratives of war and gender in twentieth-century Europe.

This was no simple contrarian return to traditional Catholicism, however. This chapter also illuminates the everyday lives of Catholic women and children and the qualitatively new experiences of industrial warfare that they encountered. Previous histories of Catholicism during the war in Central Europe remain almost exclusively focused on the adult male war effort: of soldiers at the battlefront and of priests and high-ranking clerics, especially those who embraced the "just-war" theology. In contrast, this chapter shows that the historiographically-marginalized Catholic women played a huge and vital effort in the process of total war. They helped both to increase their state's killing capacity and to heal their own societies' wounds.

Public piety on the homefront

As previous chapters have shown, public religious piety in a military context was a highly impromptu affair, particularly because of the lack of priests available to minister to the spiritual needs of massive military forces. By contrast, public piety at the homefront showed much more established lines of continuity with pre-war norms. Despite impressionistic accounts of cultural critics and disillusioned believers who wrote that

---

[6] Belinda Davis, *Home Fires Burning: Food, Politics, and Everyday Life in World War I Berlin* (Chapel Hill: University of North Carolina Press, 2000); Healy, *Vienna*.

religious belief had fallen away quickly after 1914, homefront religious observance actually remained constant throughout the war years, with the 1960s being the moment of real religious change.[7]

Statistical evidence of public piety often referred to such measures as the reception of communion at Easter time (a mandatory requirement of the faith) and the number of yearly communion receptions per individual Catholic. In Münster in Westphalia in northwestern Germany, a city of around 100 000 inhabitants during the First World War, the percentage of the population receiving Easter communion began the war at sixty-five percent and ended the war slightly higher, at sixty-seven. Yearly communion receptions per individual Catholic started the war at nineteen times per year, rose slightly to twenty-two in 1915 and remained at around twenty-one or twenty-two for the duration of the war, dipped to nineteen in 1922 and then rose in the 1930s to twenty-seven times yearly.[8] Even in urban centers, the Catholic milieu was strong.

In communal measures such as attendance at Mass, statistics reveal similar homefront continuities, but also a need to look locally for particular explanations of religious behavior. In the Archdiocese of Freiburg, for example, Church attendance at Catholic parishes suggested multiple causal factors involving many parishes. The cathedral in Freiburg suffered a steep decline in attendance during the war, from a height of nearly 12 000 in 1914 to a low of around 8000 by the end of the war, much of which reflected the cathedral's status as the main point of contact for visitors to the city and Catholic soldiers from the main barracks, both of which found traveling opportunities limited after 1914. Other parishes in the Freiburg archdiocese, however, experienced overall stasis during the war, including modest declines and modest increases in parishes such as St. Martin, St. Urban, St. Johann, and Sacred Heart, with a new parish opening in Littenweiler. Public religious life on the homefront reflected grim determination but not large-scale abandonment of the Church.[9]

One must account for declining official Church membership, but as part of a more complicated story than a simple exit from the Church. For instance, there was a wave of formal exits by parishioners: in Germany, over 100 000 Catholics left between 1919 and 1923. However, this was less than the comparatively massive exodus of Protestants, which numbered around 1 million in Germany in the same time period.[10] Perhaps

---

[7] Altermatt, *Katholizismus und Moderne*; Benjamin Ziemann, *Sozialgeschichte der Religion: von der Reformation bis zur Gegenwart* (Frankfurt a.M.: Campus Verlag, 2009).

[8] Liedhegener, *Christentum und Urbanisierung*, 223–39.

[9] Chickering, *The Great War*, 489–90.

[10] Felix Raabe, "Die Katholiken und ihre Verbände in der Zeit der Weimarer Republik," in Gatz, *Laien in der Kirche*, 194.

more susceptible to the appeals of socialism than others in the Catholic milieu, Christian trade unions showed remarkable growth and strengthening during the war, especially in the industrialized areas of western Germany. The initial years of the war, when workers could be drafted without concern for their labor contributions to the war effort, saw a rapid decline in membership, from 341 735 in 1913 to 178 907 in 1916. The Auxiliary Service Law of 1916 saw trade unions officially recognized, and the Christian trade unions received increased political support through such advocates as Adam Stegerwald and Heinrich Imbush. This clout also led to a surge in membership: in 1918, the number of Christian trade unionists had risen to 538 559, and by 1919, the number was over a million: officially, 1 000 070. The First World War strengthened the corporate position and power of the Christian trade unions.[11]

Nonetheless, suggestive new patterns of change were already taking place, especially in the area of male–female loyalty to the Church. Again, cities like Münster showed that men were leaving the Church in greater numbers than women.[12] Long stigmatized as a feminine religion, Catholicism during the war accentuated these trends toward gender imbalance in the Church. The tale of Catholic women during the war, however, is a much more complicated story.

Family values and female sexuality in wartime

The importance of the Catholic ideal of the Virgin Mary as an essential and ambiguous notion of religious gender roles can hardly be overstated. The Virgin Mother emphasized both virginity and childbirth, heavily stressing female purity as a condition of saintliness: an aspiration for all women. The Virgin Mary provided a powerful symbol for Catholic lay women through the institution of motherhood, and Mary's virginity was also an inspiration for celibate female believers. By giving birth, Catholic women replicated the birth of Christ, bearing soldiers who would be sacrificed for a higher ideal. Catholic women implored the Virgin Mary as the ultimate human source of connection with the divinity of Christ. Motherhood remained a strong ideal for Catholic women. The Virgin Mary, embodying belief in both chastity and motherhood, provided a perfect symbol of the ambivalent duality of feminine Catholicism.[13]

---

[11] Aschoff, "Von der Revolution," 190–1.
[12] Liedhegener, *Christentum und Urbanisierung*, 238–9.
[13] For the centrality of the cult of the Virgin Mary to Catholic history, see Michael P. Carroll, *The Cult of the Virgin Mary: Psychological Origins* (Princeton, NJ: Princeton University Press, 1986). For a brilliant, path-breaking work on Marian popular

Individual women's religious reflections on sexuality remain difficult to recover, especially where they conflicted with Church norms.[14] Celibacy and virginity remained the stereotypical ideal for Catholic women, especially in three prominent roles in the public sphere: as teachers, nurses, and nuns. These roles were not mutually exclusive. Catholic nuns, in particular, were especially prominent as teachers and nurses, involved in the caritas network of care, which attempted to lessen the harsh conditions of the war. Lay women could also approach the Catholic feminine ideal, especially through chaste roles as teachers and nurses. Unlike that of their male counterparts, female teachers' celibacy was legally mandated in Germany, a situation that would change only in the Weimar Republic.[15]

For Catholic women as a corporate group, the war presented an opportunity for religious renewal. In contrast to more self-consciously progressive women's groups on the left of the political spectrum, Catholic women's groups during the war stressed a concept of renewal that respected traditions from the past, and in many ways attempted to strengthen an idealized pre-war conservatism. Catholic corporate women's groups, most prominently the Catholic Women's League (*Katholischer Frauenbund* [KFB]) in Germany, argued that female purity and strengthened domesticity were not only a form of spiritual social regeneration but also a concrete war aim and a philosophical contrast to the degeneracy of the Central Powers' enemies. These critiques drew on anti-French arguments, particularly regarding modern women's fashion. Hedwig Dransfeld, the head of the KFB, emphasized a "German style and German essence" that reflected "physical and psychological health" in contrast to a "Gallic culture of decay." German Catholic women represented their French counterparts as typifying decadent weakness, frivolity, and overall cultural degeneration.[16] By contrast, German women argued that they were guardians of traditional social mores that preserved modern society against disorienting decay.

At the War-Women's Day organized by the KFB in Frankfurt am Main in 1915, the KFB highlighted many of the intertwined issues associated with sexual morality and the Catholic concept of the family. The KFB

---

religiosity with special relevance to Central Europe, see Blackbourn, *Marpingen*, xxi–xxxiv, 3–41.

[14] Beil et al., "Populare Religiosität und Kriegserfahrungen," 298–320.

[15] Irmgard Niehaus, "'Die Krone unserer Berufswürde' Die Auseinandersetzung um den Lehrerinnenzölibat im Verein katholischer deutscher Lehrerinnen und im Katholischen Deutschen Frauenbund," in *Katholikinnen und Moderne*, ed. Gisela Muschiol (Münster: Aschendorff, 2003), 43–67.

[16] Breuer, *Frauenbewegung im Katholizismus*, 131.

tapped into perennial generic laments about the decline of the family and morals and spoke out against wartime prostitution, sexually-transmitted diseases, and especially the military use of field bordellos. The KFB argued that it strove toward "a religious renewal" through such actions as religious mission campaigns, distribution of religious literature, and the strengthening of women's associations aimed at improving social conditions. The KFB further argued that, "Especially the responsibility of mothers should experience the most profound strengthening, so that they can remain conscious of their duties toward God, family, and Fatherland and reckon the education of their children as the first, most important, and most distinguished task of life."[17]

Expressed in corporate organizations, religious women's groups emerged as staunch defenders of tradition, often echoing the voices of the patriarchy. Franz Hitze, a Catholic Center Party deputy in the Reichstag and generally a progressive social reformer, founded the Select Committee on Population. Hitze argued against birth control, free love, and promiscuity, which would cause a "shock to the moral order." According to Hitze, any act of contraception was "a sacrilege... a revolt against nature" and a way of "denuding marriage of its moral dignity." In this he echoed the Prussian Minister of the Interior, Friedrich Wilhelm von Loebell, who spoke of the need for women to bear more children as a "holy task" and a "moral crusade." Overall, efforts at pronatalism in Germany were part of an ideological campaign, a cheap form of social policy designed to shore up declining birthrates, which had been noticeable across Europe before 1914 but became a matter of military concern during the war years.[18] Such efforts received the backings of Protestant and Catholic politicians.[19]

Viewed at a personal individual level, budding sexuality was a natural phenomenon that often caused feelings of guilt in Catholic children, especially girls presented with the ambivalent figure of the Virgin Mary. Young children prepared to make their first communion and continued to grow up during wartime, taking traditional paths of religious upbringing. During times of "hunger, homelessness" and overall "crisis," even in the "bad times" of the French and Belgian occupation of the Ruhr, Charlotte Reger, from Paderborn, recalled making her first communion and being set at ease by the candles, incense, and feeling of mystery of the Catholic liturgy at the Church of St. Joseph. But the young girl's budding sexuality

---

[17] Ibid., 132.
[18] Quoted in Cornelie Usborne, "'Pregnancy is the Woman's Active Service.' Protanalism in Germany during the First World War," in Wall and Winter, *The Upheaval*, 395–6.
[19] Martin Fassbender, *Des deutschen Volkes Wille zum Leben* (Freiburg: Herder, 1917).

caused her to feel guilt and shame. With the requisite confession before a priest approaching, she worried about what sins she had committed that, if she did not confess them, would land her in purgatory or in hell. Like others in her class, she fantasized about a teenage communion ministrant with curly hair, "yet so unreachable as the moon." She also worried that she was inflaming her lust by looking at naked pictures found in Meyer's *Konversationslexikon* dictionary and the *grosse Brockhaus* encyclopedia, especially anatomical figures and nude portraits of Greek and Roman mythological characters.[20] Her guilt remained intertwined with her faith.

Children

In Central Europe, religious children both embraced and rejected the war that enveloped their lives and their relationships with authority figures.[21] The recorded contemporary recollections of Catholic children, such as the colorful drawings and incipient diary of a young Yves Congar, serve as a visible reminder that children were most concerned about how the war affected their parents and loved ones away from home.[22] Children's toys reflected the militarization of society and of warfare, especially toy soldiers, artillery pieces, planes, tanks, and ships.[23] Children, however, were not simply sheltered away at home. Some of them, as servants and Mass assistants for military chaplains in the field, served at the front and repeatedly came under enemy fire. Particularly in occupied areas, military chaplains used children to forge local connections with the occupied populations.[24]

With men requisitioned for war service, more women became school teachers in Central Europe, which marked a decisive change in pedagogical leadership, especially in contrast to the Entente Powers. In the pre-war era, around eighty percent of German school teachers were men, compared with forty percent in Britain and twenty-five in France. As Andrew Donson has argued, the war created a paradoxical situation of educational freedom and advancement in Central European pedagogy.

---

[20] DTA 1294,9–1294,10, Charlotte Reger, Tagebuch, pp. 3, 23, 35–9. For a contemporary young Catholic man's guilt over looking at nude bodies, see the reflections of Franz Huberl (pseudonym) in Scheule, *Beichten*, 88–9.

[21] The case of children's historical evidence during the Great War must be treated with analytical care. Few personal materials remain outside of drawings and school essays (prompted by teachers). Letters and diaries written by older children often recreated the war after the fact. For an excellent reflection on children's experience, see Rollet, "The Home and Family Life," 345–8.

[22] Yves Congar, *Journal de la Guerre, 1914–1918*, ed. Stéphane Audoin-Rouzeau and Dominique Congar (Paris: Cerf, 1997).

[23] Rainer Rother, *Der Weltkrieg.*   [24] Houlihan, "Clergy in the Trenches," 157–8.

In contrast to the pre-war authoritarian pedagogy of memorization and a strict curriculum, teachers used much more flexible instruction methods, often focused on current events related to the war, such as analysis of newspaper articles and penny dreadfuls. The teachers allowed their students freedom in the application of the content of such articles, so long as the content itself remained loyal to war aims of supporting the state.[25]

During the Great War, religious children experienced a newfound ability to act without parental or familial oversight. As the primary domestic figures in the nexus of Kinder–Küche–Kirche, religious women had been the main childcare-givers in the pre-war era. Now, however, state authorities told them it was their duty to serve in factories, mines, and other places related to the war effort. With so many parental figures thus absent, childcare was outsourced to other parties. Members of the extended family, especially grandparents, took on primary care roles. The strains of food procurement, however, limited the physical ability of elders to care for others.

Those without sufficient family networks turned to the arms of the Church. Religious women, including nuns and lay women, formed an important part of this network of care. They supervised massive programs of childcare for children whose primary caregivers were otherwise occupied in the war effort. Most often, this included daycare, schools, orphanages, and homes for foundlings. They also provided aid for single women with children. In children's minds, religious women as educators and caregivers fit easily into the role of "assistant mother-caregivers" (*Mitpflegemütter*), stressing the fulfillment of motherly functions while maintaining a sense of distinct religious calling that separated them from the children's actual biological mothers. In the words of one child of the era temporarily sent away to a school in Roskilde, Denmark, the teachers at her school were "all single women... it appeared that at this time there that this profession was bound together with a type of celibacy."[26]

Nuns and religious lay women not only cared for children in a passive sense but actively focused the children's efforts on contributing to the war effort. Children remembered these experiences as foundational in their experience of religiously-focused school and daycare. Margaretha Witeschnik-Edlbacher, who attended the Sacré Cœur primary school

[25] Andrew Donson, *Youth in the Fatherless Land: War Pedagogy, Nationalism, and Authority in Germany, 1914–1918* (Cambridge, MA: Harvard University Press, 2010). For the percentage of male teachers, see p. 135.

[26] Christa Hämmerle, ed., *Kindheit im Ersten Weltkrieg* (Vienna: Böhlau, 1993), 36.

in Vienna's Third District, remebered religious women and children organizing collections of money, food, clothing, and raw materials. Pedagogically, teachers also encouraged children to write essays, draw pictures, and otherwise contribute to propaganda efforts in support of their state cause. Here, children were both subject and object, demonstrating that they were doing their part in a wide social effort, and at the same time emphasizing to soldiers that children were part of a separate idyllic homefront of peace and prosperity that needed to be defended against aggression. More sentimentally, nuns and religious women organized children's letter-writing campaigns and the sending of care pacakages (*Liebesgaben*) in order to bolster morale. Care packages usually consisted of some tobacco products, chocolate or other sweets, seasonal objects such as Christmas trees, warm clothing such as scarves and mittens, and wholesome entertainment, usually in the form of edifying literature such as novels and collections of sermons. Much of the reading material had a nostalgic bent, focused on the peace of the homeland, but it also included stirring patriotic preaching. In any event, much of the literature was filled with religiously-tinged language and themes of Christian devotion, sacrifice, humility, charity, and love.[27]

The newfound sense of youth independence was a powerful influence on the growth of the youth movements that would flourish in the interwar period. Not simply a rejection of religion and authority, the youth movements in Central Europe brought more direct agency to young people, who were participating more fully in Church-related religious life through events such as pilgrimages, nature hikes, and youth festivals. Such events were often outside the direct control of the Church hierarchy, but nonetheless involved both lay and religious leaders and themes. In conjunction with related movements associated with nature and liturgy, Catholic youth movements saw rapid growth in the interwar period. The religious youth movements were a vibrant, flourishing outgrowth of the Great War.

Some children experienced the war years as a time of innocent obliviousness to the war, or adapted their play to the new, socially-expansive militarization. Much more often, especially long after the fact, children remembered the war years with a retrospective seriousness that saw the era of 1914–45 as a depressing background to their lives. Maria Balley, born in Vienna before the Great War, remembered the era as "unforgettable and decisive for our development." In her old age, she wrote that, "We had to take a backseat to being proper children. We were all much too serious."[28] During the war and the interwar period, Balley remembered

---

[27] Ibid., 43–61.   [28] Ibid., 42.

that her mother, like other Viennese mothers, took her urban children
to the comparatively well-provisioned rural areas to scrounge for food
("*aufs Land hamstern*"), a foraging process that generated urban–rural
conflicts. On one occasion, Balley recorded that they only brought back
"limited amounts" to the city: a liter of milk, two eggs, two kilos of potatoes – a "poor yield" that was purchased through trade goods, as currency
exchange was not viable. Such measures often led families to resort to
"war kitchens," in which a mish-mash of "questionable" food products
found their way into communal soup pots.[29]

Children, especially rural children, remembered how the Great War
introduced strangers into their land, especially refugees and prisoners
of war. Familial structures were changing, with absent fathers and overworked mothers who were caring for the entire household. New familial
actors, especially POWs, were used for rural farm labor all over Central
Europe, and became integrated as members of family units. Hermine
Kominek (née Brunner) remembered her youth growing up on a farm in
Trasdorf in Lower Austria. At seven and a half when the war broke out,
she was old enough to recognize the distinctly unusual and grim changes
that it caused. The harsh forced labor of Romanian POWs at the gunpowder factory at Moosbierbaum (they were fed "only black 'coffee,'
cooked turnip leaves, and probably a piece of bread, too") resulted in
mass starvation and dysentery, creating situations in which "every sadist
could run riot" on the prisoners, beating them to death for no reason at
all. Village children were "confronted with the most horrible pictures,"
seeing "dead bodies lying in ditches by the roadside" to be picked up
daily by a horse-drawn wagon. The few survivors would beg for food in
the villages.[30]

Forced labor, when organized industrially for war production, often
meant impersonalized connections and total social disregard for POWs.
Elsewhere, however, especially on rural farmsteads, POWs became
integrated into family units. In contrast to the harsh treatment of
Romanian gunpowder factory workers, Kominek described Russian
POWs who worked all day laboring in the farm fields before going home
to their sleeping accommodations inside Austrian homes. She described
the entire village eagerly anticipating the return of the Russian men,
who would sing their evening prayers communally on their way home,
which fascinated the Austrians. Kominek wrote that, "Gradually, the
prisoners were slowly integrated into 'their' families, so that by the
end, almost everyone could sleep in 'his' house, sometimes even with

---

[29] Ibid., 36.   [30] Ibid., 62–7.

peasant women."[31] Of course, as Kominek's testimonial alludes to, enemy POWs also caused moral panic among authority figures in rural villages, especially when they formed sexual liaisons and had children with native women. Reintegration of soldiers into post-war societies would prove an unsettling problem for traditional conceptions of paternal authority in traditional societies.[32]

The nostalgia and reality of family

For religious soldiers and their families, the homefront was a nostalgic ideal, both inspiring and delusive. It was a reminder of pre-war times and provided hope that the future could return to a state of tranquility and domestic bliss. The ideal of women in war created a "gendered war culture of patriotic duties," in which previously private, domestic female actions became public, civic virtues.[33] As seen through the everyday history of Freiburg during the war, religious women were at the forefront of bold new political ideas of emancipation and social charity, as well as being the disadvantaged recipients neglected by the system, in which charity was a last, desperate option.[34] In the capital cities of Berlin and Vienna, and also London and Paris, "family and household structure was profoundly disturbed by the war." This disturbance occurred not only through the death and wounding of family members, but also through declining birthrates, reconfigured social relations (both strengthening and breaking social bonds), and overall transformation of domestic arrangements.[35]

Often remembered nostalgically, the Catholic milieu figured prominently in memoir recollections of religious believers. These writings remembered the specifically religious content of their past experiences in usually positive terms of peaceful domesticity, in which women played a leading role. Born in 1915 in the town of Neustadt, Hartmut Schiller's earliest memories of childhood were anchored in the nearby parish church, "because Mother instilled in us in her lovely way a truly Christian life and wakened early our religious interest." His recollections were structured by religious turning points, especially the Christmas

[31] Ibid., 64–5.
[32] Maureen Healy, "Civilizing the Soldier in Postwar Austria," in Wingfield and Bucur, *Gender and War*, 47–69.
[33] Jean H. Quataert, *Staging Philanthropy: Patriotic Women and the National Imagination in Dynastic Germany, 1813–1916* (Ann Arbor: University of Michigan Press, 2001), 272. See also Karen Hagemann and Stefanie Schüler-Springorum, eds., *Home/Front: The Military, War, and Gender in Twentieth-Century Germany* (Oxford: Berg, 2002).
[34] Chickering, *The Great War*, 469–517.
[35] Rollet, "The Home and Family Life," 320.

season (and the singing of "Transeamus") and the Marian month of
May. Childhood games involved groups of children pretending to be a
priest ministering to the faithful. Schiller remembered a vibrant associational network of Catholic organization, including the "Marianische
Kongregation, Gesellenverein, Jugendverein, Borromäusverein, Kath.
Kaufmännischer Verein. Kath. Meisterverein, Kath. Arbeiterverein, Not-
burgaverein, DJK, Kreuzbund, Jungborn, Quickborn, and later St.
Georgs-Pfadfinder, Sturmschar, Jungschar, Neudeutschland and surely
some others that I've forgotten."[36] The milieu's network of associations
remained active and vital in interwar Europe.

The war would temper teenage enthusiasms, but the emotions found
other outlets of expression. Hanna Grünwald, most likely a Protestant,
wrote in short diary phrases punctuated by superfluous exclamation
points. In mid-summer 1914, she wrote of an invitation to a dance party:
"Hopefully it'll be nice!! Gertrud may come along!!! It's heavenly! I look
forward to it enormously!!!" Then the war began and her diary became
increasingly filled with short, laconic descriptions of troop movements,
battle reports, casualty notices, food shortages, and general homefront
misery. By August 1916, she still employed exclamation points, but the
mood was decidedly more grim: "Today it's now two years since the war
broke out, and always no more end in sight! It's too terrible! How long
should it yet last! It can't go on like this! But we must hold on! It *can't*
last so long! How it should end, no one knows!"[37]

In Germany, the rhetoric of defensive war drove up ideological support for protecting homefront and contributed to the linking of home and
battlefield events. During the war, the *Katholischer Frauenbund*, the main
confessional association for Catholic women, founded in 1903, became
linked with larger associational trends for all German women.[38] The
middle-class women's movement, the Federation of German Women's
Associations (BDF) founded the National Women's Service (*Nationaler
Frauendienst*) on July 31, 1914, with the aim of "'mobilizing women for
patriotic work on the homefront.'" At first, the National Women's Service concerned itself with nursing care, food supplies, relief for soldiers
and families, and the jobless. However, it soon widened in scope, eventually embracing child and youth welfare and the protection of infants
and homeless new mothers. This was only possible because the Women's

---

[36] DTA 135, Tagebuch von Hartmut Schiller, pp. 11–16. By contrast, the devotions
to the Sacred Heart of Jesus did not please him. He also ominously mentioned that
the Catholic associational life was very fragmented and was only unified under the
Nazis.
[37] DTA 700/1, Hanna Grünwald Tagebuch, May 29, 1914, August 1, 1916, 1, 45.
[38] Breuer, *Frauenbewegung im Katholizismus.*

Executive Secretariat of the SPD had joined in August 1914, along with the Women Worker's General Secretariat of the Free Trade Unions. Manpower losses following the huge slaughters of 1916 resulted in the Patriotic Auxiliary Service Act (*Hilfsdienstgesetz*) of December 6, 1916, calling for compulsory service for men, but not for women. The Central Office for Women's Labor (Spring 1917) advocated for women's work in the war industry and the army auxiliary force (*Etappenhilfsdienst*), close to combat zones.[39]

The war often left women widowed or temporarily without income, including the mothers of dependent children. Catholic women often wrote pleading letters to members of the clergy, begging for information about their men in the military and asking for money to support their families, especially in the latter years of the war when want became particularly pressing. In January 1918, Rachele Benuzzi, a mother in Lansbeck, Tyrol, wrote to the military chaplain of her late husband's unit, the 4th Tyrolean Kaiserjäger Regiment, begging for a supplement of 80–100 kronen promised to her by her husband. She referred to herself as an "abandoned widow with a child, alone on the street without any money . . . I desperately need the money."[40]

Family networks provided important sources of comfort and emotional support.[41] On both sides of the trenches, many couples' relationships contained religiously inspired elements.[42] Of course, extant records of familial and spousal personal correspondence often highlight only idealized model relationships, not dwelling on "messy" relationship topics such as infidelity, abortion, and frustration with marriage. Police records, court files, and censors' files all add layers of meaning, with stories of conflict, betrayal, crime, adultery, faithlessness, and abandonment. The strained social net provided by the state tended to create disincentives for divorce, especially as single women with children found decreasing sources of support. In Berlin, the annual divorce rate for the entire population declined during the war years, going from 2323 divorces in 1913 to 1295 in 1917; in 1919, the rate returned to the near-pre-war level of 2222. Some divorces stemmed from hasty war marriages that were made to increase social benefits (through a separation allowance from the state) or to legitimize children.[43] Religiously-motivated relationships tended to emphasize the positive aspects of relationships and to increase social bonds.

---

[39] Hagemann and Schüler-Springorum, *Home/Front*, 9–10.

[40] TLA, TLVA, 4. Tiroler Kaiserjäger Regiment, Gruppe VI, Ktn. 14, Letter of Benuzzi to Gasser, 2.3.1918.

[41] Rollet, "The Home and Family Life," 328–42.   [42] Hanna, *Your Death*.

[43] *Statistik des Deutschen Reiches*, vol. 276 (Berlin 1922), p. xxxii and vol. 39 (Berlin, 1918), p. 49, quoted in Rollet, "The Home and Family Life," 343–5.

Religious families were not blind to the war's utterly shattering destruction. Although religious women were not combatants in the Great War, in keeping with the notion of total war, they were nonetheless deeply involved as participants in the production of violence, as well in attempts to soothe its destructive effects. Descriptions of combat were not sanitized, reflecting both homefront bonds of solidarity and the belief that religious faith could endure the most horrifying situations. In April 1916, at the height of the Battle of Verdun, a young soldier on the Western Front, Heiko Fleck, stationed 100 meters from Fort Vaux, wrote to his mother of the dreadful conditions, which were "simply ghastly murder." Heiko described the omnipresent shriek of artillery and sweeping machine gun fire, which claimed endless lives, leaving bodies destroyed and unburied for months on end – a situation made worse for the living by the lack of cover and torturous thirst. He concisely described clouds of poison gas and flamethrower attacks as "the most highly refined war materials of modern technology or human bestiality." He wrote, "If only this frightful war would end soon!" and added that although "Life does not hold out long" in a place like Fort Vaux, the question of "how long" was known only by "dear God." Heiko's mother, Anna, engaged in correspondence that both comforted and emboldened her son, promising to send him cigars and cigarettes, yet also asking if he had helped to storm Fort Douaumont. She mirrored his descriptions of depressing conditions, writing that while shopping for provisions in Stuttgart, "everything was very expensive." She returned home overtired, but his letters from the front filled her with new strength. Nevertheless, she wrote, "Where there is war, there is misery," and while she bemoaned the "such sad continued murder," she nevertheless urged, "Pray, my dear son, from the depths of your heart and God will give you mercy and comfort."[44]

It would get worse for Heiko and his family. In autumn 1916, he was transferred near Péronne as part of the effort to shore up the Allied offensive on the Somme, and he wrote that his experiences near Fort Vaux had been superseded by those at the Somme. "That is no longer war but rather a reciprocal destruction with technical power, what should a fragile human body have to do with it?" Nevertheless, he prayed to hold out for twelve days and urged his homefront community to pray for him, saying one or two daily rosaries, hoping that he would survive the Somme campaign. He "found trust and comfort in prayer in the hours of horror." Heiko survived the Somme and experienced an ecumenical Christmas service in 1916, with sing-alongs, Christmas trees, and "only one wish:

---

[44] Bibliothek für Zeitgeschichte (BfZ) NL 97.1/33, Letter, April 8, 1916, Heiko to mother; NL 97.1/37: Letter, n.d., ca. Summer 1916, Heiko to mother and sister; NL 97.1/99 Letter, April 7, 1916, mother to Heiko.

peace." On New Year's Eve 1916, he wrote to his mother and sister that he only wanted to be at home with them, sitting near them on the sofa, singing, talking, praying together, "then bury myself in the pillows and sleep and sleep and never awaken." Stationed not far from the English lines, he wrote that, "The rosary is often my only comfort."[45]

As Heiko's war continued into 1917, he became a lieutenant and received the Iron Cross. He went on leave in May, traveling to Leuven, Brussels, Valenciennes, and Arras, first making sure to stop in the Cologne Cathedral for the May veneration of Mary. In his letter of May 12, 1917, he wrote of a passing fighter pilot that, "He who hasn't made war as a Front-Pig [*Frontsau*], doesn't know how good he has it." Nonetheless, Heiko remained cheerful, sending his "hearty greetings and kisses" to his family and friends. This letter arrived unstamped by the military post office; it was to be his final letter home. Heiko had been carrying it in his breast pocket, and it was there that it was stained with blood from his fatal wound, received near Monchy-le-Preux. On June 12, Heiko's family received a suitcase containing his final effects, which became objects of family veneration and religious relics in their own right: his blood-stained last letter and garments, his ring, and his rosary.[46] The Great War deprived families of their loved ones, but religious faith became one way of maintaining a connection for believers.

Catholic belief in Divine Providence, especially over the long term, helped relativize the Great War's impact. Maria Dorfmann, an elderly Bavarian peasant woman, wrote in 1916 of her husband, Sepp, then dead 18 years, with a longing to be reunited with him. Their hard work together in the pre-war period formed the substance of her life, in which the Great War was a depressing but not earth-shattering episode.[47] Similarly, Ottilie S., born 1903, lived a hard life in Innerstetten. Her father died in 1918 and her mother worked in agriculture while raising nine children. In the interwar period, the family survived by gathering mushrooms and wild berries. Although the war colored her memories of childhood, on a personal level, the Great War was not the defining crisis that determined her life. In Ottilie's view, the central decisive event of her life was her unplanned pregnancy in 1924.[48]

---

[45] BfZ, NL 97.1./51, Letter, October 3/4, 1916, Somme. Heiko to mother and sister; NL 97.1/52, Letter, October 9, 1916, Somme, Heiko to mother and sister; NL 97.1/65, Letter, Decemeber 24, 1916, St. Emilie (Somme), Heiko to mother and sister; NL 97.1/67, Letter, December 31, 1916, Heiko to mother and sister.

[46] BfZ, NL 97.1/96, Letter, May 12, 1917, "Als Erdwurm" to mother and sister.

[47] Michael Mitterauer, ed., *Kreuztragen. Drei Frauenleben* (Vienna: Hermann Böhlaus, 1984), 32–3.

[48] Ibid., 95–132.

Figure 7 Female mourners, All Souls' Day 1916 (BfZ)
"Women and children, often marginalized in religious histories of the
Great War, were in fact key members of the community of believers
connecting homefront and battlefront."

In retrospect, the homefront ideal was a powerful means of nostalgia. Both during and after the war, an idyllic home and peaceful childhood became an escape from the war, as well as fuel for the desire to return to a pre-war world. Numerous contemporary accounts and memoirs referred to the pleasant memories of childhood. Catholic children growing up during the war idealized their family life. Religious rites of passage such as first communion and confirmation loomed large as markers of believers' life stories. Most pointedly, Catholic children remembered recurring holidays, Christmas above all. Children fondly remembered the preparation of special meals of salted potatoes, goose, and white sausage with sauerkraut; the anticipation of opening presents on Christmas Eve (with their parents' ringing of a bell the signal for them to enter the room and see the decorated tree); the singing of Christmas Carols; attendance of Christmas Eve Mass; and the overall sense of ordered, peaceful domesticity.[49]

During the war, however, the reality of religious marriage and family life was often under direct siege. Leading Church advocates voiced public fears about the spread of vice through prostitution, decrying especially the field bordellos set up by military authorities. Official marriages, scrupulously confirmed in the pre-war era, took on a feeling of rushed formality. Church officials fulminated at moral laxity and constantly tried to curb its excesses, but the Church also resigned itself to such occurrences as part of the temporary depravity of war. This underscored a perennial Church theme: the need for a sinful society to renew itself, turning toward a more calm, well-ordered, organic, and harmonious society.[50]

The example of Berlin shows how much the Church rhetoric about the increase of wartime vice was a delusional moral panic. In fact, annual illegitimate births in Berlin dropped substantially during the war, from 10 017 in 1913 to 4278 in 1917, a decrease of 57.3%. Married couples in Berlin also had fewer children, declining from 42 511 in 1913 to 19 463 in 1917, a drop in the birthrate of 54.7%. The overall proportion of births outside of wedlock in Berlin remained constant through the war years, at around 22–23%, although the German average increased slightly, from 9 to 11%.[51]

Especially in the opening weeks of the war, soldiers rushed to have marriages validated. The tiny military religious bureaucracy of the Apostolic

---

[49] DTA 1132, "Erinnerungen" von Kristina Margarthe Anja Kronthaler, pp. 17–20. For other memories of Christmas, see DTA 135, p. 14, as well as Hämmerle, *Kindheit im Ersten Weltkrieg.*

[50] Max Scheler, "Zur religiösen Erneuerung," *Hochland* 16 (1918): 5–21.

[51] *Statistisches Jarhbuch des Deutschen Reiches,* vol. xxvi (Berlin, 1915) and vol. xl (1919), p. 4, quoted in Rollet, "The Home and Family Life," 322.

Field Vicariate in Vienna was overwhelmed, receiving tens of thousands of such requests as the soldiers left for the front. Military chaplains were nominally empowered as the official pastors of soldiers, but by 1916, a military decree relinquished this right.[52] The Church had moved earlier on this issue, in the autumn days of 1914, empowering civilian pastors with the jurisdiction to conduct marriage ceremonies for soldiers and their brides. Doing away with a convoluted pre-war process consisting of three separate ecclesiastical steps, the Church issued same-day marriage dispensations to those who swore an oath, as long as their papers were correctly presented at the local magistrate's office and the bride's local parish.[53] Church and state bureaucracies struggled to keep pace with the new dimensions of war, even in its early phase.

Contentious homefront: the politics of food

Under the conditions of total war, food supply became a contentious political issue, and religious belief complicated questions of loyalty to the cause, especially for women on the homefront. Food procurement was an essential element of domesticity, as well as a way in which women could demonstrate their loyalty to the state through efficient methods of food preparation for their families. Yet, during the course of the war, when it became apparent that the state could not effectively guarantee food supplies, women began to doubt the legitimacy of the patriarchy, and the figure of the emperor in particular. Political grievance and claims of citizenship were acute problems for the wartime state, and women were deeply active in this process of delegitimizing the imperial states in Central Europe.[54]

At the outbreak of war in 1914, the German bishops had removed fasting restrictions. Catholics in Austria-Hungary, however, were not excused from fasting.[55] For all believers between the ages of twenty-one and sixty, Catholic dietary restrictions required abstaining from meat on Fridays, fasting during the season of Lent, and fasting before reception of communion at Mass. Soldiers obtained dispensations from these dietary strictures in time of war,[56] but non-combatants made food procurement and consumption a contentious political issue.

---

[52] *Wiener Diözesanblatt* (1916), 82. For the overwhelming number of marriage requests, see ÖStAKA, AFV, Ktn. 160–3.

[53] "Zulässigkeit beschleunigter Eheschließungen," *Reichspost*, July 30, 1914, p. 7.

[54] Davis, *Home Fires Burning*; Healy, *Vienna*.

[55] E. Ille, "Fastengebot – Feiertage," *Korrespondenzblatt der katholischen Klerus Oesterreichs* XXXIV, Nr. 4: February 25, 1915: 136.

[56] *Wiener Diözesanblatt* (1915), 29–31.

Reflecting the increasingly totalizing aspect of modern war, Catholic women on the homefront stressed that they, too, were intimately involved in the war effort. They argued that both their participation in their own right and their family links to fighting soldiers should enable them to receive special permissions and protections from Church and state laws applying to normal peacetime society. The issue of fasting, for instance, became a source of both religious devotion and social conflict. Meatless Fridays throughout the year, combined with special days of fasting (especially during the Lenten season), strained homefront women's resources and ability to plan. The Allied global blockade only deepened the acute food shortage, but intrastate distribution methods also made it worse. Not only meat itself but also animal products such as *Schmaltz* (rendered animal fat) were increasingly off limits or unavailalbe, although women attempted to make concessions to religious requirements by substituting plant oils for animal fats.[57] Although some Catholic women scrupulously tried to observe pre-war regulations, most were more concerned about feeding their families in any way possible and ignored religious dietary laws that did not seem appropriate to the new wartime familial situation.

By 1918, even Catholic authorities were starting to admit that the new realities of war were making some pre-war fasting norms an impossible ideal. Indeed, the Diocese of Vienna continued to issue the normal regulations on fasting, but at the same time acknowledged that urban citizens were having difficulties obtaining the basic foodstuffs of life even in times of non-fasting.[58]

But if urban areas were struggling to find food, many rural regions were comparatively much better provisioned. Catholic husbands and wives continued to correspond about the daily requirements of farm life. The letters of Johann Schutz, a Bavarian farmer, were full of religious prayers: invocations reflecting concern over the running of the farm's agricultural rhythms, especially hay and milk production and the birth of new livestock. This correspondence reflected a deeply pious trust that family and farm would continue to find favor with God.[59] Rural food production affected different regions in disparate ways, but on the whole, rural regions were better fed than urban ones.

In the Habsburg capital of Vienna, women and children had become political actors who were critical of the Imperial state, voicing increasing disillusionment with its inability to provide the basic foodstuffs essential

57 *Wiener Diözesanblatt* (1915), 29–31, 50.   58 *Wiener Diözesanblatt* (1918), 9ff., 124.
59 BfZ, NL 12.5, Johann Schutz to Karoline, letters of March 18, 1917, January 24, 1918, and August 26, 1918.

to life.[60] Food became a politicized issue, with citizens distrusting the legitimacy of Central European monarchies that could not ensure basic state functions in wartime. There were profoundly suggestive regional disparities in the Habsburg and Hohenzollern Empires, indicating that the rural, predominantly Catholic regions of Central and Eastern Europe suffered less food deprivation than urban areas. In Austria-Hungary, the most pronounced divide was between more industrialized Austria and more agricultural Hungary, with the urban Viennese deeply resentful of black-marketing and the perceived withholding of food. Even within the "Austrian" half of the Dual Monarchy, Viennese citizens deeply resented the better-provisioned agricultural regions of lower Austria, going so far as to engage in violent foraging expeditions to procure food from rural Austrian farmers.[61]

Similar trends continued in Germany, where urban regions like Freiburg and Berlin saw a breakdown and fragmentation of state services throughout the war[62] Bavarian Catholic farmers resented fighting a war for "Prussia and big capitalists," and remained tied to local, regional loyalties of farm and faith, peppering their war correspondence with details of how to keep family farms running. In times of shortages, farmers withheld their food products from distant urban markets, as well as state requisitioning agents.[63] Rural regions in which Catholics were statistically overrepresented simply had more food to eat; when discussing the breakdown of imperial states, the urban–rural divide produced regional cleavages.

Statistically speaking, more Catholics came from rural agrarian backgrounds, and in a conflict in which food sources became contentious political issues, Catholic families often had more to eat. Furthermore, these larger rural families could absorb the loss of a member, even a paterfamilias, more easily, without major disruptions to the collective rhythms of life. Such indications of these themes can be seen in the condolence letter written from the Kruger family to Frau Krista Scholl, the wife of a Bavarian peasant, Stephan, killed on June 22, 1915 in Ban de Sapt in den Vogesen. Referring to her support network of children and her farmstead, a member of the Kruger family wrote that, "You can console yourself more than a similarly unfortunate lady, because you don't have any worries about food." Frau Scholl kept her Catholic faith and

---

[60] After declining steadily throughout the war, by June 1918, rations of potatoes in Vienna were down to half a kilogram per person per week, and new restrictions threatened. Healy, *Vienna*, 305.

[61] Ibid., 43–61.   [62] Chickering, *The Great War*, 208–75.

[63] Ziemann, *Front und Heimat*.

the war did not hurt her socio-economic status as a prosperous peasant. In 1917, she donated 300 marks to her local church in Oellingen, for a series of Sacred Heart devotions to the memory of her husband.[64] Especially as recorded in the traces of peasant women, peasant rhythms of life often did not see the Great War as a socially-atomizing, world-reorienting experience.[65]

Female religious authority and challenges to the patriarchy

The Great War unleashed tremendous spiritual energy and opportunities for personalized religious experiences, some of which were pointed challenges to the paternalistic clerical hierarchy of the Catholic Church. As previous chapters have shown, women played important parts in fighting both for and against continued devotion to the state cause of victory. Religious women also materially and spiritually bolstered the soldiers, blurring the boundaries between homefront and battlefront. Especially in rural villages, religious women used folk remedies to supplement official forms of religious devotion, tightening the bonds of affection between themselves and their soldiers in battle.

In times of peace, the Catholic patriarchy was highly skeptical of female religious autonomy, but the war unleashed many new channels of such autonomy, which could not be easily controlled as the Church was busy with crises on every front. During the war, female visionaries, seers, prophets, and folk healers all flourished, and pre-war trends were exacerbated. In one of the most prominent instances, the seventy-year-old visionary Barbara Weigand from Schippach gathered a following around her intensely personal blend of spirituality. Her appeal drew on the cult of the Sacred Heart, which flourished across Europe and formed a trans-regional form of militarized devotion in the region of Tyrol that helped to unite Germans and Austrians (or Tyroleans).[66] Ecstatic visions drew on a tradition of religious seers but found new resonance in pre-war Europe, which was industrializing, and in which the feminizing Catholic Church ran up against bounds of centralizing ultramontane patriarchy.

---

[64] BfZ, NL Knoch 1914–1918, Letter of October 10, 1915. For the note about the 300-mark donation, see BfZ, NL Knoch 1914–1918, Abschrift, p. 177.

[65] Mitterauer, *Kreuztragen.*

[66] Claudia Schlager, "Waffenbrüderschaft im heiligsten Herzen Jesu: Die deutsche und österreichische Herz-Jesu-Verehrung im Ersten Weltkrieg und die Propagierung des Tiroler Vorbildes," in *Der Erste Weltkrieg im Alpenraum*, ed. Hermann J. W. Kuprian (Innsbruck: Wagner, 2006), 165ff.

Poor, socially disadvantaged women and children became religious authority figures through mystical experiences, often including apparitions of the Virgin Mary. They usually articulated critiques of the current Church and society, promising retribution for sinful behavior and unbelief, including skepticism about the visions themselves. The 1917 Fátima apparitions represent the most famous of a flood of religious visions that occurred during times of crisis and war in twentieth-century Europe.[67] On May 13, 1917, during the Catholic Church's traditional month of Marian devotion, peasant girls in Fátima, Portugal reported seeing visions of the Virgin Mary. The poor shepherd children Lúcia Santos and her cousins Jacinta and Francisco Marto claimed that the vision denounced the war, called for repentance, and uttered prayers for peace. The appearances occurred on the thirteenth day of each month, culminating in the October 13 "Miracle of the Sun," in which a crowd of tens of thousands of people witnessed unusually luminous behavior and movement of the sun, a fact confirmed by even the anti-clericals and non-believers in the crowd. The vision was interpreted by much of the crowd as a prophetic fulfillment, but others claimed it was either a meteorological occurrence or the result of eyes staring too long at the sun.[68] An invigorated twentieth-century Catholicism based on the Marian cult would form an essential feature of Central and Eastern European Catholic identity well beyond the years of the First World War.[69] Following investigation by the Church, which declared the apparitions officially "worthy of belief" in 1930, Fátima became a site of pilgrimage, and it remains so today. An attempt was made on Pope Saint John Paul II's life on May 13, 1981, the anniversary of the original Fátima vision, and he attributed his survival to the Virgin Mother's intervention, and eventually placed one of the assassin's bullets in the shrine at the altar of Fátima.[70]

During the Great War, however, ecastatic visions in Central Europe met with skepticism and ultimately repression by Church and state authorities. Barbara Weigand had chosen in her twenties not to marry and to devote herself to the Church, although she did not join a religious order. Weigand's mystical visions of the Virgin and the saints often occurred in church and coincided with Sacred Heart festivals, beginning in the 1880s and continuing into the 1920s.[71] Pointed theological critiques in prominent publications accused Weigand of having "a totally

---

[67] For the Marian apparitions during the First World War, see Blackbourn, *Marpingen*, 327–8.
[68] Jenkins, *The Great and Holy War*, 170–2.
[69] Monique Scheer, "Rettet Maria Deutschland? Die Diskussion um eine nationale Marienweihe zu Beginn des Kalten Krieges," in Korff, *Alliierte im Himmel*, 141–56.
[70] Jenkins, *The Great and Holy War*, 370.   [71] Schlager, *Kult und Krieg*, 290ff.

false version of the Sacred Heart devotion" and press campaigns were mounted against her both before the war and during the conflict. The "Seer of Schippach" continued undaunted, however, founding a movement that by 1915 had raised 500 000 marks for the establishment of a pilgrimage grotto akin to Lourdes. The Ordinariat in Würzburg attempted to halt construction on multiple occasions, beginning in November 1915, and in November 1916 invoked the aid of police. Opposition to Weigand's movement mounted when her visions became tied to pronounced national-political goals and made mention of the current monarchs of Germany and Austria-Hungary, Field Marshal Hindenburg, and other notables. As her pointed prophecies of victory failed to materialize, authorities intervened more decisively to halt construction of the pilgrimage grotto. On January 7, 1915, the first day of a three-day national festival of Sacred Heart devotion, Weigand described seeing a row of saints and the Virgin Mary leading her devotees from purgatory directly into Heaven. Weigand's prophecy, claimed to recount the words of the Virgin Mary, was recorded as follows:

Now, believe too, that German and Austrian soldiers will triumph! Not in vain was the Love-Community [*Liebesbund*; Weigand's term for her following] formed in Germany, not in vain should the sign of the Love-Community build the Victory- and Peace Church [i.e., the pilgrimage grotto] in Germany. Germany and Austria owe their victories hitherto only to those men that led you to My Son [i.e., Jesus Christ], and that cared that the Love-Community spread widely.[72]

The role of female folk seer, especially in isolated areas of Central Europe, drew on long-standing traditions. Religious studies of everyday life in the Dual Monarchy, for instance, recorded that mountainous, Alpine regions contained villages with marked religious "continuities into late antiquity," especially through female religious authority figures in Romanen and Ladine ethno-religious customs. In these areas, the nineteenth century had seen stigmatics such as Maria von Mörl of Kaltern, Domenica Lazzari of Lazzari, and Kresztentia Niglutsch of Lana, as well as the mystic peasant daughter Ursula Mohr of Eppan and more shadowy figures like the "sick, blind woman" of Bergdorf Jenesien, near Bozen.[73]

Regional studies of Tyrol during the Great War have begun to investigate Church-approved forms of religiosity, including conflicts between Church and state hierarchies, for instance over the issue of whether church bells should be melted down for the production of armaments. Drawing on historical anthropologies, these regional studies should be reconciled with deep traditions of local folk piety and their adaption during the process of modern war, especially during flashpoints in which,

---

[72] Ibid., 297–303.   [73] Klieber, *Jüdische, Christliche, Muslimische*, 106.

from a patriarchal Church point of view, strange women acting indepen-
dently threatened the social order.[74]

Association movements and nursing care

Catholic religious orders showed the extent to which religious women
contributed to the war effort, blurring boundaries between homefront
and battlefront. Catholics in Germany accounted for only around one-
third of nominal religious believers in the majority Protestant empire.
Thus, Catholic religious women were over-represented in the vital area
of caritas nursing care: compared to around 12 331 Protestants, 17 200
Catholic religious women served as nurses, of whom 7000 worked in staging areas close to the battlefront. Of this latter group, 255 died in the line
of duty. In all, around 1000 Catholic religious women became grievously
sick or wounded in the service, and 28 were made prisoners of war.[75]

The religious orders were a fundamental part of the Church's membership, and the strong presence of religious women in particular highlighted their fundamental contribution to the war effort. Even within
Catholicism, women performed caritas outreach at a greater rate than
their male counterparts. Religious orders were part of a strong network
of care that emerged during the war and provided an increased presence for the Church as a source of social welfare. Incomplete statistical data nonetheless reveal several interesting dimensions to Catholic
religious care. At first glance, men and women from religious orders
in Germany served in nearly equal numbers: 11 717 men and 11 713
women. However, on further examination, the statistics also suggest that
the Catholic patriarchy could have been attempting to conceal or suppress
the numbers of religious women. In actuality, they were even greater.
The statistics for the German Empire both contained more unknown
categories for religious women and excluded women from the heavily
Catholic region of Bavaria. In all likelihood, many more religious women
served the war effort but were not statistically recorded by the Catholic
hierarchy.

Differences emerged because men were more closely aligned with the
state hierarchy, through direct service in the military. Of 11 717 male
members of religious orders in 1919, nearly seventy-five percent, or 8422
to be precise, served the state in some official capacity. Over half, 5302,

---

[74] Houlihan, "Imperial Frameworks of Religion," 165–82; Rettenwander, *Der Krieg als
Seelsorge.*

[75] Birgit Panke-Kochinke, *Unterwegs und doch daheim. (Über-) Lebensstrategien von
Kriegskrankenschwestern im Ersten Weltkrieg in der Etappe* (Frankfurt am Main: Mabuse
Verlag, 2004), 24–5. By comparison, 92 000 German women unaffiliated with any
particular religion served as nurses in the Red Cross.

served as soldiers, although these were lay brothers and novitiates who had not received ordination. Of the remainder, 2089 served in hospitals and 1031 as military chaplains. During the war years, besides their participation in state-sponsored institutions like military chaplaincy, the male religious orders in Germany established 115 of their own hospitals to care for war victims, eventually caring for 464 181 people during the war.[76]

Religious women established more independent networks of care through the Church than did men. Although the total number of religious women in Germany in 1919 is not available, more religious women served the war effort in an auxiliary capacity as nurses: to reiterate, around 11 713 women, compared to 8422 men. In addition to their state participation, female religious orders established 556 of their own hospitals, which provided a disproportionate amount of care to wounded soldiers, numbering 6 386 794 in total. Religious women themselves accounted for 177 deaths and 576 serious illnesses, while their male counterparts numbered 906 killed in combat, 2166 wounded or seriously ill, and 512 missing. These figures are a rough estimate: the number of sick and wounded people cared for by some male religious orders (Carmelites, Capuchins) went unreported, for example, despite these orders' strong presence in terms of number of personnel. Thus, one must underscore that the official contemporary statistics likely undercounted the number of Catholic religious women who served.[77]

Caught between imperatives of Church and state, male religious orders faced a manpower crises, as their lay brothers and unordained novitiates could be called up for active duty as soldiers. The Jesuits were perhaps the most pointed example of a male religious order caught up in modern warfare. Technically outlawed in Germany until the outdated statute was removed in 1917, Jesuits in fact served in the German armed forces as soldiers and military chaplains from the beginning of the war. Perhaps the most famous, Rupert Mayer, was grievously wounded as a military chaplain, receiving the Iron Cross (First Class) for his service with the 8th Bavarian Reserve Regiment. Mayer became a staunch opponent of Nazism, drawing upon his war service and wounding as an alternative model of heroic Christian devotion.[78]

As part of a broader reenergization of Catholic associational life, Catholic women's and children's movements saw marked growth and

---

[76] Krose, *Kirchliches Handbuch für das katholische Deutschland*, 9 (1919–20), 393–8. See also Erwin Gatz, ed., *Geschichte des kirchlichen Lebens in den deutschsprachigen Ländern seit dem Ende des 18. Jahrhunderts: Die Katholische Kirche*, vol. 7: *Klöster und Ordensgemeinschaften* (Freiburg: Herder, 2006), 288–9.

[77] Krose, *Kirchliches Handbuch für das katholische Deutschland*, 9 (1919–20), 393–8.

[78] Rita Haub, *Pater Rupert Mayer: Ein Lebensbild* (München: Neue Stadt, 2007). For the context of Jesuitism in Germany, see Healy, *Jesuit Specter*.

consolidation because of the war. In the Archdiocese of Cologne, association membership grew from 558 associations with 190 000 members
in January 1920 to 652 associations with 200 000 members by the next
year. In the "Association of Catholic Women and Mothers," women paid
monthly dues of 10 pfennigs, received the periodical *Die Monika,* and
pledged themselves to pray the daily Association prayer, attend monthly
meetings of the congregation, take communion with the Association,
and pray for deceased members. The Association "put itself under the
protection of the Most Holy Virgin and Sorrowful Mother of God."
Women obtained new opportunities for leadership in these Church-
affiliated organizations, provided they submitted to overall patriarchal
conceptions of authority in a selfless, communal fashion. In the words of
the Association's fivefold intertwined founding principles: "The purpose
of the association is to help every member to become a.) a practical pious
Catholic woman of firm faith, b.) a loving and true spouse of the man,
c.) a soundly-educated, life-skilled mother of children, d.) a practical
housekeeper, e.) a sacrificial, smart helper of fellow humans in need."[79]

Catholic authorities took very seriously the problematic social disorder caused by the spectacle of suffering of poor, hungry, and desperate
women and children. Under the direction of Agnes Neuhaus, a centralized association for this purpose, originally founded in 1901 and operating out of Dortmund, extended its reach to 144 local chapters across
Central Europe. By 1919, the association's 34 455 contributing sponsors,
established 42 homes with around 3000 beds, caring for 8610 "neglected
and defenseless children, girls, and women" providing "a refuge, a place
of care, of education, of spiritual improvement."[80]

The war opened large opportunities for Catholic women to participate
as leaders in religious organizations, especially in mid-level roles and positions that had some degree of supervision from the male clerical hierarchy. But there were outstanding leadership examples that would provide
inspiration for more emancipated Catholic women later in the twentieth
century. Socially-prominent aristocratic Catholic women often served as
ideal organizers and examples. Baroness Angela Marie Katharine Freiin
von Petzoldt of Munich, for example, continued a pre-war Catholic
tradition of social-caritative efforts. In the late nineteenth century, the
Baroness held meetings with Pope Leo XIII, who helped her culti-
vate transnational charity networks associated with the well-being of the

---

[79] AEK, CR I 22.20,1, "Normalsatzung für Vereine kath. Frauen und Mütter in der
Erzdiözese," and "Jahresbericht des Verbandes der kath. Frauen- und Müttervereine in
der Erzdiözese Köln."
[80] AEK, Gen I 23.37,1, "Jahresbericht 1919 des Gesamtvereins katholischer Fürso-
rgeverein für Mädchen, Frauen, und Kinder." By 1929, the number of local chapters
had grown to 380. See AEK, Gen I 23.37,1, "Jahresbericht, 1929."

youth, creating refuges for orphan and wayward girls. The Baroness continued her efforts during and after the war, raising money and creating opportunities for disadvantaged youth, until her death in 1929.[81] Other Catholic aristocratic women stepped headlong into the military administrative state, usually as emissaries and symbols of the homefront, but nonetheless possessing a great deal of social capital. After making a personal visit to Austro-Hungarian troops at the battlefront, Archduchess Blanka reported to the Ministry of War that the number of chaplains was insufficient to properly serve the religious needs of the army.[82]

In their labor relations, Catholic women in Central Europe found themselves caught up in the inefficiencies of military command autonomies that unleashed anarchic competition and fragmentation of concentrated efforts.[83] In a 1917 open letter circulated to the female religious orders in Cologne, Cardinal Felix von Hartmann acknowledged that labor resources were stretched thin in Germany, with women being called to work in factories and thus having insufficient time to attend to infants and school children. Cardinal Hartmann called upon Catholic nuns to do their part by supporting the girls and women who had joined the labor force. Hartmann advocated a program of "caritative-effective" care designed to supplement a network of nurseries, childcares, and school programs run by Catholic institutions, as well as to provide free-standing homes for children, soup kitchens, and supplemental aid to families with children.[84]

One of the most important areas of female religious labor was nursing. Especially through their nursing, Catholic lay and religious women formed an important part of the caritas network that both sustained the war effort and tried to ameliorate it. Religious organizations, along with state and non-governmental organizations such as the Red Cross, provided a layer of care that attempted to heal the wounds of war. The Catholic ideal of female chastity fit particularly well with the professional ideals of nurses, although romances with patients certainly did happen. However, the celibate nurses became emotional focal points for soldiers, transferring their affection toward caring female figures who represented notions of home and family.[85]

---

[81] DTA 1100,1, Baronesse Angela Marie Katharine Freiin von Petzoldt.

[82] ÖStAKA, NFA, AOK, Qu. Op. 1916, Ktn. 1682 (betr. 48739) (KM, q. Zu. Nr. 19323); cf. KM, 9. Abt (1916), Ktn. 983:11–32 (reg. 19323).

[83] John Horne, ed., *State, Society, and Mobilization in Europe during the First World War* (Cambridge: Cambridge University Press, 1997); Wall and Winter, *The Upheaval*.

[84] AEK, Gen I 23.19,1, January 19, 1917, "Rundschreiben an die weiblichen Ordensgenossenschaften in der Erzdiözese Cöln."

[85] Daniel, "Women," 1:89–102.

Figure 8 Caritas hospital network (BfZ)
"Religiously-based hospital care was a key form of the caritas network."

Religious women as nurses became deeply involved in their patients' lives. As in previous wars, they comforted the sick and dying. The new horrors of industrial war, however, presented new aspects of the human condition, with bodies disfigured by poison gas, flamethrowers, and assorted artillery shells. Furthermore, advances in medicine made it possible for more soldiers to live and linger in grievous conditions that would have been considered immediately mortal and therefore untreatable in previous wars.

Religious women serving in the hospital network faced a particularly difficult dilemma of care. On the one hand, they tried to maintain the clinical, impersonal professionalism demanded by the functional role of nurse: a clinical, professional role. On the other hand, however, religious nurses became intimately involved as friends and sometimes lovers of their patients, offering comfort and a sense of return to homefront peace to soldiers scarred by war.[86]

Writing from the Eastern Front in Eylau, Hilda Galles, a Red Cross nurse and likely Protestant, wrote of the difficulties that could develop in relationships with patients when flirtatious or romantic attachments

[86] Panke-Kochinke, *Unterwegs und doch daheim*, 110–38.

were involved. Writing home to her parents regarding her hospital service, Galles alluded to class and power dynamics in her interactions with the officers, which made them more difficult to care for. She wrote that, "The care of officers is decidedly more difficult than that of the enlisted men. The officers, although most of them are married, often want more than hospital care. They are so lonely and lovesick and they want to flirt. That is dangerous because in the end, I am not made of stone. However, you can be assured that I am inapproachable, not exactly to my advantage."[87] Galles corresponded with her parents frequently, arranging supplemental food packages, clothing, and amusing diversions for the soldiers under her care. After seeing the burial of one of the religious sisters serving as a hospital nurse, the third or fourth to die in a few months, Galles wrote of her sisters' full devotion to their society's effort in a total war, which was nonetheless underappreciated by the patriarchy: "Yes, if people at home would only recognize more the work of the sisters, and then no one would denigrate them. We are fighting a fight in the truest sense of the word."[88]

As Galles's own correspondence reveals, however, religious women were hard-pressed to inform the homefront fully about what was going on, due to fatigue and self-censorship. Because of the enormous strain placed on the insufficient hospital networks, nurses and doctors found themselves constantly overworked, with little free time. In the time available, they did not want or were not able to reveal the true horrors of war in their letters home. Hilda's correspondence with her parents through terse field postcards contrasts sharply with the personal searing images of war that she recorded in her diary. Her postcard of September 16, 1915 succinctly stated to her parents that, "Have a lot to do! I cannot write. Have been for 6 days an operating nurse in a field hospital in Brest-Litovsk." Her diary of the same period, however, records the experiences in vivid detail and is worth quoting at length, especially for the contrasts with her communication to the homefront:

In the letters one may not write anything negative, in order not to unsettle the people at home. And actually everything here is negative and correspondingly horrifying. [Of the area around Brest-Litovsk], now it's one field of ruins. Everywhere there are blazes, everywhere shells explode... On the ground on stinking straw in their dirty uniforms lay endless rows of sick and wounded Russians, Germans, Poles, Austrians, Czechs, etc. All mixed together. There was no window, no ventilation... My boss [the chief surgeon] greeted me warmly... I had to administer narcotics, monitor the pulse and instruments. And then we began!

[87] BA-MA, MSG 2/1718, Letter, Hilda to mother, November 24, 1914.
[88] BA-MA, MSG 2/1718, Letter, Hilda to mother and father, September 23, 1915.

It was chiefly about amputations and brain operations. Shrapnel and bullets had to be removed. I worked as if in a trance. One wounded soul after another was laid on the table, and [the chief surgeon] operated at a frantic pace. When I announced that breathing and pulse had stopped . . . he was furious and flung our expensive instruments on the ground. The orderlies had to collect and quickly clean them . . . In the courtyard was a tower of amputated limbs, covered by a swarm of flies. Next! And so it went on under lamplight and candlelight until the surgeon had to stop from exhaustion. For me that was not the end. I went with the students and the orderlies to the sick and wounded, distributing morphine injections and trying here and there to give a bit of calm and comfort . . . It was difficult, bitterly difficult, finally to leave the dark room. On all sides, I was grabbed firmly, and the orderlies had to free me by force. All cried out, "Sister, Sister dear, don't go! Stay by us!" I would have liked to cry, but I wasn't able to do it any more. It had to be . . . At the first light of dawn, it began again. Our first duty was to take out of the hall those who had died the previous night. I had to declare if they were dead, and they were taken away. New sick and wounded were brought in and laid on dirty straw, regardless of whether a wounded or diseased man had died there. It was Hell![89]

Hilda's recorded correspondence broke off in late November 1915, when she wrote to her parents that she was applying to leave the Red Cross.[90] Like their male counterparts, even the most resolute women could not endure seeing the horrors of combat wounds for long. Field hospitals were the most disturbing sites of bodily destruction. The network of hospitals extended deep into the homeland away from the battlefront, involving religious women in the process of palliative care in the drive to total war.

The numbers of religious women had risen dramatically in the nineteenth century, lending strength to the appearance of a feminizing Catholic Church. In the period from 1853 to 1909 in archdioceses of Vienna and Salzburg, the number of nuns rose from 340 to 4573 and from 190 to 1044, respectively. New female orders such as the "Gray Sisters," founded in Prague, and the Society of the Daughters of Heavenly Love, founded by Franziska Lechner from Bavaria, often began and operated with few financial means and sometimes encountered opposition within the Church. In Lechner's case, she began her order in 1869 without startup capital and by her own dynamic example attracted a following of similar women devoted to her ideal of Christian service. By 1871, the Daughters of Heavenly Love was operating in Vienna, Budapest, Troppau, and Brünn; by the time of Lechner's death in 1894, the society counted over 500 members, operating in thirty-one houses

---

[89] BA-MA, MSG 2/1718, Feldpostkarte, September 16, 1915; Diary, September 17, 1915.
[90] BA-MA, MSG 2/1718, Letter, Hilda to mother and father, November 23, 1915.

in the Dual Monarchy, now including Prague, Sarajewo, Toponár, and Berzencze. Written in 1893, shortly before Lechner's death, the twenty-fifth-anniversary celebratory publicity reveals the growing network of institutionalized charity that would become crucial in the First World War, when state resources were stretched beyond limits:

In Marian institutions 66 656 jobless young women taken in, taught, and cared for; in the institutes there were raised 9069 orphans and boarding pupils and 14 227 external students were taught; in the childcare centers were 13 422 children; in the trade schools were 15 715 students; in Sunday schools were 8247 servants; in the refuge house of St. Joseph in Breitenfurt were 294 old people unfit for work and in the reconvalescent house were 2901 convalescents. The number of the poor, that through the Society enjoyed full care and education, numbered 1350 daily. The days of care for these people ran to 9 184 306 since the founding. Besides the girls in Sunday school, 4275 poor children received free education.[91]

Recruitment to the orders rose after the war, which contributed to the growth of the Church's caritas network. Although figures from the war remain fragmentary, in 1920 there were sixty-two female religious orders with 15 024 members; by 1938, this had risen to seventy-two female religious orders with 19 555 members, a gain of nearly thirty percent.[92] Catholic women, and the social aspects of religious care, remained an essential aspect of dealing with the war's devastation. The interwar period demonstrated their central social role more than ever before.

Conclusion

For Catholic women, the Great War opened up decisive new fields of action, while maintaining a traditional and conservative ideology. In many ways, Catholic women in Central Europe began altering the practices of daily life only in the period after 1918. As Richard Bessel has shown for Germany, during the immediate post-war years, traditional marriage rates in rural areas more than doubled.[93] The institution of marriage was another source of continuity, as war-torn societies clung to a pre-war idea of domesticity and traditional values, seeking stability and order.

The Weimar Republic, and the emergence of the New Woman, introduced a powerful new ideal that shook society thoroughly. Indeed, from the viewpoint of women's history, the Nazi period was a reaction against

---

[91] Klieber, *Jüdische, Christliche, Muslimische*, 125–8.
[92] Gatz, *Klöster und Ordensgemeinschaften*, 309.
[93] Richard Bessel, *Germany after the First World War* (Oxford: Clarendon Press, 1993), 228–42.

the emancipated excesses of Weimar, especially its liberal views on sexuality and the role of women.[94] After the shattering experiences of the Nazi regime, Central European women struggled heroically to rebuild their societies and their families from the devastation of two world wars. As part of a pan-European trend, the vast social changes of the Second World War and the 1960s were more decisive than the upheavals of the First World War in altering religious women's social lives.[95]

On a pan-European level, broad swaths of Catholic religious women looked to their religious faith as a way of dealing with the upheavals of the war. One must be careful to avoid a singular "women's" experience of the Great War, however, as the example of female Catholics has shown: the war unleashed a variety of religious experiences. The figure of the Virgin Mary as a saintly inspiration was a fundamental source of Catholic identity that reflected the ambivalences of gendered attitudes toward women. Catholic women as virgins and as mothers contributed fervently to the war efforts of their respective states as nurses, teachers, industrial workers, administrative officials, and scores of other occupations. It was on the local level, however, that pre-war continuities and devotions were most apparent.

Catholic women from rural agrarian regions remained largely devoted to local concerns, above all focused on the care of family farms, but new trends were emerging. With male workers killed and maimed, POW labor supplemented the missing men, and returning soldiers had to reacclimate to their societies. New patterns of family life and farm labor were beginning, but these changes would become most disruptive only after the Second World War and the upheavals of the 1960s. The Great War did not decisively detour the Central European Catholic road to modernity.

---

[94] Birgit Sack, *Zwischen religiöser Bindung und moderner Gesellschaft. Katholische Frauenbewegung und politische Kultur in der Weimarer Republik (1918/19–1933)* (Münster: Waxmann, 1998).
[95] Hugh McLeod, *The Religious Crisis of the 1960s* (Oxford: Oxford University Press, 2007).

6   A voice in the wilderness: the papacy

In modern history, and especially during the era of total war, the papacy has been seen as suffering a decline of influence. Perhaps this was put most starkly in Stalin's infamous quip, "How many divisions does the Pope have?" During the Great War, the papacy certainly did not have the military force it had possessed in earlier eras; however, its moral force was still strong. Indeed, after the loss of the papal states with the formation of Italy in 1870, the Church gained influence as a more impartial spiritual institution, even as it lost political territory.[1]

Presiding during a world war, the pope elected in the conclave of 1914, Benedict XV, remains one of the twentieth century's lesser-known popes in historiography, an "unknown pope" in the words of his most prominent biographer.[2] Often dismissed as a mere steward during a troubled period, Benedict demonstrated the power of religious tradition as an adaptive, not static or reactionary, phenomenon. On the one hand, his diplomatic efforts were aimed toward a preservation of a pre-war sense of order, an international *status quo ante bellum*, culminating in his famous Peace Note of August 1, 1917. On the other, however, while Benedict kept the pre-war ideal in mind, both his thoughts and his actions reflected his adjustment to the new circumstances. During the war, the Church became a non-partisan diplomatic actor, devoted its material resources to soothing the afflicted, refocused its organizational structure with a new Code of Canon Law, and began to confront new social movements that emerged because of the war, most famously fascism and communism. Thus, unlike previous papacies, Benedict engaged with the modernity of the Great War. Far from reactionary retreat or idle indifference, it was a period that set the tone for the Church's vigorous grappling with modernity during the twentieth century. In many ways, the Great War

[1] Frank J. Coppa, *Politics and the Papacy in the Modern World* (Westport, CT: Praeger, 2008).
[2] Pollard, *The Unknown Pope*. More recently, see Antonio Scottà, *Papa Benedetto XV: la Chiesa, la Grande Guerra, la pace (1914–1922)* (Rome: Edizioni di storia e letteratura, 2009).

allowed for growth and consolidation within the Church; it was not a time of senseless and futile waste.

The diplomatic setting

At the outbreak of the Great War, the Holy See was not inclined toward benevolent neutrality and did not maintain official diplomatic relations with the liberal democracies on the Allied side. Among the Entente Powers, the Holy See maintained diplomatic ties only with tsarist Russia, and it was deeply suspicious of the ideological advance of Orthodoxy in Eastern Europe. The suspicion was mutual, and no papal nuncio was permitted to serve in St. Petersburg. The Holy See did maintain diplomatic relations with Belgium, the state whose identity would focus much of the world's moral outrage, with Cardinal Mercier serving as an outspoken voice of courage under occupation. However, at the start of the war the Holy See had official relations with the main Central Powers of Austria-Hungary and Germany, the latter officially through emissaries in both Prussia and Bavaria. Leading German Catholic politicians in the Central Powers, most prominently Matthias Erzberger of the Catholic Center Party, had strong connections to Rome. They used their positions as conduits of information, engaging in both official and unofficial acts of diplomacy.[3] After Franz Joseph's death in November 1916, the new Kaiser of Austria-Hungary, Karl, made failed diplomatic overtures for peace in the infamous "Sixtus" Affair, which has led some present-day Catholics to try to canonize Karl as an apostle of peace.[4]

Most conspicuously among the Entente Powers, the Holy See did not have official diplomatic relations with France, long considered the "eldest daughter" of the Church. Culminating a rising tide of nineteenth-century anti-clericalism stemming from the French Revolution, relations with France were officially severed in 1905 after the state policy of laicization, entailing the separation of Church and state, took effect. After the war, the canonization of Joan of Arc on May 16, 1920 did much to reestablish French relations with the Holy See and bring reconciliation.[5]

The Eastern Front in particular unleashed a form of religious warfare that continued through the twentieth century. In Central and Eastern Europe, war blended into revolution in 1917, and revolution into counter-revolution, thus blurring the boundaries between war and civil

---

[3] For the background of Holy See diplomacy among the warring powers, see Pollard, *The Unknown Pope*, 85–111.
[4] Elisabeth Kovács, Pál Arató, Franz Pichorner, and Lotte Wewalka, eds., *Untergang oder Rettung der Donaumonarchie?*, 2 vols. (Vienna: Böhlau, 2004).
[5] Becker, *War and Faith*.

war. A highly ideological crusade against communism was just beginning, and religious sentiment played an important part in twentieth-century ideological warfare. Catholic leadership in the crusade against communism began during the Great War, when future popes had confrontations with the specter of Bolshevism. During the Polish–Soviet War, the papal nuncio in Warsaw was none other than Achille Ratti, the future Pope Pius XI (1922–39). Ratti personally witnessed the Red Army advance on Warsaw, remaining defiantly in the city to see the Bolsheviks stunningly halted at the Battle of Warsaw. During the same period, Eugenio Pacelli, the future Pope Pius XII (1939–58), served as papal nuncio to Bavaria and thus saw the rise and fall of the Bavarian Socialist Republic in Munich. Besides witnessing the upheaval of revolution that shook the organic conceptions of traditional society, Pacelli formed a personal grievance against the revolutionaries when they confiscated his beloved Mercedes-Benz automobile.[6] One could also point to the Catholic perceived horror of the Bela Kun regime in interwar Hungary.[7] Such close brushes with communism made the Vatican leadership highly defensive against any hint of it, keeping interwar politics at a high level of ideological combat and making compromises with declared anti-communist authoritarian regimes more amenable to Catholic sensibilities.

Soothe the afflicted

In contrast to previous centuries of blatant political diplomatic games, during the early years of the Great War, the Holy See remained relatively impartial, nearly bankrupting itself through its devotion to its caritas network of care, especially for POWs, displaced persons, and children.[8] In October 1916, Benedict XV directly appealed to Catholics in the United States for money to feed the children of Belgium. The children were a moral rallying point, but the funds raised were in fact used to provide food to entire populations in the war zones. Benedict XV repeated the process of Catholic appeal for many war-torn regions: Lithuania and Montenegro in 1916 and 1917, Poland and Russia in 1916, and Syria and Lebanon every year from 1916 to 1922. In the latter case, the Christians of the Holy Land formed a symbolically poignant and vulnerable group, especially since the Holy See's relations with the Sublime Porte, not friendly to begin with, had deteriorated during the course

---

[6] Hubert Wolf, *Papst und Teufel. Die Archive des Vatikan und das Dritte Reich* (Munich: CH Beck, 2008), 16–93.
[7] Hanebrink, *In Defense of Christian Hungary*.
[8] Pollard, *The Unknown Pope*.

of the war. Christians in these regions were subjected to mistreatment, famine, and disease, most infamously culminating in the genocide of the Armenians that began in earnest in April 1915. After failed interventions by the Apostolic Delegate in Constantinople and the Holy See's diplomatic effort to get Germany and Austria-Hungary to bring pressure on the Ottomans, Benedict sent a direct letter to the Sultan on September 10, 1915, appealing to him as Caliph of Islam, a fellow world religious leader.[9] The personal intervention, however, did little to halt the killing of the Armenians, which proceeded in a series of massacres that were heavily dependent on local conditions and administrative structures of the Ottoman Empire's provinces.[10]

In the aftermath of the Great War, Benedict XV stressed the need for all peoples to help the children of Central Europe by giving money to the Save the Children Fund, which he described as "a charity which enfolds in its kindly embrace all men, without distinction of race or nation, whosoever bear within them the image of God." In his encyclical *Annus Iam Plentus* of December 1, 1920, Benedict called for Catholics to "turn their hearts in pity towards the children of Central Europe, who were so severely afflicted by hunger and want that they were wasting away with disease and were face to face with death . . . We call loudly upon Christian peoples to give us the means whereby we may offer some relief to the sick and suffering children, of whatsoever nationality they may be."[11]

In Germany and elsewhere, the First World War and the interwar period represented a decisive moment in the history of organized social welfare. During and after the war, religious groups such as the Deutscher Caritas Verein (DCV) and the Reichsverband der katholischen Wohltätigkeitsorganisationen in Österreich opened up new opportunities for the Church to extend its reach into social-welfare programs when the state could not fill the gap. The state became involved in people's lives on an unprecedented scale, but this was not always enough to remedy the war's hardship. One should not downplay the deprivation, suffering, and social fragmentation that occurred in the war. However, one should also recognize that both during and after the war, when the state could

---

[9] Ibid., 115–16.

[10] For a thorough examination of the Armenian genocide, see Raymond H. Kévorkian, *The Armenian Genocide: A Complete History* (New York: I. B. Tauris, 2011). For a succinct overview of the genocide contextualized in terms of Turkish state-building, see Uğur Ümit Üngör, *The Making of Modern Turkey: Nation and State in Eastern Anatolia, 1913–1950* (Oxford: Oxford University Press, 2011), 55–88.

[11] http://www.vatican.va/holy_father/benedict_xv/encyclicals/documents/hf_ben-xv_enc_01121920_annus-iam-plenus_en.html (last accessed October 31, 2014).

not provide for its people, religious organizations stepped in to fill some important gaps, especially when no other organizations could.[12]

The caritas network of the Church formed an intermediary institution between public and private efforts of welfare or charity. The First World War represented a decisive step forward in the organizational history of the group as a major social-welfare actor. Indeed, the Caritasverband, "previously second-rate in its impact," developed through the Great War and the Weimar Republic into "one of the most powerful and influential organizations in the sector of public welfare and charity in Germany."[13] In the years 1915–22, all thirty dioceses in Germany for the first time received a nationally-coordinated branch of the Caritasverband, and it made even more rapid progress on the local and regional level: the number of local branches increased from 33 in 1915 to more than 2000 in 1918. Membership showed corresponding increases: the number of directly active Caritasverband members increased from around 5000 in 1913 to 35 045 by October 1921, and the number of related associational members reached over 600 000.[14] In 1916–17, the Caritasverband had a yearly income of 100 000 marks, but its expenditures to the needy exceeded this. Experiencing steady growth through the war years, by 1919–20 its income had increased to around 650 000 marks, still barely outpacing expenditures.[15] With declining state contributions from 1924 to 1932, it achieved financial autonomy, balancing its financial inputs and outputs. It ensconced itself as a major player on the social-welfare scene.[16] Especially given the post-war deprivation and Weimar Germany's institutional struggles to care for veterans, widows, and orphans, Church welfare organizations filled essential gaps, and Catholic women were both key agents and recipients of this help.[17]

Framing the conflict

Early in the war, Benedict XV forecast that it would be a bloody, hard-fought contest, filled with the most advanced forms of technological destruction. His views proved prophetic, and set the tone for Catholic interpretations of the conflict. Ironically, given the papacy's often reactionary anti-modernism, the pope expressed similar views to many avant garde cultural elites' beliefs about the war, but with an important difference: the war, for him, ultimately solidified a spiritual interpretation of

---

[12] Maurer, *Der Caritasverband.*   [13] Ibid., 258.   [14] Ibid., 174–75, 186.
[15] Ibid., 148–73, 212–13.   [16] Ibid., 212, 218.
[17] Robert W. Whalen, *Bitter Wounds: German Victims of the Great War, 1914–1939* (Ithaca, NY: Cornell University Press, 1984).

metaphysical belief in God. After his election to the papacy in September 1914, he wrote in his encyclical of November 1 (All Saints' Day):

On every side the dread phantom of war holds sway: there is scarce room for another thought in the minds of men. The combatants are the greatest and wealthiest nations of the earth; what wonder, then, if, well provided with the most awful weapons modern military science has devised, they strive to destroy one another with refinements of horror. There is no limit to the measure of ruin and of slaughter; day by day the earth is drenched with newly-shed blood, and is covered with the bodies of the wounded and of the slain. Who would imagine as we see them thus filled with hatred of one another, that they are all of one common stock, all of the same nature, all members of the same human society? Who would recognize brothers, whose Father is in Heaven?[18]

The Pope argued, however, that the common human community, especially embodied by the institution of the Church, would serve as a force for unity and peace. But it was not an egalitarian vision. Benedict cited traditional passages of biblical authority, including the famous passage in Romans 13:

Hence, therefore, whenever legitimate authority has once given a clear command, let no one transgress that command, because it does not happen to commend itself to him; but let each one subject his own opinion to the authority of him who is his superior, and obey him as a matter of conscience. Again, let no private individual, whether in books or in the press, or in public speeches, take upon himself the position of an authoritative teacher in the Church. All know to whom the teaching authority of the Church has been given by God: he, then, possesses a perfect right to speak as he wishes and when he thinks it opportune. The duty of others is to hearken to him reverently when he speaks and to carry out what he says.[19]

The notion of Catholic obedience to authority was well grounded to soldiers at the micro-level. In the words of a field manual distributed to the troops by the Catholic Garrison Office in Cologne, "Military service is service to the king, and service to the king is service to God. God has determined you for this." This particular booklet reached mass publication status, with over 180 000 copies distributed to German soldiers by 1915.[20]

In his pontifical role as Bishop of Rome, Benedict XV stressed the importance of the entire Church submitting to the authority of bishops. He wrote in the encyclical, "Let those who have so unfortunately failed

---

[18] http://www.vatican.va/holy_father/benedict_xv/encyclicals/documents/hf_ben-xv_enc_01111914_ad-beatissimi-apostolorum_en.html (last accessed October 31, 2014).
[19] Ibid.   [20] Cöln, *Vor Gott ein Kind*, 4.

in their duty, recall to their minds again and again, that the authority of those whom 'the Holy Spirit hath placed as Bishops to rule the Church of God' (Acts 20:28) is a divine authority. Let them remember that if, as we have seen, those who resist any legitimate authority, resist God, much more impiously do they act who refuse to obey the Bishop, whom God has consecrated with a special character by the exercise of His power."[21] Benedict identified the key role of bishops in spreading the message of the Church, but did not recognize an inherent problem in this arrangement: bishops had multiple loyalties and their personal sense of Catholicism was a complicated mix of local, national, state, and ecclesiastical identities.[22] In the event, many of the bishops did not obey Benedict's direct commands during the war, especially the command to advocate for peace: they were in service of state aims of victory.[23] The Church's cardinals wrote to the Pope, most often in service of their particular state cause. Cardinal Désiré Mercier of Belgium and Cardinal Louis Lucon of Rheims, for instance, both wrote to Benedict describing the destruction that was occurring in their archdioceses and imploring his aid in stopping it.[24] Images of destroyed churches figured prominently in cultural propaganda, usually preferred by one side as evidence of the other's barbarity. The Pope, however, emphasized the universality of suffering, reflecting inherent human sinfulness common to all sides.

When the Pope offered only prayers and wishes for a restoration of peace, the bishops were bound to be disappointed at the lack of more direct action. In a similar way, given his public writings, the Pope was dismayed at the particularist views of high-ranking clerics, who refused to put the needs of the universal church first. Benedict XV, however, was taking steps to provide immediate, tangible aid to those suffering the scourge of war; he was also attempting to diplomatically intervene to bring the war to an end.

---

[21] http://www.vatican.va/holy_father/benedict_xv/encyclicals/documents/hf_ben-xv_enc_01111914_ad-beatissimi-apostolorum_en.html (last accessed October 31, 2014).

[22] The problem was perhaps most acute for the bishops of the ethnically-mixed polity that was the Habsburg monarchy. For a fascinating study of the bishops' attempts to synthesize Catholic universalism with more ethnic particularity, see Gottsmann, *Rom und die nationalen Katholizismen.*

[23] For an example of a medal (War Cross for Civil Service, 1st Class) awarded by Kaiser Karl to Cardinal Friedrich Gustav Piffl of the Archdiocese of Vienna, see "Allerhöchste Auszeichnung," *Wiener Diözesanblatt* (August 27, 1917), 1.

[24] http://www.vatican.va/holy_father/benedict_xv/letters/documents/hf_ben-xv_let_19141208_cum-de-fidelibus_it.html, http://www.vatican.va/holy_father/benedict_xv/letters/documents/hf_ben-xv_let_19141016_c-est-avec-un_it.html (both last accessed October 31, 2014).

Figure 9 Destroyed church in Biglia (Lipusch)
"Ruined sacred spaces were both elements of propaganda and sites of continued devotion."

Material aid

The Pope's efforts to provide care to those suffering from the war were successful both ideologically and materially. Through its vast diplomatic connections across the world, the Vatican's network of information exchange reported on the conditions of war, as well as facilitating the exchange of goods and repatriation of people. In a highly polarized global conflict, this was an important development.

Benedict XV nearly bankrupted the Church in an effort to give aid to the needy whose lives the war had altered. Displaced persons and POWs were two categories of people to which the Pope devoted particular attention. Shortly before Christmas 1914, the papal decree published in *L'Osservatore Romano* announced the need to provide "spiritual and material assistance to prisoners."[25] Although the Vatican had made earlier attempts, this decree began the formation of a vast humanitarian relief network, comparable to the efforts of the International Red Cross, for which the Great War was a decisively positive moment, vastly expanding its operation and providing it world-wide recognition as a non-partisan actor.[26] By spring 1915, the Vatican's Prisoners' Work Office (*Opera dei Prigionieri*) was set up in the offices of the Secretary of State, with branch offices in Switzerland, Germany, and Austria. By the war's end the office had dealt with 600 000 pieces of correspondence regarding 170 000 inquiries about missing persons. The Holy See became the channel of correspondence for 50 000 letters to and from prisoners and their families, which resulted in repatriation requests for 40 000 sick POWs.[27]

Using its network of nuncios, especially in Brussels, Munich, and Vienna, the Holy See's local bishops and members of the clergy became involved in helping to lessen the suffering of sick and wounded POWs. Benedict tried to provide POWs with chaplains of all their various faiths, attempting to ensure that regular religious services were available. Beyond mere religious metaphysics, however, the Holy See became involved as an advocate for improving conditions in POW camps. Engaging in delicate local diplomacy with military and state administrators, Church officials intervened to stop maltreatment of prisoners when possible and attempted to make POW facilities clean, safe, and provided with decent food. In the camps, contact with the outside world was especially problematic, as channels to the homefront were highly suspect to military

---

[25] *L'Osservatore Romano*, December 23, 1914, quoted in Pollard, *The Unknown Pope*, 113.
[26] See Caroline Moorehead, *Dunant's Dream: War, Switzerland, and the History of the Red Cross* (London: HarperCollins, 1998).
[27] Pollard, *The Unknown Pope*, 113.

authorities; thus, neutral organizations like the Catholic Church and
the International Red Cross were often prisoners' only channel of communication. The most contentious issue was the exchange of prisoners
between the warring powers, some of whom were particularly hostile
to and suspicious of the motives of the others. Despite repeated Vatican attempts, for instance, POW repatriation never took place between
Austria-Hungary and Italy.[28]

Pastoral responsibility for POWs became another area in which the
Church's resources were stretched between the conflicting needs of military and civilian ministry. Even high-ranking Church administrators were
unsure about whether the ultimate responsibility for POW ministry was to
be directed by the needs of the military or the needs of the Church. Often,
compromises were worked out in an impromptu, haphazard manner that
suited local conditions and particularities. For instance, according to a
decree of the Bavarian Ministry of War in 1916, Cardinal Bettinger of
Munich-Freising reiterated to his clergy that responsibility for ministering to POWs as laborers was the job of the clergy where the prisoners
were conducting their work, not that where the camp was located.[29]

Highlighting the ambiguity of their position between Church and state,
when captured, military chaplains continued to perform functions that
were substantially similar to those they carried out when behind their
own lines: performing Mass, distributing communion, hearing confessions, and caring for the wounded. All of these functions were performed
mainly for the captured POWs of the chaplain's own state. Other soldiers became functionally different upon capture, profoundly altering
their social role as producers of state-organized violence. Only medical
personnel performed similar functions as before capture, although often
for the state that had captured them, healing the bodies of their ostensible
enemies.[30] Although some Catholic POW chaplains ministered to enemy
troops, most continued to care for the minds and souls of their own soldiers. In any case, medical personnel had clearly defined roles: to heal
the physical body. Chaplains' more ambiguous roles as morale-builders,
comforters, friends, and spiritual ministers reflected their complicated
functionality.

---

[28] Ibid., 113–15.
[29] See EAM, Ktn. 383: Militärseelsorge Akten, VN 381a: Kriegsgefangenenseelsorge im
I. WK, Nr. 16344 ex 2.2.1916, Letter, February 14, 1916, Pfarramt Bockhorn, Pfarrer
Nickl an Kardinal von Bettinger.
[30] Ingo Tamm, "'Ein Stand im Dienst der nationalen Sache': Positionen und Aufgaben
ärztlicher Standesorganisationen im Ersten Weltkrieg," in Die Medizin und der Erste
Weltkrieg, ed. Wolfgang U. Eckart and Christoph Gradmann (Pfaffenweiler: Centarius,
1996), 11–21.

POW camps involved Catholic chaplains in a network of exchange that transcended national boundaries. When captured in battle, Catholic chaplains accompanied the troops of the Central Powers into captivity, but chaplains were also responsible for ministering to captured enemy troops in POW camps within Central Europe. In such cases, the chaplains shared their ministry with members of the clergy from the homefront, such as when the future Chancellor of Austria, Monsignor Ignaz Seipel, serving as a theology professor, assisted the Feldkurat Joachim Mayr in providing religious ministry to the POW camp in Anif, near Salzburg.[31] Members of the clergy on the homefront also had to reconcile their ministry with captured enemy clergy members, who were naturally viewed with great suspicion by military authorities.

It was hard to determine whether such cooperation from the homefront clergy became a form of military chaplaincy. On one level, the issue was clear-cut: only members of the clergy who were commissioned officers approved by their ecclesiastical and military authorities could be named chaplains. In the absence of these official chaplains, however, other clergy members exercised exactly the same functions, although without the title. One of the primary areas where this occurred was in the ministry of POWs in the homeland. In the reserve hospital in Munich, for instance, the cleric Hubert Glas substituted for the officially-appointed chaplain, the cathedral vicar Joseph Ebert, in ministering to wounded French POWs in Munich. Glas received a monthly compensation of 180 marks from the Bavarian State through the office of the First Army Command.[32]

After the treaty of Brest-Litovsk, waves of Habsburg POWs returned home to be viewed with suspicion by the high command, wary of subversive Bolshevik influence acquired during captivity. The army administration subjected its returning POWs to a further measure of Habsburg captivity, intended as a quarantine to root out possible Bolshevik influence.[33] Austro-Hungarian chaplains were commanded with surveying, assessing, disciplining, and reintegrating these returning troops. By this late stage in the war, however, the Habsburg forces were well disposed to revolutionary and pacifistic sentiments, and chaplains were unable to alter their

---

[31] ÖStAKA, AFV, Ktn. 216, Pastoralbericht Joachim Mayr, November 1915.
[32] BHStA, Abt IV, MKr. 13847, p. 72: Kommandantur der Haupt- und Residenzstadt München an das Reserve-Lazarett München B. et al., April 3, 1915.
[33] Reinhard Nachtigal, "Die Repatriierung der Mittelmächte-Kriegsgefangenen aus dem revolutionären Rußland: Heimkehr zwischen Agitation, Bürgerkrieg, und Intervention 1918–1922," in *Kriegsgefangene im Europa des Ersten Weltkriegs*, ed. Jochen Oltmer (Paderborn: Schöningh, 2006), 239–66; Alon Rachamimov, *POWs and the Great War: Captivity on the Eastern Front* (Oxford: Berg, 2002).

opinions.[34] A closer examination of the chaplaincy's effort illuminates some of the problems of reintegration of the returning veterans.

Overall, soldiers refused to accept the army's insistence on a quarantine to quell Bolshevik elements in the camps of those returning home (*Heimkehrer*). Further, during their internment in Russia, some Austro-Hungarian soldiers had gained Russian partners and children, who were refused admittance into the Habsburg monarchy, generating intense animosity against the regime.[35] In the *Heimkehrer* camp in Ozortków, Feldkurat Cyril Vycudilik reported that growing dissatisfaction with the Habsburg regime was related to what he referred to as the "stomach question" (*Magenfrage*); that is, the failure of the Habsburg state to provide many of its citizens with sufficient nourishing food. The chaplain reported that, "through such circumstances in the Army provisioning, the soldiers were first made into Bolsheviks here in Austria." Demonstrating a Catholic anti-Semitism related to the food question, Vycudilik believed that Jewish shops had plenty of food.[36] Returning to Vycudilik's earlier assertion, however, other chaplains agreed that it was precisely the army's treatment of its returning veterans as potential Bolshevik subversives that fomented dissatisfaction with the authorities.[37] Overall, in line with recent narratives of Habsburg history that revise the view of a centrifugal disordered polity, Alon Rachamimov asserts that Habsburg soldiers' critiques of their treatment in *Heimkehrer* camps were couched in terms not of socialism or nationalism but of "'civic spirit,' i.e., direct criticism of specific practices and specific policies of the Habsburg State." Thus, Austro-Hungarian POWs had civic conceptions similar to those of their counterparts from other combatant nations, such as France and Germany.[38]

Capture in battle resulted in heavily-dramatized post-war heroic narratives of survival and triumph under adverse conditions. These accounts blended easily, even after the Second World War, into a stereotypical

---

[34] Cornwall, *Undermining of Austria-Hungary*; Richard Georg Plaschka, Horst Haselsteiner, and Arnold Suppan, *Innere Front: Militärassistenz, Widerstand, und Umsturz in der Donaumonarchie 1918*, 2 vols. (Vienna: Verlag für Geschichte und Politik, 1974).

[35] ÖStAKA, AFV, Ktn. 247: Pastoralbericht September 1918 HK Lager, Feldpost 354, Feldkurat Stefan Varga.

[36] ÖStAKA, AFV, Ktn. 247: May 1918 Pastoralbericht, HK Lager in Ozortków, Cyril Vycudilik. For the politics of food in Austria-Hungary, see Healy, *Vienna*. One of the leading historians of captivity on the Eastern Front has made the argument that Jewish civilians in Eastern Europe provided captured soldiers of their own religion with better food and personal care than was the norm for non-Jewish captives. See Rachamimov, *POWs and the Great War*, 50, 151.

[37] ÖStAKA, AFV, Ktn. 247: HK Lager 215, Pastoralberichte 2. Hälfte Monats Mai.

[38] Rachamimov, *POWs and the Great War*, 196.

depiction of Russia as a lawless, savage, untamed land.[39] Although some of these stories were certainly embellished attempts at adventure tales, there were elements of truth about the lack of adequate POW care in the East. Some of this was a structural problem resulting from the overwhelming numbers of captives: of the war's 8.5 million POWs, around 2.77 million were Austro-Hungarians and 2.8 million Russians, lending credibility to the argument that, "captivity was one of the quintessential war experiences" for Russian and Austro-Hungarian soldiers. This fundamental condition of imprisonment became marginalized because it was less shocking than the new narrative of ghastly industrialized combat on the Western Front, where far fewer prisoners were taken, which became a dominant historical remembrance of the conflict.[40]

The tsarist state infrastructure was not able to deal adequately with its prison population even before the logistical strains of new industrialized war added to the pressures that overwhelmed the state system. The confusion between the collapse of the old tsarist system and the establishment of the new Bolshevik regime in an atmosphere of disorder and civil war compounded the prison problems exponentially.[41] The Catholic Church was deeply involved in the ever-shifting effort to allocate resources on the homefront and battlefront.

Diplomatic offensive

Benedict XV's efforts to end the war began in the early days of his papacy in September 1914 and continued throughout the conflict. On the first anniversary of Austria-Hungary's declaration of war on Serbia, July 28, 1915, after Italy entered the war and it became clear that the belligerents were locked in conflict, Benedict issued an Apostolic Exhortation, "To the Belligerent Peoples and their Rulers," imploring, "Abandon the mutual threat of destruction. Remember, Nations do not die; humiliated and oppressed, they bear the weight of the yoke imposed upon them, preparing themselves for their comeback and transmitting from one generation to the next a sad legacy of hatred and vendetta." Benedict argued that the conflict should be solved by peaceful methods. He wrote to the

---

[39] Karl Drexel, *Feldkurat in Sibirien, 1914–1920*, 3rd edn. (Innsbruck: F. Rauch, 1949). Cf. Liulevicius, *War Land*.

[40] Rachamimov, *POWs and the Great War*, 3–4, 221–30.

[41] Lipusch, *Österreich-Ungarns katholische Militärseelsorge*, 120–6; Georg Wurzer, "Die Erfahrung der Extreme: Kriegsgefangene in Rußland 1914–1918," in Oltmer, *Kriegsgefangene*, 97–125. Cf. Rachamimov, *POWs and the Great War*. Further, the religious care of Orthodox POWs from Russia was almost wholly neglected by German authorities. See Jochen Oltmer, "Unentbehrliche Arbeitskräfte: Kriegsgefangene in Deutschland 1914–1918," in Oltmer, *Kriegsgefangene*, 67–96.

belligerents, "It is not true that this conflict cannot be resolved without the violence of arms . . . Blessed be he who first raises the olive branch of peace and extends his right hand to the enemy offering reasonable conditions for peace. The equilibrium of the world and prosperity and secure tranquility of nations rest on mutual benevolence and the respect of the rights of and dignity of others, rather than on a multitude of armies and a formidable ring of fortresses."[42] But the belligerent powers continued in their belief in peace through victory and force of arms.

The Papal Peace Note of August 1, 1917 was one of the war's most visible attempts at a brokered compromise, a highpoint of the Vatican peace efforts. Addressed to the leaders of the belligerent nations, the Peace Note began with a proclamation of "complete impartiality towards all parties to the strife, as befits the universal Father who loves all his children equally." Benedict stated that he would continue to act "without respect of persons or discriminating between faiths" and that he had a "mission of peace . . . to neglect nothing, so far as within us lies, which might aid in hastening the end of this disaster." The opening preamble ended with a rhetorical flourish: "Is the civilized world to become nothing more than a heap of corpses? Shall Europe, so rich in glory and achievement, precipitate itself into the gulf and commit suicide, as if seized by universal madness?"[43]

As a starting point and foundation, Benedict argued that the "moral power of justice must take the place of the material power of force." The Peace Note advocated a common reduction of armaments that was "simultaneous and proportionate," with each side only keeping those arms necessary to maintain public order. A Court of Arbitration would be established to maintain peace, although the Peace Note was ambiguous and vague on the subject of how the court's decrees would be enforced for those parties who did not accept them or who refused to acknowledge the court's legitimacy. Nonetheless, after establishing the supremacy of law, according to the Note, freedom of the seas would proceed accordingly. Regarding claims of compensation and indemnities, the Peace Note called upon all parties to "renounce them utterly" because there were "no other means of solving this problem." The moral foundation of such an assertion was that "wholesale slaughter" was "incomprehensible" and thus could not be quantified. Immediately contracting its previous moral justification, the Peace Note then offered a qualification: "if there are

[42] Pollard, *The Unknown Pope*, 117–18.
[43] For the full text of the Peace Note, see Spencer Tucker and Priscilla Mary Roberts, eds., *The Encyclopedia of World War I*, 5 vols. (Santa Barbara, CA: ABC-CLIO, 2005), 5:1499–500.

contrary reasons and special claims in particular cases, these must be considered in accordance with justice and equity."[44]

The Peace Note's answers to questions of territoriality proved especially troublesome. For the belligerent powers, Benedict XV essentially advocated a return to status quo ante, with a secure, independent Belgium completely evacuated by Germany. The Peace Note argued that "French territory must be evacuated" but neglected to specify whether this included the German annexations of Alsace and Lorraine, conquered in the aftermath of the Franco-Prussian War and a major source of French grievance. For disputed territorial questions between main belligerents (the Note mentioned Italy, Austria, Germany, and France), Benedict stated that the parties in question should "examine their claims in a spirit of conciliation." Mentioning newly emergent political disputes, as well as historical grievances (the Note mentioned "Armenia, the Balkan States and those countries which once formed the Kingdom of Poland"), the Note stated that, "the aspirations of the peoples would be judged by the standard of what is just and possible, and particular interests would be brought into harmony with the general well-being of the great human family."[45]

Idealistic and ambiguous, the formulations were ultimately disregarded by all belligerent nations. As part of the deal-brokering for Italy's entry into the war, secret negotiations in the April 1915 Treaty of London had insisted that the Great Powers would not negotiate with the Holy See. Benedict XV was not invited to the post-war peace conferences. Ironically, however, because of both sides' mutual suspicion of the Holy See during the war, the papacy became more convincing as a non-partisan institution devoted to spiritual, universal concerns instead of meddling in worldly politics. This was a continuity from the 1870 loss of the papal states during the formation of the Italian state, as the Holy See now had basically no actual territory outside Vatican City and could become a moral institution. The Great War increased the prestige and believability of the papacy as a spiritual institution.[46]

At the time, however, the Peace Note failed to achieve an end to the war. Responses to the Peace Note highlighted the powers' mutual suspicion. *The Times* of London headlined the Peace Note as a "German Peace Move," while Clemenceau described the plan as "a peace against France." Woodrow Wilson rejected the note because he argued that German militarism meant that Germany's leaders could not be trusted: "We cannot take the word of the present rules of Germany as a guarantee

---

[44] Ibid.   [45] Ibid.
[46] Atkin and Tallett, *Priests, Prelates, and People*; Coppa, *Politics and the Papacy*.

of any thing that is to endure."[47] The Central Powers' responses were similarly disappointing. Kaiser Karl of Austria-Hungary and Matthias Erzberger of the German Catholic Center Party would make strong peace efforts of their own during the war.[48] However, such efforts were exceptional and only highlighted how firmly in political and administrative control was the German high command, particularly the growing military dictatorship of Hindenburg and Ludendorff. Engineered by Erzberger and the Catholic Center Party in conjunction with the Social Democrats and other progressive parties, the German Reichstag made a huge step toward peace and democracy with its famous Peace Resolution of July 19, 1917. The resolution called for a peace governed by international arbitration, with key provisions including no annexations and no indemnities. Unfortunately, the progressive resolution underscored the deeply reactionary roots of German military autocracy, being ignored by the German high command as well as the Allies. Nevertheless, although practically ineffectual, it helped force German Chancellor Theobald Bethmann-Hollweg from office, to be replaced by Georg Michaelis, who was more subservient to the wishes of Hindenburg and Ludendorff. The military autocracy remained firmly in place.[49]

Micro-level public responses were similarly disheartening. From the altar of the church of La Madeline in Paris, a preacher told his congregation, "Holy Father, we do not want your peace." Some Italian newspapers changed Benedict's regnal name from Benedetto ("blessed") to Maledetto ("accursed") and accused him of spreading defeatism. Both British and Italian newspapers blamed Benedict's Peace Note for the lack of resistance by the Allied armies at the looming disaster of Caporetto.[50] On the homefront, bishops continued in service of state interests and filtered the words of the pope accordingly. Early in the war, in January 1915,

---

[47] Pollard, *The Unknown Pope*, 126–8. Wilson's American version of a world "made safe for democracy" envisioned Wilson in a messianic role of peace-bringer. The famous Fourteen Points, however, owed much in style and content to Benedict's Peace Note.

[48] Petronilla Ehrenpreis, *Kriegs- und Friedensziele im Diskurs. Regierung und deutschsprachige Öffentlichkeit Österreich-Ungarns während des Ersten Weltkriegs* (Innsbruck: Studien Verlag, 2005). For a biography of the leading Catholic Center politician and leading force in the peace movement, ultimately murdered by nationalist fanatics, see Klaus Epstein, *Matthias Erzberger and the Dilemma of German Democracy* (New York: Howard Fertig, 1971).

[49] Wolfgang Steglich, *Die Friedenspolitik der Mittelmächte, 1917/18* (Wiesbaden: F. Steiner, 1964); Wolfgang Steglich, ed., *Der Friedensappell Papst Benedikts XV. vom 1. August 1917 und die Mittelmächte. Diplomatische Aktenstücke des Deutschen Auswärtigen Amtes, des Bayerischen Staatsministeriums des Äussern, des Österreichisch-Ungarischen Ministeriums des Äussern und des Britischen Auswärtigen Amtes aus den Jahren 1915–1922* (Wiesbaden: F. Steiner, 1970).

[50] Pollard, *The Unknown Pope*, 128–31.

Benedict had offered the bishops a "Prayer for Peace" to be distributed in their respective countries. They did distribute it, but for their own patriotic purposes; one bishop went so far as to add unauthorized words to the pope's prayer: "On conditions honorable to our Fatherland."[51] Disingenuously, Catholic papers like *Reichspost* did not announce that there were legitimate peace offers on the table, either from the head of the Catholic Church or by prominent Central European politicians. One of the leading Catholic papers in Central Europe merely reported secondhand that figures such as Woodrow Wilson saw "No prospects of peace." As reported in the paper, Wilson claimed that "he would be the first to undertake the necessary steps, whenever the indications of a lasting peace should become known."[52]

For their part, military authorities attempted to suppress the Pope's prayers for peace. In many belligerent countries, authorities discouraged pacifistic sentiments as defeatist and thus bad for collective morale. In 1915, for instance, the Austro-Hungarian 5th Army Command and the overall Commander of the Southwestern Front demanded the retraction of the prayer for peace that Catholic chaplains were saying as part of evening religious services. Military authorities argued, "for disciplinary reasons," that prayers for peace were bad for morale, and forced the Apostolic Field Vicariate to substitute them with a "War Prayer for His Majesty [the Kaiser]."[53] However, Catholic literature distribution networks sometimes defied the wishes of military censors by continuing to distribute the Pope's prayers, and in July 1918 some Catholic military chaplains gave the Pope's pacifistic prayers to their soldiers.[54]

Many Catholic newspapers, like *Reichspost* and the Diocesan newspapers, which were firmly in control of the bishops and monitored by state censors, actually refused to print the Peace Note. Instead, they engaged in discussions that obfuscated the peace offers that were already on the table. Most prominently, these included the July 19 Peace Resolution of the Reichstag and the Papal Peace Note of August 1. The diocesan newspaper of Vienna for 1917 listed only mentions of prayers for peace, not the actual papal diplomatic initiatives. For instance, the paper noted that the Archbishop, Cardinal Friedrich Gustav Piffl, had declared Christmas Day 1917 an official day of prayer for peace.[55] Similarly, a Mass of Peace was announced on June 29, 1918, as a measure for transnational clerical

---

[51] Ibid., 113.   [52] "Keine Friedensaussichten," *Reichspost*, August 10, 1917, p. 4.

[53] ÖStAKA, NFA, AOK, Qu. Abteilung, Op. Akten 1915, Ktn. 1561, Op. 75733 (SWF Kdo. R. Nr. 14049 5 AEK), "Friedensgebete – Zur Entscheidung vorgelegt."

[54] ÖStAKA, AFV, Ktn. 244, Bericht über Andachten, August 1918.

[55] "Friedensbittag am 25. Dezember (Sr. Eminenz)," *Wiener Diözesanblatt* (1917), 172.

unity: "Thus will the Catholic priesthood of the entire world in unity with the Pope represent the sacrifice of atonement and represent love, powerfully affecting the Heavenly Heart." The papal prayer for peace was read at all such services, which also included a time for adoration of the Eucharist.[56]

Outside of the direct control of the bishops, however, the word about peace was getting out. At the beginning of 1918, for instance, the German Jesuit journal *Stimmen der Zeit* printed the entirety of the Papal Peace Note of August 1, 1917, with editorial commentary.[57] It represented a scant hope for peace, but was one of the only voices of reason, especially among the public authorities of Central Europe. It was a particularly courageous move for a Jesuit journal as the Jesuits had remained technically banned in Germany until 1917.

Overall, among the losing powers, the Catholic Church focused on rebuilding efforts during the war. Organic family values, united through love and Christ, helped heal the devastation, blending with tropes of the cult of the Sacred Heart: "As the Lord consecrated, protected, and led them with special love, so should the members of the Heart of Jesus let families lead their practical Christian lives through the love of the Savior." More ominously, these religious family-values arguments were often expressed in religious terms of *völkisch* ideology: "Because the family is the cell of the Volk's organism [*Volksorganismus*], so must the family recover at the heart of salvation, thus should our peoples convalesce."[58] Such talk of blood sacrifice and the heart of Christ blended easily with the Catholic cult of the Sacred Heart.[59]

Despite this turn toward the family and rebuilding, Catholic papers were still focused on the conditions of war, and sustaining support for it. Notices calling for war materials (war bonds, clothing, raw materials) appeared frequently alongside reports of battlefield victories and the need to hold out for further victories.

Benedict XV was sensitive to the diplomatic currents. Even when his own Peace Note failed to gain traction, he recognized that Woodrow Wilson was becoming a figure for peace, symbolizing the importance of America to ending the conflict. He urged to the Habsburg Empire to seek peace by appealing to Wilson: "In the present international situation, it is not England or France but the President of the great American

---

[56] "Friedensmesse am 29 Juni 1918," *Wiener Diözesanblatt* (1918), 75–6; "Reichsgebetstag um den Frieden," *Wiener Diözesanblatt* (June 9, 1918), 67.
[57] Franz Ehrle, "Die päpstliche Friedensnote an die Häupter der kriegsführenden Völker vom 1. August 1917," *Stimmen der Zeit* 94 (1918): 1–28.
[58] "Familienweihe an das Herz Jesu," *Wiener Diözeansblatt* (1918): 67ff.
[59] Schlager, *Kult und Krieg*.

Republic alone: only he can bring about peace or the continuation of the war, and he wishes to dictate the peace in the time that remains of his presidential term."[60] Benedict was well aware that the world had seized upon Wilson as a diplomatic savior, and the Pope advocated for peace wherever possible, without primary regard for his own ego and failed Peace Note.

Benedict's shifting attitudes toward the Habsburg monarchy also demonstrated his sense of political realism. Before the war, the Holy See had maintained a strong support for the Habsburgs. The Habsburg monarchy maintained a lineage back to the thirteenth century, hundreds of years longer than even the Romanovs, the symbols of supposedly feudal and backward Russia. The Habsburgs had been one of the strongest forces for political unity in Central Europe, consolidating a bewildering array of regions, languages, and peoples under the auspices of one dynasty. Redefining themselves as a fundamentally Catholic power, the Habsburgs became champions of the Counter-Reformation, resisting the centrifugal tendencies of the growing Protestant movement. Religion became intertwined with ethnicity and nationhood as complicated variables of identity representing increasingly unsettling influences on the stability of the Habsburgs' political arrangement.[61] Nevertheless, many faiths besides Catholicism found official representation at the turn of the twentieth century – perhaps most strikingly, Islam. Following centuries of ideological hostility, famously including two failed Ottoman sieges of Vienna in 1529 and 1683, after the annexation of Bosnia-Herzegovina the Habsburg Army incorporated Muslim units into its ranks. Benedict XV supported the Habsburgs as the best possible means of unifying the disparate lands and peoples of East-Central Europe. In particular, he advocated Habsburg Catholicism as a bulwark in the Slavic lands, against the encroachment of Eastern Orthodoxy.

During much the Great War, Benedict strongly advocated for the continued existence of Austria-Hungary as the best possible political solution to the organization of the lands and peoples of East-Central Europe – a sentiment that reflected the consensus of both the Allied Powers and the nationalist movements within Austria-Hungary.[62] As late as October 1918, Benedict XV continued to lobby for the Habsburgs, even as

---

[60] Quoted in Pollard, *The Unknown Pope*, 132.

[61] Steven Beller, *A Concise History of Austria* (Cambridge: Cambridge University Press, 2006); Robin Okey, *The Habsburg Monarchy, c. 1765–1918* (Houndmills: Macmillan, 2001).

[62] For two good recent revisionist works on the viability of the Habsburg political framework, see Cohen, "Nationalist Politics," 241–78 and Kwan, "Nationalism and All That," 88–108.

Entente views shifted toward viewing the state as unviable. However, Benedict and Cardinal Gasparri, the Holy See Secretary of State, eventually sensed the winds of change and began to rethink their views. When they saw that the Habsburg Empire would collapse, they focused the Holy See's efforts on supporting Poland as a strong Catholic state that would counterbalance both Germany and Russia.[63] The Holy See recognized that the ideological opposition of atheistic Bolshevism was the paramount new danger for Catholic interests, and that Poland would be fundamental to halting the influence of the Soviet Union.[64] The Polish–Soviet War, with its culminating Battle of Warsaw, which halted the Bolshevik advance, was a showcase for the material clash of opposed ideologies; it was also a conflict that would have a formative influence on the papal nuncio in Warsaw, Achille Ratti, the future Pope Pius XI.

Code of Canon Law

In the midst of the battlefield carnage, the Catholic Church was being reborn in the twentieth century in ways drastically different from its image of archaic exhaustion in literary modernism. The 1917 or Pio-Benedictine Code of Canon Law (codex iuris canonici) was begun under Saint Pius X and officially enacted during the reign of Benedict XV. The code was a major achievement in ecclesiastical law and Church governance. Under one approved centralized standard, it published the first complete version of Church law in the history of the Church, thus coordinating and collating what had been hitherto a bewildering array of disparate provisions known as the Body of Canon Law (corpus iuris canonici). The 1917 code was the first major overhaul of Canon Law since the Council of Trent had ended in 1563.[65]

Officially promulgated during the end of the war, in practical terms such a major historical adaptation of Church tradition occurred only slowly, and mostly in the interwar period, diffusing from clergy to lay parishioners. Promulgated on May 27, 1917, the new Code of Canon Law took effect one year later. It included 2414 individual canons, subdivided into five main books: "General Norms," "On Persons," "On

---

[63] Pollard, *The Unknown Pope*, 132.

[64] Neal Pease, *Rome's Most Faithful Daughter: The Catholic Church and Independent Poland, 1914–1939* (Athens: Ohio University Press, 2009).

[65] For full text of the canons and introductory commentary, see Peters, *The 1917 or Pio-Benedictine Code*. The code would remain in force through most of the twentieth century, with a revised version issued in 1983 under Pope Saint John Paul II. The 1983 Code of Canon Law is the present legal code for the Catholic Church.

Things," "On Procedures," and "On Delicts and Penalties." Condensing and clarifying many disparate provisions in Church history, the code centralized and reinforced the authority of the Pope and the Roman Curia over the Church. The new code especially strengthened the power of the centralized Church regarding the appointment of bishops. Overall, as John F. Pollard has written, "Along with Infallibility, it was a pillar of modern papal primacy."[66] Thus, as the war on the Western Front was grinding on, the Catholic Church emerged refocused and reenergized, with 1917 a key milestone of development.

The war also affected Church–state relations within the empires of Central Europe. This was perhaps most acutely seen in Germany. In the Land of Luther, and especially amid the surge of nineteenth-century nationalism, which included leading liberal politicians, anti-Catholicism became central to the nationalist self-definition. One of the Church's most visible orders, the Jesuits, had remained officially outlawed since the *Kulturkampf*. Jesuits had fought in imperial units, and had been military chaplains and hospital personnel, since 1914, but the anti-Jesuit ban officially continued until 1917, when it was finally repealed by the Reichstag.[67] But Catholic suffering in wartime Germany created a shared blood brotherhood with Protestant believers. Even the Prussian-dominated Reichstag saw that the war had created a new sense of Christian community. After the Central European empires fell, Church–state relations were negotiated anew with the successor states. This entailed a complex and delicate balance between loyalty to Rome and loyalty to the newly created states, some of which veered toward fascism.[68]

Appeals from the faithful and a personalized papacy

The figure of the pope was symbolic of Catholicism and all it stood for. Millions wrote to Benedict XV personally. Catholics and non-Catholics offered him their plans for peace.[69] Many wrote to him in order to make him aware of a certain situation, hoping he could personally intervene to change what military and political leaders seemed unable to. Some Catholic faithful wrote to attest to sightings of Marian apparitions, as in one anonymous letter about the Black Madonna of Częstochowa in early 1914. Apparitions of the Black Madonna would also be reported on

---

[66] Pollard, *The Unknown Pope*, 194.   [67] Healy, *Jesuit Specter*.
[68] For an overview of the complicated Catholic arrangements with the old and new regimes in the era of the world wars, see Atkin and Tallett, *Priests, Prelates, and People*, 195–264.
[69] For collected examples of these letters, see ASV, Segretaria di Stato, Spoglio, Benedetto XV, Carton Nr. 2.

September 15, 1920, which supposedly stopped the advancing Bolshevik forces on the Vistula.[70]

Consequently, Catholic soldiers and members of the clergy were often faced with explaining or defending the pope, sometimes even to co-nationals who happened to be of a different religion, particularly Protestant. The chaplain Jakob Ebner, for instance, noted that on Christmas Eve, 1915, his Protestant commanding officer was focused on confessional difference, not the ecumenical peace appropriate to the season. The commander, Colonel von Grüter, asked his chaplain, "Isn't it true, Herr Priest, that the pope does not need to confess? He is infallible?" Chaplain Ebner managed a diplomatic reply to his commander, noting, "I taught him otherwise." Ebner patiently explained the difference between the pope as a person who needed to confess and the pope speaking *ex cathedra* in his position, a basic tenet of the dogma of papal infallibility.[71]

Despite the stubborn opinions of statesmen locked in their quest for peace through victory, the pope's message of peace was reaching a broad audience. Many religious believers on the homefront continued to uphold a firm line of peace through victory, especially voiced in the bishops' screeds. Fire-breathing was easier for those who were not under fire in the trenches. It was among religious soldiers that the pope's message of peace particularly resonated. It was especially striking to see the changes in attitudes as soldiers' initial hard-line views softened throughout the war into universal longings for peace. Karl Döhl, for instance, was a peasant in the Austro-Hungarian Army who went to war inflamed with hatred against the French in particular. Döhl's diary from 1914 recorded sentiments full of religious national hatred: "O God, stand by us and save us from the barbarians [the French]! They are not worth pardon, they must be beaten down like wild animals." By February 1915, Döhl's attitudes had begun to shift. He noted in his diary, "The decree with which the Holy Father ordered a day of prayer for peace." The Pope's message decreed a day of prayer on February 7, 1915. It was a day full of Catholic sorrow, stressing the universality of devastation, grief, and mourning. As recorded by Döhl, the instructions received by believers were as follows: "His Holiness, Benedict XV, depressed by the view of the storm of war that shatters young lives, throws families and cities into mourning and leads nations into its whirlwind . . . invites clergy and people to accomplish some kind of work for the expiation of sins that

[70] ASV, Seg. di Stato, Guerra 1914–1918, 244.A.1.b, Fasc. 78–9, p. 303: Anon., Letter "Il 'Kaiser,'" ca. August 9, 1914.
[71] EAF, NL 44 (Jakob Ebner Tagebuch), p. 448, entry of December 24, 1915.

are the just punishment of God." Benedict's orders were founded in a Catholic globalism that transcended the nation-states paralyzed by war: "in the whole Catholic world, humble prayers should be brought to the Lord, in order to invoke from his mercifulness the desired peace." Regarding specifically Catholic rituals for the day of prayer for peace, the pope prescribed saying a *Miserere Mei Deus (da pacem)*, praying the rosary, and offering 40 hours of prayer according to the Roman Ritual.[72]

Other soldiers, too, absorbed the Pope's messages for peace and carried their sentiments into the post-war world. During the war, Carl Havenith was a lay brother of a German Catholic order and served on the Western Front with Infantry Regiment 173 and later IR 49; after the war, he became an ordained priest. Havenith's diaries document the profound horrors of trench warfare, as well as his daily Catholic devotions, revealing his intimate spirituality. For instance, he systematically marked the days on which he said his rosary, attended Mass, received communion, and made confession.[73] Toward the end of the war, loyally serving Germany to the end, Havenith's diary testified to the soldiers' widespread longing for peace. While still recording his daily personal religious rituals and his belief in God, Havenith noted the increasing discontent with the military situation as the Allied armies advanced. As the war dragged on, soldiers longed for peace in whatever form it might take. On October 18, 1918, Havenith wrote, "Everyone has hope in the new popular government [*Volksregierung*], because they will give us peace. Meanwhile, the Allies always move forward. At Cambrai battle raged again. Unfortunately, our troops do not want to go forward any more. They have gone through too much and now want peace, therefore they do not stand firm as in the past four years."[74]

This longing for peace, and particularly the message of the Pope as a leader of the Church and an outspoken advocate for transnational peace, would resonate with religious believers in the interwar period and set the stage for national reconciliations and European community building after 1945. After the Great War, Carl Havenith became a peace activist and opposed Nazi race ideology and the idea of pure blood, instead advocating that all humanity had mixed blood. Immediately after the war, Havenith attended and presented at the International Catholic Peace Conferences held in Freiburg, Paris, and Vienna, where he met

---

[72] Dokumentationsarchiv Lebensgeschichtlicher Aufzeichnungen (DLA), 1. Weltkrieg, Briefe, Tagebücher. Karl Döhl, "Kleine Kronik von Verhangnisvollen Kriegsjahre 1914," p. 3, "Der Bettag am 7. Februar 1915," pp. 20–2.

[73] Archiv des Erzbistums Köln, NL Havenith; Bundesarchiv-Miliärarchiv Freiburg MSG 2/2812–2813.

[74] AEK, NL Havenith, Heft 2, p. 172: entry of October 12, 1918. Cf. BAMA.

with other activists whose outlooks had been shaped by the Great War. In Vienna, in 1922, he delivered a paper on the peace efforts of the papacy, which met with in thunderous applause and saw Havenith jubilantly raised up and carried out on the shoulders of his fellow attendees.[75] Religious peace movements would continue to influence the formation of a common European useable past, particularly in the post-1945 era.[76]

Religious soldiers continued to loyally serve the military cause, yet kept alive their inner wishes for peace. Michael Panni, a miner's son from Budweis enlisted with the k.u.k. 91st Regiment and later the 45th *Landsturm* Regiment, served the Habsburg Army in Serbia and Italy. On November 28, 1915, he wrote of attending a field Mass and inwardly thanking God that he was still alive and praying for peace to arrive soon. Seasonal highpoints of the Church liturgical year often brought the wish to return home to peace. By January 17, 1916, Panni's earlier hatred against his enemies was fast disappearing. He noted succinctly in his diary, "May God grant peace everywhere." By June 29, 1917, his wishes for peace were becoming more public, voiced during field Masses and not kept to himself.[77]

Military chaplains, the stereotypical fire-breathers of modernist literature, in fact were often local advocates for peace. Fridolin Mayer, a chaplain serving in northern France, noted in his diary, "What will the New Year bring? Everyone has the word, 'Peace' on his tongue, and wishes Peace to himself and to others for the New Year. Will 1917 live on in world history as a year of peace? In 1914 I was an optimist for 1915, in 1915 I was an optimist for 1916 and now, on New Year's Eve, I am a pessimist for 1917."[78]

Soldiers, military chaplains, nurses, and diplomats wrote to the Pope, often giving eyewitness accounts of the devastation. They implored the Holy Father either to intervene directly to stop the destruction or else to circulate the information they were providing to those politicians in power who could stop the madness. Typical was the letter from Justin Mulson, a French military chaplain, written on May 8, 1915. Mulson began by stating emphatically that he was writing in his own name, "without having consulted either my ecclesiastical superiors or my military bosses." He centered his letter on the profound new realities of industrial battlefield death: "Dear Holy Father, see this distress: thousands of unburied bodies." This was distressing not only because of the Church

---

[75] AEK, NL Havenith, Heft 1: Lebenslauf von Pfarrer Carl Havenith; cf. *Stimmen der Zeit* (1923): 165.
[76] Kaiser, *Christian Democracy.*   [77] Panni, *Das Tagebuch des Michael Panni*, 50, 65, 171.
[78] EAF, Na 16/1: Krieggstagebuch 1914–1918 von Fridolin Mayer, p. 428.

requirements for Christian burial but also because of the physically foul air of the battlefield, which spread contagion. Attesting to the Pope's growing reputation for fostering care for POWs, Mulson begged him to intervene with the belligerents "to suggest to them a solution more Christian, more humane and compatible, however, with the cruel necessities of the war."[79] Alas, practical solutions were difficult to obtain.

Nevertheless, multitudes wrote to implore the Pope personally. Rose Ball of Sandusky, Ohio, wrote, "Your Holiness, Dear Holy Father: My heart aches for all the sorrows caused by the war, particularly do I sympathize with the Bl. Sacrament, for all the sacrileges committed against it thru all the terrible crimes committed during the war, how his heart must be bleeding for the heaven-crying sins committed! May the Lord have mercy on us all." Begging forgiveness for her presumptions, Ball continued, "Do you not suppose that the anger of God would be appeased if the whole Catholic world would atone by doing penance by fasting for nine days or attend a novena of Masses? Or better still if every priest of the Universe was commanded to offer up the sacrifice of holy Mass the most efficacious of gifts a certain day and the faithful attending milled their prayers with the holy church and offering the spotless lamb the passion of our Lord in reparation for all the sins of the world, and beg for mercy, pardon and peace?"[80] Seeking to avoid traditional diplomatic channels and using the Pope as a source of direct appeal to the enemy belligerents, another petitioner wrote to him in hope of making an appeal for peace to Kaiser Wilhelm. Arthur M. Edwards, a retired US Army Major, Vancouver Barracks, Washington, DC, wrote a one-act verse play, "The Conversion of Kaiser Wilhelm," and sent a copy to Benedict XV, appealing to him to send it directly to the Kaiser. In Edwards's view, the Kaiser was the "chief obstacle" to "a world made glorious by the principles of a safe and sane democracy," which would "hasten the coming of a brotherhood of nations." Edwards believed his work reflected "the justice and the mercy" of the "Gospel of Christ." He implored the Holy Father: "If you change the attitude of the main cause of all this uncivilized and barbarous war, you can bring to the world a peace which shall be safe for all mankind. I would be pleased to have Kaiser Wilhelm read this drama which tempers justice with mercy and have him remember that I am seeking by this method the greatest good to the greatest number, in the best and most ideal way. Please forward the enclosed copy for his

[79] ASV, Seg. di Stato, Guerra 1914–1918, 244B.1.a, Fasc. 41:14–28, Letter from Justin Mulson, Aumônier au Grope de Braucardiers de Corps, Secteur postal 80, letter to Pope, May 8, 1915.
[80] ASV, Seg. di Stato, Guerra 1914–1918, 244.A.1.b., Fasc. 64, pp. 123r–124v: Letter of October 19, 1917 from Rose C. Ball, Sandusky, Ohio, USA.

information, (if agreeable in the interests of the whole human race)."[81] The parenthetical statement in the original document was in fact the key motivation.

Benedict XV's wishes for peace highlight the complicated layers of authority that existed within the Catholic Church. Scholars have long noted that after exposure to combat, most soldiers at the front quickly turned to thoughts of peace, and for many combatants this happened early in the war. In one of the Great War's most celebrated episodes, the "Christmas Truce" of 1914, enemy troops on the Western Front fraternized with each other in an informal, spontaneous ceasefire that began on Christmas Eve and continued through the next day. British, French, and German units buried the dead and held communal religious services between the trenches. They sang Christmas songs, exchanged gifts, shared meals together, and in some cases played soccer in no-man's-land. After Christmas, the soldiers returned to killing each other. Thus, the "Christmas Truce" was often sentimentally portrayed as a last gasp of civilized decency that quickly fell out of place in a brutal industrialized war.[82]

Episodes like the "Christmas Truce" highlight the complicated issues of authority and agency that influenced the desires for peace during the Great War. At both the top and the bottom of the Church hierarcy, believers early and fervently wished for peace at any cost – a return to normalcy and universal brotherhood. Such pacific desires were widespread among lay believers, who mostly wanted the war to end quickly so that they could be reunited with their families and local communities. Even within the hierarchical Catholic Church, however, intermediary layers of authority prevented peace. Safe at the homefront, Roman Catholic clergy members, particularly the bishops in service of disparate state aims, would not abandon their belief that their respective states were engaged in a just war of defense against aggression. This intransigent collective belief refused to yield, thus prolonging the war. In this mindset, achieving victory was the only guarantor of collective security and validation of the sacrifices already incurred. The theology of the clergy and bishops was in many ways a theology that served Caesar.

By contrast, the Pope and ordinary everyday Catholic believers held remarkably similar beliefs about the need for peace and reconciliation. Through his visible efforts at charity and peace, the Great War made

---

[81] ASV, Seg. di Stato, Guerra 1914–1918, 244.A.1.b, pp. 131–53: Arthur M. Edwards, Maj. USA Retired, Vancouver Barracks, Washington, August 22, 1917.

[82] Stanley Weintraub, *Silent Night: The Story of the World War I Christmas Truce* (New York: Free Press, 2001).

Benedict XV and the Catholic Church a more believable, humanitarian, and universal institution committed to engaging the modern world.

Conclusion

Benedict XV was an effective steward of the Catholic Church during the Great War, serving as an adaptor of tradition. A more purely reactionary pope, in the model of Pius IX, for example, would likely have been content to retreat inward, to denounce the modern world and the Great War as a just punishment for great sinfulness. Benedict XV adopted such language in terms that ironically resonated with the avant garde modernists, denouncing the war as the "suicide of civilized Europe." But the Pope did not stop there, self-righteously fulminating against modernity. While Benedict XV certainly believed that the Great War was a repudiation of certain aspects of the modern condition, he progressively adapted the Church to the new world and the challenges that confronted it, many of which had been caused by the Great War. The Code of Canon Law, originally proposed under Saint Pius X, was finally published in 1917, taking effect in 1918. A monument of the Church's legal and ideological structure, which had remained uncodified since the Council of Trent in the sixteenth century, the Code of Canon Law would remain in force for most of the twentieth century, until it was modified in 1983 by Saint John Paul II. It was a milestone in centralizing Church law.

Beyond the purely Catholic world, however, Benedict reached out to all the peoples of the world to remedy the universal suffering that the war had caused. He nearly bankrupted the Holy See by paying for efforts to aid victims of war, especially displaced children, displaced persons, and POWs. The vast Catholic network of diplomatic contacts proved invaluable for efforts at information and prisoner exchange between the Great Powers.

Benedict's attempts at peace, culminating in the Peace Note of August 1, 1917, set a diplomatic tone of unbiased mediation, although at the time all sides suspected him of favoring the enemy. Nevertheless, Benedict moved forward with his efforts to try to end the war, ably assisted by his Secretary of State, Cardinal Pietro Gasparri. In a move nearly unprecedented in Church history, Cardinal Gasparri remained as Secretary of State to the new pope, Pius XI, thus ensuring a smooth, continuous transition. In contrast to the Holy See's previous history of territorial-based politics when the papal states existed, in the twentieth century the Church began to assume a role as a more purely moral, non-governmental symbolic force that lent strength to its universalistic claims in the modern world. The Church began to move out of its diplomatic isolation. While, on the eve of war in 1914, the Church had maintained contact almost exclusively with authoritarian governments in Europe, in the interwar period the Church established official diplomatic relations with Western liberal democracies. This was perhaps most apparent in France, a long-standing "daughter of the Church," with whom the Holy See had severed diplomatic relations as a result of the official separation of Church and state in 1905. By 1922, helped by the canonization of Joan of Arc and the triumphant French victory during the Great War, France resumed official diplomatic relations with the Holy See.[83]

The papacy was not simply a disinterested voice for peace, however. More ominously, the Church also contributed to continuing ideological warfare in the interwar period. As with much else in the Great War, the conflict did not end neatly in 1918. Adding flames to the smoldering socialist movement in the nineteenth century, the rise of Bolshevism after 1917 seemed to confirm the worst fears about the hostility of the militant proletariat. Benedict XV and key leaders in the Church hierarchy witnessed the emergence of a proudly atheistic regime in the Soviet Union, convinced of its role as a leader in a world-historical movement. Achille Ratti, the future Pope Pius XI, saw the Bolshevik armies halted at the Battle of Warsaw during the Russo-Polish War. Eugenio Pacelli, the future Pope Pius XII, witnessed the brief attempt to establish a Bavarian Socialist Republic. Both of these popes would be important voices in the Church's twentieth-century crusade against communism, which continued through the fall of the Soviet Union.[84]

Despite a small number of important scholarly works, the papacy of Benedict XV remains relatively unknown, partially due to the unassuming nature of Benedict himself.[85] By contrast, the strong personalities of Saint Pius X, Pius XII, Saint John XXIII, and Saint John Paul II, for instance, make greater impact concerning the qualities of papal leadership. Benedict XV was, however, the head of a very traditional institution adapting to the unprecedented pressures of industrial warfare, and was an effective leader of the Church.

As this chapter has shown, the papacy of Benedict XV deserves greater attention as part of a study of Catholicism during the Great War. Despite the fact that the Central European powers lost the Great War, Catholicism and its leadership during this time remain essential to understanding the development of twentieth-century Europe's religious history. Particularly for Central Europe, the pontificates of Pius XI and Pius XII are widely scrutinized for their involvement with the developing Nazi regime.

---

[83] Becker, *War and Faith.*   [84] Coppa, *Politics and the Papacy.*
[85] Pollard, *The Unknown Pope.*

Studies of Nazism rightly stress the Great War's fundamental formative experience on Germany's road to the Third Reich. Future studies of Catholicism in the twentieth century must continue to examine the role of the "unknown Pope," Benedict XV, who managed the crisis of the Great War and guided the Church as a humanitarian institution into an era of complicated world affairs.

7   Memory, mourning, and the Catholic way of war

The war on the Western Front ground to a halt with the Armistice of November 11, 1918. That day was also the Feast Day of Saint Martin of Tours, a notable patron saint of soldiers, who was especially worshipped not for his military prowess but rather for his peacemaking and social devotion to the needy. Sixteen centuries after his death, the stories of Saint Martin had powerful resonance in the aftermath of the First World War as Europe tried to heal itself. Due to his associations with both France and Hungary, and his travels through Central Europe, he became a pan-European figure of veneration during the Middle Ages. In the aftermath of the First World War, his stature gained new currency due to this coincidence with the Armistice on the Western Front.

Traditional religious imagery played a key role in helping European society make sense of the war. Religion, along with classical and romantic tropes, allowed communities of bereaved to mourn the loss of loved ones. This occurred on a mass scale, as more people simply had to deal with violent death and destruction, approaching what Jay Winter has termed a "universality of bereavement" as European society attempted to assuage its grief. Traditional imagery and languages of mourning thus played a fundamentally healing role, strengthening social bonds and emotional ties. Hence, as Winter noted in his classic study, war memorials after 1918 involved dual motifs: "war as *both* noble and uplifting *and* tragic and unendurably sad."[1] War memorialization involved this duality in an ever-shifting process of balance between the two interests. It was only after the Second World War, not the First, that European society changed its attitudes toward war memorialization, invoking more abstract imagery and universal values.[2]

[1] Winter, *Sites of Memory*, 5, 85.
[2] Laurence Van Ypersele, "Mourning and Memory, 1919–45," in Horne, *Companion*; Jay Winter, "Commemorating War, 1914–1945," in *The Cambridge History of War*, vol. 4: *War and the Modern World*, ed. Roger Chickering, Dennis Showalter, and Hans Van de Ven (Cambridge: Cambridge University Press, 2012), 310–26.

The religious aspects of commemoration have often been subsumed under the heading of "nationalism," especially in Germany a vengeful nationalism, dedicated to redeeming the political loss of the First World War.[3] There were, however, other valences of loyalty. Scholars coming after the transnational turn have begun to note other sources of social identification. Regarding religion in war, the subject is still underdeveloped, yet there are exciting avenues of possibility. For instance, in contrast to the plethora of public and utilitarian aspects of memorialization at schools, hospitals, train stations, and especially public monuments, as Jay Winter has noted, "Catholic commemoration was more sacred than secular."[4] As previous chapters have shown, this fits with the different Catholic time scale of the twentieth century.

This chapter highlights the Catholic aspects of the process of memory and mourning. Its approach is fundamentally transnational, showing the importance of the nation as a locus of sacrifice, but also underscoring the importance of cross-regional, local, familial, and personal ties – all of which are seen through primarily Catholic frames of reference. This web of associations helps to show the insufficiency of the nation-state as the sole focus of symbolic representation for societies coming to terms with the destruction of the First World War. Indeed, precisely by examining the losing powers, one sees most starkly that collective defeat did not mean disenchantment and dissolution. The Catholic powers of Central Europe relied on an adaptation of traditional forms to help them cope with the new horrors of war.

Recent comparative histories have stressed that the Great War was the moment at which older mourning practices confronted the new fact of the absence of the bodies of those killed in the war. Soldiers were often buried on site in makeshift graves in military cemeteries; consequently, civilian cemeteries had to incorporate symbolic forms to acknowledge the real and symbolic loss of tangible bodies.[5] A Catholic way of war helped to make this absence more bearable. The communion of saints, particularly notions of saintly intercession, embodied by the Virgin Mary above all, helped religious believers make sense of the sacrifice in a Catholic way that stressed sorrow and healing on a universal scale.

---

[3] For one of the most powerful statements of this view, see George L. Mosse, *Fallen Soldiers: Reshaping the Memory of the World Wars* (Oxford: Oxford University Press, 1989).

[4] Winter, "Commemorating War," 311.

[5] Carine Trevisan and Elise Julien, "Cemeteries," in *Capital Cities at War. Paris, London, Berlin, 1914–1919*, ed. Jay Winter and Jean-Louis Robert (Cambridge: Cambridge University Press, 1997–2007), 428–67.

Returning home

Soldiers returned from combat and attempted to reintegrate into society. As numerous studies have shown, the demobilization process was incomplete, as soldiers returned to societies that the Great War had permanently changed. Yet public piety in interwar Europe did not immediately decline after the failure to achieve quick victory in 1914. Returning home from service on the Western Front, chaplain Jakob Ebner's diary entry of December 8, 1918 recorded churches full of anxious people in the town of Winterberg and elsewhere. Many current and former soldiers were in attendance at Mass, and priests' sermons were addressed, "To the Homecoming Warriors."[6] In the interwar era, massive social problems still threatened Europe: disease, conflict, famine, and death. Enforcing the peace of Versailles, and repaying Germany for its harsh occupation during the war, French and Belgian troops occupied the Ruhr from 1923 until 1925. The troubles of the war continued, and the churches were not empty. The story of religious consolation and diminishing returns on those beliefs was a complicated, variable process that occurred in disparate sectors of publicly-observable practice.

In the immediate post-war era, the Catholic Church at a local level was torn between proclaiming a moral panic and providing a calm reassurance of stasis. Church periodicals were filled with themes of loss of paternal authority and extra-marital relationships causing the spread of sexually-transmitted disease, a habit learned from soldiers away from home, particularly at brothels, some of which had even been sponsored by the military. Against all society, local clergy members vented against rampant consumerism and materialism that excluded religiously-based spiritual values. In Catholic regions like Tyrol and Bavaria, the clergy conceived a need for a mission to reintegrate soldiers into religious life and spoke of a dangerous split between Church ideals and local practice that could potentially destabilize society.[7] Transnationally, however, as Oswald Überegger has argued, Church rhetoric about moral panics in rural societies in the immediate post-war phase obscured the fact that soldiers returning home were largely successfully reintegrated in the 1920s. In the words of a Church periodical, the returning troops in regions like Tyrol and Bavaria "found their rest again" in the societies they

---

[6] EAF, NL 44, Jakob Ebner Tagebuch, p. 834, December 8, 1918: Mass in town of Winterberg, Mass in Pfarrkirche, Hirtenbrief read out "an die heimkehrenden Krieger."

[7] Oswald Überegger, *Erinnerungskriege: der Erste Weltkrieg, Österreich und die Tiroler Kriegserinnerung in der Zwischenkriegszeit* (Innsbruck: Universitätsverlag Wagner, 2011), 216.

had left, and performed "apparently faultlessly their religious duties." Benjamin Ziemann's research on rural Bavaria further undermined the Nazi myth of a "front-community" of battle-hardened men permanently transformed through their experience as soldiers.[8]

Depending on the socio-political needs of disparate communities, religiously-based visions of collective sacrifice wavered between consolation and agitation. In a pastoral letter of 1919, the Austrian bishops announced to soldiers, "what you patiently suffered for, is secured in a better world [in Heaven] and finds there its eternal remuneration."[9] Such rhetoric was meant to soothe souls and validate the many sacrifices of war.

Notions of collective sacrifice, however, could also agitate communities. English and German military chaplains, for example, reminded communities that the dead would not rest easily and that political mobilization had to continue. The political context mattered greatly. In the English case, chaplains motivated their listeners to maintain the peace that victory had achieved, while in the German case, chaplains agitated for a renewed war that would achieve a more just peace.[10]

In contrast to most of the bishops, military chaplains had seen the horrors of war firsthand, sometimes renouncing them utterly and questioning their own role in the war. For instance, the Jesuit chaplain Karl Egger wrote in his memoirs of the self-doubt common to chaplains who had seen the slaughter of battle and felt themselves complicit. Addressing himself and his priestly fellows, Egger wrote in a highly self-critical fashion:

Hey, chaplain! Didn't you desire the spawning of this hell? Through your inflammatory words, didn't you give nourishment to glowing hatred in the hearts of men? You servant of the crucified Prince of Peace, weren't you of the Devil, from the beginning departing from all good spirits, in terrible self-infatuation, a henchman of murderers?

It appears to me as if the eclipsed soul is fraught with the ruins of the collapsing building of my war outlook. The common cry: no more war! appears as the only light. I damn the terrible experience of the war! How does it help me? I become yet more confused. I feel that I'm spiritually falling apart, fury and disgust in the heart! Everything blood, all sacrifices in vain! Cursed cloaca of the collapse! Damned hyenas, vampires of war![11]

---

[8] Ibid., 217. See also Ziemann, *Front und Heimat*, 390–1.

[9] Überegger, *Erinnerungskriege*, 213–14.

[10] Patrick Porter, "Beyond Comfort: German and English Military Chaplains and the Memory of the Great War, 1919–1929," *Journal of Religious History* 29, no. 3 (2005): 258–89; Alexander Watson and Patrick Porter, "Bereaved and Aggrieved: Combat Motivation and the Ideology of Sacrifice in the First World War," *Historical Research* 83, no. 219 (2010): 146–64.

[11] Egger, *Seele im Sturm*, 229.

Trying to make sense of his spiritual crisis, Egger found his role as a rural pastor. Rocked by inner turmoil, to outward appearances he lived his life readjusted as a normal priest taking care of parishioners, as documented through a photo-album memory book. Such accounts composed in retrospect could easily slip into constructed nostalgia of a pre-war idyll.[12] In the interwar period, rosy reminiscences longed for a pre-1914 "world of yesterday." In the post-1945 era, they could also reach back to before the First World War, but the more thorough destruction of the Second also made the interwar years seem a relative haven of peacefulness and comfort.

Making sense of the sacrifice incurred in loss, Catholics closest to the centers of power showed most acutely the eternal religious dilemma of deference to state authority: giving to Caesar what was Caesar's and giving to God what was God's. At the end of the war, Ludwig Berg, the Catholic chaplain at Kaiser Wilhelm II's headquarters throughout the war, documented both the continuity and the change in sharp detail. In one of the Kaiser's last disquisitions before he left Germany for exile in Holland, he nervously and hypocritically commented on the situation of Pope Benedict XV, potentially threatened by revolutionary unrest in Rome. Venting his own fear of the crowds and the upheavals taking place in Germany, the Kaiser told Berg that, "The Pope should have ample machine guns in the Vatican, and a few of those machine guns could clean the rabble from Saint Peter's Square." Changing his mind, he immediately went on to state that the Pope was compelled to be a Christ figure because of religious belief: "And if the rabble really caught the Pope and killed him, he must be like his Lord and Master; Christ died for his beliefs. The Pope must also be prepared, if he is truly serious as an advocate for truth, to die as a martyr for truth and justice." Berg highlighted the differences between temporal and metaphysical leadership, juxtaposing the Kaiser's verbal outbursts with his actions that led to his flight to Holland on November 10: "The Kaiser is not up to his great task, in view of the great danger to his life, and is not prepared to die as a martyr for Germany and for his kingdom."[13] Berg's diary highlights that association with state power tempted Catholics to support it. Sharing privileged accommodations at the heart of military power, and eating well as much of the population starved, Berg was biased toward loyalty to the Kaiser and his military regime. Even as late as November 1918, in a meeting with Cardinal Faulhaber, Berg's sermons and philosophy

---

[12] Cf. ibid., with AASI Vienna, Autobiographie des P. Karl Egger, S.J., "Aus meinem Leben," pp. 48–63.

[13] Betker and Kriele, *Pro fide et patria!*, 809–10.

highlighted the traditional themes the necessity for believers to fight "for
faith and fatherland," a theme from which he never wavered while in
his position at the Kaiser's headquarters; this theme was the organizing
principle of Berg's war diary and his notion of service.[14] Yet by dismiss-
ing the Kaiser as a false martyr, a Catholic believer like Berg could carve
out a space for religion that transcended the political order of monarchy.
Especially after the Armistice, Berg reiterated the role of religion as a
source of comfort and healing. On November 15–16, 1918, soldiers at
the train stations leaving the front to return home told Berg that they had
forgotten how to pray, and he responded with the traditional comforts of
religion that would smooth over the ephemeral political reordering: "Now
I can understand you. When you return home again to wife and child,
old memories will help you pass over difficult times. Our Lord God is still
always the old one."[15] Religion, and its conceptions of ordered domesticity, would continue to be a source of stability in the post-war world of
the Catholic believer.

Catholic women and the dolorous conception of war

A transnational Catholic way of war helped Europe to grieve and mourn
the devastation. In contrast to the stereotype of the churches as zealous
jingoistic cheerleaders for war, the Catholic way of war showed the adaptation of Catholic tradition to the new circumstances of industrial warfare. The revised Roman Missal of 1920 offered key insights. The Mass
in Time of War (*Missa tempore belli*) represented the Church's official
liturgical guidelines for church services during war. Although the Bible
certainly contained much Old Testament sanction for chosen-people violence visited on one's fellow humans, these passages were not at all a part
of the Mass in Time of War. This Mass was based on universal grief
and consolation, not on divine-right chosen-people nationalism. As prescribed in the Roman Missal, the Old Testament readings were drawn
from the lamentations of the prophet Jeremiah, particularly Chapter 42.
There, the army leaders of Israel implore the prophet to speak to the
Lord and say, "Grant our petition; pray for us to the LORD, your God,
for all this remnant. We are now few who once were many, as you well
see." Jeremiah speaks to God and waits ten days for a response. The
prophet then returns with the Lord's answer to the people of Israel: "If
you remain quietly in this land I will build you up, and not tear you down;
I will plant you, not uproot you; for I regret the evil I have done you. Do
not fear the king of Babylon, before whom you are now afraid; do not

[14] Ibid., 780–2.   [15] Ibid., 794.

fear him, says the LORD, for I am with you to save you, to rescue you from his power."[16]

This was a striking theology, at odds with a representation of the Great War as apocalypse and utter incomphrensability. It portrayed God as a humane, approachable, and regretful God, divined through the offices of Jeremiah the prophet, which also had the important additional benefit of emphasizing the intercessory priestly hierarchical culture of the Catholic Church. This was not a theology of God as wholly other, mysterious, inscrutable, as in emerging forms of Protestant Dialectical Theology. The Mass in Time of War offered a picture of the Great War as a less-than-radical break with previous time, not a wholly-other period of incomprehensibility. The important point was that the war was not the apocalypse itself. This was further reinforced by the Gospel reading for the Mass in Time of War, a selection in which Christ's disciples ask him how to discern the apocalypse and the Second Coming of Christ. The disciples ask Jesus, "[W]hat sign will there be of your coming, and of the end of the age?" Jesus eventually responds with the familiar passage counseling the need to avoid false Messiahs, instead looking for a time when, "Nation will rise against nation, and kingdom against kingdom; there will be famines and earthquakes from place to place," which Christ likens to the beginning of labor pains. Importantly, however, Jesus qualifies, "You will hear of wars and reports of wars; see that you are not alarmed, for these things must happen, but it will not yet be the end."[17] In the Mass in Time of War found in the Roman Missal, the Church acknowledged war of great devastation and suffering as an inherent part of the fallen human condition. But, in the official Catholic liturgy, the Great War was relativized and normalized; it was not the apocalypse and the end of all time.

Making sense of Christian sacrifice, the Catholic motif of the Pietà had such resonance because it focused attention on families and brought women to the forefront of communities of suffering. In contrast to nineteenth-century monuments of heroic martial masculine virtue that emphasized the bombast of battlefield victory, the Pietà was explicitly feminine, humane, and humble. In an age of mass suffering, the Pietà was an effective and evocative symbol to the masses. The Pietà did not explicitly condemn war, but it called attention to the suffering and sacrifice involved. It allowed survivors to mourn the fallen, linking their

---

[16] Jer. 42:1–2, 7–12, quoted in *Missale Romanum: ex decreto sacrosancti Concilii tridentini restitutum s. Pii V. pontificis maximi jussu editum, aliorum pontificum cura recognitum, a Pio X. reformatum et Benedicti XV. auctoritate vulgatum* (Ratisbonæ: F. Pustet, 1920), 101.

[17] Matthew 24:3–8, quoted in *Missale Romanum*, 102.

sacrifice with that of Christ. Catholic women were not mere symbols in this memorialization process; they were agents in the process of historical remembrance. Perhaps most pointedly, Ruth Schaumann created a stone Pietà in 1929 for the German Catholic Women's League. Placed in the crypt of the Frauenfriedenskirche in Frankfurt, the Pietà contained a specifically female inscription: "In praise of our husbands, sons, brothers, fathers, R.I.P." Schaumann's Pietà contained no image of a soldier, but other works did make this symbolism explicit, putting a dead or dying soldier into the arms of a female mourner.[18] As never before, explicitly classical imagery incorporated women into monuments as ordinary, everyday mourners, as in Friedrich Bagdons's 1923 design for the cemetery entrance at Freudenstadt, in which a dead soldier lies in the lap of a seated naked woman.[19]

Mothers and fallen soldiers emphasized the universality of suffering, as well as reinforcing the Catholic image of the Virgin Mary as mother of Christ and special patron for human suffering. The Soldier's Remembrance Chapel in the Church of Saint Nicholas in Cologne, the major Catholic city in the heavily Catholic Rhineland, was sculpted by Johannes Osten around 1920. The chapel showed the body of the fallen Christ surrounded by the Virgin Mary, Mary Magdelene, and John, all standing above the inscription, "Help us, O dolorous Mother, in our sorrow."[20] Far away, on the idyllic shores of Lake Constance, the Church of St. Nikolaus displayed beautiful stained glass windows, designed by Albert Figel in 1920, that showed explicit parallelism between the female caritas network of empowered women as healers of society's wounds, definitively framed in terms of Christian sacrifice and Marian devotion. A main window's inscription proclaimed, "In struggle and need, help us for all time, Mary." The window's imagery portrayed a wounded soldier in the foreground, comforted by a Red Cross sister. Subtly shrunken in the background, in a picture-within-a-picture, a grieving Mary caressed the body of the fallen Jesus, newly taken down from the cross. Thus, the window reinforced that female nurses were equivalent to the Virgin Mother Mary, examples of charity and devotion, newly recognized as essential to healing the nation's wounds and care for the Christian heroes.[21] Otto Hitzberger's 1927 wooden Pietà in the Laurentiuskirche

---

[18] For an overview of the Pietà as motif in war memorials, see Winter, *Sites of Memory*, 90–3. For a discussion of Schaumann's work, see Volker G. Probst, *Bilder vom Tode. Eine Studie zum deutschen Kriegerdenkmal in der Weimarer Republik am Beispiel des Pietà-Motives und seiner profanierten Varianten* (Hamburg: Wayasbah, Original-Ausg edition, 1986), 158–9, 366.

[19] Probst, *Bilder vom Tode*, 160–2, 368.

[20] Ibid., 189–90, 388.   [21] Ibid., 266–7, 446.

in Berlin embodied Christian sacrifice in contemporary sculptural styles, directly in the heart of one of the main urban centers of modernist thought. Josef Limburg's 1927 marble Heroes' Altar in the Church of St. Ludwig in Berlin-Wilmersdorf, while not specifically a Pietà motif, was an example of traditional imagery in a modernist setting, showing a triumphant Christ rising from the crucifixion on a monument dedicated to the fallen of 1914–18.[22] In rural regions outside of the major metropolitan areas, a plethora of traditional roadside shrines, altars, and chapels became new sites for mourning the fallen of the Great War.

The figure of the widow represented an intriguing and problematic image for post-war societies. As Erika Kuhlman has argued in a path-breaking work on widowhood, "War widows perpetuated war – a defining characteristic of the nation-state – when they performed their gendered roles as women and mothers in need of male protection; they threw a wrench into the war machine when they felt betrayed by their governments, or when they perceived their losses collectively as humans, across national boundaries."[23] On an ideological level, however, Catholic women identified with the Virgin Mary as the supreme symbol of womanhood and of sainthood. The concept of Christian sacrifice made loss more understandable and endurable.

A family history of death

Beyond the justifications for war lay the reality of families struggling to cope with personal losses. Perhaps the ultimate change in ascriptions of sacrifice concerned Kaiser Franz Joseph. In 1914, the Central Powers' propaganda machine had made much of the fact that Austria-Hungary and Germany had gone to war to avenge Serbia's dishonor to the Habsburg monarchy. Franz Joseph died on November 21, 1916, to be succeeded by his great-nephew Karl, the last Habsburg emperor. Having ruled since 1848, Franz Joseph was, for many of his subjects, the personal embodiment of everything the Habsburg monarchy stood for, and his death was a highly symbolic end of an era. By 1916, the Habsburg patriarchy was crumbling. Initial outpourings of grief in the Catholic press reflected the symbolic associations of the throne-and-altar alliance, but this was not shown in war monuments and memorials. Despite the rage of hurrah patriotism that had accompanied the need

---

[22] Ibid., 132–3, 347–8.
[23] Erika A. Kuhlman, *Of Little Comfort: War Widows, Fallen Soldiers, and the Remaking of the Nation after the Great War* (New York: New York University Press, 2012), 5–6. For a classic account of the state's neglect of German soldiers, widows, and orphans, see Whalen, *Bitter Wounds*.

to defend the monarchy, during and after the war, memorials did not include members of the Habsburg family. The monarchy had been a symbol of declining resonance even before the war, but the Habsburg state's failure to provide food in time of war highlighted the monarchical patriarchy's impotence.[24] After the war, especially in the losing powers, grief and bereavement became highly personalized, as collective symbols lost their meaning at the state level.

More locally, however, religious thought helped to inform grieving families. During and after the war, families relied immensely on the Catholic clergy and laity for information on their family members' deaths and burials. Through the military and administrative hierarchies, military chaplains, priests, nuns, and religious nurses were often the families' point of contact for information about lost loved ones. As a military chaplain, Friedrich Gasser of the Fourth Tyrolian *Kaiserjäger* Regiment received numerous letters testifying to families' persistence of belief despite the death of loved ones. This correspondence of belief continued even late into the war, when its successful outcome seemed increasingly doubtful for the Central Powers. In March 1918, a grieving mother, Frau Morandini, wrote a postcard to Gasser in which she declared, "I send you my warmest thanks for your note about the death of my dearest son. It is for me a difficult loss; it is painful for me. In my suffering, there is comfort that at least he was given a Christian burial not in enemy hands but here in Tyrol. May the dear God take him up and grant him eternal rest."[25] Similarly, in a pleading letter written on All Souls' Day 1917, a civilian father, Rudolf Otto von Ottenhud of Vienna, wrote to Chaplain Gasser asking for assistance in identifying and repatriating his son's body, located in the soldiers' cemetery at Monte Buse. Otto wrote that, "It would be a great comfort for us to know that the last remains of our unfortunate child are buried in home soil, so that we can be united with him in the grave when God calls us away [to the afterlife]."[26]

Whenever possible, religious figures sought to comfort families that their loved ones had died quickly, usually painlessly, and had received full rites of Christian burial. Letters from clerics were meant to console:

[24] Laurence Cole and Daniel L. Unowsky, eds., *The Limits of Loyalty: Imperial Symbolism, Popular Allegiances and State Patriotism in the Late Habsburg Monarchy* (New York: Berghahn Books, 2007); Healy, *Vienna.*

[25] TLA, 4. Tiroler Kaiserjäger Regiment, Gruppe VI, Ktn. 14: Feldpostkarte, Frau Morandini to Gasser, March 14, 1918; TLA, 4. Tiroler Kaiserjäger Regiment, Gruppe VI, Ktn. 14: Feldpostkarte, Franz Linser to Gasser, March 17, 1918.

[26] TLA, 4. Tiroler Kaiserjäger Regiment, Gruppe VI, Ktn. 14, November 2, 1917 (All Souls' Day) letter from Rudolf Otto v. Ottenhud, Vienna, to Gasser.

they did not speak of the agonizing horrors of poison gas, dismember-
ment by artillery shells, or painful disfigurement. When religious letters
addressed the issue of soldiers' suffering, clerics would mention that the
deceased had died valiantly doing his duty, in heroic sacrifice for the
greater good, thus imitating Jesus Christ. Clerics reported that soldiers'
last words focused heavily on traditional tropes of family and homeland.
As reported by chaplains, soldiers mentioned their loved ones, most often
their mother or wife, while trying to convey the message that they were
going to a better spiritual place and would continue to watch over and
protect the family.[27]

It was easier to give this reassurance in hospital settings on the homefront. There, clergy could be found to administer last rites and burial
procedures, even after death. At battlefront hospitals and in the midst of
battle, this standard of religious care was often simply not possible, as
the growing size of industrial armies rapidly outpaced the religious care
network there. Chaplains rationalized that they had often given units
departing for battle a general absolution. At the front, clerics performed
individual and mass burials, sometimes giving the burial rites long after
death.[28] The publicized mass media image of death, however, was traditional in the extreme. Photos of cemeteries showed well-ordered rows
of graves, often with flowers and personal inscriptions. Comrades often
stood mourning at the graveside, thus assuring those at home of a continuity of heroic devotion.

During and after the war, family networks of consolation continued to
uphold religious faith as a source of meaning, making the loss of their
loved ones more comprehensible. This can be seen in the condolence
letters written from the Kruger family to Frau Krista Scholl, the wife of
a Bavarian peasant, Siegfried, killed on June 22, 1915 in Ban de Sapt
in den Vogesen. During the war, Siegfried maintained a conscientious
devotion to his religious practice. In his letters home, he wrote that he
had prayed the rosary three or four times daily and that he "prayed
diligently... almost every day and night."[29] Religion was a strong component of the Scholls' marital bonds. Writing from the battlefield on
the anniversary of his engagement during the harvest festival, Siegfried
wrote to Krista that, "it's 11 years since we became engaged. Now I live
in such a dangerous time. I pray every day that God will lead me home
again. You and the children do that, too."[30] After Siegfried was killed in

---

[27] Ludwig Esch, z.Z. Felddivisionspfarrer "Der Feldseelsorge. Schwierigkeiten und
Erfolge," *Stimmen der Zeit* 92 (1916): 400–1.
[28] Ibid., 416.
[29] BfZ, NL Knoch 1914–1918, Letter of October 29, 1914, November 3, 1914.
[30] BfZ, NL Knoch 1914–1918, Letter of November 7, 1914.

battle, his family network consoled his wife with their shared religious faith. Krista's brother-in-law, Gerhard Zahn, wrote to her that he was "very regretful" for her loss, as Siegfried was a "good man and truly careful father." Gerhard recognized that for Krista, Siegfried's loss was "very painful and bitterly hard for you," and he could scarcely imagine that someone with whom they lived so closely "had to give up his life for the Fatherland and that God could determine such a terrible unhappiness for us." Nevertheless, Zahn believed that duty to homeland was paramount and God's will prevailed – although it was inscrutable – and that believers had to help each other. Despite the sadness and pain, he wrote, "And yet we must all console ourselves again. What God does, is done for good, that is, no one can overcome God's inscrutable resolution." In a gesture of Marian piety that underscored the role of the consoling mother, Gerhard wrote, "Console yourself thus, dear sister-in-law, because even in the greatest pain, we are helped by the heart of the Mother of God. Poor [Siegfried], he rests in peace."[31] The Scholl family kept its religiously-framed memory of the sacrificial devotion of Siegfried Scholl, especially through legacies of indulgences for the saying of Mass. For a one-time or regular fee, beneficences could ensure that Catholic believers who had died were remembered as part of the liturgy, linking them with the communion of saints that had formed the Catholic community from its origins in antiquity.

During and after the war, having a Mass said for a fallen soldier was a quick and easy form of remembrance and honor that respected religious faith. For larger fees, the remembrance could continue for longer periods of time. Honoring the death of her husband, Krista Scholl donated 300 marks to her local church in Oellingen for a series of Sacred Heart devotions to his memory, which continued long after the war was over. When Scholl herself died in 1963, her family set up a similar devotion of 300 marks to her memory, keeping the tradition going.[32] The Catholic community network of memory continued.

Any item with a personal connection to the dearly departed became a religious relic for believing Catholic families. Such items included bits of clothing, rings, and even the bullets or shell fragments that had killed the soldier. These relics were treasured by religious family members as a form of connection to the deceased. The family of Heiko Fleck, killed in 1917, noted that his final unsent letter home was stained "with his heart's blood" from the bullet that had killed him, thus reinforcing the imagery of the cult of the Sacred Heart of Jesus, bursting with the

---

[31] BfZ, NL Knoch 1914–1918, Letter of July 15, 1915.
[32] BfZ, NL Knoch 1914–1918, Letter of October 10, 1915. For the note about the 300 mark donation, see BfZ, NL Knoch 1914–1918, Abschrift, p. 177.

blood of the Savior.[33] Central to modern Catholic imagery, the symbols of the Sacred Heart in particular reinforced the language of Christian sacrifice, underscoring the belief that the individual had died for a higher, communal purpose, in imitation of Christ. The Great War was a decisive moment in the emergence of such symbols in the Catholic imaginary.[34]

Medievalism was also a large part of Catholic memory and mourning culture, which attempted to draw on traditional motifs. There were certainly areas of overlap with Protestant Christianity, especially in medievalism's emphasis of the martial virtues of chivalry. This attempted to humanize representations of war, thus establishing continuities of civilization in defiance of the atomizing, senseless nature of industrial carnage. Catholic believers also drew upon additional layers of their religious belief structure, indebted to the medieval era. The Church as a medieval society provided a simplistic vision of an organic community in which everything was religiously ordered and stability reigned. It was a powerful antidote to terrifying visions of modern society and the horrors of war it had unleashed.[35] Especially in the formation of a German nation-state led by a version of liberal Protestant nationalism, Catholicism had been a convenient foil, denounced as superstitious, feminine, medieval, and un-German; it was precisely these qualities, however, that made Catholicism a rich source of traditional stability in the minds of believers. In particular, the intercessory saint culture and the notion of the Virgin Mary as feminine protector provided extra layers of comfort for Catholic believers struggling to understand the cataclysm of the Great War.[36]

Votive tablets placed in churches and religious shrines were another source of religiously-based memorialization, invoking especially the healing powers of women. In thousands of Catholic churches across Europe, believers thanked the community of saints for interceding on behalf of their loved ones, and often implored their continued assistance in the future. The Virgin Mary and Saint Joseph (patron saint of a happy death) figured prominently in prayers to the saints, as did Saint Jude, the patron saint of hopeless causes.[37] Soldiers' saints were especially venerated, particularly those who became pacifists, like Saint Martin of Tours, or who suffered wounding persecution by the Roman military, like Saint Sebastian (easily recognizable as a body pierced by arrows), or who refused to harm their fellow Christians, like Saint Maurice of the famous Theban Legion. Militant saints were also invoked in representations in prayers

---

[33] BfZ, NL 97.1/96 (Fleck), Letter, May 12, 1917, "Als Erdwurm" to mother and sister.
[34] Busch, *Katholische Frömmigkeit*; Schlager, *Kult und Krieg*.
[35] Stefan Goebel, *The Great War and Medieval Memory: War, Remembrance, and Medievalism in Britain and Germany, 1914–1940* (Cambridge: Cambridge University Press, 2007).
[36] Gross, *War against Catholicism*.
[37] Nikitsch, "... den unsern Jammer," 223–62.

and on memorials, particularly to lend strength to the claim that the deceased had fought a good fight; these included Saint George, slayer of the dragon, and Saint Michael, the archangel who leads the forces of God against the forces of Satan in the Book of Revelation.[38] Benjamin Ziemann has noted, however, that the use of Saint George could also be read not merely as militant Christianity but, in the context of popular piety, as an admonition for soldierly purity in the face of danger, thus representing a plea for returning soldiers to guard themselves against morally lax behavior.[39]

The bodily destruction of mass industrial warfare tested the limits of believers' rational understanding of a well-ordered universe. The major conceptual hurdle was battlefield violence that prevented bodies from being recovered. Some men simply disappeared. Some were blown apart and completely destroyed, some lost in the mud and dirt of the trenches, while others simply went missing. Catholic chaplains close to the front were well aware of the issue. Jakob Ebner, serving on the Western Front, recorded in his diary the questions he received from fighting soldiers about death and burial in the new type of war:

Who wants to search for the unforgotten and find them and record their names, they who lie forward in the trenches, shaken and smothered through heavy shellfire or through explosions?... Who searches together for those who have been ripped to pieces by explosions or shellfire or who have even been pulverized into atoms? Who can recognize Father and Son in the mass graves of this war of movement, in which the brave rest united beside – and sometimes on top of – each other?[40]

Of special importance in a conflict in which so many were killed by artillery, some to be completely obliterated, was another prominent female saint, Saint Barbara. This patron saint of artillery, engineers, miners, and any Catholics who faced the dangers of sudden, violent death, especially by explosions, figured prominently both during and after the conflict.[41] Saint Barbara would help to comfort those families who had no body to mourn.

Far from being an antiquated relic of a pre-modern religious behavior that the war had supposedly destroyed, the cult of saints as intercessory figures demonstrated the vitality of popular Catholicism in interwar Central Europe.[42]

---

[38] Meinhold Lurz, *Kriegerdenkmäler in Deutschland*, 6 vols. (Heidelberg: Esprint, 1985), 4:389; Vogt, *Religion im Militär*, 425.

[39] Ziemann, *Front und Heimat*, 450–2.

[40] EAF, NL 44, Jakob Ebner Tagebuch, entry of June 19, 1916, pp. 510–11.

[41] http://www.catholic.org/saints/saint.php?saint_id=166 (last accessed October 31, 2014).

[42] Mooser, "Katholische Volksreligion," 144–56.

Figure 10 Bricolage grave, Saint Barbara (Lipusch)
"This grave incorporated an artillery shell, which could represent either the profession of the soldier or his cause of death. Patron saints, such as Saint Barbara (for miners, trench diggers, and artillery), helped believers to make sense of the new forms of death and destruction."

Scriptural readings for the Catholic Requiem Mass emphasized passages that promised individual salvation for the believer, but as part of a larger community. The Gospel and liturgical language drew especially from John 11:25–6, and its story of the raising of Lazarus from the dead: "Jesus told her, 'I am the resurrection and the life; whoever believes in me, even if he dies, will live, and everyone who lives and believes in me will never die. Do you believe this?'" After the priest sprinkled the coffin with Holy Water, the absolution for the Requiem Mass emphasized the Catholic community in particular, as the priest intoned, "Grant, O Lord, we beseech thee, this mercy unto thy servant deceased, that, having in desire kept thy will, he may not suffer in requital of his deeds: and as a true Faith joined him unto the company of thy faithful here below, so may thy tender mercy give him place above, among the Angel choirs. Through Christ our Lord. Amen."[43] During and after the war, prayers at soldiers' gravesides and memorial services at home spoke in universal terms of common suffering. In a common prayer book issued to German Catholic soldiers by the Archdiocese of Cologne, the "Prayer for the Fallen" reminded soldiers that, "The best prayer that you can perform for the fallen is the reception of holy communion for them, offering up a plenary indulgence that is bound with it." The instructions continued: "By prayer for the fallen, do not think merely on your fallen comrades, rather also on the fallen enemies. Death led them all before the same judge, before whom you also must one day stand and who can now be well-disposed to you whenever you pray for friend and enemy."[44] For Catholic believers, prayer communities of the living Catholic faithful could continue to affect metaphysical relations between Heaven and Earth, ensuring individual and collective salvation.

Especially in publications, the overall language of prayer moved back toward traditional forms, away from the jingoistic corruptions and omissions that were widespread in time of war. In one notorious example early in 1914, Dietrich Vorwerk, a Protestant pastor and author, altered the Lord's Prayer to read, in part, "Our Father, from the height of heaven / Make haste to succor Thy German people. / Help us in the holy war, / . . . Lead us not into the temptation / Of letting our wrath be too gentle / In carrying out Thy divine judgment."[45] Another German propaganda variant of the Lord's Prayer altered it to speak in the guise of a "Russian Our Father." Beginning, "Our Father, Who art in

[43] http://www.usccb.org/bible/john/11 (last accessed October 31, 2014). *Missale Romanum: ex decreto sacrosancti Concilii tridentini restitutum s. Pii V. pontificis maximi jussu editum, aliorum pontificum cura recognitum, a Pio X. reformatum et Benedicti XV. auctoritate vulgatum*, 130.
[44] Cöln, *Vor Gott ein Kind*, 35–6.
[45] Quoted in Jenkins, *The Great and Holy War*, 12–13, trans. Jenkins.

Figure 11 Snowstorm burial (Lipusch)
"During a snowstorm, a military chaplain buries a soldier with funeral rites."

Petersburg, Thy name be destroyed, Thy kingdom disappear, Thy will be done neither in Heaven nor on Earth."[46]

It is perhaps a case of omission that best highlights religion's instrumentalization for state aims during the Great War. During the conflict, a highly romanticized picture booklet of the "Our Father" went line by line through the prayer, representing the text through painted images of wartime Christianity. Tellingly, however, the booklet left out a key message of the prayer, one of the core principles of Christianity: "as we forgive those who trespass against us."[47] This message was a prime symbol of the aggressive public war theology, which had no place for forgiveness, especially for perceived wrongdoing. By contrast, in the post-war years, the somber traditional forms of prayer returned, the "Lord's Prayer" regaining its traditional lines in place of jingoism.

[46] Marius Meinhof, "Gebete im Ersten Weltkrieg," in *Glaubenssache Krieg. Religiöse Motive auf Bildpostkarten des Ersten Weltkriegs*, ed. Heidrun Alzheimer (Bad Windsheim: Verlag Fränkisches Freilandmuseum, 2009), 100–1.
[47] Siegmund Rudl, *Kriegsvaterunser: Andenken an den Weltkrieg für alle Mitkämpfer und ihre Angehörigen* (Prague: Bonifatia Verlag, 1917), 17–19.

Suicide, spiritualism, and Catholic prohibitions

Specific forms of belief and action around death and mourning during the Great War explicitly contravened official Catholic practice. Suicide and spiritualism were two of the most widespread and visible. Catholic reactions to these occurrences show the flexibility of tradition, as well as its complete negation.

The practice of suicide was the ultimate rejection of the interpretation of heroic sacrifice, and explicitly condemned by the Catholic faith as a mortal sin. In a military setting, however, Catholic prescriptions sometimes had to be disregarded. The military hierarchy supported the Church hierarchy strongly on the issue of suicide. In order to sustain the collective morale of the army, many officers strongly counseled chaplains to admonish the soldiers against committing suicide. The words of the commander of the German 3rd Army Corps couched the injunction in terms of patriotic duty: "It is to be made clear to the troops that it is always an act of cowardliness to throw one's life away, especially in these times, where our life belongs to our King. Whoever commits suicide now, sins not only against his God, but also against his King and his Fatherland."[48] Catholic chaplains interpreted an increase in suicides as a sign of decreasing collective will. Andreas Farkas, a chaplain in the k.u.k. 25th Infantry Regiment, ascribed a string of "desperate and intentional suicides" to frustration about the lack of winter clothing for the troops, currently stationed in freezing conditions.[49]

Catholic teachings against suicide were extremely severe in theory, but often adaptable in battlefield practice. According to Canon Law, suicide was a mortal sin that denied immortality to those who committed it. Correspondingly, suicides could not be buried in consecrated ground with believers who had died in a state of grace.[50] The official pre-war Catholic field manual for Austria-Hungary held to this doctrine, as did a Prussian field manual that appeared late in the war.[51] In actual practice, however, chaplains ameliorated the official regulations on suicide. Catholic chaplains interpreted self-inflicted death as one of the unfortunate realities of the brutality of war. The chaplain Benedict Kreutz, the future leader of the Deutscher Caritas Verein (DCV), showed no hesitation in his diary when he reflected on burying suicides. Kreutz granted

---

[48] BA-MA, PH 32/147: Feldseelsorge, Bd. 1, July 7, 1915 letter of III. Armeekorps Commanding General.

[49] ÖStAKA, AFV, Ktn. 216, Pastoralbericht, Andreas Farkas, November 1915.

[50] From the 1917 Code of Canon Law, see Canons 1240 and 2350, found in Peters, *The 1917 or Pio-Benedictine Code*, 421–2, 746.

[51] Albert, *Handbuch*, 303–6; Bjelik, *Handbuch*, 29–30. Cf. CIC, Cann. 1230–1240, found in Peters, *The 1917 or Pio-Benedictine Code*, 409–22.

them a Catholic military burial on multiple occasions. For instance, an infantryman, Xaver Lutz, drowned himself in a river on May 2, 1917, supposedly fearing a transfer to the Eastern Front. Even more conclusively, two days later, a *Landwehr* artilleryman, Victor Vögele, hanged himself. Kreutz gave Catholic burials to both servicemen.[52] Similarly, Karl Laska, a chaplain with the Austro-Hungarian 5th Army, wrote in his monthly pastoral report to the Apostolic Field Vicariate in Vienna that he regularly accorded burials of suicides the same honors as other military burials.[53]

Along with suicide, spiritualism was another topic that conflicted with Catholic doctrine. During and after the Great War, Catholics participated in séances and forms of spiritualism designed to get in touch with the dead. These paranormal practices began during the war, as people saw the ghosts of their relatives and close friends. Ghosts of soldiers killed in battle appeared at the homefront and ghosts of their loved ones appeared to soldiers in a network of spiritual family aid. Believers usually perceived these ghosts as trying to help the living, sometimes simply giving notification that they had died, easing the uncertainty of not knowing. Often couched in terms of rumor and hindsight, occult publications in Central Europe were filled with stories such as that of "Frau W. from S.," who on the afternoon of October 30, 1914, suddenly felt "great unrest and bodily weakness," overcome by a vision of her husband lying with his chest torn open at the edge of a forest; on November 6, Fraw W. received a telegram informing her that her husband had indeed been killed in a forest near Ailly on the afternoon of October 30, dying from artillery shrapnel in his chest.[54] Sometimes, ghosts or spirits actively intervened to change the behaviors of the living, either imploring them to lead better moral lives or immediately saving them from imminent death. In a case of the latter, a dragoon recounted the time in November 1915 when he was moving to administer a final mercy shot to one of his horses wounded in an attack and a ghostly vision of his dead mother appeared, luring him away from the struggling animal. Moments later, a shell burst on the horse, ripping it to pieces and destroying the ground where he would have stood had it not been for this vision, which he was convinced had saved his life.[55]

[52] Wollasch, *Militärseelsorge im Ersten Weltkrieg*, 118.
[53] ÖStAKA, AFV, Ktn. 217, Pastoralbericht, Karl Laska, December 1915.
[54] Bruno Grabinski, *Das Übersinnliche im Weltkriege. Merkwürdige Vorgänge im Felde und allerlei Kriegsprophezeiungen* (Hildesheim: Franz Borgmeyer, 1917), 32.
[55] Ibid., 30. For a recent examination of ghost stories, see Tim Cook, "Grave Beliefs: Stories of the Supernatural and the Uncanny among Canada's Great War Trench Soldiers," *Journal of Military History* 77, no. 2 (2013): 521–42.

Actively contacting the dead was strongly outlawed by the Catholic Church, which deemed spiritualism a form of superstitious "black magic" that ran contrary to the rites of the Church. In the Catholic conception, once the dead had been given burial rites, they could not be summoned on command by the living.[56] For the most part, Catholics obeyed the prohibitions, allowing their dead to rest in peace. There were, however, exceptions, as religious believers sought comfort in any contact whatsoever with their loved ones. In other instances, Catholics ventured into spiritualistic practices out of scientific interest or for entertainment. In many cases, believers sought the approval of Church authorities for participation in such affairs, writing that their ventures into spiritualism and the occult complemented, and did not negate, their dogmatic beliefs – but permission was usually denied when such requests reached higher levels of authority. In a 1927 letter to Cardinal Schulte of Cologne, C. Flössel asked for a dispensation "because of the scientific method of my research," which, for the previous six years, had investigated such phenomena as "parapsychology and related areas," "hypnosis and occult science," and "spiritualism sessions." Flössel wrote that, "It is certainly prohibited through Church decrees to take part in these kinds of things, and that is fully correct since a great deal of mischief [*Unfug*] is done there," but that his experience as a university professional complemented his "absolutely strong Catholic position." He declared that, "I stand with conviction on the fundamentals of Catholic dogma and fulfill with conscientiousness all of my religious obligations."[57] History does not record the Church response to his petition.

Other Catholics wrote that spiritualism and occult practices complemented their faith at a more personal level. They were also aware that such feelings ran counter to established Church decrees, and in some cases sought clerical permission to continue hybrid forms of spirituality. In a 1930 letter to Cardinal Schulte, Adolf Overzier described his spiritualistic convictions in detail, writing:

For the past half year, we have a little circle that meets every two weeks in order to do so-called table-turning [*Tischrücken*] on a spiritualistic basis. I submit that we have never talked with evil spirits or with strangers, rather only with our dead relatives and acquaintances, in particular with our parents. The result of this is that our faith has deepened itself even more, that we considerably remember them more now than was earlier the case through having Masses said for them and lighting candles. In short, for my wife as well as for me, the religious

---

[56] "Spiritismus, Teilnahme an solchen Sitzungen verboten," *Wiener Diözesanblatt* (1917), 90.

[57] AEK, Gen I 22.12, Letter, April 30, 1927, C. Flössel to Cardinal Schulte.

emotional life [*das religiöse Gefühlsleben*] has become deeper and more intimate than before.[58]

Overzier wrote of his awareness of Church prohibitions and tried to pay obeisance to them, framing his interest in terms of entertainment:

Now I can understand that conjuring spirits, black magic, and how one likes to call all these things, are fundamentally outlawed by the Church and must be. But I cannot comprehend how wonderful entertainment evenings [*Unterhaltungs-Abende*] somehow should violate the commandments of God or the Church. My last confessor explained that it was not sinful. On occasion, I have talked with others here and there about this point, and I have consequently experienced that the views are different.

In order to clear my conscience fully now, I humbly request that Your Eminence would briefly notify me if these good and nice entertainment evenings are sins for me and my wife.[59]

Particularly striking in this correspondence is Overzier's wavering between assertions of self-justification and the collective guilt imposed by Church law. Cardinal Schulte's office responded quickly to offer an interpretation of the "entertainment evenings": "The answer should read: 'No to everything,' i.e., that all the events in the request are not allowed."[60] Such responses highlighted that when Catholics chose to appeal to the authority of the clerical hierarchy, a hard-line authoritarian and inflexible answer was usually given in terms of established doctrine and dogma, especially regarding issues like suicide and superstition. When Catholics exercised their individual initiative at a lower level, however, they had a great deal more freedom of action to enact their beliefs.

Catholic reconciliation and exclusion

Beyond the bishops, scholars must look locally to individual believers and the social bonds of corporate groups, stemming from beliefs and emotions that do not always fit conventional narratives. After the guns of the Western Front fell silent, the Catholic Church provided a transnational means of reconciliation in ways unimaginable to the embittered national chauvinists, especially those from defeated Protestant Prussia. Some German Catholics, however, certainly did feel an embittered sense of defeat and betrayal, perhaps most notably Bishop (later Cardinal) Michael von Faulhaber of Munich, who had been heavily involved in the leadership of Bavarian chaplaincy during the Great War. Nevertheless, the most comprehensive study of the "stab-in-the-back" legend

---

[58] AEK, Gen I 22.12, Letter, September 5, 1930, Adolf Overzier to Cardinal Schulte.
[59] Ibid.   [60] AEK, Gen I 22.12, Antwort of 18.9.1930.

emphasizes the decisive influence of the Protestant social–moral milieu in advancing a sense of religiously-charged nationalist disappointment.[61]

By contrast, due to the transnational character of the Catholic Church and its self-justified universalisitic mission, Catholic understandings of being allowed for healing and reconciliation. The influential German Jesuit journal *Stimmen der Zeit* accorded prominent space to essays written by Paul Doncœur, a French Jesuit who had served in the war as a French army chaplain and who had been severely wounded at the Somme. Doncœur claimed that a visit to Lourdes had miraculously healed his wounds, allowing him to rejoin his regiment and participate in the final push to victory in 1918. In the conclusion to one of his articles published in 1922, Doncœur emotionally wrote of the necessity of Catholicism as a force for reconciliation in a fallen world:

Despite everything that can temporarily separate us here below [on Earth], it is nevertheless a wonderful thought that there are millions of souls all over the world who strive to give honor to the same Heavenly Father. We become aware that we are brothers, born of the same blood that flowed out of the same heart at one and the same Calvary. May this feeling of the unity of all sons of the Church triumph over all the obstacles that battle against love and unification. It was for them [i.e., all sons of the Church] that our Savior prayed in high priestly prayer: may they be one.[62]

Doncœur's Catholic sensibility was not exultant in service of the winning power; he struck a chord among the German Jesuits of the losing side. German Protestants had a much more difficult time reconciling their religious faith across national borders.[63]

While Catholics from the losing powers could conceptualize themselves as both universal and national, nevertheless, the Great War caused religious differences to diminish in some areas and exacerbated them in others; the cleavages were not split along simple lines of secularization or belief. Particularly in Germany, the sacrifice shared by both Protestants

---

[61] See Barth, *Dolchstoßlegenden*, 150–71, 340–59, 555.

[62] Paul Doncœur, S.J., "Die Gegenwartshoffnungen der Katholiken Frankreichs auf religiösem Gebiete," *Stimmen der Zeit* 103 (1922): 200. "Trotz all dem, was uns hier unten einen Augenblick auseinanderreißen kann, ist es doch ein herrlicher Gedanke, daß auf der ganzen Welt die Seelen nach Millionen zählen, die alle für die Ehre desselben himmlischen Vaters sich mühen. Da erwacht in uns das Bewußtsein, daß wir Brüder sind, geboren aus demselben Blute, das aus demselben Herzen floß auf ein und demselben Kalvarienberg. Möge dieses Gefühl der Zusammengehörigkeit aller Söhne der Kirche triumphieren über all die Hindernisse, die sich der Liebe und der Vereinigung entgegenwerfen, für die unser Heiland betete im hohenpriesterlichen Gebet: Ut sint unum." The phrase "high priestly prayer" refers to the last discourse of Christ, recounted in John 17:1–26.

[63] Houlihan, "Local Catholicism," 233–67.

and Catholics helped convince them that they were one nation, whose loyalty to the state was more paramount than its religious differences. In the land of the Protestant Reformation, this was a huge conceptual shift. One of the most prominent Catholic philosophers in Central Europe, Max Scheler, wrote of the "Peace between the confessions" that had occurred as a result of the Great War. Scheler claimed that, "There can be no more doubt: out of the dark depths of our historical past, only when we all know to master the newly awakened opposition of parties, putting religious confession on a new path . . . only then is it possible to avoid the bloodiest civil war and restrain the fall of the empire and the Bolshevisation of Europe . . . The question today is becoming clear to us, in order to avoid this, it means peace between the religious confessions in this fuller sense."[64]

The darker side of inclusion was, of course, exclusion. In Germany, religious differences between Christians and Jews became accentuated as Jews were made scapegoats. The majority Christian society desperately grasped for reasons why its shared sacrifice had resulted in defeat, eventually developing the notion of treason by inner enemies: a Jewish–Bolshevik conspiracy that had stabbed the German Army in the back.

The relationships between Nazism and different forms of religion have long been a subject of scholarly interest. Examining the specifically Catholic affiliations of the early Nazi movement, Derek Hastings has persuasively argued that historians need to reexamine the overlap and indeed continuities between the pre-war and interwar periods, particularly regarding the rise of the Nazi Party in Munich. As Hastings notes, "Building on the distinctive tradition of Catholic anti-ultramontanism and opposition to political Catholicism in Munich, the party was able to skillfully deploy the interconfessional ideal of Positive Christianity within an overwhelmingly Catholic context. It embraced the principle of religious Catholicism and thus distinguished itself from other *völkisch* groups, pitching itself ultimately as the most viable option for *völkisch*-oriented Catholics in Munich." The early Nazi movement developed among a plethora of other *völkisch* groups with strong religiously-inspired affinities for the rebirth of organic national communities in the aftermath of the Great War. Hastings shows that while the Catholic Church as a corporate organization was strongly opposed to Nazism, nonetheless, on a local level, individuals and groups could freely identify parts of their religiously-inspired faith, affirming that their values coincided with political movements. Furthermore, Hastings shows that the Nazi

[64] Max Scheler, "Der Friede unter den Konfessionen," *Hochland* 18 (1920–21): 140–7, 464–86.

movement underwent a change in its religious attitudes: the very early Nazi movement of 1919–23 had considerable affinities with certain elements of Munich Catholicism. However, the Nazi Party became more anti-religious over time and lost Catholic support, especially after Hitler's decision to join the Kampfbund in September 1923. Thus, instead of looking at Nazism as either a political religion or a religious politics, it is important to identify the local context and change that the party experienced over time in its relation to local Catholicism in Munich.[65] Even in rural, isolated regions of Germany like the Black Forest, there were structural factors such as the breakdown of *Vereine* in the 1920s that allowed Catholics on a local level to support Nazism as a heterogeneous mass party with national appeal. However, one must not overstate the case. Even in 1930, around half of the Black Forest's inhabitants still remained loyal to the Catholic milieu, voting with the Center Party and not with the Nazi Party.[66]

Although the war between the Great Powers had ended, a new war against Bolshevism was beginning, with real-world revolutionary attempts in cities such as Berlin, Budapest, and Munich.[67] Catholic military chaplains continued to serve in counter-revolutionary *Freikorps* units marauding in the Baltic regions, while battles were fought between paramilitary units in the former areas of the Austro-Hungarian monarchy, such as on the border between Carinthia and Slovenia.[68]

With historical hindsight, stormclouds of nationalist hatred and revenge politics were gathering in the interwar era. Perhaps this can be most acutely seen in the death of Matthias Erzberger. The leading German Catholic Center politician who helped direct the July 19, 1917 Reichstag Peace Resolution, Erzberger was especially hated by ultranationlists for his role in signing the Armistice in the railway car at Compiègne in November 1918, becoming one of the so-called "November criminals." After numerous attempts, Erzberger was finally murdered by a fringe right-wing group on August 26, 1921 in Bad Griesbach in the Black Forest. A news report from *Reichspost* in the immediate aftermath wrote that, "Erzberger was stamped by his opponents as the representative of an all-too-weak peace policy." Besides the Reichstag

[65] Derek Hastings, *Catholicism and the Roots of Nazism: Religious Identity and National Socialism* (Oxford: Oxford University Press, 2009), 183.

[66] Oded Heilbronner, *Catholicism, Political Culture, and the Countryside: A Social History of the Nazi Party in South Germany* (Ann Arbor: University of Michigan Press, 1998), 227.

[67] Bernhard Duhr, "Die Wurzeln des Bolschewismus. Eine ernste Mahnung auch für uns," *Stimmen der Zeit* 99 (1920): 402–13.

[68] Gerwarth, "Central European Counter-Revolution," 175–209; Houlihan, "Stab-in-the-Back Myth?," 67–89.

Peace Resolution, commentators used the occasion to highlight the papal peace initiatives, especially Benedict XV's Peace Note of 1917, and Erzberger's role in facilitating transnational Catholic peace overtures.[69] Erzberger's memoirs of the Great War culminate in an ironic sense of doom given his eventual assassination: their final pages contain descriptions of numerous assassination attempts, but Erzberger wrote of his belief that God protected him, and that he had helped bring peace to Germany.[70] Erzberger's role in the events of November 1918 underscored that, as one veered closer to the fringe elements of the German right, there would always be a feeling that Catholics were less German and less devoted to the nation than the ultranationlists wished.

If one traces longer continuities of Central European history, however, one sees that Jews, not Catholics, were the marginalized scapegoats of the First World War.[71] In fact, the Great War was a profound moment of Catholic assimilation into Germany. Sustained shared sacrifice during industrial warfare had integrated Protestants and Catholics in Central Europe as never before into a shared blood brotherhood unknown since before Martin Luther. As religion and nation became fused in the ideological imaginary, racialized thinking implied that non-Christians were of a different race, not true members of a national community. Lingering religious sentiment played a strong role in the ideological imaginary of inclusion and exclusion, ultimately culminating in the genocide of the Jews during the Second World War.

Catholic philosophy of war

The Catholic dolorous philosophy of war was present at the very beginning of the conflict and helped make a consoling interpretation of it after it was lost for the imperial powers of Central Europe. Although Catholics were certainly involved in some of the jubilance of the August days of 1914, from peasants at the village level to the highest ranks of clergy in the public sphere, there remained a strong strand of existential despair about the human condition on Earth. While Protestant circles certainly embraced parts of this focus on human sinfulness and the fallen condition, Catholic philosophies of war tended away from legitimizing one form of government or nation-state as divinely ordered. Thus, when imperial powers lost the war and new political orders were created, the conceptual leap was not as jarring for the ordinary Catholic believer.

---

[69] "Erzberger Ermordet!", *Reichspost*, August 27, 1921, p. 1.
[70] Matthias Erzberger, *Erlebnisse im Weltkrieg* (Stuttgart: Deutsche Verlagsanstalt, 1920), 383.
[71] Smith, *Continuities of German History*.

Protestant–Catholic differences in early war philosophy and post-war interpretation were striking. Written in the heady days of July 1914, an editorial in the prominent Austro-Hungarian Catholic paper *Reichspost* declared, "As long as there are human beings, there will be wars on Earth. As long as goods like homeland, freedom, and honor are held in esteem; as long as nations have interests on securing the economic and political interests of the Fatherland . . . there will be wars down here [on Earth]." The article declared a conception of humanity in a fallen and imperfect condition, based on original sin, and with a view of life on Earth as a dolorous journey: "Earth is not a paradise; the first-born of Creation are not Angels. Guilt and error sprawl everywhere in this valley of tears enormous passions nest in the small heart of man, and the nobly minded must always defend the battlefield against those of base passions; in the name of truth and justice, nations must always take up the sword against national lies and national injustice." In this Catholic philosophy of war, history was cyclical and not subject to great change, based on the perpetual condition of fallen humankind: "The pages of History speak a bloody language. National peace was the ideal; national war almost always the rule . . . The places change, the motives change, the forms change; but the thing remains . . . History teaches that dreams of eternal peace are illusions. War is bound up with the lives of nations, just as hardship and suffering are bound up with the existence of the individual . . . Tears are almost more necessary to people than smiles."[72] Right at the outset of war, this was a philosophy of history that contrasted particularly with the optimistic, linear philosophy of German Protestantism – especially the powerful version of chosen-people nationalism. When the conflict stagnated, and victory seemed ever more distant, Catholic philosophy allowed for less traumatic conceptual shifting from the expectations promised at the war's beginning.

After the war was lost for the Central Powers, this Catholic philosophy of war provided continuity in a confusing new world. Arguing that the Catholic Church was a fundamentally conservative force and that the Great War had brought no new revelations to believers, Peter Lippert, S.J., wrote in *Stimmen der Zeit* that, "The forms of government of states, the economic systems, the conditions of production, and the distribution of goods are meaningless in themselves for the goals and tasks of Christianity, and thus also meaningless for priests and pastors."[73] Drawing on the shifting sentiments of the Catholic bishops, based on natural-law

---

[72] "Der Krieg," *Reichspost*, July 30 (1914), Nr. 355, p. 1.
[73] Lippert, "Klerus, Krieg, und Umsturz," 84.

philosophy, this line of thought did not sanctify any one form of government. Thus, fallen monarchies, destroyed empires, and failed states were of lesser consequence to the religious believer. This also left open the option to transfer one's loyalties to new authoritarian states. Horrified at the terrors of atheistic communism, by default this favored Catholics shifting their political sentiments toward clerico-fascist alliances, which were on the rise across Central and Eastern Europe.[74] The Church's anti-communism in the post-1918 period would also become a focal point of Catholic identity in the post-1945 period, as well as serving as a source of common European political and cultural integration at Europe's supposed "zero hour" in 1945.[75]

Writing in 1922, the French Jesuit and former French military chaplain Paul Doncœur reflected the transnational dimensions of wartime sacrifice and memory. Around the time of the Armistice on the Western Front, Doncœur recalled advancing over captured German lines and admiring the large wooden cross erected there, which bore the inscription, "Here resting with God lie seven French warriors, fallen for their Fatherland." Validating that this sacrifice happened for Catholic believers on opposite sides during the war, Doncœur wrote that, "Certainly, these men fell 'for their Fatherland,' in the nicest sense of the word – for its spiritual rebirth." Doncœur transnationally linked the soldiers' blood sacrifice to the devotion of Christ as founder of the Catholic religion: "We Catholics . . . believe in the power of salvation through blood; we know that in this fundament the basis of our hope lies decided in this sacrifice offered to God." Doncœur was firmly restricted in this Catholic interpretation of the war, writing "it was the only explanation" for witnessing the unfolding of the process of salvation through the war. He asked his readers, "What success did the war have in hindsight on religious life?", and it was a loaded question. He argued that the war brought success "not in a sudden and all-encompassing upheaval of the country, in a mass conversion [*Massenbekehrung*], born out of the divine power of miracles [*göttlichen Wundermacht*]." Doncœur wrote that the "voice of God" was found always in the "conversion of souls only as a result of the deep-seeded work of mercy." Reconciliation, healing, and mercy would be the order of the day, manifested in small acts of everyday devotion. Doncœur did not minimize the "extraordinary lengths and difficulties of this test" that the sufferings of war had brought European society. He affirmed that some of superficial faith would turn away from belief in

[74] Martin Conway, *Catholic Politics in Europe, 1918–1945* (London: Routledge, 1997).
[75] Kaiser, *Christian Democracy*.

divine order after witnessing and living through destruction on a mass scale. He wrote of the force of Catholic belief as a fundamental stabilizing factor for society after the period of feverish panic, believing that "one saw the old sobriety coming back again." For France or Germany, for victors or losers of the conflict, Doncœur wrote that the war's effects were common to all Catholics. In religious minds, faith in a universal magisterium of believers would triumph over national enmity.[76]

Of course, such sentiments spoke to an idealization of pre-war life and a projected hope of a return to peace. In some ways, the war had not ended. New enemies had already appeared, especially a competing movement of international solidarity, the rise of socialism and its claims of materialistic atheism, which threatened the fundamentals of Catholic belief structure. For Catholics in the interwar period, the danger of Bolshevism was a war to be fought on all fronts. It had entered a decisive phase in 1917, after the Bolshevik Revolution in Russia, and it was one form of combat that did not end neatly on November 11, 1918.[77]

Religiously-minded soldiers and their families in the Central Powers often lost belief in the cause of state. They kept believing, however, in the metaphysical presence of God in their lives. Erwin Meier, a German soldier serving on the front lines in northern France late in the war, wrote in his diary on September 28, 1918 that, "It is right that we lose the war! The fraud is too big!" After describing the packet of bread that he had received from his mother, he further reinforced the family longings and homefront sense of community that animated the minds and hearts of religious believers, who prayed for their family members and appealed to the intercessory saint culture of the Church for continued protection. Meier wrote, "In Champagne and between Argonne and Maas, there is since yesterday a defensive battle. I suspect that my brother is there. God protect him."[78] Networks of intercession triumphed over nationalist loyalties.

In the interwar and post-war periods, the domesticity and imagined tranquility of home became a powerful vision of nostalgia. Believers longed for a return to peace and serenity, to childhood, to a time undisturbed by the social suffering of war. In her memoirs, Kristina Margarthe Anja Kronthaler, living in Freiburg im Breisgau, wrote of her childhood in Schweidnitz, in Silesia, with fond, idealized nostalgia: "Often I dream of Schweidnitz, city of my childhood, which was a happy one . . . I know

---

[76] Paul Doncœur, S.J., "Die Gegenwartshoffnungen," 104–13. For an assessment of the Great War's effect on French Catholicism, see, above all, Becker, *War and Faith*.

[77] Bernhard Duhr, "Die Wurzeln des Bolschewismus," 402–13.

[78] DTA 260, " . . . Und alles tanzt. Kriegstagebuch eines Kriegsfreiwilligen, 1914–1918," p. 212.

in the dream that I am in my hometown, but I do not find the way home to my parents' house. Then I wake up lost." In evoking her local identity as a Silesian, she reached back to a regional identity with loyalty to Empress Maria Theresa (d. 1780). She declared that Silesians retained loyalties to Austria and to the local area, despite being "Forced Prussians" (*Musspreussen*). Katharina recalled an interwar atmosphere of devotional piety, in which her family attended Mass every Sunday, with her father going to services daily. She particularly remembered the May festivities, when the churches were "filled with believers, who sang with zeal" and when there were devotions to the Virgin Mary centered on May altars decorated with flowers and burning candles.[79] Such nostalgic visions were key sources of comfort, providing alternative dreams that helped religious believers cope with the unsettled new socio-political realities of the interwar period.

Local war memorials and fragmented national memories

The Central Powers' official memorialization of the war was a contested process that faced a huge conceptual hurdle for the states that lost. On a local level, however, memorials in small communities across Europe demonstrated the persistence of traditional religious imagery and messages.[80] Soldiers' bodies were often buried at the front or else missing, sometimes completely destroyed. These memorials helped Catholics from the losing powers understand the phenomenon of mass death, legitimizing suffering and sacrifice. In the minds of religious believers, the war was seen not as a new form of destruction beyond comprehension, but rather as another episode in the shameful history of human sinfulness. Lists of names, usually in alphabetical order, emphasized the equality of sacrifice.[81]

Official commemorations in Catholic areas gravitated toward universal religious moments, especially the Feasts of All Saints (November 1) and All Souls (November 2). Before, during, and after the war, the days of early November retained a powerful symbolic resonance in the popular mindset, particularly since much of the fighting seemed to stop during this autumnal time in 1918. Catholic believers went to the cemeteries, lit candles, and honored the memory of all the dead, the communion of saints, and the entire community of the faithful departed. Traditional

---

[79] DTA 1132, "Erinnerungen," pp. 1–17.
[80] Van Ypersele, "Mourning and Memory," 580–1.
[81] Winter, "Commemorating War," 310–26.

belief in religious salvation would overcome even the new horrors of industrial war.

Especially in overwhelmingly rural regions, in the interwar period the Catholic Church seized control of war memorials, interpreting the sacrifices of the fallen in explicitly religious terms and dominating the public-sphere discourse about the war. This began with the quantitative presence of war memorials. As Oswald Überegger has calculated for the region of Tyrol, around ninety percent of war memorials were in churches, religious cemeteries, or on church property. Regarding the more symbolic language of Tyrolean monuments, between 1918 and 1938 the overwhelming majority of iconography was religious, which meant Christian, and usually Catholic: 33.8% of monuments had purely religious imagery, while a further 23.7% had some combination of religious iconography and more military or civilian motifs.[82]

In a world in which the monarchy had been dissolved as a political entity, the Church was still vastly important to the military in maintaining an aura of legitimacy grounded in the throne-and-altar alliance. Chaplains held positions of honor at regimental gatherings, helping to consecrate flags and imbue the proceedings with a sense of divine approval. In the interwar period, military chaplains were essential figures at ceremonies that blended military veterans' associations and local patriotism.[83] Flag consecration ceremonies drew in rural participants from widespread areas. Such events often began with solemn church services but also usually included celebratory elements at which young and old could socialize in a festive atmosphere. As Benjamin Ziemann has noted, Catholic ordinariates in Bavaria often unsuccessfully attempted to forbid the conjunction of church services with festive remembrance events and flag consecration parties, but the ceremonies went on anyway, in a show of local patriotism with religious initiative.[84]

With regard to war memorials, however, the Church in Bavaria laid down a much more decisive opinion, refusing to consecrate any war memorials, or to conduct the requisite ceremonies, if the activities did not have primarily Christian leanings – and the rural communities usually submitted to the Church's wishes in this regard.[85] In rural regions in Central Europe, such local memorials were mostly situated on church grounds, often incorporated as part of the church itself. All across

---

[82] Überegger, *Erinnerungskriege*, 131–44.
[83] Lurz, *Kriegerdenkmäler in Deutschland*, 4:391–2. For photographs of chaplains leading interwar remembrance ceremonies at veterans' associations, see DAG, Sch. 29–34: Fotos.
[84] *Bayerischer Krieger Zeitung*, July 20, 1921, September 5, 1921, quoted in Ziemann, *Front und Heimat*, 425ff.
[85] Ibid., 438–61.

Central Europe, memorials to the Great War carried more Christian motifs than those recalling the nationalist wars of the nineteenth century, as religion provided a means of consolation to the bereaved attempting to cope with the war's destruction.[86] In particular, Bavarian Marian piety swelled during the war, reaffirmed by a papal decree from Benedict XV, becoming an excellent vehicle for post-war bereavement, as encapsulated by the Christian form of the Pietà.[87] Centered in Marian devotions to the rosary, the Bavarian pilgrimage church of Altötting swelled with around 300 000 annual visitors in the interwar years. Soldiers and their family networks made vows that if they emerged from the war alive, they would all go on pilgrimages to give thanks. The swelling number of pilgrims made clear that many religious families took such vows seriously.[88]

At Bavarian sites of memory such as Altötting, Cardinal Michael von Faulhaber, who had been integral to Bavarian chaplaincy during the war, made the war experience a foundational element of his post-war preaching. During a May 3, 1925 address to former Bavarian soldiers who had made the pilgrimage to Altötting, Faulhaber implored his listeners to "Honor those who fell on the field of honor! But shame those who fell on the field of shame!" The latter part was directed against the perceived laxness of moral behavior during the war, especially sins of incontinence such as sexual infidelity and drunkenness. Militarizing the message, such diatribes had presentist implications for their living audience. Faulhaber even used the same contrast between the "Field of Honor" (*Feld der Ehre*) and the "Field of Shame" (*Feld der Schande*) during an April 27, 1919 sermon for Easter communion held in front of middleschool students who had not experienced the war as soldiers. Faulhaber's message showed a continuity of form centered in war experience and remembrance. During a speech to members of the *Katholischer Gesellenverein* in Munich's Bürgersaal on March 16, 1919, Faulhaber emphasized that the experience of war reconciled humanity's conscience to God because the omnipresent closeness of death was a guide for leading moral lives. Twenty years later, in the Munich Cathedral, during the May 30, 1939 dedication of a memorial to military chaplains and candidates for the priesthood who had fallen in the Great War, Faulhaber argued that religion was the source of customary power that solidified society, especially through devotion to the flag and the morality of perseverance (*Durchhaltemoral*), again couching his speech in war terms. For Faulhaber, the Great War was a permanent moral lesson, applicable to future generations.[89]

---

[86] Lurz, *Kriegerdenkmäler in Deutschland*, 4:221. Cf. Winter, *Sites of Memory*, 78–116.
[87] Ziemann, *Front und Heimat*, 448–50.   [88] Ibid., 257–8.
[89] Klier, *Von der Kriegspredigt*, 137–45.

Especially for many rural regions in which the Catholics of Central Europe were a preponderant majority, memorialized historical remembrance was firmly rooted in local contexts and webs of meaning. Bavaria, for instance, officially declined to participate in German national remembrance and the national hero cult. Throughout the Weimar period, Bavaria did not celebrate the National Day of Mourning (*Volkstrauertag*) decreed for the sixth Sunday before Easter, which was arranged by the National League for the Maintenance of German War Graves (*Volksbund für Deutsche Kriegsgräberfürsorge*). Instead, after 1926, the Bavarian Catholic Church created a day of mourning on the second Sunday in November, within the octave of All Souls, thus keeping with a more Catholic sensibility that did not celebrate the German nation. This explicit depoliticization also helped to prevent people from questioning the political frameworks and underlying social conditions that had caused the war in the first place.[90]

Care of official monuments and war graves tended to reinforce transnational themes. During the war, governments set up institutions like the German and Austrian Black Cross (*Schwarzes Kreuz*) to look after war graves, create monuments to the fallen, and monitor official military cemeteries. In the immediate post-war years of rampant inflation and socio-economic distress, these organizations often had little funding, and they only began to enact practical reforms in the mid-1920s and later. Furthermore, negotiating the care of soldiers' graves on the territories of former embittered combatant states was nearly impossible diplomatically.[91]

Photos of Vienna's central cemetery taken in 1920 reveal an air of exhaustion in the capital, with the soldiers' section looking "completely dilapidated." Only in 1925 did this begin to change, with a central monument established by Anton Hanak, prominently featuring a Pietà motif of a mourning woman with outstretched arms, sinking to her knees. This portrayal did not heroicize or glorify war, but focused on individual loss and mourning, applied as a shared suffering common to all those who had lost loved ones.[92]

---

[90] Ibid., 455–61.

[91] KAS, 22/27: Österr.Militär-Witwen u. Waisenfond 1915–1919, Kriegsgräberfürsorge Schwarzes Kreuz Statuen Buchlein, "Bestimmungen für den Allgemeinen Kriegsgräber-Tag in Österreich 1917 vom 31. Okt. bis einschl. 2. Nov 1917" (Genehmigt mit Erlaß des k.u.k. Ministeriums des Innern, Zl. 48.477).

[92] Thomas Kahler, "'Gefallen auf dem Feld der Ehre.' Kriegerdenkmäler für die Gefallenen des Ersten Weltkriegs in Österreich unter besonderer Berücksichtigung der Entwicklung in Salzburg bis 1938," in *Steinernes Bewußtsein I. Die öffentliche Repräsentation staatlicher und nationaler Identität Österreichs in seinen Denkmälern*, ed. Stefan Riesenfellner (Vienna: Böhlau, 1998), 386–7.

Locally-based historical monuments, however, often did retain themes of traditional heroism, showing how local power identities operated within larger imperial frameworks.[93] Tyrol, for example, was a staunchly Catholic region that reached back into the nineteenth century, establishing its local identity in regional terms where defeat in war did not matter. The local patriot Andreas Hofer, leader of an uprising against Napoleon, was paramount in the Tyrolean pantheon of heroes. Despite the failure of Hofer's actions (he was ultimately captured and executed by Napoleonic forces), he was a powerful symbol of the fight for freedom. Nineteenth-century monuments to Hofer became sites of local Tyrolean pilgrimage, especially by military units. New monuments prominently featured the Christian motif of a central cross placed upon an altar, to which the Tyrolean Book of Honor (*Tiroler Ehrenbuch*) in Innsbruck added lists of the dead, containing the names of all the fallen.[94]

In localities across Central Europe, veterans' associations, especially at the regimental level, played a key part in creating monuments that combined heroism with Christian sacrifice. Local regimental histories also tapped into deep lines of continuity with past generations of military sacrifice. Of special importance to the area around Salzburg, for example, Infantry Regiment Nr. 59 "Archduke Rainer" drew on the legacy of regimental pride during the Napoleonic Wars, particularly with the establishment of the main "Rainer" monument, an obelisk in the Salzburg cemetery, in 1882. The monument represented 2127 soldiers and 46 officers buried in the communal grounds, who had died throughout the Napoleonic conflicts. As a result of the Great War, new monuments and inscriptions appeared around the Salzburg area, testifying to the expansion of suffering: "Every tenth man fell!" A memorial tablet on the main Salzburg post office identified places of sacrifice in Pontebba and Ciadenis, calling out specific mountains on which actions had been fought. This linked the regiment back to its roots fighting in the mountain areas of Salzburg and Tyrol.[95]

More ominously, there were transnational scenes of memorialization that focused on pan-German loyalties. Plans for monuments included gestures to Nordic heroes' groves of trees (*Ehrenhain*). In 1921, the Salzburg sculptor Leo von Moos dedicated a memorial tablet to the fallen members of the Germanic Jahn gymnastic association. The relief showed two gymnasts locking hands in a circle around a wreath of honor for the

---

[93] Houlihan, "Imperial Frameworks of Religion," 165–82.
[94] Rettenwander, *Der Krieg als Seelsorge*; Überegger, *Erinnerungskriege*.
[95] Kahler, "Gefallen auf dem Feld der Ehre," 392–405. For a military chaplain's account of the Rainer Regiment's travails in the Great War, see Spitzl, *Die Rainer*.

fallen, with the inscription: "To the sacrifices for the German Volk and Fatherland, 1914–1918." Around the edges of the tablet were columns of bronze oak leaves, with swastikas in the corners and the inscription, "Our honor is fidelity" (*Unsere Ehre Heisst Treue*) – symbols and words that would become infamously adopted by Himmler's SS.[96]

Even in a small country such as the Austrian successor state, war memorials took on extremely localized meanings.[97] As in Germany, despite so much wartime emphasis being placed on the need to defend the monarchy, war memorials almost never displayed direct references to this institution. Much more prevalent was the notion of sacrifice for the *Heimat*, which, especially in the fragmented successor states of the Habsburg monarchy, was often a vague notion of a localized ethno-national fatherland.[98]

The process of "staging the past" in the successor states in the Habsburg Empire showed that contested processes of national identity formation drew heavily on Christian imagery.[99] The traditional Habsburg literature on nationalism argued that the Czech nationalist movement was one of the most centrifugal forces seeking autonomy from the Habsburg yoke.[100] Even during the late stages of the war in September 1918, however, some Habsburg units containing soldiers from Bohemia did not subscribe to the centrifugal nationalism that was a characteristic of the Czech nationalist movement, celebrating the potentially inflammatory Feast of Saint Wenceslas in a spirit of quiet devotion.[101]

The new Czech state selectively promoted the memory of former soldiers who served its current political interests. Thus, the members of the famous Czech Legion that had fought in Russia became heroes in a struggle of national liberation, while the many Czech and Slovak soldiers who fought for Austria-Hungary were largely forgotten in official commemorations. In 1928, the Czech Legionaries established a national memorial on Vítkov Hill in Prague, which contained a museum and a mausoleum for the remains of the fallen Legionaries. Overall, it would serve as a "temple of the political and cultural renaissance" of the new nation. Furthermore, the new Czech and Slovak states deliberately excluded

---

[96] Kahler, "Gefallen auf dem Feld der Ehre," 402–3.   [97] Ibid., 365–409.

[98] For a comparison with Austria-Hungary, see Lurz, *Kriegerdenkmäler in Deutschland*, 3:107–8, 131–2, 158.

[99] Bucur and Wingfield, *Staging the Past*.

[100] Oscar Jaszi, *The Dissolution of the Habsburg Monarchy* (Chicago, IL: University of Chicago Press, 1971); Z. A. B. Zeman, *The Break-Up of the Habsburg Empire, 1914–1918* (Oxford: Oxford University Press, 1961).

[101] At least, it was reported so by the unit chaplain. ÖStAKA, AFV, Ktn. 233: Sept. 1918 (misfiled), Ersatzbatallion k.u.k IR 102, Pastoral Report of Karl Sobek.

important national minorities from official memory, namely the respective German and Hungarian minorities. In Heroes' Square in Budapest, a new portion was dedicated to the Tomb of the Hungarian Unknown Soldier. Outside of Budapest, however, monuments to territories lost at the Treaty of Trianon were established, thus agitating fantasies of irredentism.[102]

Of course, in some areas, religious national relations were much tenser. When Vienna slowly became more socially fragmented as the politics of food became less able to sustain survival, ethnic hatred and mutual suspicions became inflamed, especially between Germans and Czechs.[103] One could find similar instances on the battlefield, where troops from the Sudetenland at a field hospital showed "tepidity" about participating in Catholic religious services together – in contrast to troops from Poland and Croatia, and even POWs from Italy.[104] In other instances, however, even in the heart of the disintegrating Habsburg capital, German and Czech Catholics recuperating in a hospital could coexist relatively peacefully in communal services conducted using both German- and Czech-language liturgy and music.[105] Other battlefield units reported late into the war that Germans and Czechs participated together in combined religious services with eagerness and no apparent sign of national enmity.[106] All of this underscores the need to look at battlefield religion locally, at a micro-level, away from the convenient generalizing narratives of national identities and imperial instability.

After the war, despite Thomas Masayrk's avowed preference for a separation of Church and state and a desire to move away from anything symbolically representing the Catholicism of the old Habsburg Empire, even the new secular Czechoslovak state used religious figures in its state commemorations. Such symbols drew on nationalist sensibilities, even if they were problematic for the image of the new state. In many of these interwar Czechoslovak commemorations, Saint Wenceslas served as a compromise national figure, a counterweight to the separatist symbolism of the Protestant Jan Hus.[107] Even within the new Czechoslovak state, however, there were important subgroups whose religious devotions are

[102] Van Ypersele, "Mourning and Memory," 577–81.   [103] Healy, *Vienna*, 265–6.

[104] ÖStAKA, AFV, Ktn. 240, Pastoralbericht of Oskar Schuchter, April 1918, Feldspital Nr. 404.

[105] ÖStAKA, AFV, Ktn. 244, Pastoralbericht of Richard Seyss-Inquart, July 1918, Reservespital Nr. 12 (Vienna). The chaplain was the brother of Arthur Seyss-Inquart, the later prominent Austrian Nazi Chancellor. See also ÖStAKA, AFV, Ktn. 246, Pastoralbericht, September 1918 Reservespital in Kremsier.

[106] ÖStAKA, AFV, Ktn. 244, Pastoralbericht of Franz Cech, July 1918, IR 75; ÖStAKA, AFV, Ktn. 244, Pastoralbericht of Josef Roskopal, July 1918, 6. Kav. Div, 11. Armee.

[107] Paces, "Religious Heroes."

not accurately captured by a generic portrait of imperial decline and fall. The Slovak population of Czechoslovakia, for instance, still remained suspicious of the Hus cult and the Prague government in general, and became invigorated by the idea of a separate, explicitly Catholic state. Slovakian Catholic nationalist hopes would be realized in the clerico-fascist regime headed by Monsignor Jozef Tiso.[108]

The supposed defection of k.u.k. Infantry Regiments 28, 35, and 75, composed mostly of soldiers of Czech ethnicity, highlights how the military performance of Austro-Hungarian units became entangled in inter-war memory politics. Eager to blame Czechs for the dissolution of the Habsburg monarchy, and to conceal the poor strategic decisions of the high command, Austrian politicians condemned the units, arguing that the regiments in question had defected to the Russian side, readily abandoning the Habsburg lines in the battles of Esztebnekhuta in April 1915 and Zborow in July 1917. Similarly, interwar Czech politicians agreed that units had defected, but instead praised them for it, arguing that they were the vanguard of a triumphant nationalist political movement away from the decrepit Habsburg state. In reality, however, a recent military history of the regiments in question reveals that the Czech units performed loyal service to the Habsburg military, holding the line well, especially given a difficult tactical situation. The units did not betray the Habsburg Army and did not defect, but that did not stop them from becoming a political football in the interwar period.[109]

The case of Polish Galicia represented one promising area of wartime Catholicism and its aftereffects on popular piety, viewed locally and nationally. To the last days of the war, even after the Habsburg Empire had officially fallen, Polish chaplains eagerly petitioned the war ministry asking to serve in the Imperial forces and even in the forces of the Republic of German-Austria. Even as centrifugal ethno-national tensions were at their height, the Habsburg monarchy found a supply of Catholic chaplains who exhibited loyal "dynastic-patriotic sensibility" (*dynastisch-patriotische Gesinnung*). War ministry officials turned back such aspirants by telling them that the empire no longer existed and that they should seek to serve within the armed forces of the new Polish nation.[110]

During the war, both German and Austro-Hungarian sources testified to the exemplary piety of Galician civlians and troops. Austro-Hungarian chaplains observed the intense faith of enemy POWs, ethnic Poles serving

---

[108]   Burleigh, *Sacred Causes*, 258–62.

[109]   Richard Lein, *Pflichterfüllung oder Hochverrat? Die tschechischen Soldaten Österreich-Ungarns im Ersten Weltkrieg* (Vienna: Lit, 2011), 417–21.

[110]   ÖStAKA, LV 1918–1919, 16 LW Seelsorger, Ktn. 2398:20 702, 20 741, and 20 742, petitions of Alexander Bogdanowicz, Boleslaus Gawel, and Josef Liska.

in the Russian Army, who expressed their thanks for the opportunity to worship and receive holy communion.[111] Bavarian Catholic chaplains commented favorably on the religious observance of Galician Catholic Poles on the Eastern Front throughout the war, contrasting them with German units from various parts of the Wilhelmine Empire.[112] Similarly, German chaplains commented that Polish civilians regularly and eagerly participated in Catholic services offered to German troops stationed near Rozana.[113]

The national affinities of Catholic Poles on the eve of the First World War have raised complicated trajectories of loyalty, which continued into the post-war period. Polish peasants made sure that rural myths and religious beliefs became part of the imagery of the new Polish nation-state.[114] Precisely because ethnic Poles had fought against each other for the Triple Entente and the Central Powers, one single Polish national collective memory did not suffice to explain the sacrifices made during the Great War. Similar stories of complicated ethnic allegiances existed for many of the new nations of East Central Europe in the interwar period. Christianized nationalism, far from being disillusioned during the First World War, was poised for a flourishing in the interwar period.[115]

In Austria, the town of Mariazell provided one of the best examples of the power of transnational Catholicism as a site of memory and mourning, continuing the medieval tradition of Catholic pilgrimage to Jerusalem, Rome, Santiago di Compostella, and Aachen. Well into the twentieth century, groups making pilgrimages to the famous town drew on the pomp and circumstance of the medieval and baroque eras. The disruptions of the world wars did not diminish Central European enthusiasm for visitations to Mariazell. In 1957, the town celebrated the 800th anniversary of its official establishment as a pilgrimage site, now with a backdrop of Cold War politics, with the Communists replacing the

---

[111] ÖStAKA, AFV, Ktn. 230, Pastoralbericht June 1917. Chaplain Julian Ogarek, stationed in Graz, reported that his sermons reflected a Catholic sensibility and were received favorably: "Das Thema derselben ist immer beinahe gleich: 'Gebet, frommes Leben, Geduld, Vertrauen an göttl. Vorsehung und göttl. Willen, Arbeitsamkeit, das rechte katholische Leben.'"

[112] EAM, NL Faulhaber, Ktn. 6777, 4.4.1917 Letter from Sebastian, Divisionspfarrer, Stab. 5. Preuß. Res. Div.

[113] BA-MA, PH 32/267 Seelsorgesbericht, January–February 1917, Etappenpfarrer Greis.

[114] Bjork, *Neither German nor Pole*; Keely Stauter-Halsted, *The Nation in the Village: The Genesis of Peasant National Identity in Austrian Poland, 1848–1914* (Ithaca, NY: Cornell University Press, 2001).

[115] Hans-Christian Maner and Martin Schulze Wessel, eds., *Religion im Nationalstaat zwischen den Weltkriegen 1918–1939: Polen, Tschechoslowakei, Ungarn, Rumänien* (Stuttgart: Steiner, 2002); Martin Schulze Wessel, ed., *Nationalisierung der Religion und Sakralisierung der Nation im östlichen Europa* (Stuttgart: Steiner, 2006).

Ottoman Turks as the projected enemy. The Archbishop of Salzburg, Andreas Rohracher, celebrated a Mass for the occasion, in which he declared, "There is no coexistence between Christianity and Communism." A variety of Catholic figures gathered in Mariazell for celebratory Masses, including German Chancellor Adenauer, Austrian Chancellor Leopold Figl, Cardinal Innitzer from Vienna, Cardinal Wendel from Munich, Cardinal Feltin from Paris, and General Francisco Franco. The Hungarian Revolution of 1956 gave a sense of historical continuity and repetition of familiar themes: now refugees from Central and Eastern Europe headed to Mariazell were fleeing Soviet atheism instead of the Islamic Turk. The later bishop of Eisenstadt, Stephan László, became an official Vatican spokesman for refugees in Austria and made Mariazell a key site of organizational visits, with Masses conducted in Hungarian language and vestments. Cardinal József Mindszenty, the Prince Primate of Esztergom and the symbolic leader of Hungarian Catholic resistance to fascism and communism, died in exile in 1975. He was buried in the crypt of the Laudislaus Chapel in Mariazell, where his remains rested until 1991, when they were transferred to Hungary after the fall of the Iron Curtain.[116]

In the immediate aftermath of the Great War, the Catholic Church focused on the reintegration of soldiers into peacetime society. Official religious faculties delegated to military chaplains in time of war ceased in February 1919, most prominently through the stoppage of general absolution or communal absolution of individual sins without prior individual confession.[117] Across Europe, survivors erected votive chapels and shrines, thanking God for the safe return of the soldiers. Communal bonds of family and faith helped religious believers make sense of a world shattered by war. Alongside the persistence of religious belief, however, the world the soldiers returned to had undergone irrevocable changes. As always, tradition adapted to the needs of the present and projected future.

Conclusion

The Catholic philosophy of war helped to lessen the collective sting of defeat for Central European religious believers. The disparate historical remembrances of the conflict showed that the nation mattered as one type

---

[116] Christian Stadelmann, "Mariazell," in *Memoriae Austriae*, ed. Emil Brix, Ernst Bruckmüller, and Hannes Stekl (Vienna: Verlag für Geschichte und Politik, 2004), 2:304–35.
[117] *Acta Apostolicae Sedis*, 11:74–5.

of collective, but it was not the only or even most important locus of identity for religious believers. Even at the national level, defeat in 1918 was also a moment of (re)birth for nations such as Poland and Czechoslovakia. Catholic belief even helped former opponents like France and Germany reconcile.

Catholic belief structures provided tangible means of comfort for the faithful. Battlefield relics, liturgies of comfort, and a dolorous philosophy of war helped believers understand the war in traditional terms. Collective loss was certainly an important part of ascriptions of sacrifice but, especially at a local level, most believing Catholics cared more about their family members than about an overarching cause. The intercessory saint culture in particular gave believers the idea that they and their departed loved ones were, now and forever, involved in a metaphysical community of salvation rooted in their belief in "one, holy, Catholic, apostolic Church," as the formation of the Credo put it. Thus, defeat in war was rendered less onerous. Numerous Catholic portrayals of everyday life testified to the flourishing piety that existed in the interwar years. Defeat for Central European Catholics did not equal disillusionment.

Therefore, the figure of Saint Martin and the quiet Western Front on November 11 is both appropriate and misleading. The representation testified to the powerful belief in the community of saints, which served as a comfort mechanism for religious believers trying to make sense of the war. The image also misrepresented the nature of the Great War, which was unsettled on the Eastern Front and at home. Christian believers in Central Europe faced the new danger of Bolshevism both outside and inside their borders.

Catholic beliefs about death and memory from the Great War centered on local communities in mourning. Founded in the faith of families, notions of saintly intercession helped believers connect to the bodies and souls of their fallen loved ones who were no longer there. The Virgin Mary, in particular, highlighted the feminine and familial dimensions of the human condition, linked to divine intercession through the sacrifice of Christ. This familial-focused grieving showed the resilience of Catholic tradition, adapted to explain the destruction and loss of the Great War.

Conclusion

Pope Benedict XV, the "unknown pope" of the Great War, died on January 22, 1922, after a short illness. The conclave elected a new leader, Pope Pius XI, who, in his position as papal nuncio, had seen the Bolshevik armies advance on Warsaw during the Polish–Soviet War; the Church endured, its leadership increasingly turning to authoritarian alliances that would confront the specter of Bolshevism. Papal funerals were and are symbolic points of reflection for the Church, and the choice of an end date to this study is deliberately arbitrary. Since this book has argued for continuities and adaptations of traditions, especially in the everyday lives of ordinary Catholics, such a stopping point represents a narrative convenience.

Chronologically, the story could have easily extended further. The Franco-Belgian occupation of the Ruhr and the Beer Hall Putsch in 1923 would have been another leap along the road to Hitler's accession to the chancellorship of Germany. In Austria, the decisive shift to authoritarianism happened with the Justice Ministry fire of 1927, which helped lead to civil war in 1934. Indeed, explicating the full political legacy of two fallen empires, Habsburg and Hohenzollern, would require treating the histories of their individual state components, as well as the transnational, national, local, familial, and personal levels. Although the empires fell in Autumn 1918, this book has shown how this political narrative of historians' convenience does not correspond to the lived religion of believers who experienced the Great War. The Catholic story of the twentieth century does not fit the standard story of the Great War as an epic moment of disillusioning modernism, either in 1914 or in 1918. Indeed, the persistence and adaptation of Catholic tradition helps lend strength to the claim that the period from 1914 to 1945 is best seen as a continuum, a "Second Thirty Years War."[1] In helping make sense of the

---

[1] Winter, "Commemorating War," 310–26.

twentieth century, this book has demonstrated a transnational Catholicism of lived religion, destabilizing a master narrative of disillusion for the losing powers' cultural history.

One must underscore the deprivation and distress that the war caused, especially to people from Central Europe, who lost the war, saw empires fall, and endured suffering on a vast scale. Precisely for these reasons, however, religion provided a comfort mechanism, helping believers interpret and live with a radical upheaval and loss that tested the powers of human endurance. As studies of everyday life have indicated, the chaos of the Great War continued into the interwar period.[2] Revolution and counter-revolution spread across the continent. Despite what literary portrayals of spirituality would show, Catholics continued to practice their beliefs in public, demonstrating piety in religious services across Central Europe. Churches were filled to overflowing. Economic crises caused by blockade and inflation did not stop. Diseases like cholera and Spanish influenza continued to scourge populations. Pastoral letters from bishops extolled the virtues of sacrifice. Numerous sermons emphasized the need for civilians to reincorporate returning soldiers into civil society as fathers, brothers, and leaders. Catholic sermons also emphasized the role of women as special guardians of virtue, family values, and a return to normalcy. The wish for peace and domestic tranquility was nostalgic, but a powerful motivator nonetheless.

On a pan-European level, Catholicism during the interwar era showed an incredible vitality. Marriage rates skyrocketed, especially in rural regions. Ordinations for the priesthood and recruitment to religious orders increased dramatically, rising above pre-1914 levels. New religious movements, with varying degrees of clerical control, incorporated lay believers into activist roles, in which religious faith was an essential part of the public message. The youth movement and the liturgical movement were two prime examples; both were especially strong in Central Europe. Indeed, as Martin Conway has observed, the interwar years were "the apogee of a particular model of Catholicism forged in the pre-1914 era and which – in comparison to the much more divided structures of the Protestant faith – constituted a creative and remarkably effective response to the challenges presented by the more urbanised, educated and pluralist character of European society."[3] In the immediate aftermath of the Great War, Catholicism had achieved a marked increase in relative social-political power, with Orthodoxy hobbled by the advance of Bolshevism and Protestantism in Germany reeling from the Weimar Republic's shattering of the throne-and-altar alliance.[4] Just after the Great War, as

---

[2] Chickering, *The Great War*; Healy, *Vienna*.   [3] Conway, *Catholic Politics*, 2.
[4] Burleigh, *Sacred Causes*.

Philip Jenkins has written, "The Catholic Church especially seemed to have done well, to the point that, fairly or otherwise, a popular German saying declared, 'Luther lost the war!'"[5]

Interwar Europe saw the expanded growth of a religiously-inspired Catholic politics seeking a third way between socialism and capitalism. Writing in the Jesuit journal *Hochland* in the immediate period after the Great War, Carl Muth, the journal's founder and leading light, spoke of the search for a way between the extremes of socio-economic barbarisms, from both the left and the right. This line of political theorizing had roots in Pope Leo XIII's famous encyclical *Rerum Novarum*.[6] The Catholic "third way" was a major source of pre-1914 continuity that developed fully only after 1945. Membership in Catholic workers' movements and Christian trade unions rose dramatically during the war.[7] The development of Christian Democracy, with transnational Catholic networks in particular, served as a basis for pan-European integration that would culminate in the European Union. In a shattered post-1945 Europe, Christian-influenced politics assumed a place of "hegemony by default."[8] Central to the war-making efforts in both world wars, the industrial areas of northern France and western Germany were heavily Catholic regions that gave rise to transnational Christian values and to leaders like Robert Schuman and Konrad Adenauer, whose networks and experiences helped to foster informal and, later, formal politics. Thus, the European Coal and Steel Community, which formed the basis of the European Union, was a prime example of Franco-German reconciliation at the heart of European integration.

There was, of course, an exclusionary dark side to notions of integration and identity. Indeed, the persistence of traditional religiosity, including Catholicism, helped lay the groundwork for the rise of Hitler and genocidal anti-Semitism.[9] The confrontation with the emerging Bolshevik regime and the threat of revolutionary upheaval across Europe made Catholics more amenable to compromise with authoritarian regimes who promised to deal with the Red menace and restore traditional values of organic community. The churches were sources of complicity as well as resistance to Nazism. In the post-1945 period, the Cold War reitereated the conviction that religious believers and their societies were again in danger, under threat from atheistic communism in a global war of

---

[5] Jenkins, *The Great and Holy War*, 193.

[6] Carl Muth, "Die neuen 'Barbaren' und das Christentum," *Hochland* 16 (1919): 585–96.

[7] Aschoff, "Von der Revolution," 190–1. From 341 735 in 1913 to over 1 million in 1919, the rising membership of Christian trade unions showed that key sectors of Catholic workers found themselves in a stronger religiously-based corporate order during the war.

[8] Kaiser, *Christian Democracy*, 163–90.   [9] Hastings, *Catholicism and the Roots of Nazism*.

dominance. While the threat of Bolshevism loomed large in the Cold War, the nature of Catholic anti-Semitism waned. It was only after 1945, and especially in the 1960s during the formulation of the Second Vatican Council (1962–65), that Catholics, shaped by many former Jewish converts such as Monsignor John Maria Oesterreicher, abandoned long-held racial anti-Semitism. In line with a broader ecumenism toward a global community, Catholics now viewed Jews as brothers, not enemies.[10]

As this book has shown through a history of everyday mentalities, wartime Catholicism presented an array of tangible practices and spiritual beliefs that allowed Catholics to adapt to the war's upheaval. On the eve of the Great War, Catholics in Germany and Austria-Hungary came largely from rural regions, deeply embedded in traditional agrarian ways of life, although Catholic industrial workers assumed an increasing share of importance as a part of the modern world influenced by the war. Most peasants and workers greeted the war not with cheers but with sorrow and deep concern, driven by the question of who would bring in the harvest in Autumn 1914. Ordinary Catholics' pessimism formed a pointed contrast to the hurrah patriotism of the bishops and prominent members of the clergy. This jingoistic war theology, while an important part of the Catholic experience of war, nonetheless inappropriately limited representations of what the war meant to most believers.

From the war's outset, the Catholic philosophy of dolorous, cyclical history relativized it as just one episode in the history of human folly, which made adjustment easier when defeat came to the Central Powers. In particular, Catholic natural-law philosophy allowed believers to rapidly adjust their political loyalties. Catholic theology during the war emphasized the deep continuities and ancient roots of the Church, thus contextualizing the Great War and minimizing its horrors. A Catholic theology of community also generated exclusionary practices, in its extreme case reinforcing traditional anti-Semitism, which would lead to genocidal complicity in the Second World War.

At the forefront of battle, Catholic military chaplains, the stereotypical fire-breathers of literature, were in fact much more complicated and interesting historical figures. As official representatives of the military-administrative links between Church and state, chaplains were liminal figures who performed duties of both propagandistic agitation and soothing comfort. In numerical terms, chaplaincy was overwhelmed by the scale of mass industrial war. However, they left many records behind, and their sensitive grappling with issues of religiosity shows that they adapted their ministry sensitively to the local needs of the front. Often

[10] Connelly, *From Enemy to Brother*.

questioning the war's higher purpose, chaplains' reflections show the need to approach battlefield religion with a keen sense of individual context and personal spirituality beyond stereotype. Invigorated by the war, some former chaplains would advance in the ranks of Church–state politics, turning to political authoritarianism, perhaps most notoriously in the case of Jozef Tiso, the leader of Slovakia. Other chaplains, like Benedict Kreutz, the leader of the Deutscher Caritas Verein (DCV), became focused on charity and healing, rather than political agitation.

At the battlefront and the homefront, the Catholic tangibility of sacramental objects drew on folk practices and forms of pagan spirituality, thus embracing both traditional devotional cultures of popular religion and elements of "superstition" outside of doctrine and dogma. The idea of intercession and a devotional culture of sainthood gave Catholics many linkages between homefront and battlefront and between the living and the dead. This was particularly the case with adoration of the Virgin Mary, the model of family-centered Christian devotion, which accentuated feminine spirituality and represented the comforts of home.

Long neglected in previous religious histories of the war, Catholic women were an essential part of the war effort, both practically and symbolically. In some ways, the ideal of Catholic purity/motherhood embodied by the Virgin Mary was an ambiguously-gendered symbol of sexuality: the symbol was a powerful motivator toward a return to peacetime normalcy. The return to the pre-war world was of course impossible, and in key ways, women and children became new socio-political actors, taking agency as never before and forming an integral part of the new post-war societies. Most prominently, driven by the failures of the state to adequately provide enough food, Catholic women assumed new roles as members of a caritas network providing for people affected by war, in many cases helping where the state could not reach. The interwar years saw tremendous increases in social welfare, and religiously-based organizations dominated by women played a key role in this major transformation.

Pope Benedict XV, marked as an "unknown pope" even by his biographers, played a key role in a Catholic history of the war. His famous efforts at creating a peace were not futile, even though they appeared so based on the Peace Note of August 1, 1917. In the midst of national enmity, even among Catholics, the Pope's efforts symbolized the transformation of the Church into a non-partisan political actor. In contrast to previous reactionary popes' hostility toward the modern world, Pope Benedict XV reached out in a spirit of communicative action. Through Benedict's charity efforts, which nearly bankrupted the Holy See, the Church made strides toward becoming a humanitarian actor, which continued into the interwar period and beyond. Led by the pope, the Church cared for POWs, displaced persons, and children in war-torn regions, and generally sought to ameliorate the devastation of war. A new Code of Canon Law in 1917 helped pave the way for a more efficient and centralized Church bureaucracy, poised for a period of renewal and growth in the interwar period.

During and after the war, Catholic forms of memory and mourning highlighted ways in which traditional religious modes of thought comforted and consoled the populations of Europe. The Mass in Time of War was based in universal grief and the Creator's regret, not exclusive divine-right nationalism, especially in its Protestant-German variant of supposed linear destiny. Indeed, the Mass in Time of War embodied a distinctly different sensibility than a Protestant Sonderweg. This was especially consoling to Catholics from powers that lost the war. Feminine and familial forms of representation, centered in the Pietà motif and the Virgin Mary mourning Christ on the cross, helped to reinforce that individual religious believers were parts of larger social communities of intercession. The Catholic way of understanding war and peace stressed community and social bonds, not atomizing, abstract, incomprehensible nihilism.

Remarkable strides have been made recently in the historiography of the Great War, showing the analytical influence of holistic war-and-society concepts. More than ever, even traditional trumpets-and-drums histories now take into account the cultural factors of ideology and the social bonds that link fighting soldiers with broader networks of mass societies conducting war, perhaps most pointedly including women and children, who have often been marginalized actors in military history. These more encompassing portraits more accurately depict whole societies as producers of mass violence on an industrial scale.[11] Yet, when analyzing the cultural history of the Great War, religion has often been completely left out of the discussion or marginalized to an unwarranted extent. Especially for the losing powers, Germany and Austria-Hungary, cultural histories of warfare stress the grand narrative of the cultural avant garde or the war jingoism of the national episcopates.

As this book has shown, however, future, more accurate representations of the war's cultural history will continue to illuminate a spectrum of religious beliefs and practices. This variety of religious experiences formed an essential component of the worldviews of vast majorities of the people who experienced the Great War on a pan-European level. Adrian Gregory has recently argued that the question of enduring faith

---

[11] Chickering et al., *War and the Modern World*.

during the war defies a definitive answer because of three factors: an inability to characterize the pre-war backgrounds, disparate war experiences, and source bases that include observer biases.[12] Similarly, this book shares skepticism about a final answer for questions of religious endurance related to standard Great War themes such as consent and coercion, as well as enthusiasm and remobilization. Yet studies of religion during the Great War challenge the deeply ingrained master narrative of cultural disillusionment, anomie, and nihilism. By portraying a wide variety of experiences, including religion, one can better understand the cultural history of the twentieth century.

Current popular-media discussions of public piety in modern Europe refer often to the image of an empty church, using this to symbolize the decline of public religion.[13] Contemporary photos of interwar Europe, however, tell a different story. Photos of a Catholic Mass at an anonymous church, likely in Baden or Württemberg, during the opening of the National Assembly of the Weimar Republic on February 26, 1919, show a packed house, with every seat filled. Religious belief did not trickle away to nothing after the August experiences of 1914, and was alive and well in Europe even for the losing powers after the convenient narrative end point of the Armistice of November 11, 1918. Measured in yearly Easter communion reception, as well as weekly Mass attendance, communal statistics of public piety from urban centers in medium-sized cities like Münster and Freiburg show that religious practice remained fairly constant through the war years and actually increased through the 1920s and 1930s.[14] Even major urban centers like Berlin, Paris, and London, the preeminent sites of artistic modernism, saw developments that cast doubt on notions of urban environments as inherent engines of secularization. Statistics showing declining church attendance (often measured from solely Protestant sources), especially following trends emerging from the nineteenth century, need to be balanced by such "counter-statistics" as increases in church burials and a "steady rise in per capita rates of church marriage, Sunday school attendance, and baptism among working-class Londoners."[15] Public piety in interwar Europe did not vanish after the Armistice.

In Germany, the war showed Catholicism breaking out of its minority ideological ghetto of the Catholic milieu, which had in many ways

---

[12] Gregory, "Beliefs and Religion," 437.

[13] George Weigel, *The Cube and the Cathedral: Europe, America, and Politics without God* (New York: Basic Books, 2005).

[14] Chickering, *The Great War*, 489–90; Liedhegener, *Christentum und Urbanisierung*, 223–39.

[15] Gregory and Becker, "Religious Sites and Practices," 388.

Figure 12 Church service, Weimar Republic (BfZ)
"This Catholic service on the opening of the Weimar Republic
(February 26, 1919) showed that public piety had not vanished in
interwar Europe. Catholic believers relied on their faith to illuminate
their past, present, and future."

remained a strong component of the pre-1914 Catholic worldview in Germany.[16] Ideologically, the shared suffering of the war had made the Catholic milieu less hostile toward fellow Christians, but when nationhood became tied with religion, this helped to solidify boundaries that excluded non-Christians. In the interwar years, rates of priestly ordination and Catholic marriage rose to exceed their pre-1914 levels. New revival movements, increased attendance at processions and pilgrimages, and rising numbers of seminarians and female religious believers were strong structural factors that demonstrated increased participation rates and devotion to Catholic causes. The Catholic milieu continued to serve as a focal point of orientation for the daily lives of religious believers through a network of associations and organizations that represented cradle-to-grave activities with religious affiliation. Represented by the Catholic Center Party in Germany and the Christian Social Party in Austria, religion was still a powerful force politically on the state level, even for the defeated powers.

Debates in German church history have questioned the extent to which the Catholic milieu declined in the 1920s and 1930s, but the milieu was still alive and well during and immediately after the Great War. Industrialization, urbanization, and the experience of war, especially among young men, helped change certain parts of the pre-war milieu. Certainly, the experience of war helped Catholics imagine a world in which religion was one possible answer to existential life questions of belief and conduct, but not necessarily the absolute or only way. However, especially in rural areas and among young women, the Catholic milieu remained strong, supported by new pastoral methods and mass demonstrations of loyalty to the Church. Such demonstrations were often not directed by the clergy, as had usually been the case in the pre-1914 era. Ultimately, the Catholic milieu's persistence, and its totalizing aspirations over a community, would bring it into conflict with the Nazi regime, fighting a battle over the control of loyal souls.[17] Marian apparitions, stigmatics, and charismatic visionaries continued into the early Cold War era in Central Europe, reflecting not only political conflict, but also the persistence of religion during periods of social turmoil.[18] Only in the face of rampant consumerism, rapid technological modernization, and

---

[16] Roland Haidl, "Ausbruch aus dem Ghetto? Katholizismus im deutschen Heer 1914–1918," in Krumeich and Lehmann, *"Gott mit uns,"* 263–71.

[17] Michael E. O'Sullivan, "An Eroding Milieu? Catholic Youth, Church Authority, and Popular Behavior in Northwest Germany during the Third Reich, 1933–1938," *Catholic Historical Review* 90, no. 2 (2004): 236–59.

[18] Monique Scheer, *Rosenkranz und Kriegsvisionen: Marienerscheinungskulte im 20. Jahrhundert* (Tübingen: Tübinger Vereinigung für Volkskunde, 2006).

the post-1945 German "economic miracle" did the Catholic milieu in Central Europe irrevocably decline.[19]

During the Great War, the ideology of German national suffering was based on a consistent shared sacrifice that fused Christianity and nationhood, and ominously excluded non-Christians from the ideological contract. In a majority-Catholic society like Austria-Hungary, the loss of the Habsburg monarchy signaled the fragmentation of Catholic politics in Central and Eastern Europe. Political Catholicism was alive and well, and bent on authoritarian restoration of organic society against the new threat of Bolshevism. The loss of the monarchy, however, highlighted that for believing Catholics, their religious faith was a personal matter, tied to social bonds of family, not high-ranking bishops and monarchs.

On a general level, decline in religious pious practice in Catholic Europe only occurred on a large scale as a post-1945 phenomenon, and especially after the large-scale social reordering of the 1960s. Scholars must continue to uncover traditional forms of religious belief, often from agrarian regions of Europe, that did not neatly coincide with either avant garde cultural interpretations of the war or the elite opinions of religious clerics, categorized nationally. One cannot equate the Central Powers' eventual defeat in the Great War with the declining relevance of organized religion. Though recognizing that defeat played a large role in ascribing certain collective notions of sacrifice, religious believers in the Central Powers derived multiple levels of meaning from their religious faith. Scholars need to examine more micro-level histories, including religious histories that highlight family relationships, personal religiosity, and communal commitments that did not end in 1918 with military defeat. For many Central European religious believers, although their empires may have lost the war, their religious faith did not fall under the rubric of disenchantment.

A book about everyday mentalities must contextualize the place of religion in the modern world. Especially for the Great War as a formative moment for artistic modernism, the secularization thesis remains a dominant master narrative.[20] Yet there are efforts to rethink the relationship between religion and modernity. Charles Taylor's *A Secular Age* is a

---

[19] Mark Edward Ruff, *The Wayward Flock: Catholic Youth in Postwar West Germany, 1945–1965* (Chapel Hill: University of North Carolina Press, 2005). For an excellent overview of historiographic debates on the Catholic milieu, see O'Sullivan, "From Catholic Milieu," 837–61.

[20] This is largely because, as Jeffrey Cox has argued, no master narrative of comparable explanatory power has emerged to displace the secularization thesis. See Jeffrey Cox, "Master Narratives of Religious Change," in *The Decline of Christendom in Western Europe, 1750–2000*, ed. Hugh McLeod and Werner Ustorf (Cambridge: Cambridge University Press, 2003), 201–17.

theoretical call to "understand better belief and unbelief as lived conditions, not just as theories or sets of beliefs subscribed to."[21] Seen in these terms, religious believers from the losing powers need further study.

The present book is not a polemic meant to deny that modern Europe has undergone vast religious shifts in terms of public piety in the twentieth century. If objectivity is a chimerical "noble dream" for the historical profession, nevertheless the present work is written as a provisional quest for more empirically-grounded debate on the topic of religion during the Great War.[22] The author hopes that this book will stimulate other researchers to trek to the archives and add their findings about everyday religiosity, to see how these results complicate the picture of the war's cultural legacy on a pan-European level. If one can vastly oversimplify: Did Catholics from Central Europe experience the war in a fashion similar to Robert Graves, Jaroslav Hašek, Ernst Jünger, Karl Kraus, Wilfred Owen, Erich Maria Remarque, Siegfried Sassoon, and others from the literary modernist master narrative that dominates the cultural history of the Great War? This book has argued, "No."

Successionist linear narratives do not account for the adaptation and persistence of religious traditions, and religious histories, even from the early modern era, continue to inform conceptualizations of modernity.[23] In a landmark work, Paul Fussell argued that the cultural history of the Great War was a watershed moment in the emergence of the concept of irony in public discourse about war.[24] As the present book has shown through its invocation of the losing powers, one of the greatest ironies of the Great War was that Catholicism, the stereotypically archaic and even anti-modern religion, adapted to the circumstances of modern war quite well. Indeed, Catholicism adjusted to modern war better than more self-consciously "progressive" versions of Christianity on the eve of the Great War. Catholicism endured, comforting its adherents much more than religion's cultured despisers believed to be the case.

Scholars must not equate the Central Powers' eventual defeat with the supposed declining relevance of religion, and attendant instrumentalization of wartime religion in service of state aims. Although defeat played a

---

[21] Taylor, *A Secular Age*, 3, 8.

[22] The author underscores Peter Novick's remarks about the provisional nature of ambitious works: "In casting my net as widely as I have, in exploring so many complex interactions, I have inevitably raised more questions than I have answered. This is as it should be in a work which attempts to open rather than close a subject: to stimulate others to inquire into areas on which I have touched lightly, and to reconsider and revise my conclusions." Peter Novick, *That Noble Dream: The "Objectivity Question" and the American Historical Profession* (New York: Cambridge University Press, 1988), 17.

[23] Brad S. Gregory, *The Unintended Reformation: How a Religious Revolution Secularized Society* (Cambridge, MA: Belknap Press of Harvard University Press, 2012).

[24] Fussell, *The Great War and Modern Memory*.

large role in ascribing certain collective notions of sacrifice, especially on the level of the nation, religious believers in fact derived multiple levels of meaning from their religious faith, demonstrating complex notions of historical remembrance. Many Catholic believers, especially from rural regions across Europe, have found themselves as voiceless historical subjects in a conflict whose reigning cultural trope is disillusioned futility. While patterns of European religiosity in the twentieth century have obviously changed in terms of public observance, one must not assume that the First World War was the point of shift. In fact, the Catholic modernity began after the Second World War, not the First, as part of a broader trend, with the 1960s the moment of real change and the Second Vatican Council of 1962–65 the decisive transformation in modern Catholicism.[25] The Catholic story of twentieth-century Europe does not fit with standard narratives of the Great War's legacy.

Seen through the experience of the losing powers, Catholic public religiosity in Europe changed in the twentieth century, but the Great War was not the decisive cataclysm. One cannot understand Catholics of the Great War in terms of anachronism, a convenient story of decline and fall, framed in terms of the cultural avant garde. While not necessarily agreeing with their beliefs, scholarship of wartime Catholicism must try to understand Catholics as they understood themselves. Whether speaking about artisans and craftsmen in an age of industrialization or about religious believers in an age of secularization, one needs to contextualize the lived realities of historical actors. E. P. Thompson once movingly wrote of the need to rescue historical working-class figures from the "enormous condescension of posterity."[26] As a legacy of the Great War that has done so much to shape notions of modernity, it is time to relieve the Catholics of Europe from a similarly predestined historiographical fate.

---

[25] McLeod, *Religious Crisis.*

[26] E. P. Thompson, *The Making of the English Working Class* (New York: Vintage, 1966), 12. Cf. Gregory, "The Other Confessional History: On Secular Bias in the Study of Religion," 149.

Sources

ARCHIVES

Archivio Segreto Vaticano (ASV)
   Segretaria di Stato, Guerra 1914–1918
   Segretaria di Stato, Spoglio, Benedetto XV

Archivum Provinciae Austriae Societatis Iesu (AASI)
   Autobiographie des P. Karl Egger, S.J., "Aus meinem Leben"

Archiv der Bayerischen Franziskaner (ABF)
   PA I: Polykarp Schmoll Tagebuch

Bayerisches Hauptstaatsarchiv (BHStA)
   BHStA, Abt. IV, MKr.
   1. Bayerische Reserve Division, Bd. 100: Tagebuch, Richard Hoffmann

Bibliothek für Zeitgeschichte Stuttgart (BfZ) (Names are pseudonyms to protect
   privacy and comply with archival regulations)
   Fotosammlung, WK1, Ktn. 214, Religion – Feldgottesdienste
   NL Knoch 1914–1918
   NL 12.5, Schutz
   NL 97.1, Fleck

Bundesarchiv-Militärarchiv (BA-MA)
   PH 32: Militärseelsorge
   MSg 1/161
   MSg 2/1718
   MSg 2/2813
   MSg 2/5799
   MSg 2/5800

Diözesanarchiv Graz (DAG)
   NL Bischof Dr. Ferdinand Pawlikowski (Militärvikariat)

Diözesanarchiv Sankt Pölten (DASP)
   NL Rössler, Bischofskonferenzen

Deutsches Tagebuch-Archiv, Emmendingen (DTA) (Names are pseudonyms to
protect privacy and comply with archival regulations)
DTA 135, Hartmut Schiller, Tagebuch
DTA 138a, Gotthard Gruber, Tagebuch
DTA 260, Erwin Meier, Tagebuch
DTA 700/1, Hanna Grünwald, Tagebuch
DTA 1100/1, Baronesse Angela Marie Katharine Freiin von Petzoldt, Tage-
buch
DTA 1132, "Erinnerungen" von Kristina Margarthe Anja Kronthaler
DTA 1294/9–1294/10, Charlotte Reger, Tagebuch

Dokumentationsarchiv Lebensgeschichtlicher Aufzeichnungen, Vienna (DLA)
(Names are pseudonyms to protect privacy and comply with archival regu-
lations)
Kurt Döhl, Tagebuch
Andrea Hartl, Tagebuch

Erzbischöflichesarchiv Köln (EAK)
NL Carl Havenith
CR I
Gen I

Erzbischöflichesarchiv München-Freising (EAM)
NL Michael von Faulhaber
Militärseelsorge (Akten des Domkapitulars Buchberger)

Erzbischöflichesarchiv Freiburg (EAF)
NL Jakob Ebner
NL Fridolin Mayer

Erzbischöflichesarchiv Wien (EAW)
Bischofsakten Friedrich Gustav Piffl
Bischofskonferenzen
Praesidialia

Konsistorialarchiv Salzburg (KAS)
NL Matthias Ortner
22/27: Österr.Militär-Witwen u. Waisenfond 1915–1919, Kriegsgräberfürsorge Schwarzes Kreuz Statuen

Österreichisches Staatsarchiv-Kriegsarchiv (ÖStAKA)
Apostolisches Feldvikariat (AFV)
Kriegsministerium (KM)
Militärkanzlei Seiner Majestät (MKSM)
Neue Feldakten (NFA)

Tiroler Landesarchiv (TLA)
4. Tiroler Kaiserjäger Regiment
Tiroler Landesverteidigungsakten (TLVA)

PERIODICALS

Acta Apostolicae Sedis
Armeeblatt
Amtsblatt für die Erzdiözese München und Freising
Der Champagne-Kamerad. Feldzeitung der 3. Armee
Hochland
Kirchliches Handbuch für das Katholische Deutschland
Kölnische Volkszeitung
Korrespondenzblatt der Katholischen Klerus Österreichs
Pastoralblatt für die k.u.k. Katholische Militär- und Marinegeistlichkeit
Reichspost
Der Schuetzengraben
Stimmen der Zeit
Wiener Diözesanblatt

PUBLISHED PRIMARY SOURCES

Adam, Karl. *The Spirit of Catholicism*, trans. Justin McCann. New York: Crossroad, 1997 [1924].

Albert, Franz. *Handbuch für die katholischen Feldgeistlichen des Preußischen Heeres.* Vilnius: Verlag der 10. Armee, 1918.

Bächtold, Hanns. *Deutscher Soldatenbrauch und Soldatenglaube.* Strassburg: Tübner, 1917.

Betker, Frank and Almut Kriele, eds. *Pro fide et patria! Die Kriegstagebücher von Ludwig Berg 1914/18: Katholischer Feldgeistlicher im Grossen Hauptquartier Kaiser Wilhelms II.* Cologne: Böhlau, 1998.

Bielik, Emerich (sic). *Geschichte der k.u.k. Militärseelsorge und des Apostolischen Feld-Vicariates.* Vienna: Selbstverlag des Apostolischen Feld-Vicariates, 1901.

Bjelik, Emmerich. *Handbuch für die k.u.k. katholische Militärgeistlichkeit.* Vienna: Selbstverlag des Apostolischen Feldvikariats, 1905.

Cöln Katholisches Pfarramt. *Vor Gott ein Kind, vor dem Feind ein Held. Gedanken, Gebete und Lieder zur Massenverbreitung unter die katholischen Mannschaften des Heeres und der Flotte.* Cologne: Bachem, 1915.

Congar, Yves. *Journal de la Guerre, 1914–1918,* ed. Stéphane Audoin-Rouzeau and Dominique Congar. Paris: Cerf, 1997.

Delahaye-Théry, Eugène. *Les Cahiers Noirs. Notes quotidiennes écrites d'October 1914 à Novembre 1918 par une Lilloise sous l'occupation allemande.* Rennes: Éditions de la Province, 1934.

Egger, Karl. *Seele im Sturm: Kriegserleben eines Feldgeistlichen.* Innsbruck: F. Rauch, 1936.

Eppstein, John. *The Catholic Tradition of the Law of Nations.* Washington, DC: Carnegie Endowment for International Peace, published by the Catholic Association for International Peace, 1935.

Erzberger, Matthias. *Erlebnisse im Weltkrieg.* Stuttgart: Deutsche Verlagsanstalt, 1920.

Fassbender, Martin. *Des deutschen Volkes Wille zum Leben*. Freiburg: Herder, 1917.

Faulhaber, Michael von. *Waffen des Lichtes. Gesammelte Kriegsreden*, 5th edn. Freiburg im Breisgau: Herder, 1918.

Grabinski, Bruno. *Das Übersinnliche im Weltkriege. Merkwürdige Vorgänge im Felde und allerlei Kriegsprophezeiungen*. Hildesheim: Franz Borgmeyer, 1917.

Neuere Mystik. Der Weltkrieg im Aberglauben und im Lichte der Prophetie. Hildesheim: Franz Borgmeyer, 1916.

Weltkrieg und Sittlichkeit. Hildesheim: Franz Borgmeyer, 1917.

Gremel, Maria. *Mit neun Jahren im Dienst. Mein Leben im Stübl und am Bauernhof 1900–1930*, ed. Michael Mitterauer, *Damit es nicht verlorengeht*. Vienna: Böhlau, 1983.

Guardini, Romano. *The Spirit of the Liturgy*, trans. Ada Lane. New York: Crossroad Publishing, 1998 [1918].

Hämmerle, Christa, ed. *Kindheit im Ersten Weltkrieg*. Vienna: Böhlau, 1993.

Haugeneder, Hans. *Gestern noch auf stolzen Rossen. Tagebuch eines Kriegsteilnehmers 1916–1918*, ed. Anna Kautsky. Vienna: Hermagoras/Mohorjeva, 2010.

Hellwig, Albert. *Weltkrieg und Aberglaube: Erlebtes und Erlauschtes*. Leipzig: Wilhelm Heims, 1916.

Kovács, Elisabeth, Pál Arató, Franz Pichorner, and Lotte Wewalka, eds. *Untergang oder Rettung der Donaumonarchie?*, 2 vols. Vienna: Böhlau, 2004.

Leb, Josef. *P. Heinrich Abel, S.J., Der Männerapostel Wiens: ein Lebensbild*. Innsbruck: Marianischer Verlag, 1926.

Lipusch, Viktor, ed. *Österreich-Ungarns katholische Militärseelsorge im Weltkriege*. Vienna: Verlag für Militär- und Fachliteratur Amon Franz Göth, 1938.

Ludwig, Walter. "Beiträge zur Psychologie der Furcht im Kriege," in *Beiträge zur Psychologie des Krieges*, ed. William Stern and Otto Lipmann, 125–72. Leipzig: Johann Ambrosius Barth, 1920.

Meinertz, Max, and Hermann Sacher, eds. *Deutschland und der Katholizismus: Gedanken zur Neugestaltung des Deutschen Geistes- und Gesellschaftslebens*, 2 vols. Freiburg im Breisgau: Herder, 1918.

Missale Romanum: ex decreto sacrosancti Concilii tridentini restitutum s. Pii V. pontificis maximi jussu editum, aliorum pontificum cura recognitum, a Pio X. reformatum et Benedicti XV. auctoritate vulgatum. Ratisbonæ: F. Pustet, 1920.

Mitterauer, Michael, ed. *Kreuztragen. Drei Frauenleben*. Vienna: Hermann Böhlaus, 1984.

Ortmayr, Norbert, ed. *Knechte. Autobiographische Dokumente und sozialhistorische Skizzen*, ed. Michael Mitterauer and Peter Paul Kloß, *Damit es nicht verlorengeht*. Vienna: Böhlau, 1992.

Panni, Michael. *Das Tagebuch des Michael Panni. Kriegserlebnisse aus dem Ersten Weltkrieg*, ed. Peter Wendlandt. Rottenburg am Neckar: Mauer Verlag, 2009.

Peters, Edward N., ed. *The 1917 or Pio-Benedictine Code of Canon Law: In English Translation with Extensive Scholarly Apparatus*. San Francisco: Ignatius Press, 2001.

Pfeilschifter, Georg. "Seelsorge und religiöses Leben im deutschen Heere," in *Deutsche Kultur, Katholizismus und Weltkrieg: Eine Abwehr des Buches, La guerre allemande et le catholicisme,* ed. Georg Pfeilschifter, 235–68. Freiburg im Breisgau: Herder, 1915.

Feldbriefe katholischer Soldaten, 3 vols. Freiburg im Breisgau: Herder, 1918

Plaut, Paul. "Psychographie des Kriegers," in *Beiträge zur Psychologie des Krieges,* ed. William Stern and Otto Lipmann, 1–123. Leipzig: Johann Ambrosius Barth, 1920.

Rudl, Siegmund. *Kriegsvaterunser: Andenken an den Weltkrieg für alle Mitkämpfer und ihre Angehörigen.* Prague: Bonifatia Verlag, 1917.

Scheler, Max. *Gesammelte Werke.* Bern: Francke Verlag, 1954–.

Scheule, Rupert Maria, ed. *Beichten: Autobiographische Zeugnisse zur katholischen Bußpraxis im 20. Jahrhundert, Damit es nicht verlorengeht.* Vienna: Böhlau, 2001.

Schneider, Constantin. *Die Kriegserinnerungen 1914–1919,* ed. Oskar Dohle, *Veröffentlichungen der Kommission für Neuere Geschichte Österreichs.* Vienna: Böhlau, 2003.

Scholz, Ludwig. *Seelenleben des Soldaten an der Front: hinterlassene Aufzeichnungen des im Kriege gefallenen Nervenarztes.* Tübingen: J. C. B. Mohr, 1920.

Spitzl, Bruno. *Die Rainer: Als Feldkurat mit IR 59 im Weltkrieg,* 2nd edn. Innsbruck: Tyrolia Verlag, 1938.

Wollasch, Hans-Josef, ed. *Militärseelsorge im Ersten Weltkrieg: Das Kriegstagebuch des katholischen Feldgeistlichen Benedict Kreutz.* Mainz: Matthias Grünewelt Verlag, 1987.

SECONDARY SOURCES

Achleitner, Wilhelm. *Gott im Krieg: Die Theologie der österreichischen Bischöfe in den Hirtenbriefen zum Ersten Weltkrieg.* Vienna: Böhlau Verlag, 1997.

Altermatt, Urs. *Katholizismus und Antisemitismus: Mentalitäten, Kontinuitäten, Ambivalenzen: zur Kulturgeschichte der Schweiz 1918–1945.* Frauenfeld: Huber, 1999.

Katholizismus und Moderne: zur Sozial- und Mentalitätsgeschichte der Schweizer Katholiken im 19. und 20 Jahrhundert. Zürich: Benziger, 1989.

Anderson, Margaret Lavinia. *Practicing Democracy: Elections and Political Culture in Imperial Germany.* Princeton, NJ: Princeton University Press, 2000.

"Voter, Junker, Landrat, Priest: The Old Authorities and the New Franchise in Imperial Germany," *American Historical Review* 98, no. 5 (1995): 1448–74.

Arbeitskreis für kirchliche Zeitgeschichte, Münster. "Katholiken zwischen Tradition und Moderne: Das katholische Milieu als Forschungsaufgabe," *Westfälische Forschungen* 43 (1993): 588–654.

Aschoff, Hans-Georg. "Von der Revolution 1848/49 bis zum Ende des Ersten Weltkrieges," in *Laien in der Kirche,* ed. Erwin Gatz, 115–91. Freiburg: Herder, 2008.

Atkin, Nicholas and Frank Tallett. *Priests, Prelates, and People: A History of European Catholicism since 1750.* New York: Oxford University Press, 2003.

Audoin-Rouzeau, Stéphane and Annette Becker. *14–18: Understanding the Great War,* trans. Catherine Temerson. New York: Hill and Wang, 2002.

Barrett, David B., George Thomas Kurian, and Todd M. Johnson, eds. *World Christian Encyclopedia: A Comparative Survey of Churches and Religions in the Modern World*, 2nd edn, 2 vols. New York: Oxford University Press, 2001.

Barth-Scalmani, Gunda. "'Kriegsbriefe'. Kommunikation zwischen Klerus und Kirchenvolk im ersten Kriegsherbst 1914 im Spannungsfeld von Patriotismus und Seelsorge," in *Tirol – Österreich – Italien. Festschrift für Josef Riedmann zum 65. Geburtstag*, ed. Klaus Brandstätter and Julia Hörmann, 67–76. Innsbruck: Wagner, 2005.

Barth, Boris. *Dolchstoßlegenden und politische Desintegration: Das Trauma der deutschen Niederlage im Ersten Weltkrieg*. Düsseldorf: Droste, 2003.

Beales, Derek. *Joseph II. Against the World, 1780–1790*. Cambridge: Cambridge University Press, 2009.

Becker, Annette. "Faith, Ideologies, and the 'Cultures of War,'" in *A Companion to World War I*, ed. John Horne, 234–47. Malden, MA: Wiley-Blackwell, 2010.

War and Faith: The Religious Imagination in France, 1914–1930, trans. Helen McPhail. Oxford: Berg, 1998.

Beil, Christine, Thomas Fliege, Monique Scheer, Claudia Schlager, and Ralph Winkle. "Populare Religiosität und Kriegserfahrungen," *Theologische Quartalsschrift* 182, no. 4 (2002): 298–320.

Beil, Christine and Ralph Winkle. "'Primitive Religiosität' oder 'Krise der sittlichen Ordnung'? Wissenschaftsgeschichtliche Anmerkungen zur Aberglaubensforschung im Ersten Weltkrieg," in *KriegsVolksKunde. Zur Erfahrungsbindung durch Symbolbildung*, ed. Gottfried Korff, 149–77. Tübingen: Tübinger Vereinigung für Volkskunde, 2005.

Beller, Steven. *A Concise History of Austria*. Cambridge: Cambridge University Press, 2006.

Bergen, Doris L., ed. *The Sword of the Lord: Military Chaplains from the First to the Twenty-First Century*. South Bend, IN: University of Notre Dame Press, 2004.

Bessel, Richard. *Germany after the First World War*. Oxford: Clarendon Press, 1993.

Bjork, James E. *Neither German nor Pole: Catholicism and National Indifference in a Central European Borderland*. Ann Arbor: University of Michigan Press, 2008.

Blackbourn, David. *Marpingen: Apparitions of the Virgin Mary in Nineteenth-Century Germany*. New York: Knopf, 1994.

Blaschke, Olaf. "Die Kolonialisierung der Laienwelt: Priester als Milieumanager und die Kanäle klerikaler Kuratel," in *Religion im Kaiserreich: Milieus, Mentalitäten, Krisen*, ed. Olaf Blaschke and Frank-Michael Kuhlemann, 93–135. Göttingen: Vandenhoeck & Ruprecht, 1996.

Katholizismus und Antisemitismus im Deutschen Kaiserreich. Göttingen: Vandenhoeck & Ruprecht, 1997.

Bobič, Pavlina. *War and Faith: The Catholic Church in Slovenia, 1914–1918*. Boston, MA: Brill, 2012.

Bourke, Joanna. *An Intimate History of Killing: Face to Face Killing in 20th Century Warfare*. New York: Basic Books, 1999.

Boyer, John W. "Catholics, Christians, and the Challenges of Democracy: The Heritage of the Nineteenth Century," in *Christdemokratie in Europa in 20. Jahrhundert*, ed. Michael Gehler, Wolfram Kaiser, and Helmut Wohnaut, 23–59. Vienna: Böhlau, 2001.

Culture and Political Crisis in Vienna: Christian Socialism in Power, 1897–1918. Chicago, IL: University of Chicago Press, 1995.

Political Radicalism in Late Imperial Vienna: Origins of the Christian Social Movement, 1848–1897. Chicago, IL: University of Chicago Press, 1981.

Brandt, Hans Jürgen and Peter Häger, eds. *Biographisches Lexikon der Katholischen Militärseelsorge Deutschlands 1848 bis 1945.* Paderborn: Bonifatius, 2002.

Breuer, Gisela. *Frauenbewegung im Katholizismus: der Katholische Frauenbund 1903–1918.* Frankfurt: Campus Verlag, 1998.

Burleigh, Michael. *Earthly Powers: The Clash of Religion and Politics in Europe from the French Revolution to the Great War.* New York: HarperCollins, 2005.

Sacred Causes: The Clash of Religion and Politics from the Great War to the War on Terror. New York: HarperCollins, 2007.

Busch, Norbert. *Katholische Frömmigkeit und Moderne: Sozial- und Mentalitätsgeschichte des Herz-Jesu-Kultes in Deutschland zwischen Kulturkampf und Erstem Welkrieg.* Gütersloh: Chr. Kaiser, 1997.

Carroll, Michael P. *The Cult of the Virgin Mary: Psychological Origins.* Princeton, NJ: Princeton University Press, 1986.

Chickering, Roger. *The Great War and Urban Life in Germany: Freiburg, 1914–1918.* Cambridge: Cambridge University Press, 2007.

Chickering, Roger, Dennis E. Showalter, and Hans J. Van de Ven, eds. *Cambridge History of War, vol. 4: War and the Modern World.* Cambridge: Cambridge University Press, 2012.

Christian, William A. *Person and God in a Spanish Valley*, rev. edn. Princeton, NJ: Princeton University Press, 1988.

Clark, Christopher and Wolfram Kaiser, eds. *Culture Wars: Secular-Catholic Conflict in Nineteenth-Century Europe.* Cambridge: Cambridge University Press, 2003.

Cohen, Gary B. "Nationalist Politics and the Dynamics of State and Civil Society in the Habsburg Monarchy, 1867–1914," *Central European History* 40 (2007): 241–78.

Cole, Laurence. "Für Gott, Kaiser und Vaterland": *Nationale Identität der deutschsprachigen Bevölkerung Tirols 1860–1914.* Frankfurt: Campus, 2000.

Cole, Laurence and Daniel L. Unowsky, eds. *The Limits of Loyalty: Imperial Symbolism, Popular Allegiances and State Patriotism in the Late Habsburg Monarchy.* New York: Berghahn Books, 2007.

Confino, Alon. *The Nation as a Local Metaphor: Württemberg, Imperial Germany, and National Memory, 1871–1918.* Chapel Hill: University of North Carolina Press, 1997.

Connelly, John. "Catholic Racism and Its Opponents," *Journal of Modern History* 79, no. 4 (2007): 813–47.

From Enemy to Brother: The Revolution in Catholic Teaching on the Jews, 1933–1965. Cambridge, MA: Harvard University Press, 2012.

Conway, Martin. *Catholic Politics in Europe, 1918–1945*. London: Routledge, 1997.

Cook, Tim. "Grave Beliefs: Stories of the Supernatural and the Uncanny among Canada's Great War Trench Soldiers," *Journal of Military History* 77, no. 2 (2013): 521–42.

Coppa, Frank J. *Politics and the Papacy in the Modern World*. Westport, CT: Praeger, 2008.

Coreth, Anna. *Pietas Austriaca*, trans. William D. Bowman and Anna Maria Leitgeb. West Lafayette, IN: Purdue University Press, 2004.

Cornwall, Mark. *The Undermining of Austria-Hungary: The Battle for Hearts and Minds*. New York: St. Martin's Press, 2000.

Cox, Jeffrey. "Master Narratives of Religious Change," in *The Decline of Christendom in Western Europe, 1750–2000*, ed. Hugh McLeod and Werner Ustorf, 201–17. Cambridge: Cambridge University Press, 2003.

Daniel, Ute. "Women," in *Brill's Encyclopedia of the First World War*, ed. Gerhard Hirschfeld, Gerd Krumeich, and Irina Renz, 89–102. Boston, MA: Brill, 2012.

Davis, Belinda. *Home Fires Burning: Food, Politics, and Everyday Life in World War I Berlin*. Chapel Hill: University of North Carolina Press, 2000.

Deák, István. *Beyond Nationalism: A Social and Political History of the Habsburg Officer Corps, 1848–1918*. Oxford: Oxford University Press, 1990.

Donson, Andrew. *Youth in the Fatherless Land: War Pedagogy, Nationalism, and Authority in Germany, 1914–1918*. Cambridge, MA: Harvard University Press, 2010.

Ebel, Jonathan H. *Faith in the Fight: Religion and the American Soldier in the Great War*. Princeton, NJ: Princeton University Press, 2010.

Ebner, Oswald. *Kampf um die Sextner Rotwand*. Bozen: Athesia, 1978.

Ehrenpreis, Petronilla. *Kriegs- und Friedensziele im Diskurs. Regierung und deutschsprachige Öffentlichkeit Österreich-Ungarns während des Ersten Weltkriegs*. Innsbruck: Studien Verlag, 2005.

Eitler, Pascal, Bettina Hitzer, and Monique Scheer. "Feeling and Faith: Religious Emotions in German History," *German History* 32, no. 3 (2014): 343–52.

Eksteins, Modris. *Rites of Spring: The Great War and the Birth of the Modern Age*. Boston, MA: Houghton Mifflin, 1989.

Ellis, John. *Eye-Deep in Hell: Trench Warfare in World War I*. Baltimore, MD: Johns Hopkins University Press, 1989.

Epstein, Klaus. *Matthias Erzberger and the Dilemma of German Democracy*. New York: Howard Fertig, 1971.

Eustace, Nicole, Eugenia Lean, Julie Livingston, Jan Plamper, William M. Reddy, and Barbara H. Rosenwein. "AHR Conversation: The Historical Study of Emotions," *The American Historical Review* 117, no. 5 (2012): 1487–531.

Fliege, Thomas. "'Mein Deutschland sei mein Engel Michael.' Sankt Michael als nationalreligiöser Mythos," in *Alliierte im Himmel: Populäre Religiosität und Kriegserfahrung*, ed. Gottfried Korff, 159–99. Tübingen: Tübinger Vereinigung für Volkskunde, 2006.

Forstman, H. Jackson. *Christian Faith in Dark Times: Theological Conflicts in the Shadow of Hitler.* Louisville, KY: Westminster/John Knox Press, 1992.

Frings, Manfred S. *The Mind of Max Scheler: The First Comprehensive Guide Based on the Complete Works.* Milwaukee, WI: Marquette University Press, 1997.

Fussell, Paul. *The Great War and Modern Memory.* Oxford: Oxford University Press, 1975.

Gatz, Erwin. *Die Katholische Kirche in Deutschland im 20. Jahrhundert.* Freiburg: Herder, 2009.

"Zur Kultur des priestlichen Alltages," in *DerDiözesanklerus,* ed. Erwin Gatz, 282–318. Freiburg: Herder, 1995.

ed. *Geschichte des kirchlichen Lebens in den deutschsprachigen Ländern seit dem Ende des 18. Jahrhunderts: Die Katholische Kirche,* vol. 4: *Der Diözesanklerus.* Freiburg: Herder, 1995.

ed. *Geschichte des kirchlichen Lebens in den deutschsprachigen Ländern seit dem Ende des 18. Jahrhunderts: Die Katholische Kirche,* vol. 7: *Klöster und Ordensgemeinschaften.* Freiburg: Herder, 2006.

Gerwarth, Robert. "The Central European Counter-Revolution: Paramilitary Violence in Germany, Austria and Hungary after the Great War," *Past and Present 200,* no. 1 (2008): 175–209.

Gibson, Ralph. *A Social History of French Catholicism, 1789–1914.* London: Routledge, 1989.

Goebel, Stefan. *The Great War and Medieval Memory: War, Remembrance, and Medievalism in Britain and Germany, 1914–1940.* Cambridge: Cambridge University Press, 2007.

Gottsmann, Andreas. *Rom und die nationalen Katholizismen in der Donaumonarchie. Römischer Universalismus, habsburgische Reichspolitik und nationale Identitäten 1878–1914.* Vienna: Verlag der Österreichischen Akademie der Wissenschaften, 2010.

Götz von Olenhusen, Irmtraud. *Klerus und abweichendes Verhalten: zur Sozialgeschichte katholischer Priester im 19. Jahrhundert: die Erzdiözese Freiburg.* Göttingen: Vandenhoeck & Ruprecht, 1994.

Graf, Friedrich Wilhelm. "'Dechristianisierung.' Zur Problemgeschichte eines kulturpolitischen Topos," in *Säkularisierung, Dechristianisierung, Rechristianisierung im neuzeitlichen Europa,* ed. Hartmut Lehmann, 32–66. Göttingen: Vandenhoeck & Ruprecht, 1997.

Der heilige Zeitgeist: Studien zur Ideengeschichte der protestantischen Theologie in der Weimarer Republik. Tübingen: Mohr Siebeck, 2011.

Graves, Robert. *Good-Bye to All That.* New York: Anchor Books, 1998.

Grayzel, Susan R. *Women and the First World War.* New York: Longman, 2002.

Gregory, Adrian. "Beliefs and Religion," in *The Cambridge History of the First World War,* ed. Jay Winter, 418–44. Cambridge: Cambridge University Press, 2014.

Gregory, Adrian, and Annette Becker. "Religious Sites and Practices," in *Capital Cities at War: Paris, London, Berlin: Vol. 2, A Cultural History,* ed. Jay Winter and Jean-Louis Robert, 383–427. Cambridge: Cambridge University Press, 2007.

Gregory, Brad S. "The Other Confessional History: On Secular Bias in the Study of Religion," *History and Theory* 45, no. 4 (2006): 132–49.

The Unintended Reformation: How a Religious Revolution Secularized Society. Cambridge, MA: Belknap Press of Harvard University Press, 2012.

Greschat, Martin. *Der Erste Weltkrieg und die Christenheit. Ein globaler Überblick.* Stuttgart: Kohlhammer, 2014.

Gross, Michael B. *The War against Catholicism: Liberalism and the Anti-Catholic Imagination in Nineteenth-Century Germany.* Ann Arbor: University of Michigan Press, 2004.

Hagemann, Karen and Stefanie Schüler-Springorum, eds. *Home/Front: The Military, War, and Gender in Twentieth-Century Germany.* Oxford: Berg, 2002.

Haidl, Roland. "Ausbruch aus dem Ghetto? Katholizismus im deutschen Heer 1914–1918," in *"Gott mit uns": Nation, Religion, und Gewalt im 19. und frühen 20. Jahrhundert,* ed. Gerd Krumeich and Hartmut Lehmann, 263–71. Göttingen: Vandenhoeck & Ruprecht, 2000.

Ham, Claudia. "Von den Anfängen der Militärseelsorge bis zur Liquidierung des Apostolischen Feldvikariates im Jahr 1918," in *Zwischen Himmel und Erde: Militärseelsorge in Österreich,* ed. Roman-Hans Gröger, 13–98. Graz: Styria Verlag, 2001.

Hammer, Karl. *Deutsche Kriegstheologie, 1870–1918.* Munich: Deutscher Taschenbuch Verlag, 1974.

Hämmerle, Christa. *Heimat/Front: Geschlechtergeschichte/n des Ersten Weltkriegs in Österreich-Ungarn.* Vienna: Böhlau, 2014.

Hanebrink, Paul A. *In Defense of Christian Hungary: Religion, Nationalism, and Antisemitism, 1890–1944.* Ithaca, NY: Cornell University Press, 2006.

Hanna, Martha. *Your Death Would Be Mine: Paul and Marie Pireaud in the Great War.* Cambridge, MA: Harvard University Press, 2006.

Harris, Ruth. *Lourdes: Body and Spirit in the Secular Age.* New York: Viking, 1999.

Hašek, Jaroslav. *The Good Soldier Schweik,* trans. Paul Selver. New York: Frederick Ungar Publishing Co., 1930.

Hastings, Derek. *Catholicism and the Roots of Nazism: Religious Identity and National Socialism.* Oxford: Oxford University Press, 2009.

Haub, Rita. *Pater Rupert Mayer: Ein Lebensbild.* München: Neue Stadt, 2007.

Haupt, Heinz-Gerhard and Jürgen Kocka, eds. *Comparative and Transnational History: Central European Approaches and New Perspectives.* New York: Berghahn Books, 2009.

Healy, Maureen. "Civilizing the Soldier in Postwar Austria," in *Gender and War in Twentieth-Century Eastern Europe,* ed. Nancy M. Wingfield and Maria Bucur, 47–69. Bloomington: Indiana University Press, 2006.

Vienna and the Fall of the Habsburg Empire: Total War and Everyday Life in World War I. Cambridge: Cambridge University Press, 2004.

Healy, Róisín. *The Jesuit Specter in Imperial Germany.* Boston, MA: Brill, 2003.

Heilbronner, Oded. *Catholicism, Political Culture, and the Countryside: A Social History of the Nazi Party in South Germany.* Ann Arbor: University of Michigan Press, 1998.

"From Ghetto to Ghetto: The Place of German Catholic Society in Recent Historiography," *Journal of Modern History* 72, no. 2 (2000): 453–95.

Herwig, Holger H. *The First World War: Germany and Austria-Hungary, 1914–1918*. London: Arnold, 1997.

Holzem, Andreas, ed. *Krieg und Christentum: Religiöse Gewalttheorien in der Kriegserfahrung des Westens*. Paderborn: Schöningh, 2009.

Holzem, Andreas and Christoph Holzapfel. "Kriegserfahrung als Forschungsproblem: Der Erste Weltkrieg in der religiösen Erfahrung von Katholiken," *Theologische Quartalsschrift* 182, no. 4 (2002): 279–97.

Horne, John, ed. *State, Society, and Mobilization in Europe during the First World War*. Cambridge: Cambridge University Press, 1997.

Houlihan, Patrick J. *"Clergy in the Trenches: Catholic Military Chaplains of Germany and Austria-Hungary during the First World War."* Ph.D. Diss., University of Chicago, 2011.

"Imperial Frameworks of Religion: Catholic Military Chaplains of Germany and Austria-Hungary during the First World War," *First World War Studies* 3 (2012): 165–82.

"Local Catholicism as Transnational War Experience: Daily Religious Life in Occupied Northern France, 1914–1918," *Central European History* 45, no. 2 (2012): 233–67.

"Was There an Austrian Stab-in-the-Back Myth? Postwar Military Interpretations of Defeat," in *From Empire to Republic: Post-World War I Austria*, ed. Günter Bischof, Fritz Plasser, and Peter Berger, 67–89. New Orleans, LA: University of New Orleans Press, 2010.

Hürten, Heinz. "Die katholische Kirche im Ersten Weltkrieg," in *Der erste Weltkrieg: Wirkung, Wahrnehmung, Analyse*, ed. Wolfgang Michalka, 725–35. Munich: Piper Verlag, 1994.

Jenkins, Philip. *The Great and Holy War: How World War I Became a Religious Crusade*. New York: HarperOne, 2014.

Juergensmeyer, Mark, Margo Kitts, and Michael Jerryson, eds. *The Oxford Handbook of Religion and Violence*. New York: Oxford University Press, 2013.

Kahler, Thomas. "'Gefallen auf dem Feld der Ehre.' Kriegerdenkmäler für die Gefallenen des Ersten Weltkriegs in Österreich unter besonderer Berücksichtigung der Entwicklung in Salzburg bis 1938," in *Steinernes Bewußtsein I. Die öffentliche Repräsentation staatlicher und nationaler Identität Österreichs in seinen Denkmälern*, ed. Stefan Riesenfellner, 365–409. Vienna: Böhlau, 1998.

Kaiser, Wolfram. *Christian Democracy and the Origins of European Union*. Cambridge: Cambridge University Press, 2007.

Kévorkian, Raymond H. *The Armenian Genocide: A Complete History*. New York: I. B. Tauris, 2011.

Klieber, Rupert. *Jüdische, Christliche, Muslimische Lebenswelten der Donaumonarchie 1848–1918*. Vienna: Böhlau, 2010.

"Soziale Integration durch Religion? Die konfessionelle Milieus der Habsburgermonarchie und ihr Einfluss auf die Lebenspraxis der Bevölkerung," in *Soziale Strukturen*, ed. Helmut Rumpler and Peter Urbanitsch, 743–81. Vienna: Verlag der Österreichischen Akademie der Wissenschaften, 2010.

Klier, Johann. *Von der Kriegspredigt zum Friedensappell: Erzbischof Michael von Faulhaber und der Erste Weltkrieg: ein Beitrag zur Geschichte der deutschen katholischen Militärseelsorge*. Munich: Kommissionsverlag UNI-Druck, 1991.

Kłoczowski, Jerzy. "Katholiken und Protestanten in Ostmitteleuropa," in *Erster und Zweiter Weltkrieg: Demokratien und totalitäre Systeme (1914–1958)*, ed. Jean-Marie Mayeur and Kurt Meier, 872–912. Freiburg im Breisgau: Herder, 1992.

Knoch, Peter. "Erleben und Nacherleben. Das Kriegserlebnis im Augenzeugenbericht und im Geschichtsunterricht," in *Keiner fühlt sich hier mehr als Mensch. Erlebnis und Wirkung des Ersten Weltkriegs*, ed. Gerhard Hirschfeld, Gerd Krumeich, and Irina Renz, 199–219. Essen: Klartext, 1993.

Kocka, Jürgen. "Comparison and Beyond," *History & Theory* 42, no. 1 (2003): 39–44.

Korff, Gottfried, ed. *Alliierte im Himmel: Populare Religiosität und Kriegserfahrung*. Tübingen: Tübinger Vereinigung für Volkskunde, 2006.

Koselleck, Reinhart. *Vergangene Zukunft. Zur Semantik geschichtlicher Zeiten*. Frankfurt a.M.: Suhrkamp, 1979.

Kraus, Karl. *Schriften, vol. 10: Die letzten Tage der Menschheit. Tragödie in fünf Akten mit Vorspiel und Epilog*. Frankfurt a.M.: Suhrkamp, 1986.

Krieg, Robert A. *Catholic Theologians in Nazi Germany*. New York: Continuum, 2004.

Kronfeld, Ernst Moritz. *Der Krieg im Aberglauben und Volksglauben kulturhistorische Beiträge*. München: Schmidt, 1915.

Kronthaler, Michaela. "Caritasorganisation in Österreich bis zum Ende des Zweiten Weltkrieges," in *Caritas und soziale Dienste*, ed. Erwin Gatz, 213–26. Freiburg im Breisgau: Herder, 1997.

Krumeich, Gerd and Hartmut Lehmann, eds. *"Gott mit uns": Nation, Religion, und Gewalt im 19. und frühen 20. Jahrhundert*. Göttingen: Vandenhoeck & Ruprecht, 2000.

Kuhlman, Erika. *Reconstructing Patriarchy after the Great War: Women, Gender, and Postwar Reconciliation between Nations*. New York: Palgrave Macmillan, 2008.

Kuhlman, Erika A. *Of Little Comfort: War Widows, Fallen Soldiers, and the Remaking of the Nation after the Great War*. New York: New York University Press, 2012.

Kuprian, Hermann J. W. and Oswald Überegger, eds. *Der Erste Weltkrieg im Alpenraum: Erfahrung, Deutung, Erinnerung/La Grande Guerra nell'arco alpino: esperienze e memoria*. Bozen: Athesia, 2006.

Kwan, Jonathan. "Nationalism and All That: Reassessing the Habsburg Monarchy and Its Legacy," *European History Quarterly* 41, no. 1 (2011): 88–108.

Lätzel, Martin. *Die katholische Kirche im Ersten Weltkrieg. Zwischen Nationalismus und Friedenswillen*. Regensburg: Friedrich Pustet, 2014.

Lehmann, Hartmut. "'God Our Old Ally': The Chosen People Theme in Late Nineteenth- and Early Twentieth-Century German Nationalism," in *Many Are Chosen: Divine Election and Western Nationalism*, ed. William R. Hutchinson and Hartmut Lehmann, 85–113. Minneapolis, MN: Fortress Press, 1994.

Lein, Richard. *Pflichterfüllung oder Hochverrat? Die tschechischen Soldaten Österreich-Ungarns im Ersten Weltkrieg.* Vienna: Lit, 2011.

Leisching, Peter. "Die römisch-katholische Kirche in Cisleithanien," in *Die Habsburgermonarchie, 1848–1918*, ed. Adam Wandruszka and Peter Urbanitsch, 1–247. Vienna: Verlag für die Österreichische Akademie der Wissenschaften, 1980.

Liebmann, Maximilian. "Von der Dominanz der katholischen Kirche zu freien Kirchen im freien Staat – vom Wiener Kongreß 1815 bis zur Gegenwart," in *Geschichte des Christentums in Österreich*, ed. Rudolf Leeb, Maximilian Liebmann, and Georg Scheibelreiter, 361–456. Vienna: Ueberreuter, 2003.

Liedhegener, Antonius. *Christentum und Urbanisierung: Katholiken und Protestanten in Münster und Bochum 1830–1933.* Paderborn: F. Schöningh, 1997.

Lilla, Mark. *The Stillborn God: Religion, Politics, and the Modern West.* New York: Knopf, 2007.

Liulevicius, Vejas Gabriel. *War Land on the Eastern Front: Culture, National Identity, and German Occupation in World War I.* Cambridge: Cambridge University Press, 2000.

Lurz, Meinhold. *Kriegerdenkmäler in Deutschland*, 6 vols. Heidelberg: Esprint, 1985.

Maurer, Catherine. *Der Caritasverband zwischen Kaiserreich und Weimarer Republik: Zur Sozial- und Mentalitätsgeschichte des caritativen Katholizismus in Deutschland.* Freiburg: Lambertus, 2008.

McBrien, Richard P. *Catholicism*, rev. edn. San Francisco: HarperSanFrancisco, 1994.

The Church: The Evolution of Catholicism. New York: HarperOne, 2008.

Lives of the Popes: The Pontiffs from St. Peter to John Paul II. San Francisco: HarperSanFrancisco, 1997.

McLeod, Hugh. *Religion and the People of Western Europe, 1789–1989*, 2nd edn. Oxford: Oxford University Press, 1997.

The Religious Crisis of the 1960s. Oxford: Oxford University Press, 2007.

Meinhof, Marius. "Gebete im Ersten Weltkrieg," in *Glaubenssache Krieg. Religiöse Motive auf Bildpostkarten des Ersten Weltkriegs*, ed. Heidrun Alzheimer, 92–106. Bad Windsheim: Verlag Fränkisches Freilandmuseum, 2009.

Mergel, Thomas. "Milieu und Religion. Überlegungen zur Ver-Ortung kollektiver Identitäten," in *Sachsen in Deutschland. Politik, Kultur und Gesellschaft 1830–1918*, ed. James N. Retallack, 265–79. Bielefeld: Gütersloh, 2000.

Missalla, Heinrich. "Gott mit uns": *Die deutsche katholische Kriegspredigt, 1914–1918.* Munich: Kösel Verlag, 1968.

Mitterauer, Michael. "'Nur diskret ein Kreuzzeichen.' Zu Formen des individuellen und gemeinschaftlichen Gebets in der Familie," in *Religion und Alltag. Interdisziplinäre Beiträge zu einer Sozialgeschichte des Katholizismus in lebensgeschichtlicher Aufzeichnungen*, ed. Andreas Heller, Therese Weber, and Olivia Wiebel-Fandel, 154–204. Vienn: Böhlau, 1990.

Moorehead, Caroline. *Dunant's Dream: War, Switzerland, and the History of the Red Cross.* London: HarperCollins, 1998.

Mooser, Josef. "Das katholische Milieu in der bürgerlichen Gesellschaft. Zum Vereinswesen des Katholizismus im späten Deutschen Kaiserreich," in *Religion im Kaiserreich. Milieus, Mentalitäten, Krisen.*, ed. Olaf Blaschke and Frank-Michael Kuhlemann, 59–92. Gütersloh: Chr. Kaiser, 1996.

"Katholische Volksreligion, Klerus, und Bürgertum in der zweiten Hälfte des 19. Jahrhunderts: Thesen," in *Religion und Gesellschaft im 19. Jahrhundert*, ed. Wolfgang Schieder, 144–56. Stuttgart: Klett-Cotta, 1993.

Morsey, Rudolf. "Die Deutsche Katholiken und der Nationalstaat zwischen Kulturkampf und Erstem Weltkrieg," *Historisches Jahrbuch* 90, no. 3 (1970): 31–64.

Mosse, George L. *Fallen Soldiers: Reshaping the Memory of the World Wars.* Oxford: Oxford University Press, 1989.

Niehaus, Irmgard. "'Die Krone unserer Berufswürde' Die Auseinandersetzung um den Lehrerinnenzölibat im Verein katholischer deutscher Lehrerinnen und im Katholischen Deutschen Frauenbund," in *Katholikinnen und Moderne*, ed. Gisela Muschiol, 43–67. Münster: Aschendorff, 2003.

Nikitsch, Herbert. "'. . . den unsern Jammer, der anders brennt'. Verortungen des Judas Thaddäus-Verehrung im Ersten Weltkrieg und 'in unserer Zeit,'" in *Alliierte im Himmel. Populare Religiosität und Kriegserfahrung*, ed. Gottfried Korff, 223–62. Tübingen: Tübinger Vereinigung für Volkskunde, 2006.

Nipperdey, Thomas. *Religion im Umbruch: Deutschland, 1870–1918.* Munich: C. H. Beck, 1988.

O'Sullivan, Michael E. "An Eroding Milieu? Catholic Youth, Church Authority, and Popular Behavior in Northwest Germany during the Third Reich, 1933–1938," *Catholic Historical Review* 90, no. 2 (2004): 236–59.

"From Catholic Milieu to Lived Religion: The Social and Cultural History of Modern German Catholicism," *History Compass* 7, no. 3 (2009): 837–61.

Okey, Robin. *The Habsburg Monarchy, c. 1765–1918.* Houndmills: Macmillan, 2001.

Orsi, Robert A., ed. *The Cambridge Companion to Religious Studies.* New York: Cambridge University Press, 2011.

Paces, Cynthia J. "Religious Heroes for a Secular State: Commemorating Jan Hus and Saint Wenceslas in 1920s Czechoslovakia," in *Staging the Past: The Politics of Commemoration in Habsburg Central Europe, 1848 to the Present*, ed. Maria Bucur and Nancy M. Wingfield, 209–35. West Lafayette, IN: Purdue University Press, 2001.

Panke-Kochinke, Birgit. *Unterwegs und doch daheim. (Über-) Lebensstrategien von Kriegskrankenschwestern im Ersten Weltkrieg in der Etappe.* Frankfurt am Main: Mabuse Verlag, 2004.

Pauley, Bruce F. *From Prejudice to Persecution: A History of Austrian Anti-Semitism.* Chapel Hill: University of North Carolina Press, 1992.

Pease, Neal. *Rome's Most Faithful Daughter: The Catholic Church and Independent Poland, 1914–1939.* Athens: Ohio University Press, 2009.

Plaschka, Richard G. "Contradicting Ideologies: The Pressure of Ideological Conflicts in the Austro-Hungarian Army of World War I," in *The Habsburg Empire in World War I: Essays on the Intellectual, Military, Political, and*

Economic Aspects of the Habsburg War Effort, ed. Robert A. Kann, Béla K. Király, and Paula S. Fichtner, 105–19. New York: Columbia University Press, 1977.

Plaschka, Richard Georg, Horst Haselsteiner, and Arnold Suppan. *Innere Front: Militärassistenz, Widerstand, und Umsturz in der Donaumonarchie 1918*, 2 vols. Vienna: Verlag für Geschichte und Politik, 1974.

Pollard, John F. *The Unknown Pope: Benedict XV (1914–1922) and the Pursuit of Peace*. London: Geoffrey Chapman, 1999.

Porter, Patrick. "Beyond Comfort: German and English Military Chaplains and the Memory of the Great War, 1919–1929," *Journal of Religious History* 29, no. 3 (2005): 258–89.

"Slaughter or Sacrifice? The Religious Rhetoric of Blood Sacrifice in the British and German Armies, 1914–1919" (D. Phil, University of Oxford, 2006).

Pressel, Wilhelm. *Die Kriegspredigt 1914–1918 in der evangelischen Kirche Deutschlands*. Göttingen: Vandenhoeck und Ruprecht, 1967.

Probst, Volker G. *Bilder vom Tode. Eine Studie zum deutschen Kriegerdenkmal in der Weimarer Republik am Beispiel des Pietà-Motives und seiner profanierten Varianten*. Hamburg: Wayasbah, Original-Ausg edition, 1986.

Pulzer, Peter. *The Rise of Political Anti-Semitism in Germany and Austria*, rev. edn. Cambridge, MA: Harvard University Press, 1988.

Quataert, Jean H. *Staging Philanthropy: Patriotic Women and the National Imagination in Dynastic Germany, 1813–1916*. Ann Arbor: University of Michigan Press, 2001.

Raabe, Felix. "Die Katholiken und ihre Verbände in der Zeit der Weimarer Republik," in *Laien in der Kirche*, ed. Erwin Gatz, 193–220. Freiburg: Herder, 2008.

Rak, Christian. *Krieg, Nation und Konfession: die Erfahrung des deutschfranzösischen Krieges von 1870/71*. Paderborn: F. Schöningh, 2004.

Rauchensteiner, Manfried. *Der Tod des Doppeladlers: Österreich-Ungarn und der Erste Weltkrieg*. Graz: Verlag Styria, 1993.

Reichmann, Bettina. "Die Rolle des ungarischen Bischofs Ottokár Prohászka im Ersten Weltkrieg," in *Geistliche im Krieg*, ed. Franz Brendle and Anton Schindling, 291–311. Münster: Aschendorff Verlag, 2009.

Remarque, Erich Maria. *All Quiet on the Western Front*, trans. A. W. Wheen. Boston, MA: Little, Brown and Company, 1929.

Rettenwander, Matthias. *Der Krieg als Seelsorge: Katholische Kirche und Volksfrömmigkeit in Tirol im Ersten Weltkrieg*. Innsbruck: Universitätsverlag Wagner, 2006.

Rollet, Catherine. "The Home and Family Life," in *Capital Cities at War: Paris, London, Berlin, 1914–1919*, ed. Jay Winter and Jean-Louis Robert, 315–53. Cambridge: Cambridge University Press, 2007.

Roshwald, Aviel and Richard Stites, eds. *European Culture in the Great War: The Arts, Entertainment, and Propaganda, 1914–1918*. Cambridge: Cambridge University Press, 1999.

Rothenberg, Gunther E. "The Shield of the Dynasty: Reflections on the Habsburg Army, 1649–1918," *Austrian History Yearbook* 32 (2001): 169–206.

Rother, Rainer, ed. *Der Weltkrieg 1914–1918: Ereignis und Erinnerung.* Wolfratshausen: Edition Minerva, 2004.

Ruff, Mark Edward. *The Wayward Flock: Catholic Youth in Postwar West Germany, 1945–1965.* Chapel Hill: University of North Carolina Press, 2005.

Sack, Birgit. *Zwischen religiöser Bindung und moderner Gesellschaft. Katholische Frauenbewegung und politische Kultur in der Weimarer Republik (1918/19–1933).* Münster: Waxmann, 1998.

Sandgruber, Roman, ed. *Ökonomie und Politik: österreichische Wirtschaftsgeschichte vom Mittelalter bis zur Gegenwart.* Vienna: Ueberreuter, 1995.

Scheer, Monique. "Rettet Maria Deutschland? Die Diskussion um eine nationale Marienweihe zu Beginn des Kalten Krieges," in *Alliierte im Himmel. Populare Religiosität und Kriegserfahrung,* ed. Gottfried Korff, 141–56. Tübingen: Tübinger Vereinigung für Volkskunde, 2006.

Rosenkranz und Kriegsvisionen: Marienerscheinungskulte im 20. Jahrhundert. Tübingen: Tübinger Vereinigung für Volkskunde, 2006.

Schlager, Claudia. *Kult und Krieg. Herz Jesu – Sacré Cœur – Christus Rex im deutsch-französischen Vergleich, 1914–1925.* Tübingen: Tübinger Vereinigung für Volkskunde, 2011.

"Waffenbrüderschaft im heiligsten Herzen Jesu: Die deutsche und österreichische Herz-Jesu-Verehrung im Ersten Weltkrieg und die Propagierung des Tiroler Vorbildes," in *Der Erste Weltkrieg im Alpenraum,* ed. Hermann J. W. Kuprian. Innsbruck: Wagner, 2006.

Schorske, Carl E. *Fin de siècle Vienna: Politics and Culture.* New York: Alfred A. Knopf, 1980.

Schumann, Frank, ed. *"Zieh Dich warm an!" Soldatenpost und Heimatbriefe aus zwei Weltkriegen. Chronik einer Familie.* Berlin: Neues Leben, 1989.

Schweitzer, Richard. *The Cross and the Trenches: Religious Faith and Doubt among British and American Great War Soldiers.* Westport, CT: Praeger, 2003.

Scottà, Antonio. *Papa Benedetto XV: la Chiesa, la Grande Guerra, la pace (1914–1922).* Roma: Edizioni di storia e letteratura, 2009.

Senior, Donald and John J. Collins, eds. *The Catholic Study Bible,* 2nd edn. New York: Oxford University Press, 2006.

Shedel, James. "Emperor, Church, and People: Religion and Dynastic Loyalty During the Golden Jubilee of Franz Joseph," *Catholic Historical Review* 76, no. 1 (1990): 71–92.

Smith, Helmut Walser. *The Continuities of German History: Nation, Religion, and Race across the Long Nineteenth Century.* Cambridge: Cambridge University Press, 2008.

ed. *Protestants, Catholics, and Jews in Germany, 1800–1914.* New York: Berg, 2001.

Snape, Michael. *God and the British Soldier: Religion and the British Army in the First and Second World Wars.* London: Routledge, 2005.

"The Great War," in *World Christianities, c.1914–c.2000,* ed. Hugh McLeod, 131–50. Cambridge: Cambridge University Press, 2006.

Stadelmann, Christian. "Mariazell," in *Memoriae Austriae,* ed. Emil Brix, Ernst Bruckmüller, and Hannes Stekl, 304–35. Vienna: Verlag für Geschichte und Politik, 2004.

Stadler, Karl R. "Die Gründung der Republik," in *Kirche in Österreich, 1918–1965,* ed. Erika Weinzierl and Ferdinand Klostermann, 2 vols, 1:72. Munich: Herold, 1966–67.

Stambolis, Barbara. "Nationalisierung trotz Ultramontanisierung oder: 'Alles für Deutschland. Deutschland aber für Christus': mentalitätsleitende Wertorientierung deutscher Katholiken im 19. und 20. Jahrhundert," *Historische Zeitschrift* 269 (1999): 57–97.

Steffen, Lloyd. "Religion and Violence in Christian Traditions," in *The Oxford Handbook of Religion and Violence,* ed. Mark Juergensmeyer, Margo Kitts, and Michael Jerryson, 100–25. Oxford: Oxford University Press, 2013.

Steglich, Wolfgang. *Die Friedenspolitik der Mittelmächte, 1917/18.* Wiesbaden: F. Steiner, 1964.

   ed. *Der Friedensappell Papst Benedikts XV. vom 1. August 1917 und die Mittelmächte. Diplomatische Aktenstücke des Deutschen Auswärtigen Amtes, des Bayerischen Staatsministeriums des Äussern, des Österreichisch-Ungarischen Ministeriums des Äussern und des Britischen Auswärtigen Amtes aus den Jahren 1915–1922.* Wiesbaden: F. Steiner, 1970.

Stevenson, David. *Cataclysm: The First World War as Political Tragedy.* New York: Basic Books, 2004.

Stone, Norman. *The Eastern Front, 1914–1917.* London: Penguin, 1975.

Strachan, Hew. "Epilogue," in *The Legacy of the Great War: Ninety Years On,* ed. Jay Winter, 185–98. Columbia: University of Missouri Press, 2009.

Taylor, Charles. *A Secular Age.* Cambridge, MA: Belknap Press of Harvard University Press, 2007.

Taylor, John. "The Future of Christianity," in *The Oxford History of Christianity,* ed. John McManners, 644–83. Oxford: Oxford University Press, 1993.

Thomas, Keith. *Religion and the Decline of Magic: Studies in Popular Beliefs in Sixteenth- and Seventeenth-Century England.* New York: Scribner, 1971.

Thompson, E. P. *The Making of the English Working Class.* New York: Vintage, 1966.

Todd, Lisa M. "'The Soldier's Wife Who Ran Away with the Russian': Sexual Infidelities in World War I Germany," *Central European History* 44, no. 02 (2011): 257–78.

Trevisan, Carine and Elise Julien. "Cemeteries," in *Capital Cities at War. Paris, London, Berlin, 1914–1919,* ed. Jay Winter and Jean-Louis Robert. Cambridge: Cambridge University Press, 1997–2007.

Tucker, Spencer and Priscilla Mary Roberts, eds. *The Encyclopedia of World War I,* 5 vols. Santa Barbara, CA: ABC-CLIO, 2005.

Überegger, Oswald. *Erinnerungskriege: der Erste Weltkrieg, Österreich und die Tiroler Kriegserinnerung in der Zwischenkriegszeit.* Innsbruck: Universitätsverlag Wagner, 2011.

Üngör, Uğur Ümit. *The Making of Modern Turkey: Nation and State in Eastern Anatolia, 1913–1950.* Oxford: Oxford University Press, 2011.

Unowsky, Daniel L. *The Pomp and Politics of Patriotism: Imperial Celebrations in Habsburg Austria, 1848–1916, Central European studies.* West Lafayette, IN: Purdue University Press, 2005.

Usborne, Cornelie. "'Pregnancy is the Woman's Active Service.' Protanalism in Germany during the First World War," in *The Upheaval of War: Family, Work, and Welfare in Europe, 1914–1918*, ed. Richard Wall and Jay Winter, 389–416. Cambridge: Cambridge University Press, 1988.

van Dülmen, Richard. "Der deutsche Katholizismus und der Erste Weltkrieg," *Francia* 2 (1974): 347–76.

Van Ypersele, Laurence. "Mourning and Memory, 1919–45," in *A Companion to World War I*, ed. John Horne, 576–90. Malden, MA: Wiley-Blackwell, 2010.

Verhey, Jeffrey. *The Spirit of 1914: Militarism, Myth, and Mobilization in Germany*. Cambridge: Cambridge University Press, 2000.

Viaene, Vincent. "International History, Religious History, Catholic History: Perspectives for Cross-Fertilization (1830–1914)," *European History Quarterly* 38, no. 4 (2008): 578–607.

Vogt, Arnold. *Religion im Militär: Seelsorge zwischen Kriegsverherrlichung und Humanität: Eine militär-geschichtliche Studie*. Frankfurt a.M.: Peter Lang, 1984.

Wall, Richard and Jay Winter, eds. *The Upheaval of War: Family, Work, and Welfare in Europe, 1914–1918*. Cambridge: Cambridge University Press, 1988.

Wandruszka, Adam and Peter Urbanitsch, eds. *Die Habsburgermonarchie 1848–1918*, vol. 4: *Die Konfessionen*. Vienna: Verlag der Österreichischen Akademie der Wissenschaften, 1985.

eds. *Die Habsburgermonarchie 1848–1918*, vol. 5: *Die bewaffnete Macht*. Vienna: Verlag der Österreichischen Akademie der Wissenschaften, 1987.

Ward, James Mace. *Priest, Politician, Collaborator: Jozef Tiso and the Making of Fascist Slovakia*. Ithaca, NY: Cornell University Press, 2013.

Watson, Alexander. *Enduring the Great War: Combat, Morale and Collapse in the German and British Armies, 1914–1918*. Cambridge: Cambridge University Press, 2008.

Watson, Alexander and Patrick Porter. "Bereaved and Aggrieved: Combat Motivation and the Ideology of Sacrifice in the First World War," *Historical Research* 83, no. 219 (2010): 146–64.

Wawro, Geoffrey. *The Austro-Prussian War: Austria's War with Prussia and Italy in 1866*. Cambridge: Cambridge University Press, 1996.

The Franco-Prussian War: The German Conquest of France in 1870–1871. Cambridge: Cambridge University Press, 2003.

Weigel, George. *The Cube and the Cathedral: Europe, America, and Politics without God*. New York: Basic Books, 2005.

Weintraub, Stanley. *Silent Night: The Story of the World War I Christmas Truce*. New York: Free Press, 2001.

Whalen, Robert W. *Bitter Wounds: German Victims of the Great War, 1914–1939*. Ithaca, NY: Cornell University Press, 1984.

Williamson, George S. "A Religious Sonderweg? Reflections on the Sacred and the Secular in the Historiography of Modern Germany," *Church History* 75, no. 1 (2006): 139–56.

Wingfield, Nancy M. "The Enemy Within: Regulating Prostitution and Controlling Venereal Disease in Cisleithanian Austria during the Great War," *Central European History* 46 (2013): 568–98.

Wingfield, Nancy M. and Maria Bucur, eds. *Gender and War in Twentieth-Century Eastern Europe*. Bloomington: Indiana University Press, 2006.

Winter, Jay. "Approaching the History of the Great War: A User's Guide," in *The Legacy of the Great War: Ninety Years On*, ed. Jay Winter, 1–17. Columbia: University of Missouri Press, 2009.

"Commemorating War, 1914–1945," in *War and the Modern World*, ed. Roger Chickering, Dennis Showalter, and Hans Van de Ven, 310–26. Cambridge: Cambridge University Press, 2012.

Sites of Memory, Sites of Mourning: The Great War in European Cultural History. Cambridge: Cambridge University Press, 1995.

Winter, Jay and Antoine Prost. *The Great War in History: Debates and Controversies, 1914 to the Present*. Cambridge: Cambridge University Press, 2005.

Wolf, Hubert. *Papst und Teufel. Die Archive des Vatikan und das Dritte Reich*. Munich: CH Beck, 2008.

Zahra, Tara. *Kidnapped Souls: National Indifference and the Battle for Children in the Bohemian Lands, 1900–1948*. Ithaca, NY: Cornell University Press, 2008.

Ziemann, Benjamin. *Contested Commemorations: Republican War Veterans and Weimar Political Culture*. Cambridge: Cambridge University Press, 2013.

Front und Heimat: Ländliche Kriegserfahrungen im südlichen Bayern, 1914–1923. Essen: Klartext, 1997.

"Katholische Religiosität und die Bewältigung des Krieges: Soldaten und Militärseelsorger in der deutschen Armee, 1914–1918," in *Volksreligiosität und Kriegserleben*, ed. Friedhelm Boll, 116–36. Münster: Lit, 1997.

Sozialgeschichte der Religion: von der Reformation bis zur Gegenwart. Frankfurt a.M.: Campus Verlag, 2009.

War Experiences in Rural Germany, 1914–1923, trans. Alex Skinner. Oxford: Berg, 2007.

Zumholz, Anna Maria. "Die Resistenz des katholischen Milieus: Seherinnen und Stigmatisierte in der ersten Hälfte des 20. Jahrhunderts," in *Wunderbare Erscheinungen. Frauen und katholische Frömmigkeit im 19. und 20. Jahrhundert*, ed. Irmtraud Götz von Olenhusen, 221–51. Paderborn: Ferdinand Schöningh, 1995.

Index

Printed in the USA
CPSIA information can be obtained
at www.ICGtesting.com
LVHW021556221223
767236LV00003B/104